GEORGE MATEI **CANTACUZINO**

GEORGE MATEI

CANTACUZINO

A HYBRID MODERNIST

by DAN TEODOROVICI

Wasmuth

To his children, Marie-Lyse and Șerban

Imprint

George Matei Cantacuzino –
A Hybrid Modernist
Dan Teodorovici

This publication has been funded with support from the **Union of Romanian Architects**

Editing
Dr Sigrid Hauser

Graphic design
Dan Teodorovici

Printing and bookbinding
AZ Druck und Datentechnik, Kempten

Printed in Germany

www.wasmuth-verlag.de

ISBN 978 3 8030 0767 4

Front cover shows the *Hotel Bellona*, Eforie Nord,
Black Sea Coast (c. 1932-34). Period photograph c. 1960 (ADT).

Contents

The Eye Set Free

Foreword

by Ákos Moravánszky

"What a man touched upon, he should take with him. If he forgot it, he should be reminded. What gives a man worth is that he incorporates everything he has experienced. This includes the countries where he has lived, the people whose voices he has heard."

Elias Canetti, The Tongue Set Free

The linguistic complexity of East-Central-Europe is no more mappable than the stylistic plurality of its architecture. Today (after the canonization and institutionalization of modern architecture) it is difficult to imagine Modernism in a fluid state of emergence. Looking at the work of George Matei Cantacuzino, we are tempted to speak of *alternative Modernism* – however, in the 1920s and 1930s, only alternative Modernisms existed.

Cantacuzino was a member of the Romanian nobility. He was brought up in Vienna, and studied in Montreux and Paris. He was privileged enough to live in two centers of imperial tradition in Europe – Vienna and Paris –, having strong connections to a third metropolis – London. More than a few members of East-Central European aristocracy became catalysts of the cultural life of the twentieth century, not only in Romania. Cosmopolitanism is not only an appropriate notion under these circumstances, but can serve as a useful tool to analyze the various facets of Cantacuzino's stylistic pluralism, the range of seemingly confusing vocabularies he developed. Dan Teodorovici recognizes a "klassische Haltung" (classical attitude) in his written and built œuvre, which is another expression for humanistic thought.

Cosmopolitanism is often used in a negative sense, to describe the freewheeling bourgeois individual with no roots in the local culture, with no loyalty to the nation-state – or in reference to the luxurious lifestyles of the wealthy few. Nothing could be further from the truth in Cantacuzino's case. Intellectuals like Cantacuzino – or Elias Canetti, similarly a traveller from this region – must have realized quite early that identities are not the unchangeable, eternal essences, but invented and malleable, easily adaptable to the goals of modernity. For Cantacuzino, the rural tradition of Romania was a perfect ingredient of his vision of modernity. He saw no conflict between the general goals of modernization and the cultural significance of the vernacular artifact. In his essay *Traditionalism and Modernism* he concluded:

"Our problem is not to reduce general tendencies to regional aesthetics; on the contrary, we have to appreciate our old regional heritage as a cultural value of general interest, that we transfer into the great realm of the eternal artworks of humanity."[1]

1 Opposite:
G. M. Cantacuzino on Unter den Linden, on his voyage to Berlin as chief-architect of the Romanian Railways CFR (Căile Ferate Române), in August 1940. In the background, on the left, is a part of the Humboldt University, and the Neue Wache by K. F. Schinkel (AMLSC).

Cantacuzino's appreciation of rural tradition was not connected to nationalist imaginations of homeland, territory or roots. It was the expression of the concern for universal values such as reason, such as the constructional rationality of vernacular architecture that he admired. His cosmopolitanism is closely connected to the political collisions, to the historic transitions and competing visions that Romania and the whole of East-Central Europe underwent in the period between the world wars.

In his life, he experienced the most different facets of cosmopolitan existence, starting from the comfort of a privileged individual and ending as an exile in his own country.

Dan Teodorovici's research on Cantacuzino's architecture goes well beyond the analysis of a singular case, as a curious deviation from the aesthetics of the historical avant-garde, explained by the particular situation of East-Central Europe. The author opens a large geocultural perspective to capture a range of cosmopolitan practices in the work of this important Romanian architect and public intellectual.

A Hybrid Modernist

Introduction

"There are the traditionalists, the modernists and the others. The latter include those architects who believe that it is necessary to seek an equilibrum based on classical disciplines without rejecting modern themes and without turning one's back on tradition." [1]

George Matei Cantacuzino, On the Aesthetics of Reconstruction (1947)

On 5th May 1939 Fiorello La Guardia, then Mayor of the City of New York, praised Romanian ideals in his address at the inauguration of the Official Pavilion of Romania at the World's Fair. George Matei Cantacuzino (1899-1960) was the architect of the pavilion and was appointed an Honorary Citizen of New York. He was on the peak of his career, a leading architect and public intellectual in Romania with close colleagues and friends in Western Europe.

But the ascent of fascism, the outbreak of the Second World War, the rise of communism and the Iron Curtain broke many a vital personal connection between East and West. Dissidents were often ignored in their own countries. G. M. Cantacuzino was one of them, and as a result, was forced into oblivion. In 1977 some of his writings had been reedited, but it was not until after 1990 that he had been truly rediscovered and given more public credit in Romania. On the international level however this has been less the case.

Indeed, the Romanian cosmopolitan G. M. Cantacuzino is still one of the least known polymaths of the the twentieth century. In view of that age of extremes, both his *classical attitude*, which links Modernism to Tradition and Aesthetics to Ethics, and his intellectual integrity are remarkable. He is hereinafter called GMC, like he himself used to sign paintings or explanatory notes in his annual cultural periodical *Simetria* (1939-1947).

Being born in 1899, GMC belonged to the second generation of modernists which included the likes of Alvar Aalto and Mart Stam. He was in touch with Modernism but was independent enough to criticize its extreme aspects. He studied architecture at the École des Beaux-Arts in Paris (1920-29), starting in the atelier run by Gustave Umbdenstock, Le Corbusier's arch-enemy at the École. But soon he switched to the atelier run by two liberal professors: Georges Gromort, the architectural historian, and Roger-Henri Expert, who was active as an architect. Expert was also a member of the progressive *Groupes des Architectes Modernes* around Tony Garnier, Auguste Perret and Henri Sauvage. This movement, which sought to link Modernism and French Classicism, most probably inspired GMC. In Romania he became the unchallenged integrative figure of the moderate Modernism and still is the most prolific architectural theorist of that country. He was also professor of architectural history and theory in Bucharest, painter and curator, chief-architect of the Romanian Railways CFR, the first Romanian correspondent of *L'Architecture d'Aujourd'hui*, honorary corresponding member of the Royal Institute of British Architects, and much more. With his liberal political attitude being disapproved of by both fascists and communists, he experienced imprisonment, social exclusion and ultimately an untimely death.

This book complements the exhibition of the same title, which is the first monographic one on a Romanian architect staged outside that country. First shown by the Weissenhof Gallery in Stuttgart in 2012, it travelled to the Gallery of the General Consulate of Romania in Munich and the Architekturschaufenster Gallery in Karlsruhe in 2013.

Both the book and exhibition are based on the PhD thesis *G. M. Cantacuzino (1899-1960): Dialogik zwischen Tradition und Moderne* (Dialogic between Tradition and Modernism), completed at the Faculty of Architecture and Urban Planning of the University of Stuttgart in 2010.

This book consists of three parts. Beginning with an intellectual biography, it continues with a study in architectural theory of GMC's *classical attitude* (which is shown in italics throughout the book) and is completed by the addendum. Apart from the bibliography and further references, the addendum includes a list of architectural works, a few selected essays translated into English, some selected colour plates of paintings and watercolours, and a biography of the architect.

Offering a journey through GMC's momentous life and work, this study tries to place it within a wide architectural, cultural, economic and political context. It also seeks to reveal the corner-stones of GMC's *classical attitude* and to show how, in the words of Gilles Deleuze, they come into being along various "lines of actualization or of differentiation"[2]. Deleuze used this method in his study of the philosophy of Henri Bergson, who perhaps was the thinker who made the greatest impact on GMC.

Enthused about the *élan vital* coined by Bergson, GMC was sceptical towards epoch labels and refused to apply the term style to the dynamism of architecture. His wide-ranging architecture was concerned, throughout his entire career, with particular interest in Palladianism and various attempts at a synthesis between Modernism, late Byzantine-Romanian traditions and Classicism. The *classical attitude*, which runs through GMC's unsystematic writings like Ariadne's thread, is perhaps the key to his approach.

This study also attempts to outline his artistic and intellectual family – from Vitruvius via Andrea Palladio and Karl Friedrich Schinkel to Auguste Perret and Adolf Loos, from Heinrich Wölfflin via Jean Cocteau to Rudolf Wittkower and Sir Ernst Gombrich, from Plotinus via Henri Bergson to Albert Camus, from Michel de Montaigne via Johann Wolfgang von Goethe to Rainer Maria Rilke, Paul Valéry and T. S. Eliot. The attempt to discern "the springs which feed the river of his thought"[3] seems even more appropriate as GMC himself points to it:

"Each one of us creates his own Parnassus, his own spiritual family, the only family that we are able to choose ourselves ... or, who knows, perhaps they choose us ... these friends that live outside time."[4]

The debts I owe in this book are vast and enduring. In the first place, I am much beholden to GMC's children, Marie-Lyse Cantacuzino-Ruhemann and Şerban Cantacuzino for their confidence, friendship and generosity. They provided me with unique access to their private archive, supported the exhibition on GMC in Stuttgart and invited me time and again to work on the thesis and then on the book in London.

This being the first monograph on a Romanian architect ever to be published by a major European publishing house, this edition owes much to the interest of Ernst Wasmuth and Dr Sigrid Hauser. I also extend my gratitude to the Union of Romanian Architects in Bucharest who provided financial assistance for publishing. I am particularly grateful to Professor Virgil Onofrei for his friendship and encouragement.

To Professor Ákos Moravánszky of the *gta*, ETH Zurich, I am greatly indebted for his foreword and stimulating and encouraging conversations on the subject.

For welcoming my idea of a dissertation on the work of GMC in 2005 and for his valuable advice I am greatly indebted to Professor Helmut Bott of the Institute of Urban Planning at the University of Stuttgart. Also many thanks to Professor Klaus Jan Philipp for joining in supervising the PhD thesis.

In addition I should like to thank the following for their help and encouragement: Professor Immo Boyken, Diane de la Bruchollerie, Kyra Bullert, Professor Jean-Michel Cantacuzène, Dr Pavel Chihaia, Dr George Chira, Professor Hanna Derer, Professor Peter Derer, Michael Glück, Dr Eugenia Greceanu, Professor Theresia Gürtler-Berger, Dr Felix Heidenreich, Professor Johann Jessen, Michael Kunert, Hanns-Martin Kurz, Gunther Loydl, Ruxandra Munteanu, Liliana Mușețeanu, Professor Rolf Neddermann, Professor Ulrich Pantle, Natalie Plagaro-Cowee, Dr Adrian Pocanschi, Dr Gheorghe Săsărman, Walter Scheuerle, Dr Tilman Sperle, Thorsten Stelter, Dr Elke Uhl, Anna Vahl and Anita Wolfsteiner.

For the English version of my text based on the PhD thesis I am most grateful to Marie-Lyse Cantacuzino-Ruhemann and Sarah Straubenmüller, who helped me with the translation from the German, assisted by Fenella Fairbairn, Martina Grupe, Meghan Horváth and Caroline Ireland.

At the same time every work on GMC owes a great debt to Dr Radu Patrulius†, who studied under GMC and worked in his office in the 1940s. His three articles (1975 and 1982) laid the foundations of studies of GMC's work.

As this study draws on unknown material from archives both public and private in Romania and England, I also wish to thank the following for their help: Constantin Cheramidoglu, Judy Ghyka, Paul and Dan Marinescu, Liliana Mușețeanu, Ileana Tilea-Troiano, Irina Patrulius and Gheorghe Vecerdea†.

I owe a very special debt to the former friends or students of GMC's whom I had the opportunity to talk to: Matei Cantacuzino, Dan Corneliu, Stephan Eleutheriadis, Ion Mircea Enescu, Dr Eugenia Greceanu, Theodora Kitzulescu, Dr Zamfira Mihail, Professor Petre Năsturel, Suzana Paleologu, Rada Teodoru, Professor Aurelian Trișcu and Olympia Zamfiresco†.

Lastly, I wish to thank my relatives in Romania and my parents in Waiblingen for their patience and support.

Part I: An intellectual biography

3 Pierre Puvis de Chavannes, *Ste Geneviève watching over a sleeping Paris.* Panthéon, Paris 1898 (Photograph ADT).

Family background[1]

It is raining in Paris, and the sky is grey, of that delicate and elegant grey so typical of Paris. Two men rush into the Panthéon, cold and damp and almost deserted though it is. They stop in front of the fresco by Pierre Puvis de Chavannes (1824-1898) depicting Ste Geneviève watching over a sleeping Paris. After a few moments of awesome silence, one of the men bows his head and murmurs some words into his young companion's ear. Then, waving his arms, he obviously gives an intimate lecture on the painting.

This first encounter, so vividly introduced by his older cousin Theodor Pallady (1871-1956)[2], artist and friend of Henri Matisse, could indeed have taken place roughly in 1919 between GMC and his late great-aunt Marie Cantacuzène. For the woman painted by Puvis de Chavannes in the guise of Ste Geneviève was no other than de Chavannes's wife and model Marie Cantacuzène. And this allegory seems to tell us, amongst other things, that Paris would not be Paris without the rich artistic contributions of Francophile and cosmopolitan emigrés, for whom Paris was so generous a homeland.

Marie Cantacuzène,[3] in fact, is but one of many historically relevant figures of the widespread Cantacuzino family, who could have made an impact on GMC – as regards both the conservative trait of his personality and the aristocratic tradition of social and cultural commitment. Of this distinguished family background the following chapter aims to give a brief outline.

Byzantium

4 Coat of arms, stone floor detail from the Metropolitan Church at Mistra.

2 Opposite:
On the steps of Villa Rotonda, Vicenza c. 1928 (AMLSC).

The Cantacuzinos can be traced to the eleventh century in Byzantium, through a certain general Kantakouzenos around 1094-1107. Later followed two Cantacuzino emperors: John VI (1341-55) and Matthew (1353-57). John VI is the only Byzantine emperor whose memoirs have survived; he is the first emperor in history to have deliberately abdicated and retired to monastic life at Mistra[4] – the second and last one being Charles V (1500-1558), Holy Roman Emperor (1519-1556).[5] From 1348 until well into the fifteenth century the Cantacuzinos together with the Paleologus Families possessed the despotate of Mistra. After the conquest of Constantinople in 1453 by the Ottoman Empire, some Cantacuzinos became one of the noble Phanariot[6] families. The majority left for Crete, Serbia and the Peloponese. In the sixteenth century a number of Cantacuzinos settled in Wallachia. Later some emigrated to Moldavia, Russia, Austria or Bavaria. With their branches in Wallachia and Moldavia the Cantacuzinos established themselves as one of the most influential Romanian families until the Second World War. On the eve of or right after it most Cantacuzinos left for Western Europe or the USA.

5 *Constantin Brancovan and his four sons.* Fresco in the Horez monastery church. (Stefănescu 1928)

Wallachia

The Cantacuzinos gave to Wallachia two reigning princes: Şerban Cantacuzino (1634-1688) and his nephew Stephan (1675-1716). Together with his brothers Constantin (1639-1716) and Michael (1640-1716), Şerban[7] launched a period of enlightenment and progress, introducing, for instance, the potato and maize in Wallachia.

Constantin Cantacuzino, Lord High Steward and historian, was the outstanding humanist of this period, termed "Cantacuzino Renaissance"[8] by the historians Nicolae Iorga and Georges Balş in 1922. In 1700 Constantin designed the very first map of Wallachia, and published it in Padua, where he had studied the humanities some years before. He also produced the first attempt at a critical history of Wallachia (*Istoria Ţării Româneşti*), which was his main writing. However, it was to remain incomplete due to his violent death: together with his son, the reigning prince Stephan, he was decapitated by the Ottomans in Constantinople in 1716.[9]

After a pilgrimage to the Holy Land and Mount Sinai, General Michael Cantacuzino built the Sinaia monastery in the Southern Carpathians (c. 1682). He also endowed the Colţea Hospital in Bucharest (1695), and several churches including the Fundenii Doamnei Church in Bucharest (1699). On this gem, GMC himself wrote an article in 1931, urging the authorities to restore the then derelict building.[10]

Şerban's nephew Constantin Brancovan (1654-1714), as reigning prince of Wallachia (1688-1714) continued to promote the arts, from architecture via painting to handicraft, leading Wallachia to a cultural spring, which was to be known as Brancovan period. His major commissions include the Horez monastery (1691-93) in the Olt valley at the foot of the Southern Carpathians, his two palaces at Potlogi and Mogoşoaia[11] near Bucharest, and the Mogoşoaia Avenue. The Mogoşoaia Avenue, initially connecting the two

6 Horez monastery church. *Stone balustrade with coat of arms* (Stefănescu 1928).

7 Fundenii Doamnei church, Bucharest. *Ceiling fresco in the pronaos* (Photograph ADT)

Brancovan palaces of Mogoşoaia and Bucharest, during the nineteenth century turned into one of the most famous avenues of Bucharest and indeed of the young Romanian kingdom: Calea Victoriei (Victoria Avenue).[12]

Around the turn of the century further Wallachian Cantacuzinos stood out. One of them was particularly dear to GMC: the Romanian diplomat and French poet Charles-Adolphe Cantacuzène (1874-1949), a close friend of Stéphane Mallarmé and Paul Valéry. Cantacuzène left behind fourty-four volumes of poetry and essays and a biography of prince Charles-Josèphe de Ligne (1735-1814), the Austrian-Belgian diplomat and landscape architect Goethe was so fond of.[13]

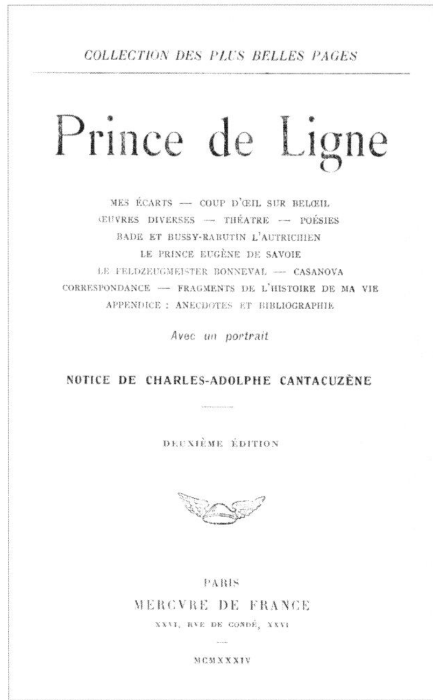
COLLECTION DES PLUS BELLES PAGES

Prince de Ligne

MES ÉCARTS — COUP D'ŒIL SUR BELŒIL
ŒUVRES DIVERSES — THÉATRE — POÉSIES
BADE ET BUSSY-RABUTIN L'AUTRICHIEN
LE PRINCE EUGÈNE DE SAVOIE
LE FELDZEUGMEISTER BONNEVAL — CASANOVA
CORRESPONDANCE — FRAGMENTS DE L'HISTOIRE DE MA VIE
APPENDICE : ANECDOTES ET BIBLIOGRAPHIE

Avec un portrait

NOTICE DE CHARLES-ADOLPHE CANTACUZÈNE

DEUXIÈME ÉDITION

PARIS
MERCVRE DE FRANCE
XXVI, RVE DE CONDÉ, XXVI

MCMXXXIV

8 Charles-Adolphe Cantacuzène (ed.): *Prince de Ligne*. Anthology of writings. Paris 1934. Title page.

Moldavia and GMC[14]

Through his father, the diplomat Nicholas Basil Cantacuzino (1864-1947), GMC found his paternal roots at Hoiseşti and Jassy in Moldavia, where some Wallachian Cantacuzinos settled during the eighteenth century. Through his mother Marcella Bibesco (1873-1957), GMC was related to another two aristocratic families: the Romanian Bibescos and the French-Belgian Caraman-Chimays. GMC's Moldavian background boasts a whole lot of outstanding political and cultural figures. They include his grandfather, the 1848 revolutionary Basil Cantacuzino (1815-1906) and his sister Maria Cantacuzène (1820-1898), the reigning prince A.I. Cuza (1820-1873), poet and translator Jean A.-C. Cantacuzène (1829-1898), architect Nicolae Ghika-Budeşti (1869-1943), French writers Anna de Noailles (1876-1933) and Marthe Bibesco (1887-1973), the pilot and president of the International Aeronautical Federation Georges V. Bibesco (1880-1941), diplomat Barbu Ştirbey (1872-1946), archaeologist and art historian Georges Balş (1868-1934), diplomat and aesthetician Matila Ghyka (1881-1965), and the painters Balasha Cantacuzino (1899-1976), Henri Catargi (1894-1976) and Theodor Pallady (1871-1956).

9 *Mogoşoaia*, Bucharest. Period postcard (AMB-JG).

10 Henri Catargi, *Landscape near Pantelimon*, Romania, 1957.

F F E

Childhood in Vienna (1899-1909)

"Dates", wrote the Viennese-born English art historian Sir Ernst Gombrich (1909-2001), "are indispensable pegs on which to hang the tapestry of history".[1] GMC too was a Viennese, and, as we shall see later, he and Gombrich happened to have some similar views on art.

GMC was born on 23rd May 1899. That year Heinrich Wölfflin published his *Classical Art*, a classic study of Italian Renaissance painters, which soon became a standard work. At the turn of the century, as Werner Oechslin pointed out, the "issue of classic was to become [...] one of the chief cultural topics of the modern age"[2]. In the same year, Auguste Choisy published his *Histoire de l'Architecture*, now a standard reference of study particularly in France.[3] In 1899 then Adolf Loos completed his Café Museum, which revolutionized Viennese architecture.

Eventually these moments refer to three cornerstones of GMC's career: classics and classicism; architectural history and theory; and, as we shall see later, the so-called "critical Viennese Modernism"[4] – particularly its crucial connection between ethics and aesthetics.

GMC's generation included the architect Alvar Aalto, historian Georges Bratianu, writer Curzio Malaparte, as well as the art historians Richard Krautheimer and Rudolf Wittkower.

In Vienna, where his father was a diplomat since 1895, GMC spent his first ten years. It was a carefree childhood. He was brought up speaking French, Romanian, and German. His parents spoke French to each other; he learned to speak Romanian from his father, and talked German to his nannies and his playmates in the Belvedere and Botanical Gardens, near the family apartment on 10 Metternichgasse.

It was not until his first visit to his Moldavian paternal grandparents that GMC for the first time heard Romanian being spoken in public. At the family country retreat in Hoisești near Jassy GMC learned to know the beauty of the Moldavian landscape. Later he discovered and embraced the whole of Romania, his commitment being documented by innumerable essays, drawings and paintings. Nonetheless, Moldavia remained his greatest love, and he concentrated his pictorial intelligence on Moldavian scenes.

Romanian too was the language of his first readings. Because of its melody and imaginative power, GMC was fascinated by the Romanian language and was recognised as an excellent author by leading writers of his day.

From his knowledge of French, GMC was to profit greatly as a student in Paris and as a passionate traveller especially from 1920 to 1940. But French was not just the language of international communication at that time, for GMC it was an intimate language: his journal (or at least the fragments which came down to us) are written in French as are his intimate letters to his wife Sanda or friends like Marietta Stern-Guetta. Apart from being a European aristocratic convention of the time, French here appears as a genuine language of love. And after the communist take-over in September 1944, GMC's preference of French in private correspondance could also be interpreted as a silent protest against political and social uniformisation, lack of

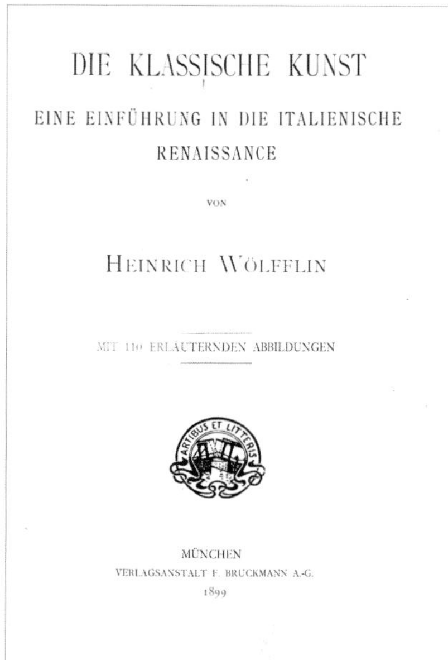

DIE KLASSISCHE KUNST

EINE EINFÜHRUNG IN DIE ITALIENISCHE RENAISSANCE

VON

HEINRICH WÖLFFLIN

MIT 110 ERLÄUTERNDEN ABBILDUNGEN

MÜNCHEN
VERLAGSANSTALT F. BRUCKMANN A.-G.
1899

12 Heinrich Wölfflin, *Die klassische Kunst*. Munich 1899. Title page.

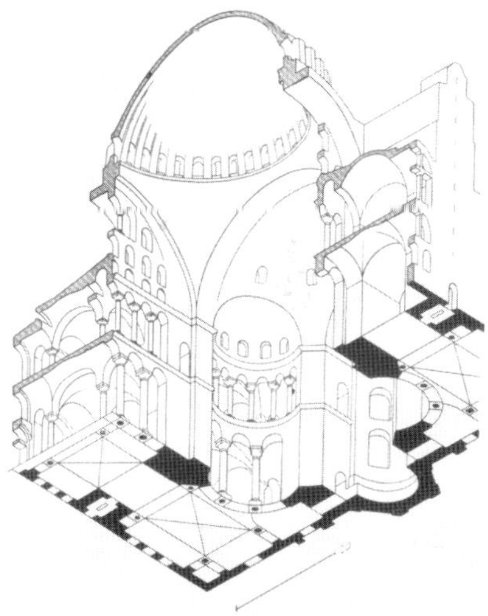

13 Auguste Choisy, *L'Histoire de l'architecture*. Paris 1899, p. 45 showing an axonometry of the Hagia Sophia, Constantinople.

11 Opposite:
Adolf Loos, *Loos House on Michaeler Platz*, Vienna (1909-1911). Façade detail (Photograph ADT).

14 Otto Wagner, *K. .k. Postsparkasse*, Vienna (1903-1912).

15 N. B. Cantacuzino (1864-1947), period photograph (AMLSC).

culture and totalitarism. The use of French in public at that time was even dangerous to the point of emprisonment, as experienced by Charles-Adolphe Cantacuzène. Unfortunately, on the very day of 1948 when the Communist authorities closed the Institut Français in Bucharest this inoffensive poet was found by the police deep in a book. He was immediately arrested and sent to the labour camp of the Danube-Black Sea-Canal. There on a winter day he froze to death. His winter coat had been stolen.[5]

German, for its part, not only enabled GMC to savour Goethe or Rilke in the original. But GMC appreciated the German moment in terms of business too. His first architectural office he founded in co-operation with August Schmiedigen, an experienced architect in Bucharest. Schmiedigen was probably a Transylvanian saxon, as possibly were the architects Eugen Eppler and Kaller, two of GMC's permanent employees in the 1930s. His favourite architectural photographer in Bucharest was also German: W. Weiss, now almost forgotten.

Around 1900 Vienna was a cosmopolitan metropolis. True, there were obvious signs of decay. But being a real "laboratory for aesthetic research"[6] Vienna experienced a cultural peak with notable schools of thought and artistic movements of cultural renewal: first, the school of art history around Alois Riegl, Adolf von Hildebrand, and Wilhelm Worringer; second, the architecture of Josef Hoffmann and Otto Wagner along with the Wagner school involving talents like Max Fabiani and Jozé Plečnik; and finally, the critical modernism led by Loos, Kraus and Wittgenstein.

In addition Vienna was Europe's temple of music and dance, of concerts and operas. GMC's parents were passionate dancers and musical cognoscenti. Nicholas Basil Cantacuzino, for instance, was reputed to have been a great dancer and singer on private chamber concerts, also entertaining Emperor Franz Joseph. GMC's parents very much appreciated the Viennese "Gemütlichkeit"[7] and metropolitan refinement, to the point that GMC's father in his memoirs remembered the fifteen years spent in Vienna as the happiest of his diplomatic career, which was to last some fifty years. On the other hand, they disapproved of the Viennese snobism, as so brilliantly sketched by Karl Kraus: "The public life of Vienna resembles a tasteless humorous magazine. Their common feature: the immobility of the figures."[8]

GMC and his brother Emanuel, who was five years his junior, profited from these conditions. It comes as no surprise that GMC throughout his life was to get along very well with his parents. His father's friendship, liberalism and judgement were to be of great value to GMC especially in the late 1930s and during the Second World War: "Papa's serenity and his peacefull judgement [...] are giving me strength to carry on."[9] Unlike his father, "the Epicurian",[10] his mother "was puritanical and severe"[11]. Her authority, though, he "did not resent"[12] – because of her beauty. In *Letters to Simon*, his autobiographical letters to Simon Bayer, an old friend, GMC maintained in 1955:

"I was born an idolater. The people who looked after me when I was very small were beautiful; the city in which I first became aware of my surroundings was beautiful, so was the house I lived in. Beauty seemed something entirely natural. I did not have to search for it."[13]

The memories of his early playmates faded away, except for the encounter with a cripple in a pram in the Botanical Garden. The sight of the boy and his arms, which "lay lifeless on his knees"[14], frightened and attracted GMC at once. Although he did not dare address him, time and again he was looking forward to seeing him. From this experience he may have learned to value normality as a privilege. At any rate he became sensitive to his surroundings and also learned to cope with being alone. Later in life he was to appreciate loneliness and silence as conditions for contemplation and creativity, very much in the same line with one of his favourite authors, Blaise "Pascal, that sombre and pitiless thinker"[15] – in his *Pensées* Pascal observed: "I have discovered that all the unhappiness of men arise from one single fact, that they cannot stay quietly in their own chamber."[16]

But some of his early experiences of loneliness also inspired him to become "essentially visual"[17]: "When I bent over the Belvedere pools, trying to give depth to reality, which meant counting the frogs at the bottom of the pools, the sky appeared, mirrored on the surface of the water. This was a lesson that taught me to opt for the superficiality of appearances."[18]

Here GMC alluded to the mirror metaphor, and then referred to Goethe's aesthetic notion: "But Goethe had a saying which you [Simon Bayer] often quoted: "*Tiefe aus Oberflächlichkeit* [Depth out of superficiality]".[19] A similar understanding of poetical mechanics we find with Cees Noteboom, who in 1993 wrote:

"*Poetry, fiction, fantasy, always deal with imaginary gardens with real toads in them,** as Marianne Moore put it in a truly unique way. Now please try to catch those toads."[20]

16 View of the apartment building at 10 Metternichgasse in Vienna. Period photograph with GMC and his mother in the central window of the raised ground floor (AMLSC).

17 *Vienna seen from the Belvedere*. Photograph Kurt Hielscher, 1931. © Christian Hamann/Wolfgang Henkel.

18 Horia Teodoru, *The Cantacuzino mansion in Hoisești, Moldavia*. Woodcut (AMLSC).

19 Claude Lorrain, *Landscape with the Embarkation of the Holy Paula Romana in Ostia*. Madrid, Museo del Prado. © Foto Marburg, image no. C 654.209.

20 *Portrait of GMC*, c. 1909 (AMLSC).

Travels

Train travels through "the Alps or Italian lakes, Moldavian valleys or the Carpathians, Lombardy or the Black Forest"[21] nurtured his fantasy and inspired him to create inner landscapes. And the figure of Sindbad the sailor, once revealed to him by his mother on the Dalmation coast, "opened up the glorious idea of adventure. [...] Sindbad completed for me the notion of the sea and from then on I loved it more. In front of it, everything seemed possible"[22]. This passion for the sea and in particular the "Mediterranean spirit"[23] as the cradle of European civilization GMC deliberately shared among others with Paul Valéry. This enduring passion can also be seen in his architectural work on the Black Sea coast, particularly at Eforie and Mamaia near Constantza. "And then later in prisons",[24] imaginary strolls through Claude Lorrain's ideal cities and landscapes were to give him consolation, with their "streets of noble architecture [...] leading to the sea"[25] and its promise of freedom: "Free man! the sea is to thee ever dear!"[26]

But his initiation into architecture he owed to the classical and baroque urban space and buildings of Vienna. On 26th June 1955 he wrote to his old friend Simon Bayer:

"When I went back to the city of my birth, Vienna, when I watched, from the Belvedere terraces the changing of the seasons, I found it difficult at first to get into my old routine. After the discovery of the sea I had experienced the luminous melancholy of Moldavia. And yet in Vienna, I was soon won over again by the strict order of the streets, by the imposing harmony of the stones and the gardens of the imperial city. I liked its air of stability and permanence, enhanced by its many cupolas and fountains, and especially by its cathedral rising high above the city, like a rock weathering all storms. I felt safe there and reassured. Sometimes I wonder if I became an architect because of those early Vienna years, because I had played in the uncompromising symmetry of its buildings, especially that of the Belvedere. For hours on end I would watch the fountains playing and see the light change the colour of the cupolas and the statues. I was thrilled by the great perspective of the streets. In some obscure way I felt the influence of a very old civilization that tried in every way to affirm its belief in human dignity. All this I learned in those early years, even if I only understood it much later.

Paris and Rome, made me even more sure of what I had learned in Vienna. Versailles and the Vatican gardens reminded me of my hours of play in the Belvedere gardens.

If, in Moldavia, I was overcome by a sense of space, I never forgot the strict and organised Western discipline which meant limitation in order to achieve depth and precision. The poetry of Moldavia, as indeed that of the sea, has always been throughout my life, a great source of inspiration, a very special part of my world of memory. And yet it was the discipline inherent in the Western world's laws of aesthetics that I wished to follow. I knew this. There was no conflict in my mind. And the result is that what I loved so much as a child remains with me today.

I am not disillusioned and I have not abandoned my first dreams. That is why I told you that I have been, and still am, a happy man."[27]

Education in Montreux (1910-c. 1914)

21 Marcella Cantacuzino (1873-1957) in the drawing-room of the Ştirbey country retreat in Dărmăneşti, Moldavia, c. 1922 (AMLSC).

In 1910 N.B. Cantacuzino was appointed state secretary at the Office of Foreign Affairs in Bucharest. Marcella with the two boys moved to French Switzerland. According to the family tradition established in the nineteenth century, GMC was to attend a humanistic high school at Montreux. For GMC this was a sudden and painful break: he was separated from his father, had to move from the carefree and cheerful vivacity of Vienna to a Calvinist provincial town, and cope with an ambiguous Romanian house teacher.

The teacher's task was to prepare him for a humanistic high school exam in Bucharest. He taught GMC mathematics, calligraphy as well as Romanian language, literature and history. On the other hand, through him GMC first experienced populist resentment. Right from the beginning the teacher in the tone of a judge accused him of being of noble birth and hence a parasite and enemy of the Romanian people. The child of ten remained outwardly unimpressed, yet "mentally aware"[1]. Somehow he felt "that truth must be somewhat different, though perhaps equally tragic"[2]. The occurrence of this enmity made him instantly "side with the accused"[3] and added to his ethical precociousness. Later in life he was to meet his teacher time and again, "dressed in various disguises"[4]. But he thought "it was salutary, this sort of opposition makes you draw in, and drawing in, you grow in depth; examining things you also examine yourself. *Quae nocent, docent* – the motto of the Cantacuzinos. [...] [The teacher] having misrepresented history, religion and morality, I was obliged to oppose his ideas on history, religion, and morality, even then as a child. From then on I have been a nonconformist and found the freedom to think for myself, independently of caste, religion or nationality.

I only believe in special cases. *Je hais la gloire et les phrases nationales*, to put it in the words of Jules Laforgue. I am not Romanian because I was born Romanian; but because, already as a child, I freely chose Romania as a theme for meditation, for devotion and love. This Romania is something entirely different from the one that exists, especially today."[5]

After having passed the school exam in Bucharest, GMC accompanied his father on a visit to his French-Belgian maternal grandmother Marie Henriette Valentine Bibesco (1839-1914). This visit, which was to exercise so profound an influence upon his life, eventually was the only opportunity to meet his grandmother. But she inspired him with love for all things French and strengthened his self-confidence:

"Of all the ghosts that have dwelt in me, she was the most imperious. Often, when I was among other people, I would hear her voice: *À la rigueur n'ayez pas de cœur, mais je vous en supplie, ayez des manières*. [...] And, whenever I went down the staircase of the various prisons I was in, it was she, my grandmother, who whispered to me *honneur d'abord*."[6]

22 École des Beaux-Arts, Paris. *Hôtel de Chimay garden*. Period postcard (ADT).

Back in Montreux, Marcella Cantacuzino moved with the children to villa Aloïse which belonged to Mlle Vincent, an elderly lady. There GMC finally felt at ease. Since there was no orthodox church around, his mother gently introduced him into religion: every Sunday morning she read a short piece

23 GMC, *Tree in Moldavia.* Watercolour, 1918 (AMLSC).

from the Bible to him. At the Montreux Lycée Municipale he enjoyed a humanistic education and learned to appreciate the Protestant work ethic. He was popular with his school-fellows, his best friend being "the son of the station-master"[7], and also on good terms with some of the teachers, in particular with Mr Poirié (History and Geography), Mr Portas (writing and drawing) and Mr Aubent (literature). All this finally reconciled him with Calvin's country,[8] before moving to Bucharest around 1914.

High school and years of apprenticeship (c. 1912-1918)

In 1916, GMC passed the *baccalauréat* at the old-established Sf Sava College in Bucharest.[1] Those years saw the beginning of some close friendships, most of them lifelong, with the lawyer Simon Bayer, poet Ion Barbu (1895-1961), architect Horia Teodoru (1894-1976) and art critic Tudor Vianu (1897-1964). In the same year, the Allies welcomed Romania on their side against the Central Powers. After the German occupation of Bucharest, the Romanian army was being reorganized under the French General Berthelot (1861-1931) near Jassy. GMC's father was sent as attaché of the Romanian legation to Russian Petrograd. He was in charge of a secret train carrying all of Romania's state treasury to the then friendly Tzarist Russia to bring it away from the Central Powers army; after the Russian Revolution the Soviet government duely confiscated the entire Romanian treasury, the best part of which is still kept by present Russia.[2] Together with high school friends, in 1917-18 GMC volunteered in fighting the Central Powers. Eventually he became the youngest sub-lieutenant of the Romanian army to have participated in the battles of Mărășești and Soveja, which were decisive in stopping the advancement of the Central Powers.[3]

After the 1918 Peace Treaty GMC together with Horia Teodoru set off journeying on foot through Moldavia with the purpose of sketching and painting. Some of their drawings and watercolours of landscapes and monuments were shown at the exhibition *Architectural Documents* staged by the Bucharest School of Architecture in January 1919.[4]

That journey could have had a therapeutical effect on the two young men. Unlike many of his generation's comrades GMC seemed to have returned healthy in body and mind from the Great War. Although he welcomed the "aesthetic opposition to the mediocre present"[5], GMC himself was far from joining the choir of "anti-bourgeois and anti-decadent intellectuals"[6], which boasted such distinct figures as Ernst Jünger and Curzio Malaparte. In fact, GMC's war experiences did lead, not to political radicalism but to liberalism. His choice was undoubtedly endorsed by public thinkers like the French professor Alain (1868-1951), whose *Mars ou la guerre jugée* (1921) remains one of the most impressive literary witnesses against war up to the present day.[7]

24 GMC, *Bistritza Church, Moldavia* Watercolour, 1918 (AMLSC).

During the summer holiday of 1912-14 GMC on recommendation of his aunt Marthe Bibesco assisted the Venetian architect Domenico Rupolo in the refurbishment of the Mogoşoaia estate. Works were undertaken in close co-operation with the Bucharest Commission of Historic Monuments. On this building site GMC's desire to study architecture took decisive shape. He was possibly inspired by the architect Nicolae Ghika-Budeşti, himself member of the Commission of Historic Monuments and older cousin of GMC's. But the one person to whom GMC felt most indebted was indeed Marthe Bibesco. There are extant letters between GMC and Marthe, which show the latter's considerable hopes of the consummate nephew and disciple, and GMC's deep affection for his aunt and mentor:

"All my aesthetic essentials, which I keep exploring and imparting to my draughtsmen and stonemasons, it is you who have instilled them in me on our strolls through Jassy, Venice or the Tuileries gardens."[8]

N.B. Cantacuzino for his part seemed to have wished his sons to embrace a diplomatic career as himself. Nevertheless, the recommendations for young diplomats he wrote in his memoirs of 1940, could have well inspired GMC in his work as an architect.[9]

The choice of the École des Beaux-Arts in Paris seemed natural: the reputation of the École was still undisputed in Romania at that time, as was, in the words of Eugène Ionesco, "le mythe de la France"[10]; Nicolae Ghika-Budeşti himself studied at the École; Matila Ghyka, the diplomat and philosopher, and Theodor Pallady, the painter – two older cousins of GMC – regularly lived and worked in Paris, as did Marthe Bibesco and Anna de Noailles. In addition, French was GMC's first language. And finally, with N.B. Cantacuzino's appointment as attaché to the Romanian legation in Paris the father and son looked forward to the prospect of seeing each other again after the troubles of the Great War.[11]

25 Marthe Bibesco (1887-1973), Romanian-born French writer and aunt of GMC's (AMLSC).

26 GMC, *Landscape with cula tower and cross.* Pencil drawing, 1926 (AGMC-PM).

27 Bucharest, intersection of Elisabeth Blvd (to the left) and Calea Victoriei. In the background is the Military Club built to the designs of Ernest Donneaud, Dimitrie Maimarolu and Victor G. Stephănescu in 1912. Period postcard (ADT).

28 Albert Galleron, *Romanian Athenaeum*, Bucharest (1886-88). Period postcard (ADT).

Francophile Romania

At the beginning of the nineteenth century the élite of the Danubian Principalities discovered in France "the great Latin sister in the west."[1] The French for their part would recognize in Romanians, as the French art historian Henri Focillon (1881-1943) noted, the "Latins of the Danube"[2]. France became the chief model of modernisation for Romania, the German model being the second one. Romania indeed was to foster her *French myth* for the best part of the twentieth century.

Francophone architects in Romania

From the late nineteenth century until the outbreak of the Second World War there were quite a few French and Swiss architects active in Romania. Some – including Cassien Bernard, Albert Callu, Jacques Carlu, Albert Galleron and Paul Gottereau – ran projects in Romania, without having close contacts with the local cultural scene.[3] Others, by contrast, settled in Romania and even succeeded in enriching the cultural scene, among them the French-Romanian architects Ernest Donneaud and Daniel Renard, and the Swiss Louis Blanc and Roger Bolomey.[4]

29 The *Mioritza Fountain* on Minovici Square, Bucharest, designed by architect Octav Doicescu and sculptor Militza Pătrașcu (1936). In the background is the Minovici Villa, built to the design of Cristofi Cerchez (1906-1907). Period postcard (ADT).

French education and Romanian architecture

Of the French educational institutions three had an outstanding international reputation: the Sorbonne, the École Polytechnique and the École des Beaux-Arts. The latter exerted a strong influence on architecture, sculpture and painting in Romania, inspiring the birth of an original Romanian architecture and the foundation of the Bucharest School of Architecture in 1897/1904.[5] Ion Mincu (1852-1912), one of its founding fathers and eminent figure of the first generation of Romanian architects,[6] studied under the influential Beaux-Arts professor Julien Guadet (1834-1908). Guadet had effectively promoted the foundation of the first regional schools of architecture in France outside Paris.[7]

Having been a mentor for Mincu very much like, for instance, Otto Wagner was for Jozé Plečnik, Guadet could well have persuaded Mincu to found a school of architecture in Bucharest. This subsequently became the laboratory and ideological centre of the Romanian *Heimatstil*. Important figures of the second (such as Petre Antonescu and Nicolae Ghika-Budești) and third generation of Romanian architects (such as Horia Creangă, Horia Teodoru, and GMC) also studied at the École des Beaux-Arts.

30 Petre Antonescu, *Architectural study in Romanian style* (Iorga 1926).

Studies at the Ecole des Beaux-Arts

Introduction

Around 1920 the École des Beaux-Arts[1] was still one of the world-wide leading schools of architecture. However, like many European universities and academies, it actually emerged weakened from the Great War. The educational system was badly affected by the huge losses of both the faculty and advanced students.[2]

The École des Beaux-Arts recovered during the 1920s. On the other hand, it failed to cope with avant-garde and modernism, which, in the aftermath of the Great War, claimed an aesthetic and moral superiority over the values and institutions of traditional civil society. In fact, it came as no surprise that modernist schools and movements wholeheartedly rejected the École as being antiquated, because its educational system depended on the study of history in order to solve contemporary problems:

"In retrospect", noted French architectural historian Bruno Foucart in 1997, "if it [the École] should have been pulled down, it should have been after the Great War, at a time [when] no one wanted it and no one was interested in history".[3]

Especially Russian Constructivism, Dutch De Stijl, and the German Bauhaus revolutionized the architectural education and scenes – first in Europe, then in Latin and North America, and finally world-wide. Internationally renowned architects like Frank Lloyd Wright or Le Corbusier rejected the École as "the great center of architectural education"[4]. Whereas in France too the the foundations of modern architecture were being re-adjusted, the walls of the Beaux-Arts stronghold were being damaged. But the École was thrown on the defensive not only by the successes of avant-garde and modernism. Financial problems and lack of space weakened her too, to the point that the reputation of the École suffered badly at the beginning of the 1930s.

So GMC's study was marked by a time of ideological upheavel. Of his own studies we only know some keynotes: the period of his studies (1920-1929), the entrance examination project, grades and main professors.

In Paris two distinct moments made a decisive impact on GMC's architectural education: in the first place, the École itself with its programme of studies, the atelier and design system, and GMC's professors, mentors and colleagues; second, the Parisian architectural movements with their disruptions and pre-eminent figures and major events. The attempt to clarify these circumstances and relate them to each other appears even more legitimate as the complex dispute over architectural renewal in Paris during the two world wars was being marked, not only by the clash of two opposed groups: the *architecture nouvelle* led by Le Corbusier and the arch-conservative Beaux-Arts traditionalists around Gustave Umbdenstock and Louis Hautecœur. But there was a third movement launched by a number of progressive Beaux-Arts professors and graduates – the so-called *Groupe des Architectes Modernes*.[5] Beyond individual focuses, these architects tried to harmonize modernism with classical architectural principles. This approach probably inspired GMC too.

32 Félix Duban, *Palais des études*, École des Beaux-Arts, Paris (c. 1832-1840). (Photograph ADT).

33 Le Corbusier, *Croisade ou la Crépuscule des Académies*. Paris 1933.
© VG Bild-Kunst, Bonn, 2014.

31 Opposite:
GMC, *X dômes de Paris*, 1925.
View of the Place de la Concorde from the Rue Royale. Pencil drawing (AMLSC).

34 École des Beaux-Arts, Paris. Palais des études, courtyard. (Photograph ADT).

The system of studies at the École

The architectural training at the École consisted of four levels: admission examination, two-partite study, and *Grand Prix de Rome*. After the successful admission examination the élèves had to pass through two classes: the *seconde* (basic studies, a sort of Bachelor), was followed by the *première* (main study, a kind of Master studies). The studies could be concluded with an internationally acknowledged diploma and was open to all nationalities. The final academic step for students, however, the *Grand Prix de Rome* competition, was reserved for French students only: "The winner of the Grand Prix de Rome stood, so to speak, at the top of the École's pyramid. Only one man a year could reach the height."[6]

This system of *seconde* and *première* rested on lectures and *concours* (design projects). Lectures were optional, with written exams solely in mathematics and the natural sciences. In order to pass from the *seconde* into the *première*, students were required a minimum of credits in the following subjects: architectural composition, construction design, mathematics, analytical geometry, stereotomy, perspective, architectural history, *éléments analytique* (graphic analysis of the classical orders), and *l'enseignement simultané des trois arts* (which comprised three concours in ornamental and nude drawing, and a concours in architectural sculpture focusing on bas-reliefs). The most demanding design project at the École was the integral *concours* in construction design. Most design projects were concerned with architectural composition. Two kinds of *concours* complemented each other in a monthly turn: *esquisses* (here: short design projects which lasted twelve hours) and *projets rendus* (comprehensive design projects that took up to three months of work).

The atelier culture

The *élèves* studied in ateliers under the supervision of a patron, whom they had chosen from the start. The patrons themselves were renowned architects, usually former *Grand Prix de Rome* winners. They were expected to be tutors, to lecture and enlighten their pupils through professional authority, an outstanding personality and excellent manners. Their supervision lessons, of which there were two or three per week, were full of revelations about architectural and cultural education.[7] The ateliers were master-classes and workshops competing with each other. They formed the heart of the École, and even more so as they were run by the students themselves. Since the foundation of the École in 1823 the ateliers established an original tradition with advanced students initiating the freshmen into a close community devoted to architecture and student life. Its features were as follows: student hierarchy, passionate intellectual discussions, intense animated working atmosphere and professional solidarity. "Old and new ones, élèves of the *première* and the *seconde* alike were brought together in the same atelier, working in a close community."[8]

Younger students were helping advanced *élèves* with drawings for imminent *concours*; in their turn, the advanced students supervised the design projects of the younger ones. "Initiation ragging, surprise parties, the Bal des

35 École des Beaux-Arts, Paris. Entrance to the Salle Melpoméne. Period postcard (ADT).

4 z'arts, pranks in the Latin Quarter, all-night work sessions, the filth and conviviality of the ateliers, casual dress and gross language, daubers' slang, graffiti, association subscriptions, drinking songs, brass bands, the costumed processions for Rougevin: [...] This atelier-lore, so much a part of the school's life, is mostly gone today."[9]

Usually projects were completed just in time. Then the *élèves* hasted with *charettes* (chariots) full of plans and canvasses from their ateliers in Montparnasse for handing them over at the *Salle Melpoméne*. If an *élève* gained a mention, a medaille, or even a *Grand Prix de Rome*, the entire atelier shared in celebrating the success. Such distinctions, as well as diplomas, were awarded in the *Hémicycle des Prix*.

36 Charles Collens, *Students with a charette full of plans on their way from an external atelier to the École des Beaux-Arts in Paris.* Drawing c. 1900.

The "spirit of design"[10]

The École trained her *élèves* in solving contemporary tasks through clear architectural compositions. The design method was called *esquisse*. In art, *esquisse* usually denotes a sketch. At the École des Beaux-Arts the *esquisse* was also a design method based on sketching. It required from the student to develop a project from a preliminary drawing. More precisely, the initial sketch had to express the student's design idea. While developping the design project in drawings on various scales, the student had to stick to the initial idea.

This design method was fundamental for the competition system. If a student wished to partake in a competition *(concours)*, he received the exposé and chose himself one of the semi-partitioned compartments *(loges)* in the drawing hall. In no more than twelve hours he had to visualise his design idea in a sketch. The students were not allowed any books or other sources of information, but were free to talk to each other. Once the preliminary drawing submitted, the student would no longer be in the position to change his design. On the other hand, he was permitted to save a copy for himself, in order to show it to his professor and develop the final design project *(projet rendu)*. The jury would judge the final project not only in terms of compositional qualities, but also if it reflected the idea contained in the initial sketch. That idea was termed *parti*. The design project was a success, only if the jury thought that the *parti* had come out well (if it was *bien trouvé*). Otherwise the student was declared out of competition *(hors du concours)*. In that case he would have wasted up to three months of studies without acquiring any credits at all.

Indeed, "the esquisse was the critical founding act of design".[11] By virtue of this design method the École trained the student in cultivating two abilities: in the first place, the critical and intellectual independence; secondly, steadfastness. Here intellectual independence stands for proposing an original design; steadfastness means to stick to it, that is to keep oneself from being distracted from it, not even by the professor. "Independence, courage and power of conception, apart from books and precedents – that is what the sketch in the loges signifies the bottom stone of the foundation of the École system – knowledge and skill, alive within a man's own personality, yielding self-independence and ability to bring imagination to bear".[12]

37 École des Beaux Arts, Paris. *View of the Cour Murier.* (Photograph ADT).

GMC's professors at the École

38 Gustave Umbdenstock, Tower of the *Nouveau Monge* pavilion, at the École Polytechnique, Paris (c. 1935), overlooking the Rue des Écoles (Photograph ADT).

Gustave Umbdenstock

The summer of 1920 saw GMC beginnig his studies at the École. He was accepted in the atelier of Gustave Umbdenstock (1866-1940) together with his friends Horia Creangă and Lucia Dumbrăveanu. It was perhaps Nicolae Ghika-Budeşti who suggested GMC to go Umbdenstock, who was a former study colleague of Ghika-Budeşti at the École. GMC probably appreciated his first *patron* as influential architect and brilliant draughtsman. By contrast, Umbdenstock's polemic and arch-conservative dogmatism and academic eclecticism could hardly have attracted GMC – especially as Umbdenstock was one of Le Corbusier's arch-ennemies.[1]

Umbdenstock's position was undoubtedly far from providing GMC with a satisfying inspiration for a question he was concerned with from the very beginning of his studies: architectural renewal, particularly in Romania. Rather, GMC must have felt attracted by the *Groupe des Architectes Modernes*, the progressive circle around Tony Garnier, Auguste Perret and Henri Sauvage. Roger-Henri Expert was a member of it. The *Groupe* was founded in 1922, and in the next year GMC left the atelier of Umbdenstock – rather unusual, already during the seconde –, in favour of the atelier run by the open-minded Expert and Georges Gromort.[2]

Georges Gromort

Committed as he was to the legacy of Quatremère de Quincy (1755-1849) and Julien Guadet (1834-1908), the great Beaux-Arts professors of architectural history, Georges Gromort (1870-1961) taught history and theory of architecture. The author of numerous writings in this field, Gromort was a passionate connoiseur particularly of Renaissance architecture, French classicism and Palladianism. Thanks to his English mother he was bilingual and attracted many students from England and the USA.[3]

From the start, GMC indulged in Gromort's books and lectures, which inspired him greatly. Later, he was himself to become a devoted professor of architectural history in Bucharest. Gromort sought in informal conversations to offer his *élèves* a reasonable and understandable access to the classical basics of architecture. This Beaux-Arts doctrine relied on a Cartesian synthesis of Aristotelian and neoplatonic principles. Beauty was considered to be the pivotal *raison d'être* of architecture, and could be achieved through well proportioned compositions. The teaching of the principles of architectural composition implied the education of taste. Taste would awaken and evolve if the *élève* would industriously keep studying classics. Gromort's chief examples came from the Graeco-Roman antiquity, Italian and French Renaissance and Classicism. He sincerely tried to give his students an enduring confidence. His character radiated a liberal attitude and calmness, which must have instantly attracted GMC, who valued intellectual independence. Also Gromort made it clear that his teaching did not aim to be easy. Therefore, he advised potential students to have a thorough look at his work and position before joining his atelier, or to choose another *patron* or mentor.

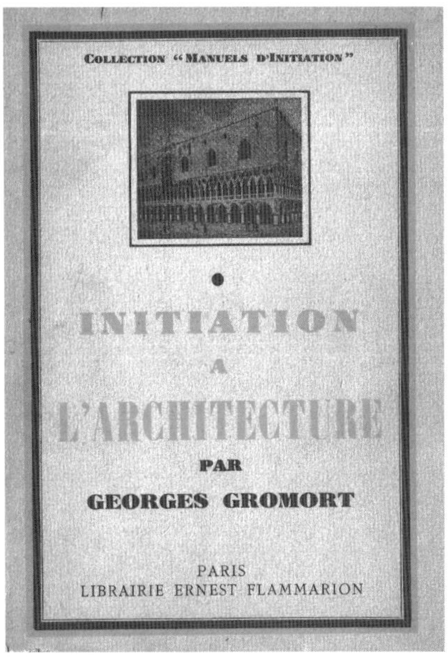

39 Georges Gromort, *Initiation à l'architecture*. Paris 1938. Front cover.

"The choice of a mentor is quite a serious matter. Therefore, before you make your choice, I would wish you to take your time and think hard, even if you can have but a general idea of the studies you would take up."[4]

Apart from Marthe Bibesco and Matila Ghyka, Gromort could have been the one mentor who might have aroused GMC's life-long passion for considering "Architecture as a theme of thought"[5]; for building up his own attitude and stay with it; for looking through architectural history for elements which stay topical and fit for resolving contemporary problems; and for taking a public stand on questions of the day. Gromort also may have introduced GMC to another discipline, to whose beauty GMC was susceptible since his childhood in Vienna and holidays at Mogoşoaia: landscape architecture. Later GMC himself was to write about and teach landscape architecture at the Institute of Urban Planning of the Polytechnic University in Bucharest. He emphasized that landscape architecture is as an integral part of the architectural design – a new approach in Romania at the time.[6]

40 Georges Gromort (1870-1961). © Académie d'Architecture, Paris.

Furthermore, Gromort promoted GMC's career in architectural journalism. He possibly recommended his élève to two institutions which were close to the École des Beaux-Arts. To *L'Architecture*, the conservative Parisian periodical, GMC contributed with the very first article published on Romanian architecture outside that country, *L'Architecture roumaine (1927)*. In addition Gromort perhaps cleared the way to the Parisian publishing house Vincent, Fréal et Cie, which published two books by GMC: the monograph on the Chrissoveloni Bank, and an anthology of historical buildings from Romania, both vernacular and religious, as the seventh volume of the *Petits Édifices* series. To the monograph on the Chrissoveloni Bank Gromort wrote the preface. It shows the professor's high esteem for his élève:

"My dear friend, it is always a pleasure to preface a beautiful work. But what a delight it is if that work involves a successful student of yours, particularly if you realize, after the effort of a number of years, that you still agree with him on so many essentials."[7]

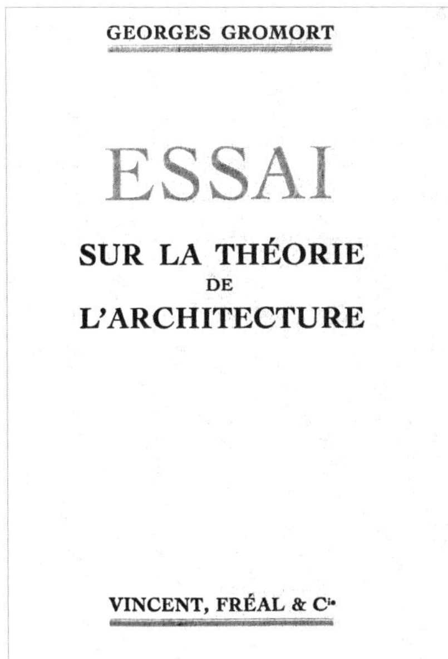

GEORGES GROMORT

ESSAI

SUR LA THÉORIE DE L'ARCHITECTURE

VINCENT, FRÉAL & Cie

41 Georges Gromort, *Essai sur la théorie de l'architecture*. Paris 1946 [1942]. Title page.

The preface also shows that the mentor aroused his students passion for Palladio, and probably for Vitruvius too. Indeed, Vitruvius and Palladio were studied at the École. Their figures were also incorporated in the decoration of the Palais d'études: a round plaque commemorates Vitruvius at the entrance to the main courtyard; and Palladio is part of the imaginary meeting of classic masters as painted in 1841 by Paul Laroche in his monumental fresco of the Hémicycle.

Throughout his entire career GMC was fascinated with Vitruvius and Palladio. On Palladio he wrote a critical essay in French (Bucharest 1928); in 1947 he produced the first ever translation into Romanian of Vitruvius's *Ten Books on Architecture*, and wrote a substantial introduction. Whilst working on *Palladio. Un essai critique*, GMC may have realized that Gromort had two essential qualities GMC attributed to Giargiorgio Trissino, Palladio's first mentor: erudition and intellectual discipline. The following passage reads as if GMC had laid out some corner-stones of his own future teaching:

"Thanks to him Palladio acquired his erudition and intellectual discipline. There is nothing more substantial that a master can give to his student."[8]

42 Paul Delaroche, Painting for the fresco in the Hémicycle of the Palais des études, École des Beaux-Arts, Paris. Detail showing architects and painters. In: P. Delaroche/ L.-P. Henri-Dupont, *L'hémicycle du palais des beaux-arts*. Tübingen 1859 (WLB Stuttgart, Sch. K. fol. 56, fig. 3). The sixth figure from the left (with his back to the viewer) depicts Andrea Palladio. The eighth figure from left shows Inigo Jones.

GEORGES GROMORT

HISTOIRE ABRÉGÉE DE

L'ARCHITECTURE DE LA RENAISSANCE EN ITALIE

OUVRAGE COURONNÉ PAR L'ACADÉMIE DES BEAUX-ARTS (PRIX BAILLY, 1914)

NOUVELLE ÉDITION ORNÉE DE 160 ILLUSTRATIONS

PARIS
A. VINCENT, ÉDITEUR
4, Rue des Beaux-Arts
M. CM. XXII

43 Georges Gromort, *Histoire abregée de la Renaissance en Italie*. Paris 1922. Title page.

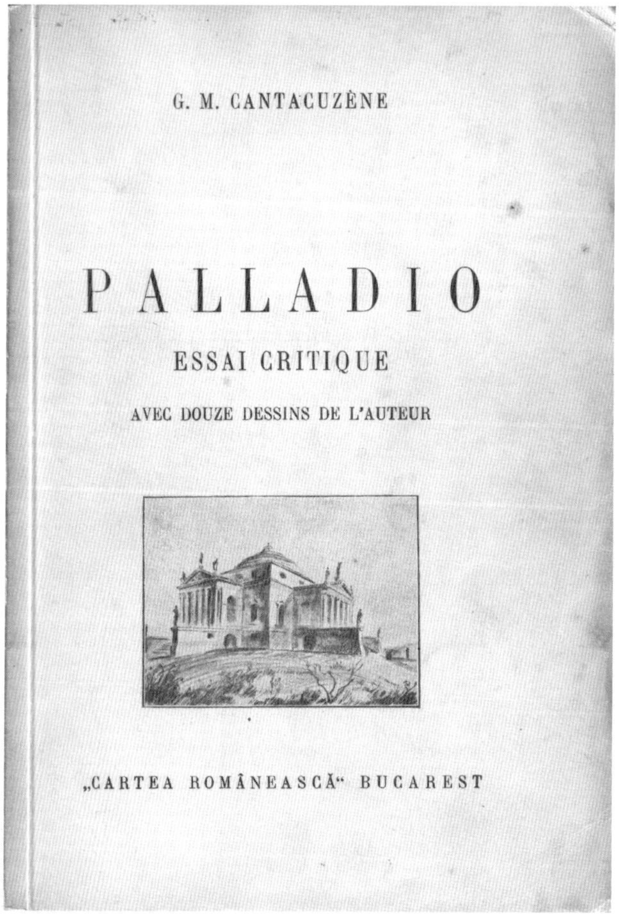

G. M. CANTACUZÈNE

PALLADIO

ESSAI CRITIQUE

AVEC DOUZE DESSINS DE L'AUTEUR

„CARTEA ROMÂNEASCĂ" BUCAREST

44 GMC, *Palladio. Essai Critique*. Bucharest 1928. Front cover.

45 GMC, *Analytical drawing of a detail from Andrea Palladio's Basilica (Palazzo della Ragione) in Vicenza*, c. 1928 (AGMC-PM)

46 Roger-Henri Expert, Atelier Building of the École des Beaux-Arts, Rue Jacques Callot, Paris, 1933. (Photograph ADT).

Roger-Henri Expert

The third Beaux-Arts professor under which GMC studied was the architect Roger-Henri Expert (1882-1955). Though a former élève of Umbdenstock, Expert was open to Modernism.[9] In the 1930s Expert became, in the words of Franco Borsi, "in a sense the most French figure – if French implies primarily rationality and elegance"[10]. Indeed Expert was a member of the *Groupe des Architectes Modernes* who attempted a synthesis between French classicism and Modernism:

"Most importantly, he blended the logical and scientific undercurrent of the architecture of the period with a retrospective affinity for Hellenism."[11]

His works include the school at the Rue de Kuss in southern Paris (1931-34), interior design of the transatlantic steamliner *Normandie* (1932-35), and a building to house external ateliers of the École at the Rue Jacques Callot in the sixth arrondissement. Expert's project was the only outbreak of the École's immobility before 1945 along with Auguste Perret's atelier building. Between the two world wars Expert was reputed as "ambassador of French taste"[12]. His major diplomatic architecture include a pavilion of the Colonial Exhibition in Paris (1931), the French Embassy in Belgrade (1934), and the theatre and fountains in the basement of the Palais de Tokyo overlooking the Champs de Mars and the Tour Eiffel for the Paris World's Fair (1937).

Undoubtedly GMC appreciated Expert's approach to architecture. He was himself to pursue at times a purist classicism and was active as a diplomatic architect. After his diploma, GMC and Expert were still close. Expert possibly recommended GMC to André Bloc, director of *L'Architecture d'Aujourd'hui*. In this Parisian modernist periodical GMC published *Tenden-*

47 Roger-Henri Expert, school on the Rue de Kuss, Paris (1931-1934). Street view. (Photograph ADT).

48 Roger-Henri Expert, school on the Rue de Kuss, Paris (1931-1934). View of the courtyard Period photograph by Salaün, in: *L'Architecture d'aujourd'hui* 4/1934, p. 18.

ces dans l'architecture roumaine (1934), devoted to the modernist works of his colleagues Horia Creangă, Octav Doicescu, Marcel Janco and Horia Teodoru. The article too presented some of GMC's own works, including the Hotel Bellona and villa Aviana on the Black Sea Coast at Eforie. Subsequently, in 1935 GMC was appointed correspondent of *L'Architecture d'Aujourd'hui* – he was in fact the very first Romanian correspondent of a European architectural review.[13]

Their paths were to cross again at the 1939 New York World's Fair, where Expert and GMC designed the official pavilions of their own country – in close promixity just opposite the Lagoon of Nations.

49 Aerial view of the Transatlantic *Normandie*. The interior was designed by Roger-Henri Expert (1932-35). Period postcard of the Companie Général Transatlantique (ADT).

GMC as a student

The grades recorded in his two surviving certificates show that GMC was a brilliant student. His projects, however, are lost, most probably due to "the saturnalia of May 1968"[1], when parts of the École's archives were destroyed by the rioting students. Of GMC's student days there are few things left: apart from his certificates, there is a photograph of his admission project, a portfolio comprising ten pencil drawings of Parisian domes and a watercolour of an interior of Georges and Marthe Bibesco's apartment in Paris.

Throughout his life GMC will stay a passionate draughtsman. For him, to draw is to communicate with nature or landscapes or cityscapes on a both intellectual and sensual level:

"To draw is, not to imitate, but to transpose what one sees. Drawing is in fact an act of intelligence."[2]

His studies lasted from 1920 to 1929. What by today's standards may appear so long a period had two reasons. The first we can ascribe to the École's system of studies, which, again by today's standards, may seem unexpectedly generous, since it allowed for and even welcomed several study tours and long-term stages in architectural offices.[3] The second reason might have been financial: most probably GMC was independent, especially from 1923 onwards, on account of his practical activity in co-operation with August Schmiedigen. Many of GMC's colleagues and friends at the École, including his Romanian comrades, worked in architectural offices.[4]

To the Parisian architectural scene in the inter-war years there can hardly be more an eloquent witness than the German architectural historian Julius Posener (1904-1996), who in the 1930s was secretary of *L'Architecture d'aujourd'hui* and probably knew GMC. In his memoirs Posener described how he was once received by the architect Léon Bazin, then partner at the atelier Albert Laprade:

"'Am I to assume, Posener,' said Bazin, 'that where you come from one undertakes his studies in a go? This is preposterous! In France one studies and then works, and goes on studying and working. Me, I am myself a student at the École for the last ten years. Meanwhile I became the right-hand man of [Albert] Laprade, but from time to time I return to the École.'"[5]

50 GMC, *Apartment of Marthe Bibesco in Paris*. Watercolour, 1931 (AMLSC).

Posener too evoked "the fraternity of the nègres [...] an international fraternity, including anyone who had one or two jobs in Paris [...] But I disapproved of the complacent way in which the term idealism was abused by

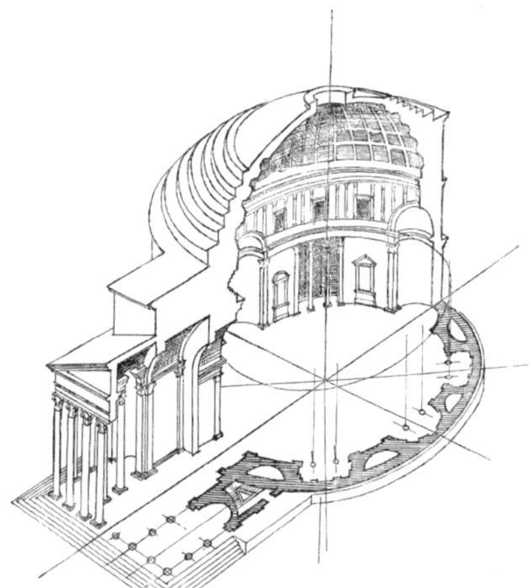

51 GMC, The Pantheon, Rome. Analytical drawing showing the main horizontal and vertical axes (*Simetria V*, 1943).

those young idlers who could afford to work for nothing. [...] The idlers at Corb [Le Corbusier] were no *nègres*, a *nègre* had no money."[6]

But GMC obviously refused to become a *nègre* or *idler*, regardless of whether this would have been with a Beaux-Arts professor or a famous modernist like Le Corbusier. Instead, GMC opted for practising architecture in a rather independent and private way: first, at Mogoşoaia, where he learned the art of a stonemason; second, through his own projects together with August Schmiedigen; and third, during private study trips and talks with his mentors, including Marthe Bibesco, Georges Gromort, Matila Ghyka and Theodor Pallady. As the École's study obligations went against the grain of his inclination to intellectual independence, from 1925 he studied the minimum necessary for securing his student status. It was not before 1927 that he finished the seconde. His focus on the première was much more determined, as he graduated on 19th February 1929 with a 1ère Seconde Medaille.[7]

The relevance of the École for GMC

One of the outstanding concerns of the École that surely must have captured GMC was the intellectual independence of the élèves – that "you must be yourself"[8].

In addition the design system based on *portfolio*, *parti*, and *esquisse* could have carried weight with GMC for his own office practice. Such practice comprised the primacy of the ground plan for the design and the concern with horizontal and vertical axes, which were meant to organize and shape the architectural composition along ground plans, sections and details into a coherent entity. This Beaux-Arts style also included, as Bruno Foucart pointed out, "a certain capacity to handle ornament, to integrate it into an analysis of approach and programme, and adapt it to functions. [...] If the École functioned, it was because it expounded a programme which asserted that there is no contradiction between modernity and history: modernity is woven from history and history is so full of possibilities that it cannot possibly be a hindrance to creation."[9]

In his comparative study of the education systems of the Beaux-Arts and the Modernist schools of architecture, *The portfolio and the diagram* (2004), Hyungmin Pai emphasized the importance of the *esquisse* for office practice:

"The logic of the esquisse was also central to office practice [...] It was [the chief's] responsibility and capacity in producing the quick sketch of the parti that distinguished him from his subordinates, who simply worked out his basic schemes."[10]

52 Auguste and Gustave Perret, *Atelier building for Chana Orloff*, 7b Villa Seurat, Paris, 1926 (Photograph ADT).

On the other hand, GMC and his Parisian and Romanian friends did not pursue something tedious and academic, but embraced modernist values. In operative terms, this bears camparison with the circle of Ion Mincu: both the latter and the group around GMC and Creangă learned the classical basics taught at the École, but took up the avant-garde tendency in Europe and introduced it in Romania – regionalism and *Heimatstil* for one thing, Modernism for another.[11] Finally GMC seemed to have been particularly captivated by the moderate modernist approach of the *Groupes des Architectes Modernes*, and from 1926 onwards he established his *classical attitude*.

The *Groupe des Architectes Modernes* and guest architects in Paris

Founded at the *Salon d'Autumne* in 1922, the *Groupe des Architectes Modernes* along with the *Section d'Art Urbain* involved some progressive Beaux-Arts professors and architects around the leading figures Tony Garnier, Auguste Perret and Henri Sauvage. They promoted attempts to root modernism in French classicism. This compound movement had some three basic ramifications: in the first place, the group around Henri Sauvage, Frantz Jourdain, Hector Guimard and Charles Plument argued for continuing *Art nouveau*; second, the circle of Tony Garnier, Auguste Perret and Michel-Roux-Spitz championned a "structural classicism"[12]; and finally, the set around Pol Abraham, Léon Azéma, Roger-Henri Expert and Pierre Patout sought to renew classicist principles through cubism up to the late 1930s.[13]

In the 1930s there emerged too a monumental Neo-classicism, pursued by architects like Léon Azéma, Louis Auguste Boileau, Jacques Carlu, Léon Jaussely, Albert Laprade, but also by Expert and Perret. As for Perret, GMC esteemed him highly as a "humanistic architect, who, unlike the majority of its colleagues, has not forgotten to accommodate man in his buildings".[14]

53 Adolf Loos, *House for Tristan Tzara*, 15 Avenue Junot, Paris (1925-26). Garden view. Period photograph.

Perret, Umbdenstock and Le Corbusier can be considered as the leading figures of the main streams of the architectural scene in Paris. Among the Parisian architectural guests, so to speak, two personalities stand out: Theo van Doesburg and Adolf Loos.[15] It is possible that GMC knew the villa built by Loos in 1926 for Tristan Tzara (1896-1963), the Romanian-born Dadaist and writer, on 15 Avenue Junot in Montmartre. Again, it is possible that together with his student-friends he attended lectures given by Loos at the Sorbonne during his stay in Paris from 1923 to 1928.[16]

Student life and cultural circles

At the École GMC befriended Georges Leconte[1], Georges Michau[2] and Georges Pingusson[3]. GMC met Leconte and Pingusson in the atelier run by Gustave Umbdenstock.

Michau became a poet, whereas Leconte won a *Grand Prix de Rome* in 1927 and became a renowned professor at the École and its Dean. His architectural works include an elegant corner apartment building on 67 Quai d'Orsay overlooking the Seine. In 1949 Pingusson (1894-1978) was also appointed professor at the École. He opened his first independent office in 1925 after finishing his studies. His *Hotel Latitude 43* in Saint Tropez (1929-32) was celebrated as one of the most impressive modernist achievements at the time, and possibly influenced GMC in his design of *Hotel Bellona* at Eforie (1932-34). In the 1920s Pingusson worked with Le Corbusier, producing some notable projects like the corner apartment building at 5 rue Denfert-Rochereau in Boulogne-Billancourt (1932-36). Pingusson's works include the *Théâtre de Menus-Plaisirs* (1930; now *Théâtre de la Comédie*), the French Embassy at Saarbrücken in Germany (1950-54; now Office of Education) and the Monument for the Martyrs of Nazi Deportation on the southern corner of the *Île de la Cité* in Paris (1961-62). Pingusson co-founded the *Association of Friends of Georges Cantacuzino*, which in 1965 commemorated GMC in Paris with a memorial at the bookshop Vincent, Fréal et Cie.

54 G. Leconte, *Apartment building*, 67 Quai d'Orsay, Paris, 1935. (Photograph ADT).

55 Georges Pingusson, Apartment building, 5 rue Denfert-Rochereau in Boulogne-Billancourt, Paris, 1932-36. (Photograph ADT).

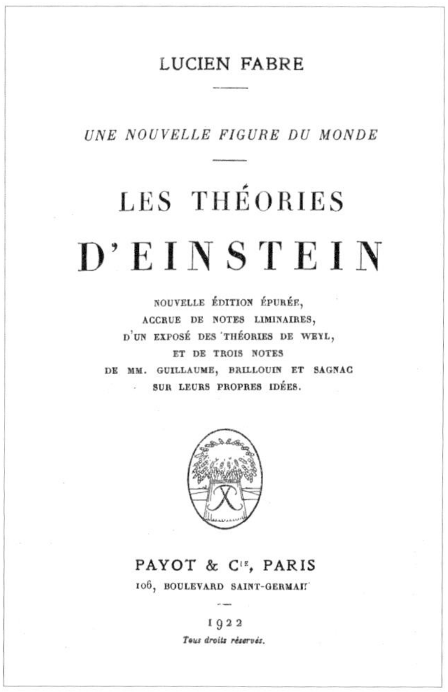

LUCIEN FABRE

UNE NOUVELLE FIGURE DU MONDE

LES THÉORIES

D'EINSTEIN

NOUVELLE ÉDITION ÉPURÉE,
ACCRUE DE NOTES LIMINAIRES,
D'UN EXPOSÉ DES THÉORIES DE WEYL,
ET DE TROIS NOTES
DE MM. GUILLAUME, BRILLOUIN ET SAGNAC
SUR LEURS PROPRES IDÉES.

PAYOT & CIE, PARIS
106, BOULEVARD SAINT-GERMAIN

1922

Tous droits réservés.

56 Lucien Fabre, *Les théories d'Einstein*. Paris 1922. Front cover.

GMC shared a flat with three Romanian friends in the Rue du Cherche Midi Nos 113-115 in Montparnasse: the architects Ion Davidescu and Horia Teodoru, and Alexander Rosetti, who became professor of literature at the University of Bucharest.[4] GMC's circle of friends also involved Georges Bratiano, the historian, liberal policitian and founder of the Young Liberals; Ion Jalea, the sculptor, and Mihai Ralea (1896-1964), the sociologist.

GMC and friends did not miss the Parisian *joie de vivre*. In Montparnasse and St-Germain-des-Près, the centres of artistic and literary avant-gardes on the Left Bank, they frequented cafés such as *La Coupole*, *Le Café de Flore*, *Le Dôme*, *La Closerie des Lilas*, or *la Rotonde*.

In such cultural strongholds the young friends plunged into the rich spiritual atmosphere enhanced by Romanian-born artists such as Brancusi, Brauner or Tzara and by their colleagues and friends such as Cocteau, Duchamp, Satie, Giacometti, Lèger, Modigliani, Picasso or Man Ray.

Thanks to his Paris-based relatives GMC had the opportunity to gain a more intimate insight into some artistic and intellectual circles.

Together with Marthe Bibesco (1887-1973) he strolled through the old Paris and Jardin des Tuileries, or met her at cafés such as *Le Vieux Colombier* or *Le Perroquet Vert*, named after one of her novels.[5] Thanks to novels like *Les Huits paradis* (1908) and *Isvor. Le pays des saules* (1923) Marthe was welcomed by the Parisian literary circles as "reigning beauty and genius"[6]. In 1946 she settled in Paris. It was Marthe who provided GMC with a more intimate approach to the works of Cocteau, Gide, Proust, Rilke and Valéry. It is possible that she also gave him deeper insight into the political situation in Europe as learned from conversations with Aristide Briand, Winston Churchill or Ramsay MacDonald.[7]

Anna de Noailles (1876-1933), the Brancovan-born French poetess, once asked GMC if he was as good an architect as she was a poet. Modestly but determined, he said yes, he was as good.[8] Anna de Noailles established herself as "reine du Tout-Paris"[9] thanks to her first volumes *Le Cœur innombrable* (1901) and *L'Ombre des Jours* (1902). Committed as she was to the romantic tradition of Baudelaire, James and Verlaine, she valued instant inspiration. Léon Blum and Jean Cocteau were among her close friends. She was elected member of the *Académie royale de langue et littérature françaises de Belgique* in 1922 and was shortlisted for the Nobel Prize for Literature in 1927, which was finally awarded to Henri Bergson.[10]

In conversations with Matila Ghyka (1881-1965) GMC was moved by aesthetic questions on proportions, the Golden Section and Neoplatonism. Ghyka was an internationally renowned cultural historian, especially in the interwar-period. His writings include *L'Esthétique des proportions dans la nature et dans les arts* (1927) and *Le Nombre d'or* (1931), both prefaced by Paul Valéry. Ghyka later became a co-editor of GMC's cultural review *Simetria*. He was also a diplomat in Berlin, Rome, Washington D.C., Madrid, Warsaw, Paris, Vienna, Stockholm and London. In London he was also Vice-President of the Free Romanian National Committee (1940-44), which opposed the Antonescu regime in favour of the exiled King Carol II. After 1945 Ghyka lectured for a short time in the USA. He died impoverished in London in 1965.[11]

It is possible that Ghyka introduced GMC to French writers Paul Morand and Lucien Fabre. For his city portrait *Bucharest* (1935), Morand drew heavily on GMC's introduction into the architecture and culture of Bucharest, both historic and contemporary.[12] With Fabre GMC became a very good friend for the rest of his life. To him GMC dedicated the essay on Palladio (1928) and the last chapter of his Middle East travel book *Moonwatch* (1938).

Lucien Fabre (1889-1952) was a French engineer, businessman and writer. A disciple of Jean Jaurès, Fabre throughout his life maintained close connections with Léon Blum and French Socialism. The anthology of poems *Connaissance de la déesse* was published in 1920 with a preface by Paul Valéry. Fabre's *Les théories d'Einstein: une nouvelle figure du monde* (1921) was instrumental in making Albert Einstein's Theory of Relativity known to the larger public. Fabre was awarded prizes such as the *Prix Goncourt* (1923) and the *Grand Prix d'Histoire de l'Académie française* (1948).[13]

In Paris GMC got fascinated by so-called decadent poets like Jules Laforgue and Jean-Paul Toulet, prominent if tragic figures of the bohemian avant-garde around 1900. They remained "intimate poets who never deserted"[14] him. They belonged to the circle which pivoted around the *Revue Blanche* periodical and received substantial support from the Bibesco family. The Parisian salon of Hélène Bibesco was frequented by writers, musicians and *Nabis* artists. This cosmopolitan circle imbued with love for Europe and devoted to the friendship between France and Germany[15] included Léon Blum, Pierre Bonard, Georges Enesco, Aristide Maillol, Anna de Noailles, Marcel Proust, Camille Saint-Saens and Edouard Vuillard. Enesco dedicated a large part of his compositions to Hélène Bibesco. Her sons, Antoine (1878-1951) and Emmanuel (187-1917), continued the family tradition of patronage of the arts. The intimate friends of the Bibesco's included Bonnard, Gauguin, Maillol, Proust and Vuillard. Antoine Bibesco, who was particularly close to GMC,[16] probably introduced him to Edouard Vuillard (1868-1940), the painter. On strolls through Versailles in April 1919 Vouillard talked to GMC about art and encouraged him to keep drawing:

"Remember that art ought be anchored in drawing. Because drawing, as Michelangelo used to say, gives you a better understanding of the world."[17]

And thanks to Pallady GMC learned to know the works of Théodore Chassériau, Pierre Puvis de Chavannes and the Fauves around Matisse. Often GMC met Pallady "in the Egyptian Galleries of the Louvre"[18]. He was particularly fascinated by Pallady's deep admiration for the "ascetic pride of Egyptian sculpture"[19]. GMC perhaps was the "sole disciple"[20] of the stoic and taciturn Pallady: Pallady too gave GMC lessons in painting in his tiny atelier overlooking the beautiful Place Dauphine, before recommending him to his Fauve friend Othon Friesz and perhaps to Pedro Aro-Jo. GMC benefited greatly from the "artistic rigour of Friesz"[21] and the apprenticeship with Pedro Aro-Jo, who taught him,

"'[W]hen you look at nature in order to paint it, do not blink, so that you see it only in vague blotches, but rather open your eyes as wide as you can.'

Open your eyes, these words I have adopted for the motto of my inner coat of arms"[22], wrote GMC in 1957 in a letter to Simon Bayer.

57 Constantin Brancusi, *The Kiss* (1909). Since c. 1926 in Montparnasse Cemetery as memorial for Tanjuscha Raschewskaia. (Photograph ADT).

58 Jean Cocteau, *Anna de Noailles*. Drawing (c.1910-1914). © VG Bild-Kunst, Bonn, 2014.

At the same time GMC profited from the rich cultural and scientific life of Paris. At the École he met art historian Charles Normand (1858-1934), the founding father of the *Société des Amis des Monuments Parisiens*.[23] The conversations with Normand enthused GMC about the historic Paris.

He almost certainly attended lectures by philosopher Henri Bergson at the Collège de France and art historians Charles Diehl and Henri Focillon at the Sorbonne. Later in Bucharest, as a professor himself, GMC warmly recommended the works of these great French scholars to his own students.[24]

In short, GMC not only committed himself to studying architecture, but also fostered what the German Philosopher Rüdiger Safranski called the "defensive concept of education"[25]. For such an approach GMC might have drawn further inspiration from the literary advise of Jean-A. Cantacuzène:

"Prepare yourself, young man, from today, through your studies an intellectual life, where you can take refuge whenever you long to."[26]

59 Henri Focillon (1881-1943).
© Roger-Viollet, photo no. 13727-5, SAEML Parisienne de Photographie.

60 Henri Bergson (1859-1941).
Period photograph.

61 GMC, *Landscape* (1938), perhaps a view of the Colentina river at Mogoşoaia (AMLSC).

62 Othon Friesz, *Coast landscape, La Ciotat (Bord de mer)*. Oil on canvas (1907). Paris, private collection © VG Bild-Kunst, Bonn, 2014.

63 Othon Friesz, Self-portrait, oil on canvas (1925). Paris, private collection © VG Bild-Kunst, Bonn, 2014.

64 Theodor Pallady, *The island St Louis, Paris*. Oil on canvas. Private collection in 1935. Photograph by Photo-Press, Bucharest. G. Oprescu, *L'art roumain de 1800 à nos jours*. Malmö 1935, p. 117.

65 Theodor Pallady, *Self-portrait* (1925). Oil on canvas. Brukenthal Museum, Sibiu © Brukenthal Museum.

MOGOSOEA
MCMXLV
G.M.C. -

Mogoşoaia

The Bibesco family acquired the Mogoşoaia estate in 1830, and for several times started to refurbish it, but this proved impossible because of economical or political crises. In 1894 Marthe and Georges Bibesco met the Venetian architect Domenico Rupolo (1861-1945) on one of his travels through Romania. Rupolo had an excellent expertise in conservation thanks to his refacing of the *Ca` d'Oro* (1896-97) on the Canal Grande and reconstruction of the campanile at St Marco (1907).[1] Finally in 1912 Marthe and Georges Bibesco commissioned Rupolo, who took GMC as an apprentice.[2]

The summer of 1920 saw GMC accepting with tremendous pleasure Marthe Bibesco's offer to take over the supervision from Rupolo. Essential parts were finished in 1927, whereas minor works continued up to 1931 due to financial problems.[3]

GMC designed the exterior staircase leading from the main entrance at the north-eastern corner of the palace to the great balcony, repaired the garden brick wall and the entrance tower, transformed the ancient kitchen into an atelier for Marthe and added a two-storey loggia to the *Villa Elchingen* – which was built in the late nineteenth century and named after Hélène Bibesco, née von Elchingen, the wife of Nicolas Bibesco and granddaughter of Napoleon's Marshall Ney. GMC also re-arranged the vast gardens originally layed out by the French landscape architect Rohan around 1870, and designed the terraces on the bank of the Colentina river.[4]

One of the key performances of GMC's is the contemporary external appearance of the palace.[5] Though still a student, he successfully opposed the Commission of Historic Monuments,[6] which was led by the well-known historian Nicolae Iorga and involved, among others, architect Nicolae Ghika-Budeşti, one of GMC's elderly cousins.

The Commission first insisted upon refacing the palace with plaster cladding similar to the original appearance as recorded by some historical accounts of European ambassadors and travellers to the court of the reigning prince Constantin Brancovan. However, after the beheading of Constantin Brancovan and his sons by the Turks in 1714 the palace was abandoned and decayed to the point that the best part of the plaster cladding was gone. Lost too were all original drawings according to which the palace was built and lavishly decorated with frescos and stuccos – their splendour was possibly similar to that of the little Fundenii Doamnei church in the northern part of Bucharest.

And this was the very reason why GMC withstood the pressure of the Commission of Historic Monuments: as both original plans and precise descriptions of the façade frescos were utterly missing, there was no reasonable way of truly reconstructing the initial external appearance of the palace. Subsequently GMC suggested that all the few surviving plaster surfaces from the façades should be removed in favour of deliberately displaying the full aesthetic qualities of the apparent brick cladding: the textile structure, gentle shadowing, vivid red and its warm contrast to the limestome elements of the balustrades, corniches, columns, and window frames.

67 Mogoşoaia (Work 1, see Addendum). Front view of palace. Photograph c. 1962.

68 Mogoşoaia (W 1), view of loggia during renovation. Photograph c.1920 (AMB-JG).

66 Opposite:
GMC, The Mogoşoaia palace as seen from the loggia of the ancient kitchen, 1945 (*Simetria VII*, 1946).

69 Mogoşoaia, view of loggia. Period photograph (AMB-JG).

HISTOIRE DE L'ART ROUMAIN ANCIEN

PAR

N. IORGA
Professeur à l'Université de Bucarest,
Agréé à la Sorbonne,
Membre de l'Académie Roumaine,
Correspondant de l'Institut.

G. BALȘ
Ingénieur,
Membre de la Commission
des
Monuments Historiques

PARIS
E. DE BOCCARD, Éditeur
1, Rue de Médicis
1922

70 Nicolae Iorga/George Balş, *Histoire de l'art roumain ancien*. Paris 1922, title page.

Also at Mogoşoaia GMC quite possibly met August Schmiedigen, the Bucharest builder-architect, whose company could well have been in charge of the stonemasonry works.

At Mogoşoaia GMC had the opportunity to use his own ideas and methods and improve his practical knowledge. There he too became aware of the vivid notion of tradition – tradition in the sense of a "deep unrest which keeps the spirit awake"[7] in a "critical counter-balance"[8]. Disapproving of a purely retrospective outlook, tradition was based on the study of outstanding works of the past – such as Mogoşoaia, which for GMC opened the gate to the Wallachian Brancovan Renaissance. To GMC, "tradition selects"[9] good from inadequate solutions and provides the architect with a set of values. From this starting point he embarked on studying the architectural history of Wallachia, Moldavia and Transylvania. In this matter he may have been inspired, among others, by the works of Nicolae Iorga, Nicolae Ghika-Budeşti, and Georges Balş.[10]

Such an analytical approach was an indispensable moment of intellectual integrity. GMC was convinced of the architect's duty to know and interact with the historical context of a particular project.

In a more practical sense, from Rupolo, Schmiedigen, and in debates with the Commission of Historic Monuments, GMC learned how to instill new life into old buildings. He practised how to develop a comprehensive design by harmonizing buildings and landscape architectural elements and vegetation. At the same time, he loved stone architecture and trained as a mason.

Finally, he came to appreciate Mogoşoaia as the best example of joy and ease in Wallachian architecture, and also as an embodiment of two themes that were to play so important a role in his career: the architectural harmonization and European spirit. Indeed, Mogoşoaia is a singular fusion of late-Byzantine-Wallachian and aquatic Venetian architecture, as well as of classical French and contemporary landscape architecture.

"Here on the flat Wallachain plane, ravaged for centuries by Tartar, Ottoman, Turkish, Bulgarian and Bosnian invaders, appeared, as if by miracle, a genuine Byzantine-Venetian palace, an architectural gem in all the glory of its eighteenth-century past. Early in the eighteenth century a Brancovan prince sent an architect to the great University School of Padua to study design and build him a palace which would combine Byzantine and Venetian traditions."[11]

In the footsteps of Aubry de la Mottraye, the French diplomat at the court of Constantin Brancovan, GMC attributed to Mogoşoaia a "European character"[12]. As a European centre Mogoşoaia was to become famous for its beauty and culture from 1927 to 1940 thanks to Marthe and Georges Bibesco. Marthe was inspired by her fatherly friend Aristide Briand who "taught her to believe that, after the horrors of war, the time had come to speak european".[13]

71 Mogoşoaia from the air (c. 1961). In the background, from the left are the ancient kitchen, the entrance tower, the village church (hidden by the trees) and the *Villa Elchingen*.

72 Mogoşoaia, detail of balcony and courtyard. Period photograph (AMB-JG).

73 Mogoşoaia, detail of stone balcony balustrade. Period photograph (AMB-JG).

74 Mogoşoaia, group photograph of Marthe Bibesco (*second from left, standing*) and George V. Bibesco (*first from right, sitting*) and their guests, the Aviation Ministers of France (J.-L. Dumesnil, *first from left, standing*), of Italy (Italo Balbo, *third from left, standing*), of England (Lord Amulree, *second from right, standing*) and of Germany (Gerd von Hoeppner, *sitting beside G. V. Bibesco*), on the occasion of the Convention of the International Aeronautical Federation in Bucharest in October 1931.

75 GMC/Schmiedigen, *The architects' office stamp*, 1928 (PMB).

Co-operation with August Schmiedigen

Architectural office

In 1923 GMC and August Ferdinand Schmiedigen opened an architectural office,[1] which enabled GMC, in spite of his youth and student status, to pursue projects of his own. Thanks to Schmiedigen, GMC progressed in his practical knowledge of building materials and learned how to manage an entire project by going through all projects phases from scratch via construction design to building site supervision. In addition, GMC wrote analytical studies on the traditional art and architecture of Romania. It was in these circumstances that the banker Jean Chrissoveloni (1881-1926)[2] called on GMC and asked him to design the Bucharest headquarters for the Chrissoveloni Bank.

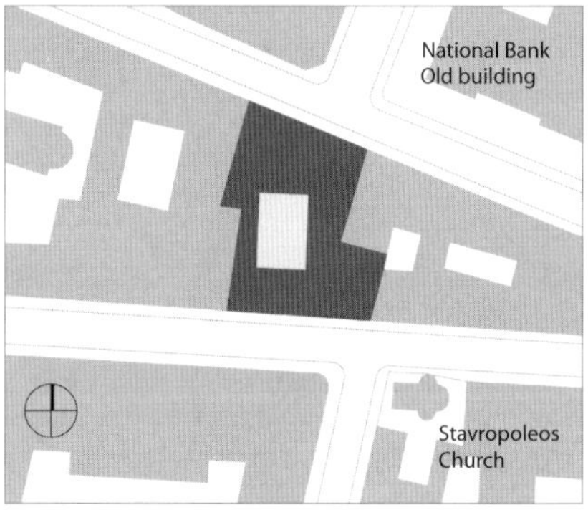

76 Chrissoveloni Bank, sitemap 1:2500 (ADT).

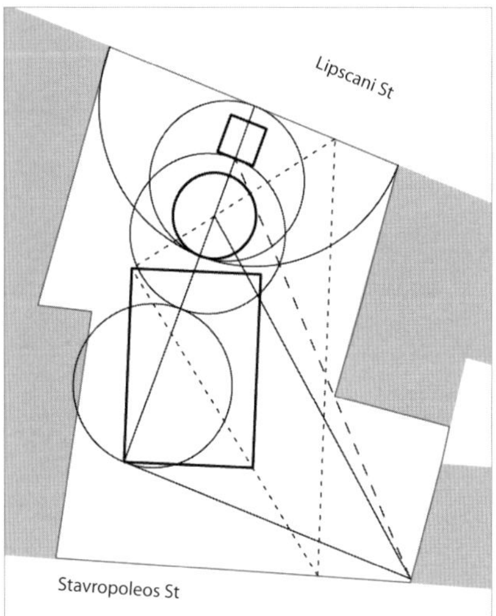

77 Chrissoveloni Bank, *Proportional study of main entrance and atrium* (ADT).

78 GMC/Schmiedigen, *Chrissoveloni Bank*, Bucharest (W 2). Front façade. Photograph W. Weiss c. 1928 (GMC/Schmiedigen 1929, plate 7).

Chrissoveloni Bank

In the inter-war period the Chrissoveloni Bank was ranked among the nine most important banks in Romania.[3] Jean Chrissoveloni desired a new representative headquarters of his bank in Lipscani, the bank district of Bucharest. He intended the building to embody not only his high professionalism, but also his social commitment and deep passion for architecture.[4]

As regards the latter, he was most probably acquainted with and approved of the architectural language GMC and Schmiedigen suggested in their design: Palladianism. One reason for this could have been his familiarity with both English and French civilisation which cultivated Classicism and Palladianism particularly for civic buildings. Jean Chrissoveloni had studied in France. Then he fostered a close business relationship with the London Hambros Bank, had English relatives and was married to Sibylle C. Youell (1881-1931), an intimate friend of Queen Mary of Romania (1875 Eastwell/Kent-1938 Sinaia).

GMC and Schmiedigen used the historical Palladianism and building typology of an urban palace as exemplified by Palladio both in his *Four Books of Architecture* and Vicentine palaces to harmonize the irregular plot and adjacent buildings – an empty space between Lipscani Street and Stavropoleos Street which lay at an angle to each other.

The architects filled the gap from street to street and arranged the building mass around the rectangular courtyard meant for public service. According to their functions, the street wings differed in depths. The main wing facing Lipscani Street accommodates the main entrance and access elements (porch, rotunda of the vestibule with access to the main staircase and elevators). Here, the rotunda mediates between the planning grids of the street wings. These subtle mechanics of design match the architects's purpose of integrating the extensive air conditioning and installations as inconspicuosly as possible.[5]

A major design feature consists in the proportioning of the rooms. It may suffice here to consider the ground floor plan. The entrance, the vestibule, and the inner courtyard have regular forms: square, circle, and rectangle respectively. The length of the entrance hall corresponds to the radius of the vestibule (c. 4 meters); its diameter has a proportion of 2 : 3 as regards the courtyard's width, with the same proportion applying to the courtyard itself (c. 12 by 18 meters). This proportion of 1,5 square is typical of the Tuscan Order and corresponds in musical terms to a fourth. It was recommended by Vitruvius and often used by Palladio.[6]

The design of the Chrissoveloni Bank is marked by two further instances typical of the best part of GMC's œuvre: the architectural fusion and the decorative theme of the tulip. Before the completion of the project, Jean Chrissoveloni died suddenly of a brain tumour, to the great grief of GMC.[7] Indeed he was grateful to have met Jean Chrissoveloni whom he acclaimed "guest at Plato's banquet"[8]. In his inauguration speech in April 1928 he said:

"The bank which we are presenting to the public today, [...] summarizes and commemorates the aspirations and ideals of a man who was particularly suited to live up to the social role of architecture.

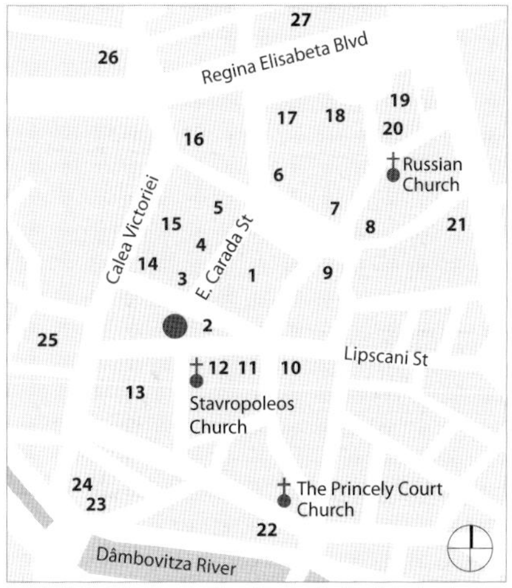

79 Site map of the Chrissoveloni Bank in Lipscani historic area of Bucharest, with a selection of banks (1850-1950) and public buildings:

1 National Bank
2 Dacia-România Insurance Company
3 Discount Bank
4 Anglo-Romanian Bank
5 Marmorosch & Blank Bank
6 French-Romanian Bank
7 Stock Exchange and Chamber of Commerce (now National Library)
8 Urban Land Credit
9 Naţionala Insurance Company
10 Berkowitz Bank
11 Fortuna Bank
12 Romanian Credit Bank
13 Post Palace (now National Museum of History)
14 Dacia Insurance Company
15 Villacross-Macca Passage
16 Rural House
17 Romanian Industry and Trade Bank
18 Generala Insurance Society
19 Industrial Credit
20 Commodities Stock Exchange
21 Rural Land Credit
22 Manuc's Han (Hotel)
23 Adriatica Insurance Company
24 Agricola Fonciera Insurance Company
25 Palace of the Savings and Loan Ban CEC
26 National Military Club
27 University of Bucharest

The site map is based on:
Pro Patrimonio Foundation (ed.): *Bucharest – Lipscani Historic Area. Panoramic Map. Banks and financial institutions 1850-1950*. Bucharest 2005.

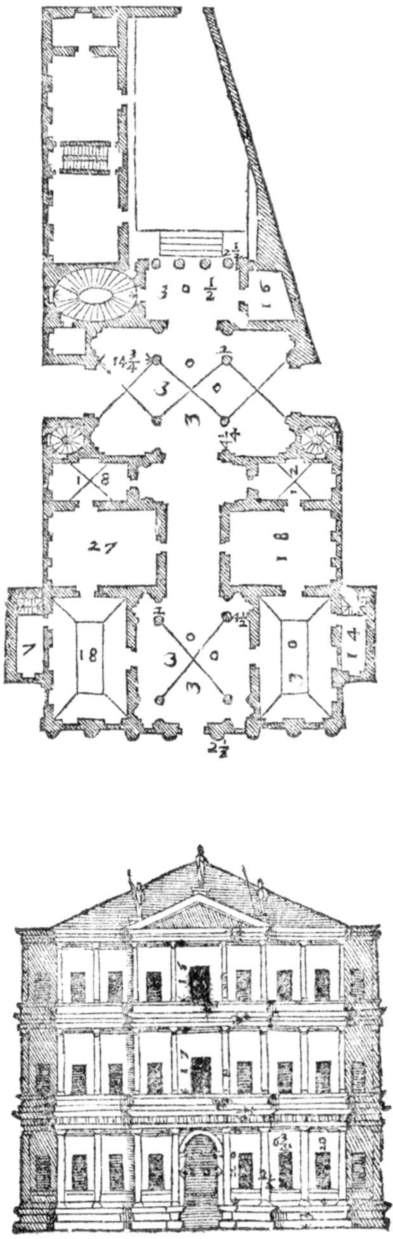

80 Andrea Palladio, *Design of an urban palace according to a pyramidal situation.* In: A. Palladio, *I quattro libri di architettura.* Venice 1601. Book II, Chapter XVII. WLB Stuttgart, Sch. K. Fol. 173.

Palladio tells us that as the great Vicentine landlords commissioned him to build their urban palaces, they did so not purely to satisfy their own needs, but also to increase the fame of their city. This very concern preoccupied Mr Jean Chrissoveloni too, in architecture as well as in finance and politics."[9]

While working on the Chrissoveloni Bank GMC undertook a "search for a contemporary discipline, [...] for 'the greatest liberty is born of the greatest rigour' (Paul Valéry)"[10]. This discipline was based on two features which had to be harmonized: one's own experience and the classical spirit as legacy of the Graeco-Roman antiquity. Palladio's attitude and work were a most conclusive embodiment of this discipline. With Palladianism being poorly represented in Romania, GMC aspired to strengthen it in that country. Gromort gave him full support:

"Undoubtedly the strong art of Palladio is as much Italian as it proved to be universal. Indeed his architecture is most suitable to various climates and regions to the point to have so brilliantly inspired the works of Jones and Wren, these two great Englishmen. For this very reason Palladio's legacy cannot be but most appropriate to enhance a latin country [like Romania]."[11]

In his inaugural GMC further observed that "the Chrissoveloni Bank is no archaeological copy. On the contrary, it is the free interpretation of some architectural memories. The main façade might recall some austere Byzantine buildings in Italy; the composition of the courtyard was inspired by the rhythm of a Veronese loggia, whereas all façades were designed according to Palladian principles of late Renaissance."[12]

The Veronese loggia GMC spoke of is none other than the two-storey *Loggia del Consiglio* attributed to Fra Giovanni Giocondo (1433-1515).[13] It could have had further significance for GMC, since the five statues of famous Veronese personalities that crown its attic include Catullus and Vitruvius, of whom GMC was particularly fond.

In Bucharest the Chrissoveloni Bank was largely recognized as an important architectural gem.[14] To accompany the completion of the project, GMC and Schmiedigen in 1929 published a comprehensive monograph at Vincent, Fréal et Cie in Paris. With the preface by Georges Gromort, it was probably very well received at the École. Conversely, modernist circles would have been likely to denounce the project as an example of anachronistic academism.

In Romania, however, where Modernism was only gradually being introduced by Marcel Janco in 1926,[15] the real hostility to the Chrissoveloni Bank was being expressed by the Heimatstil circle around the Bucharest School of architecture.[16] At that time, this circle dominated the architectural scene in Romania championing Neo-Romanism as the national style. But why take that way, GMC might have asked, as it was likely, first, to lead directly into the dead-end of provincialism; and second, far from being capable of inspiring the architectural expression of the identity of pluricultural Greater Romania? GMC from the start of his career challenged the aesthetic excesses of Neo-Romanism and its arch-conservative connotation.[17]

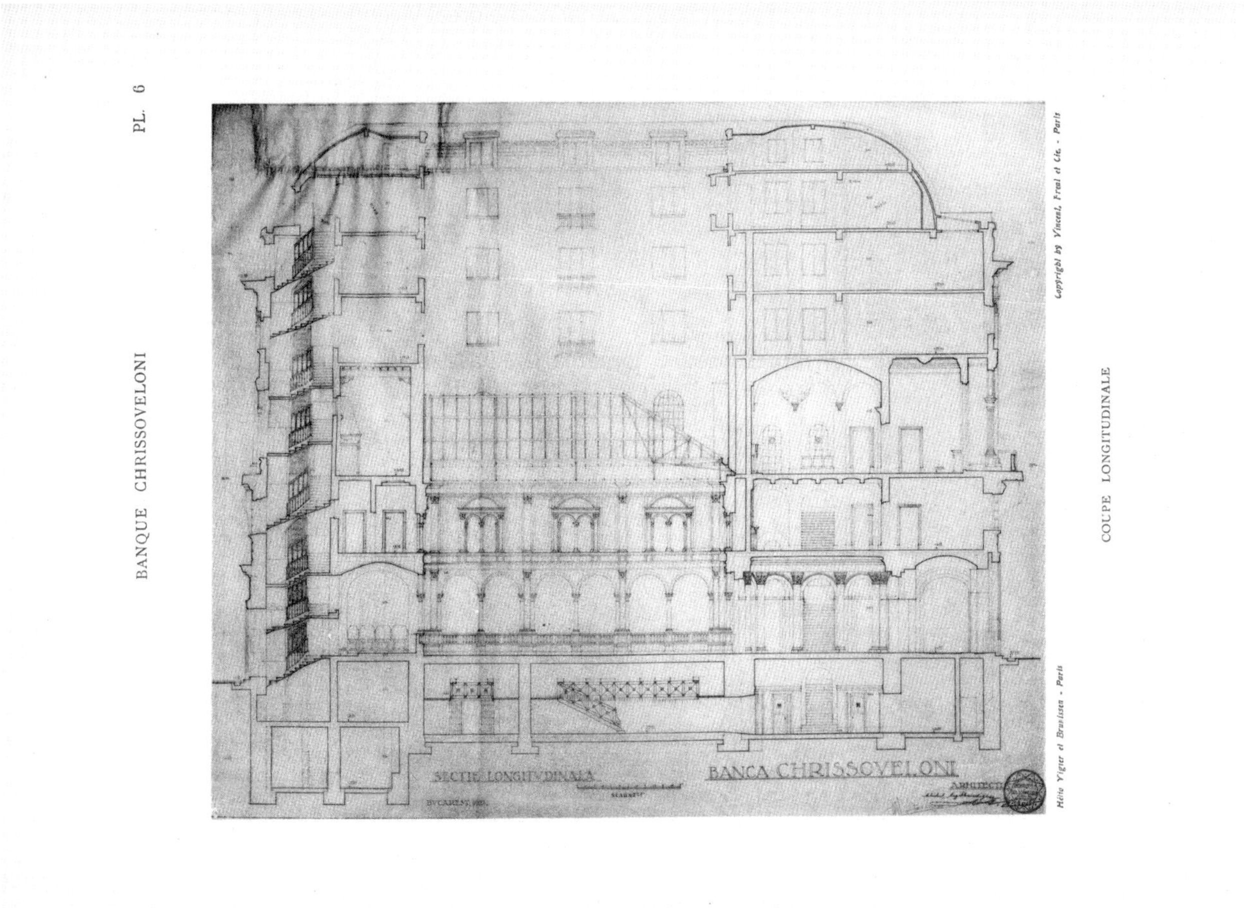

81 GMC/Schmiedigen, *Chrissoveloni Bank*, Bucharest (W 2). Longitudinal section. Pencil drawing (GMC/Schmiedigen 1929, plate 6).

82 *Loggia del Consiglio*, Verona (Photograph ADT).

83 GMC/Schmiedigen, *Chrissoveloni Bank, courtyard*. Photograph W. Weiss. (GMC/Schmiedigen 1929, plate 21).

84 GMC/Schmiedigen, *Chrissoveloni Bank, main staircase*. Photograph W. Weiss. (GMC/Schmiedigen 1929, plate 39).

Memories and design (I): On imitation

The previous passage tells of another Ariadne's thread which was to web through GMC's body of work: architectural memories. Some forty years later, while working on the pavilions of the Metropolitan Church in Jassy, GMC noted that an essential feature of his design method remained the same:

"Now, when I look back, I can see that my attitude to a work of art is the same as it was then. I was building, and building with nostalgia."[1]

To GMC, recollections, symbols, and even creativity are fruits of memory: "The world of memory is a source of life: it is creative."[2]

Or, in other words – memory is the very laboratory in which creativity unfolds. Herein GMC followed Henri Bergson and Marcel Proust. The latter, a Bergsonian himself, thought memory was a "point of intersection between spirit and matter"[3] endowed with creative power. And GMC continued:

"Memories follow the urge to live, so they carry us forward into life, into the future."[4] Here GMC compressed a passage by Bergson:

"It may be said that we have no grasp of the future without an equal and corresponding outlook over the past, that the onrush of our activity makes a void behind it into which memories flow, and that memory is thus the reverberation, in the sphere of consciousness, of the indetermination of our will."[5]

Bergson distinguished between two complementary forms of memory: a passive and an active one. The first would be a sort of archive; the second, by contrast, would be creative:

"[T]his consciousness of a whole past of efforts stored up in the present is indeed also a memory, but a memory profoundly different from the first, always bent upon action, seated in the present and looking only to the future."[6]

In *Matter and Memory* Bergson sought to counter-balance idealism and realism by moderating their excesses. With matter and memory being topical for architecture, Bergson's approach could well have had an impact on GMC's thinking about tradition and modernism. In architecture memory is connected with the relevance of the image for the design – in the sense of recalling how one has actually experienced *in situ* a particular building.[7] Therefore, an outstanding recollection tends to encourage imitation. Eventually imitation aims to profit from past experiences for present tasks.

The possible connection between image, memory, imitation, and architecture is illustrated by Werner Oechslin in his exemplary interpretation of the emerging of Palladianism. Oechslin particular links Goethe's reception of Palladio and the imitation doctrine of Quatremère de Quincy:

"Because Palladio's buildings with their dimensions and physical appearance are indeed unique, as Goethe so rightly pointed out, imitations are naturally modelled on Palladio. Yet the outcome is always something new and original, thus different from the model. This is true not only in regard of a single element or a peculiarity derived from it, but in a really comprehensive sense. For this reason the term image seems to be full of symbolic power and comprehensive to such an extent that it opens a design to all possible evolutionary fictions and variations."[8]

85 GMC/Schmiedigen, *Chrissoveloni Bank*, view of the rear façade as seen from the courtyard of the Stavropoleos Church (the church was restored by Ion Mincu from 1899-1901). Photograph W. Weiss (GMC/Schmiedigen 1929, plate 11).

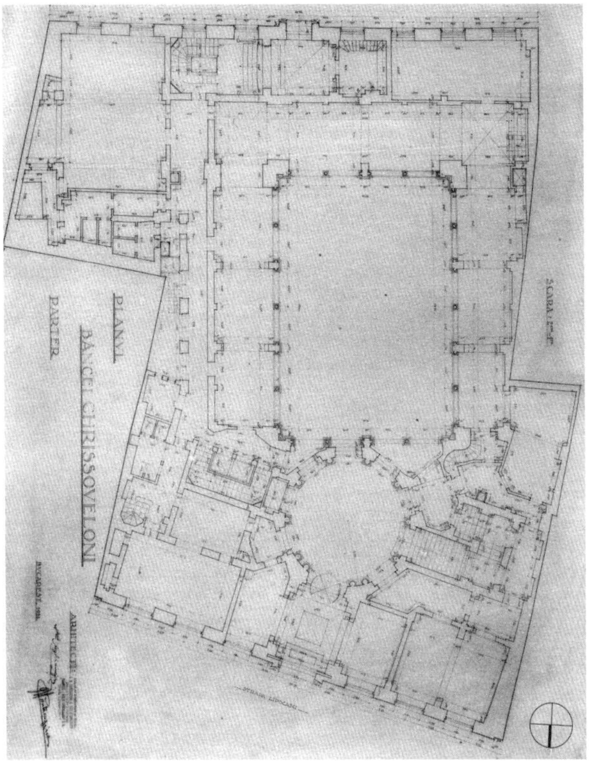

86 GMC/Schmiedigen, *Chrissoveloni Bank*, Bucharest.
Ground floor plan. Pencil drawing (GMC/Schmiedigen 1929).

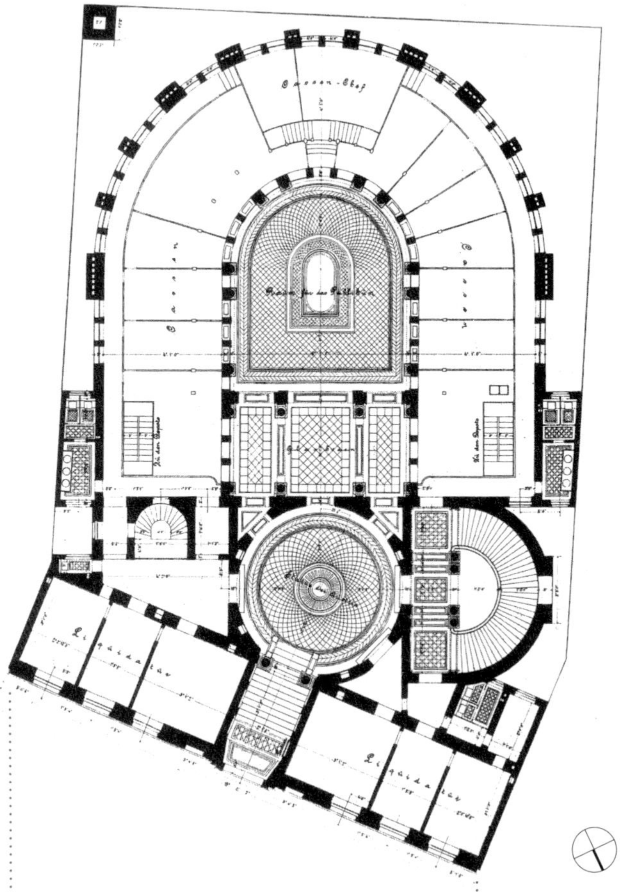

87 Above right:
Otto Wagner, *Austrian Länderbank*, Vienna (1882-1884).
Ground floor plan.

88 GMC/Schmiedigen, *Chrissoveloni Bank*, Bucharest.
Front façade. Pencil drawing (GMC/Schmiedigen 1929, plate 1).

89 Otto Wagner, *Austrian Länderbank*, Vienna.
Front façade.

In addition to GMC's fresh approach to Palladio, the Neo-Renaissance Chrissoveloni Bank reflects two further influences: the École des Beaux-Arts in Paris, and the Viennese architecture of Gottfried Semper and Otto Wagner. To begin with, the École always recommended the creative imitation of Antiquity and Renaissance through the study of classics. This outlook was cogently advocated by Antoine-Chrysostôme Quatremère de Quincy (1755-1849), the École's first and distinctly authoritative professor of architectural history.[9]

In his treatise *Essay on the Nature, Scope, and Means of Imitation in the Fine Arts* (Essai sur la Nature, le But et les Moyens de l'Imitation dans les Beaux-Arts) of 1823 he emphasized that "in the fine arts, imitation consists in producing a resemblance of a thing, but through another thing which becomes its image".[10] One of the eminent nineteenth-century French architects who championed Neo-Renaissance was Félix Duban (1797-1870), to whose design the École's Palais d'études was erected around 1840.

At the same time, GMC very much appreciated classicist Vienna as a successful fusion of Italian and French influences. For instance, Adolf Loos's conviction that the Italian model was essential for reinvigorating the metropolitan Viennese architecture, could have been influential in GMC's own quest for renewing architecture in Romania:

"We would again have beautiful monumental lines and proportions, Italian grandeur and monumentality, all things which lie in our nerves, for we are breathing in Italian air from across the Alps."[11]

In a stricter sense, the Neorenaissance approaches evident in the later projects of Gottfried Semper (1803-1879) and early ones of Otto Wagner (1841-1918) may have aroused GMC's attention too. Although Semper's "recourse to a Neo-Renaissance style"[12], as observed Hanno-Walther Kruft, showed his scepticism "about the possibility of a 'new style' for the present day"[13], it also expressed "his cosmopolitism and liberal political views"[14]. The latter could have particularly attracted GMC not just in architectural terms, but also in view of the political fragility of Romanian democracy.

Vienna also offered Wagner's rationalist urban planning and architecture. Far beyond his early works, which express his "formal commitment to the great architectural tradition of the École des Beaux-Arts"[15], Wagner was reputed as "the noblest exponent of the Viennese Renaissance"[16].

Of particular interest to GMC might have been Wagner's Austrian Länderbank (1882-84) in the Hohenstauffengasse. With its austere façades, the innovative use of glass floors and ceilings, and the open plan of the semicircular rear wing, the Länderbank was celebrated as "one of the most modern and innovative office buildings at that time in Europe."[17]

It is noteworthy that, except for the open plan, the two banks have a number of common features: a similar ground plan to cope with the irregular plot; a "dramatically staged spatial sequence"[18] based on the circular vestibule; and the urban palazzo typology, which combined a functional building of the highest technical level at the time with an external appearance of a "certain freely interpreted Renaissance"[19] as an expression of the link between utility and beauty.

90 Otto Wagner, *Austrian Länderbank.* Front façade, Hohenstauffengasse, Vienna. Period photograph.

91 GMC/Schmiedigen, *Chrissoveloni Bank,* Bucharest. Rear façade on the Stavropoleos Street. Photograph W. Weiss (GMC/Schmiedigen 1929).

92 GMC, *Italian villa* (1936). Ink drawing, reproduction (AMLSC).

93 Camille Corot, *Le Four à Briques (The Brick Kiln), c. 1840-1845*. Oil on canvas. © Staatsgalerie Stuttgart, inv. no. 2613.

Memories and Design (II): Travelling

For GMC memories were "no longer [...] valid, unless we transform them into something harmonious as well as solid and concrete"[1]. Being such a fruitful theme for art, this transformation encourages creative synthesis.[2] Therefore the interaction between memories and images lies, in the words of Oechslin, at the core of the "prolific concept of imitation as a motor of art development"[3].

The validity of an architectural image is fed by the first-hand experience of a certain building in its unique setting. Being superior to knowledge drawn from books, experience, as Gromort noted, calls for travelling in order to "search for the beauty where it is"[4].

Subsequent studies enforce travel experiences and sharpen the power of judgement. Hence theoretical studies, both preliminary and subsequent, along with personal travel experiences form the basic features of "the idea [that] comes to embody itself in that particular image"[5]. In Palladio's career GMC discerned the inspiring potential of study travels: "His main travel led him to Rome; Palladio undertook it in 1544, together with Marco Thiene. There the second miracle happened [...] as he met two artists who were to become his great collaborators, Vittoria et Veronese."[6]

At the same time, in the course of our explorations of art and architecture, it is not the critical approach which is pivotal, but the pleasure of looking and ability to admire. In these circumstances GMC recommended Goethe's view, for "the critical spirit of an artist matures but slowly, and often long after the experience of a particular work of art. This occurs when we feel the need to make distinctions and establish an hierarchy of values. But to begin with, the critical spirit is not the decisive nor the most fertile moment. The source of talent is feeding on pure joy and sincere admiration, clouded by no ulterior motive, but carried by lyric enthusiasm."[7]

Study travels, work ethics and idleness

94 GMC, *Vicenza at night*. Chalk drawing (GMC, *Palladio* 1928).

Like one of his beloved writers, Montaigne, GMC was a passionate traveller: "Travelling is renewal […] We respond to the beauty of scenery, the way a violin responds to a bow."[1] He used journeys from Bucharest to Paris and *vice-versa* for copious study travels.

Occasionally he travelled by car, often by train. Sometimes he took the Orient Express via Budapest, Vienna, Munich, Stuttgart, and Strasbourg to Paris; or he travelled on the Simplon Orient Express via the Croatian Adriatic Coast across Italy, Southern France or even Spain, before reaching Paris; from there he visited Belgium and the Netherlands.[2] He couldn't stop enthusing about the landmarks he visited.[3] In museums he explored works of Claude, Corot, Daumier, Dürer, Goya, Hokusai, Piranesi or Poussin for hours trying to decipher their craftsmanship. "Raphael's Athenian School is the height of all Art", wrote GMC later to his daughter, "but a modest landscape of Corot's means more to me in my daily meditations."[4]

At the same time he was attracted by humble places: "When I travelled through those countries, I often lingered in one city after another, without any definite purpose, except to look. Sometimes not even that. Often I stayed all day in my hotel room and only went out at night. Many places I saw only in the dark."[5]

From Paris he travelled throughout the whole of France – for which his Belgian-French grandmother inspired him such a deep love. He wandered from Mesnard to Aigue-Mortes, via the Camargue to Nîmes, or via Provence to Burgundy, Chartres, and Reims. Versailles became his "very own garden"[6].

And Vienna, that metropolitan hub between Eastern and Western, Northern and Southern Europe, was for GMC "the natural place for a rest"[7]. There he renewed his childhood memories, and explored Viennese architecture and art. He possibly visited buildings of Semper, Wagner, and Loos, and got deeply engrossed in the works of Dürer at the Albertina.

On journeys through the Apennine Peninsula he learned to appreciate that for modern man "Italy plays the same key role as Greece did for Romans in antiquity"[8]. His intellectual baggage probably included Gromort's *L'Architecture de la Renaissance en Italie*, Goethe's *Italian Journey* and *Poetry and Truth*, and Jakob Burckhardt's *Cicerone* and *Kultur der Renaissance in Italien*. Charmed by "the dawn of the Renaissance [so perfectly embodied by Simonetta Vespucci]"[9], he returned to Bucharest "laden with juicy and aromatic fruit from the Mediterranean shores"[10].

He found that the "most satisfying way of being idle is to travel"[11] since in "those moments of idleness […] we are more aware and more intelligent than at any other time"[12]. This mature insight he gained especially working on Mogoşoaia and the Chrissoveloni Bank. Both projects, extensive and demanding, gave him self-confidence. Working "with so much fervour, with so much optimism"[13], he pursued the "clear and balanced [dream]"[14] to give his spatial ideas a precise shape: "As my building rose from its foundations, I felt my confidence growing. I was totally lucid while dreaming. I understood how the dreams were turning into action."[15]

95 *Phaistos*, Crete.
Photograph GMC, 1933 (AGMC-IP).

With writing joining architecture and painting, GMC grew into an *ouvrier intellectuel* [intellectual worker] and then to a *homme de lettres*, following in the footsteps of his favourite writers such as Charles Augustin de Sainte-Beuve (1804-1869).[16]

Throughout what was to be a rather short life, and partly in difficult circumstances, GMC performed an impressive amount of work – he could bear comparison with Schinkel (1781-1841), who died at a similar age. We shall come to this later. Anyway, GMC's work ethic obviously had a playful note in it. Perhaps an echo of his happy childhood, it saved him from canonizing work into dogma. In his *Letters to Simon* he observed:

"'Thou shalt earn thy living by the sweat of thy brow.' But the brow is not made for sweat nor is the head made for bowing. Why then this punishment? Why?"[17]

Clearly GMC opposed the Old Testament determinism and overestimation of Protestant work ethic. In the same breath he addressed a Romanian proverb, which had condensed experiences from several foreign rules: "The sword won't cut off the bowed head [Capul plecat sabia nu-l taie]"[18]. On other occasions too GMC rejected fatalism and the subservient outlook which it often entails.

To work, for GMC, meant to learn industriously and duly apply the skills and techniques of the chosen profession: a self-imposed discipline, which in the first place aims for professional perfection; then it might encourage self-knowledge and surpassing oneself:

"Being requires certain conditions and one of them is restraint. You cannot achieve harmony or spirituality if you do not set limits."[19] At some other place in the *Letters to Simon* he observes in the same line: "But beauty too can isolate you, because beauty is always a source of freedom. In my pursuit of beauty I achieved greater freedom. One of the privileges of freedom is choice. We are free to choose. To choose means to commit yourself, and the greater the commitment the more difficult the freedom, but also the more heroic. The more heroic freedom becomes the more total it is. In the last stage you have to be free of your own self. [...] Isolation must not be non-participation, living in an ivory tower. Therefore not isolation, but ascension, because the heavens are above us, and our spirit is above the sky [, as Leonardo used to put it]."[20]

For GMC, self-knowledge and lucidity bind work to idleness. When man descends into the valley forever bound to carry the rock of his work up the mountain, this modern Sisyphus may experience lucid moments in which his personality lights up:

"Without a place to linger and rest, our journeys would have little meaning. Deserts too, need an oasis. It is only when we stop for a while and rest that we can hope to take stock of ourselves. The short respite between a finished piece of work and the start of another is often a period of great mental calm and serenity. You see things in the same light as a landscape after rain, when everything is clear and the distant azure can be explored. [...] And the places of respite in the course of one's life are those moments or periods when you forget much in order to feel more strongly, and when you suddenly discover your own potential – which is a way of making sure that when you really need it, you will find enough strength in yourself."[21]

So for GMC, work and idleness represented the harmonious framework of a sensitive concept of life, which goes back to ancient principles and looks for beauty and happiness. GMC's notion of beauty seems to have two meanings which are present in each other: aesthetic and existential. Beauty in arts and architecture would witness the bare spiritual necessity of separating from time, a contemplative action very much propitious to self-consciousness. Like Plotinus, GMC was convinced that "[u]gliness is just a lack of form, perhaps an aspect that offends our feelings or our mind"[22]. Plotinus himself held the view that "ugliness is but matter not mastered by Ideal-Form"[23]. Creation, in fact, offers "moments of blossoming [in which] we don heavenly clothes"[24]. Similar to Albert Camus, who believed that "[o]f all the schools of patience and lucidity, creation is the most effective"[25], GMC, grateful as he was for his artistic talent, "obeyed the vigorous discipline of art like a monk obeying monastic orders"[26]. For "a true accomplishment is always a sign of grace"[27].

96 GMC in his Bucharest studio, working on the pavilions for the Metropolitan church in Jassy, c. 1958 (AMLSC).

GMC's idea of happiness has a nuance of meaning close to the antique Greek notion of beauty – beauty as fullness and diversity in unity.[28] In his view, "happiness means maximum participation in life. This does not exclude suffering and heartache. Happiness is not static. It is an essential part of our development, in other words a state of utmost lucidity. In my own life maximum participation coincided with maximum energy."[29]

Perhaps not unsurprinsingly, GMC's approach is close to the existentialism championed by Camus: "A man's rule of conduct and his scale of values have no meaning except through the quantity and variety of experiences he has been in a position to accumulate. [...] I see then that the individual character of a common code of ethics lies not so much in the ideal importance of its basic principles as in the norm of an experience that is possible to measure." And: "Being aware of one's life, one's revolt, one's freedom, and to the maximum, is living, and to the maximum."[30]

Eventually GMC linked his work ethic and the notion of idleness in an existentialist way – the *otium graecum*, so dearly quoted by Emil Cioran,[31] being, in the words of the great German catholic philosopher Josef Pieper, "one of the corner-stones of European civilisation"[32]. In these circumstances we might be tempted to think of a somewhat paradox aphorism of Constantin Brancusi:

"Creating like a god, commanding like a king, serving like a slave."[33]

And the cities of Bucharest and Paris, which influenced GMC in a most distinct way, also have an element of idleness in their way of life. Sainte-Beuve described as follows the almost legendary Parisian way of life: "the true Parisian wisdom of life [...], that nonchalance, that grace of life even amidst work, that wisdom to know how to enjoy every hour of sunshine"[34]. Bucharest, it is a city reputed to foster a sweetness of life of its own.[35] In addition to that, GMC greatly appreciated those moments of idleness that one experiences after hard work in solitude: "the hour of the Lord"[36], as it is called according to an old Romanian Christian tradition.

97 GMC and Sanda Ştirbey on their wedding day (AMLSC).

The 1920s – a balance

The 1920s saw a time of plenty, professional and private, "full of feeling, thought, and creative possibilities"[1]. He fell in love with Sanda Ştirbey (1908-1992), and in 1926 they married. They were to have two children: Şerban, born in Paris in 1928, and Marie-Lyse, born in Bucharest in 1931.

As he became an *Architecte Diplômé par le Gouvernement Français* in 1929, he already was a well-known architect and intellectual in Romania. For some years to come he would not have to bother about new commissions.

During the first decade of his career GMC was particularly concerned with exploring traditions: vernacular, feudal-aristocratic and religious architecture in Romania on the one hand, the Graeco-Roman antiquity, Renaissance, European strands of classicism and Palladianism, on the other hand.

In his first book he proposed an *Introduction to the Study of Architecture* (Introducere la studiul arhitecturii) (Bucharest 1926), in which he outlined the *classical attitude* as his approach to architecture. The three following publication were written in French: *L'architecture roumaine* (Paris 1927); *Palladio. Essai critique. Avec douze dessins de l'auteur* (Bucharest 1928); and, edited together with Augustin Schmiedigen, *Le Palais de la Banque Chrissoveloni* (Paris 1929). The Chrissoveloni Bank was GMC's only building to be presented in a monograph. It was published by Vincent, Fréal et Cie, and lavishly illustrated with pencil drawings by GMC and Schmiedigen, as well as black-and-white photographs by W. Weiss. Weiss and Charles Cuvillier (1877-1955), the French composer, director of Théâtre de l'Odéon in Paris and amateur draughtsman,[2] joined GMC in producing the equally copiously illustrated volume *Petits Édifices* (Paris 1931) which presented an overview of traditional vernacular and religious buildings of most parts of Romania.

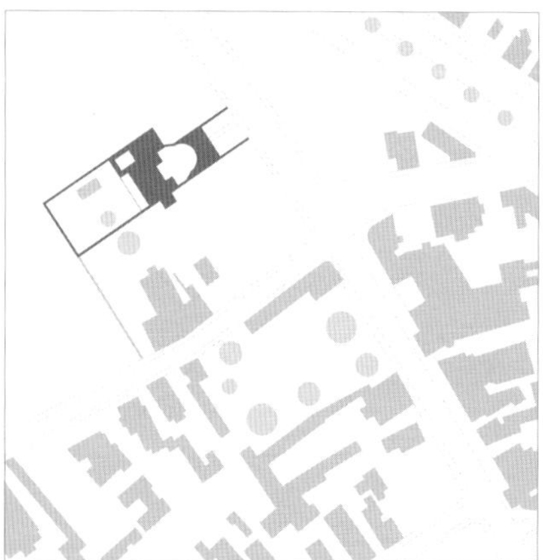

98 Site map of the Polizu estate from the late 1920s to c. 1984 (ADT).

The Polizu Estate

In co-operation with Schmiedigen GMC produced further projects, all of them committed to a traditional classicist and architectural language, including the Jockey Club (1927-29) and Polizu estate (c. 1923-25) in Bucharest.

According to Olympia Zamfiresco, a friend of GMC's and former contributor to Radio Free Europe in Munich, the Polizu house was built around 1923-25 for Marie-Angèle Massart-Polizu,[3] the mistress of Jean Chrissoveloni. Cited as one of the most beautiful estates of the inter-war period in Romania,[4] it was to be GMC's second largest villa project, next to the estate for philosopher Nae Ionesco. On Jean Chrissoveloni's sudden death in 1926, Mrs Polizu sold the estate to Queen Elisabeth of Greece, sister of the later King Carol II. She commissioned GMC and Schmiedigen to extend the villa (1928-29). In 1937 Queen Elisabeth herself sold the villa, which became the *Industrial Association Club*. After 1945, it served as *Press Club* before being transformed into the present restaurant. In the 1980s the estate was partly demolished and effectively hidden behind high-rise socialist blocks of flats.

In the Polizu design GMC certainly assimilated memories of France, Italy and Greece. Entrance to the villa was from a gateway pavilion, which was

99 Above:
GMC/Schmiedigen, *Polizu estate*, Bucharest (W 3).
Garden view, loggia made of wooden columns.
Period photograph W. Weiss (AGMC-PM).

100 GMC/Schmiedigen, *Polizu estate*, Bucharest, view of garden with pond and rear façade of cloister-like wing.
Period photograph W. Weiss (AGMC-PM).

101 GMC/Schmiedigen, *Polizu estate*, view of courtyard of the cloister-like wing. Period photograph W. Weiss (AGMC-PM).

set back from Calea Victoriei and opened via a semi-circular exedra on to an intimate *cour d'honneur*. The exedra with its sixteen composite columns recalls, for instance, the courtyard in front of the Palais d'études at the École des Beaux-Arts in Paris as well as the entrance to Raphael's villa Madama in Rome. The cloister-like wing added to the villa on the north side in order to provide a shady and cool space in hot summer days, remind one of Florentine Renaissance. In front of the atrium, the garden incorporated a rectangular pool. The Polizu estate also shows GMC interest in Mycenaen and Greek antiquity. Matila Ghyka even compared it to a Mycenaen megaron,[5] a character which might have well suited the manor of a Greek Queen. Indeed the irregular composition of the building evokes Cretan palaces.

Notable too were the six wooden columns of the loggia overlooking the garden, as preserved in a period photograph by W. Weiss. Unfortunately, they had been replaced in the process of further transformations after 1945. Crafted from smoothly polished single shafts, the wooden columns recall both the stone columns of Mino's Palace at Knossos and the Doric order. Without any basement they sprang up right from the garden terrace, four steps above the garden. As regards the Mycenaen column type, GMC rejected the sturdy shaft, and combined it with the polished slim Doric order, at once simplifying and sharpening its formal features. The anuli, for example, were deeply cut into the neck-mould, to a distance of approximately three anuli – unlike traditional anuli, which are rather close to each other. The strongly enlarged cushion pad symbolized the weight of the roof. The flat square plate of the abakus supported the balks and joists: overhanging girders consisting of coupled wooden beams with their heads profiled as reversal ogee moulding. Conveying the impression of a tectonic and playful refined elegance, the Polizu columns illustrate GMC's idea of a vivid tradition. They read like a built in footnote: first, of the cultural historical geneology of the column as included in his *Introduction to the Study of Architecture*;[6] and second, of the thesis that the ancient Greek architects created columns first of wood before transposing them into stone.

102 GMC/Schmiedigen, *Polizu estate*, front façade, Calea Victoriei, Bucharest. Period photograph W. Weiss (AGMC-PM).

Fragile harmony

The Mogoşoaia building site accompanied GMC throughout the entire decade. Eventually it proved to be a unique place of peace and quiet, which provided the perfect setting for combining industrious concentrated work and idleness. There his creative power and architectural attitude had the privilege to ripen slowly and thoroughly. Such calmness could be related to stonemasonry. Since stone, a symbol of durability, means hard work, the result can only be slowly achieved. The hard physical labour, at that time even less facilitated by electrical tools than today, calls for periods of rests, which enable one to check upon what has been achieved and think about the next steps. Any fault could be disatrous, for it would make all previous efforts futile. Working with stone requires endurance, continuity, obstinacy, and patience. The results involve the certainty of having shaped the resistant material according to one's ideas; self-confidence and balance. By learning the craftsmanship of a stonemason GMC most probably became more receptive to the art and thinking of Palladio, who himself was trained as a stonemason. At the same time, GMC followed, it would appear, Adolf Loos's recommendation to root architectural education in craftsmanship.[7]

Continuity and cultivation are instrumental too in creating landscape beauty, which to GMC is "perhaps the most beautiful symbol of wealth, most cheerful expression of civilisation and supreme luxury of society"[8]. It is also a symbol of the fragile and the ephemeral, which reminded GMC of the unstable political situation both in Romania and Europe.

"As I lived within the enclosure of Mogoşoaia, cheek to cheek with the old palace on which I worked together with my Roma comrades, I realized what a privilege it was: the privilege to work in the safe calmness of a remote world, protected from contemporary troubles by the harmony of the old yet virile walls of brick and stone, the lazy river, and the soothing shades of tranquil gardens. To plunge into time and spatial isolation gave a glimpse of eternity. But after that nothing was more troubling than the sense of fragility evoked by the Mogoşoaia atmosphere."[9]

103 Mogoşoaia, stone lion on the terrace steps overlooking the Colentina river. Period photograph (AMB-JG).

104 Mogoşoaia, terrace steps overlooking the Colentina river. Period photograph (AMB-JG).

PASAGIUL ENGLISH
VICTOR

New start and prosperity in troubled times

The political and economical context in the inter-war period

When GMC received his Beaux-Arts diploma in Paris, the timing could not have been less propitious for setting off in business. Because GMC embarked on politics, this chapter attempts to outline the political and economic background situation in Europe and Romania in relation to which one can better place his wide range of activities and his political attitude.

In 1919, Europe had lost its international hegemony to the USA. At least, the *Old world* could breathe again. Pacifism and the idea of a united Europe accompanied the attempts at securing long-term peace.[1]

There were the Treaty of Versailles, new democracies in Central and Eastern Europe along with several alliances. Cosmopolitan europeans felt the acute need to emphasize the civil and cultural foundations and common interests of their states, and vividly discussed ideas of organizing a pacified Europe. Apart from the League of Nations[2], three issues stood out: the Paneurope movement championed by Richard Nicholas Coudenhove-Kalergi; Aristide Briand's proposal for establishing a European federation, and the Briand-Kellog Pact of 1928.[3]

But national sovereignty was still the primary concern for many leading European politicians, not to speak of the population at large. A retrospective look shows that treatment of the former Central Powers by the former Allies was too harsh. Also, the League of Nations lacked the executive power to truly implement its decisions. Nonetheless, there were clear signs of approaching each other, at first place between France and Germany, best illustrated by the friendship between Aristide Briand and Gustav Stresemann.

Like other countries in Central and Eastern Europe, which realized the dream of national unity, Romania was captured by a euphoric mood, and continued democratizing and modernizing. But her foreign policy was dependent on Great Britain and France, and the home affairs remained instable on account of "the contest between democracy and authoritarianism"[4] – a contest between the king, the parliament and the political parties.[5]

The new Constitution of 1923 confirmed in principle the parliamentary system and fair elections, with the judiciary as a "separate branch of government"[6]; it introduced the universal male suffrage and granted minorities equal citizenship rights, if only thanks to the pressure of the Great Powers.[7]

In contrast other aspects added to the moments of political instability. Modelled on the outstanding personality of King Carol I (1839-1914, king from 1866-1914), the constitution provided the king with great power, so as to mediate between the great parties in times of crisis. During the 1920s the most important parties were the National Liberal Party PNL led by Ion C. Bratiano, and the National Peasant Party headed by Iuliu Maniu. Democratic control though the opposition was hindered by the extensive amount of power of the government. Parliament consisted mostly of lawyers and landlords, and was far from representing the entire population. Also, "unlike parliamentarism in Western Europe, where the government was a creation of the legislature, in Romania parliament continued to be an extension of

106 Aircraft of the Romanian Airlines LARES.
Period photograph.
Guide de la Roumanie, Bucharest 1938.

105 Opposite:
Calea Victoriei, Bucharest, c. 1930
Period postcard (ADT).

107 Woodworking industry at Lotru, Southern Carpathians. *Guide de la Roumanie*, Bucharest 1938.

the government"[8]. The latter was inclined to pursue a policy of "continued centralization of authority in Bucharest"[9], though.

In addition Romania's territory almost doubled in size in 1919. It grew into a truly multi-ethnic state, thus being called Greater Romania. In 1930, Romania had a population of some 18 million inhabitants, comprising: 71% Romanians, 7.9% Hungarians, 4.1% Germans, 4.0% Jews, 3.2% Ucrainians and Ruthenians, 2.3% Russians, 2.0% Bulgarians, 0.9% Turks, and further ethnical groups including Roma, Tartars and Serbs.[10] At the same time, the revisionist policy of Bulgaria, Hungary and the Soviet Union was an ever present threat.[11]

Since the revolution of 1848 society was virtually divided into "two general directions [which] coalesced and inaugurated a wide-ranging national debate that was to last until"[12] 1940: "Europeanists and traditionalists. The former treated Romania as part of Europe and insisted that she had no other choice but to follow the path of economic and social development already taken by the urbanized and industrialized West. The traditionalists [...] emphasized Romania's agrarian character and sought models of development based upon her own unique social and cultural heritage".[13]

The the outspoken enemies of democracy and its institutions were the Communists and the right-wing radical Legionaires. The Romanian Communist Party, founded in 1922 and declared illegal by the government two years later, was in fact insignificant until 1944-45.[14] On the other hand, the *Iron Guard* (Garda de Fier) led by Corneliu Zelea-Codreanu (1899-1938) and its followers such as Horia Sima presented a constant threat to democracy. This anti-Semitic, arch-nationalistic and Orthodox Christian fundamentalist right-wing party emerged in 1930 out of the Legion of the Arch-Angel Michael, which was formed in 1927 drawing on two anti-Semitic organizations of 1922. Especially in the late 1930s it managed to substantially increase its sympathy with and influence on the population.[15]

108 Petrol fields at Moreni. *Guide de la Roumanie*, Bucharest 1938.

In these circumstances, it comes as no surprise that the social situation was also full of contrasts. On the average, life expectancy was low and analphabetism high.[16] In 1919, the economy on the whole was agrarian.[17] "According to the census of 1930, 90.4 per cent of the rural active population had agriculture [...] as its primary source of income.[...] The majority of the peasants led a precarious material existence."[18] This is one of the reasons why the world economic depression "struck Romania with particular force".[19]

"Yet, signs of change were evident."[20] By the thorough agrarian reform of 1921 „the greater part of the land was transferred to the peasants"[21]. The country began to profit from its rich natural resources, in particular from oil. Industrialization and a modern credit system slowly improved the economic structure.

Especially the return of King Carol II in 1930 brought about a change of policy: namely a co-operation with the West, attracting both private investments and financial aid replaced the nationalist policy of "*Prin noi înșine* (By ourselves alone)"[22] pursued throughout the 1920s. In the 1930s, by contrast, "French and English capital predominated."[23]

Given the agrarian character of the country, the economy depended largely on exports, in particular to Western countries. This is particularly true for the "oil and forestry industries [...]. Foreign consumers took 82 per cent of the production of the former and 70 per cent of the latter."[24] Agricultural goods, wood and oil constituted "over 90 per cent of Romania's exports".[25]

In the late 1930s however, both France and Great Britain were no longer willing to continue importing oil and wheat from Romania. Therefore the country was literally driven into the economic embrace of Nazi Germany. Then the Wohltat Contract (1939) and the Oil-Armament Pact (1940) paved the way for Romania's joining the military alliance with Germany and Italy.[26]

In 1926 crown prince Carol was forced into exile by the authoritarian prime minister Ion C. Bratiano, who repproached him for leading a life so unappropriate of a future king.[27] After the deaths of King Ferdinand I (1865 Sigmaringen-1927 Sinaia) and PNL's leader, Ion C. Bratiano, in 1927, the infant son of the exiled crown prince Carol was proclaimed King Michael I.

Affairs were led by a regency. Instantly the country slipped into political chaos. In addition, the effects of the international economic crisis drew Romania into still higher debts. As neither the regent's council nor the government succeeded in settling the crisis, rumours and fears of dictatorship spread across the country. According to an Austrian diplomat in Bucharest, Romania was on the edge of civil war, tantamount to a "steampot without safety ventile".[28]

Due to these circumstances, leaders of the democratic opposition, high military officers, and renowned intellectuals agreed upon inviting Carol to return from his exile in Paris and seize power.[29]

Nicolae Titulesco, "the Romanian foreign minister"[30] and promoter of the balanced policy, also advocated Carol's comeback. As one of the few "Romanian political figure[s] in the inter-war period regarded in Western capitals as being of European stature"[31], Titulesco was able to convince both the Great Powers and League of Nations.[32]

109 Advertisement of the petrol company *Unirea* for the *Blue petrol Ethyl.* An American-Romanian co-operation. *Guide de la Roumanie*, Bucharest 1938.

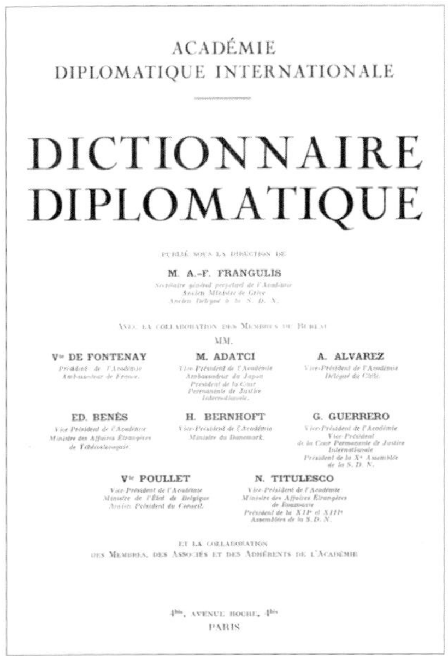

ACADÉMIE
DIPLOMATIQUE INTERNATIONALE

DICTIONNAIRE
DIPLOMATIQUE

PUBLIÉ SOUS LA DIRECTION DE

M. A.-F. FRANGULIS
Secrétaire général perpétuel de l'Académie
Ancien Ministre de Grèce
Ancien Délégué à la S. D. N.

MM.

Vte DE FONTENAY

M. ADATCI
Vice-Président de l'Académie
Ambassadeur du Japon
Président de la Cour Permanente de Justice Internationale.

A. ALVAREZ
Vice-Président de l'Académie
Délégué du Chili.

ED. BENÈS

H. BERNHOFT
Vice-Président de l'Académie
Ministre du Danemark.

G. GUERRERO
Vice-Président de l'Académie
Vice-Président de la Cour Permanente de Justice Internationale
Président de la Xe Assemblée de la S. D. N.

Vte POULLET
Vice-Président de l'Académie
Ministre de l'État de Belgique
Ancien Président du Conseil.

N. TITULESCO
Vice-Président de l'Académie
Ministre des Affaires Étrangères de Roumanie
Président de la XIIe et XIIIe Assemblées de la S. D. N.

ET LA COLLABORATION
DES MEMBRES, DES ASSOCIÉS ET DES ADHÉRENTS DE L'ACADÉMIE

4bis, AVENUE HOCHE, 4bis
PARIS

110 *Dictionnaire Diplomatique*, Paris. Front page of Vol. 1, 1933 (WLB Stuttgart). Nicolae Titulesco was co-editor.

111 King Carol II's (1893-1953) first public appearance in Bucharest after his return from exile in June 1930. (Ileana Tilea-Troiano 1998).

112 Nicolae Iorga (1871-1940), professor and founding father of modern historiography in Romania. *Guide de la Roumanie*, Bucharest 1938.

The reign of King Carol II (1930-40)

Carol's return to Romania on the 6th June 1930 may have come as a coup d'état, but in fact all went smoothly. Most Romanians and the press received Carol with enthusiasm. *The Times*, for instance, published an article titled *Rumania. Carol Made King, Return By Air From Paris, An Enthusiastic Welcome.*[1]

To begin with, Carol II managed to perform well as an integrative political figure, which he was expected to be. The young king was indeed backed by the most diverse sides – almost all democratic political parties, Freemason lodges (including politicians such as Nicolae Titulesco and Constantin Argetoianu; Carol himself was a Freemason)[2], leading economists, industrials, scientists, intellectuals and artists. They included the historian Nicolae Iorga (1871-1940), sociologue Dimitrie Gusti (1880-1955), economists Virgil Madgearu (1887-1940) and Mihail Manoilescu (1891-1950), industrial magnates Max Auschnitt (1888-1959) and Nicolae Malaxa (1884-1965), as well as journalists and writers like Nichifor Crainic (1889-1972), Nae Ionescu (1890-1940), Camil Petrescu, Mihai Ralea and Mihail Sebastian.

Alas, the unity of the *Carlists*, as they used to be called,[3] was short-termed. Much too varied were their motives and tempers. Some drifted into right-wing extremism, urging towards a cultural civic war. One of those who paved that path was Crainic with his concept of an ethnocratic state. He was joined by Nae Ionescu, professor of philosophy at the University of Bucharest. What precisely led to an open clash between Carol II and Nae Ionescu, is uncertain. One of the Ionescu's former students, the late Emil Cioran, suspected him having wanted to become a sort of a court philosopher, which Carol II obviously refused.[4]

Whatever the causes may have been, Nae Ionescu from 1933 up to his early death in 1940 vehemently fought against Carol II. Not only did he support the Iron Guard, but he also ideologically corrupted the best part of the highly gifted Young Generation, whose mentor he happened to be. Among the few young intellectuals who proved immune to the right-wing extremist poison were Eugène Ionesco and Mihail Sebastian. Not unsurprinsingly, both of them expressed their concern with this process of "rhinocerosation"[5] artistically: Mihail Sebastian in his *Journal*, posthumously published by Humanitas in Bucharest in 1996,[6] and Ionesco in his theatre play *The Rhinoceroses* (1957-58).[7]

The decade of Carol's reign was full of contrasts. Already in the early 1930s, his policy of establishing an integrative long-term democratic government was torpedoed by both the old parties and the Iron Guard.[8]

The latter's influence grew more threatening than ever in the aftermath of the elections in 1938. Being supported by all the democratic parties (not necessarily by each of their leaders), Carol II subsequently favoured the government of the *Front of National Renaissance* (Frontul Renașterii Naționale) presided by himself – virtually establishing a royal dictatorship. In the beginning, there were hopes of calming the agitated political situation, and at last the antagonist old parties were reconciled. But even the royal dictatorship failed to anihilate the Iron Guard and its violent crimes, which were discretely supported by Nazi Germany.

On the 21st September 1939, for instance, the Iron Guard murdered Armand Călinescu (1893-1939), the current Prime-Minister of the time and moving spirit behind the Front of the National Renaissance.[9]

In view of the precarious international situation, and being deserted by both France and Great Britain, Carol II's policy proved powerless. His reign ended very much like it began: "with a coup". [10] On 6th September 1940 he was again forced into exile – by General Ion Antonescu, whom Carol himself had appointed Prime-Minister in the summer of 1940, due to the pressure put on him by the Romanian High military.

113 Queen Mary and King Carol II, her son, on a rural visit in the 1930s (Ileana Tilea-Troiano 1998).

On Carol's II image according to historiography

Carol II appears to be one of the most controversial figures of Romanian history in the twentieth century. What we can resume is that the decade of his reign was full of contrasts, as was his character and action. A large part of the post 1945 historiography emphasized the negative aspects of his character, of his actions and of his reign.

Especially the Communist historiography was inclined "to demonize"[1] him, as Alexander Paleologu, the writer, politician and former Romanian Ambassador in France pointed out. Carol II was accused of having wanted to destroy the parliamentary system right from his return in 1930 and wanting to replace it with a royal dictatorship; the sympathy for Fascism; the responsibility for the territorial losses in summer 1940; and, finally, for his liaison with Elena Lupesco, a Romanian-Jewish lady.[2]

Only more recent historical studies cast doubt on the validity of this one-sided image of Carol II. Hans-Christian Maner, professor of history at the University of Mainz, for instance, points out that Carol II by no means sought to establish a royal dictatorship from the beginning. This accusation was first advanced by a number of Romanian politicians of the inter-war period, including Iuliu Maniu, the leader of the National Peasant Party, as a means of political struggle; after 1945 the Communist historiography simply took it over and cemented it.[3] *The Front of the National Renaissance* was a reaction to the dramatically increased political instability, both in Europe and Romania. Unlike the European fascisms of the day, Carol's government was authoritarian, but not totalitarian.[4] Carol sympathised with Mussolini, but disapproved of both the Iron Guard and Hitler.[5]

In a decisive moment in 1936, however, Carol gave in to Hitler's pressure and dismissed Nicolae Titulesco as Foreign Minister, this being one of his grave mistakes among others. In 1938 Carol tried to compensate for it and appointed the pro-Western Grigore Gafencu as Foreign Minister. In the spring of 1939 Gafencu undertook a diplomatic peace mission throughout Europe (ommitting Moscow, however), which was bound to bear no fruit.[6]

It is admirable that Carol was loyal to Elena Lupesco and averted all attacks and attempts to assassinate her. Together they both left for Portugal, and never set foot in Romania again.[7]

114 Dimitrie Gusti (1880-1955), professor of sociology and leading figure of cultural modernization in Romania. *Guide de la Roumanie*, Bucharest 1938.

As for the territorial losses of 1940, Carol was powerless, with poor defences and no alliance being left. Nevertheless, Romania was one of the last, if fragile, strongholds of some democratic dignity within Europe.

115 Dimitrie Gusti, *Les Fondations Culturelles Royales de la Roumanie*. Bucharest 1937. Front cover.

116 GMC, Alexander Rossetti and Horia Teodoru in the 1930s (AMLSC).

117 Advertisement of the Bucharest Museum of the Village, founded by Dimitrie Gusti in 1936 and sponsored by *The Society of Royal Cultural Foundations of Romania*. This open-air exhibition is part of the Herăstrău Park, layed out as *King Carol II Park* from 1936-1939.
Guide de la Roumanie, Bucharest 1938.

Cultural life in the 1930s

On the other hand, during Carol II's reign, Romania enjoyed a notable cultural and scientific prosperity and a cosmopolitan opening. It was accompanied by an obvious economic expansion and promoted by both state and private initiatives including the Royal Cultural Foundations launched by the king. Carol moderated the nationalist tendency of the cultural policy pursued by successive governments in the new regions of Romania after 1919. "There were certainly", in the words of the Romanian historian Lucian Boia, "a few good years of economic dynamism and flourishing culture."[18]

The cultural and scientific life was copious and diverse. There were of course the antagonist groups of the Europeans and traditionalists; there was the Young Generation; there were the aforementioned Carlists; there were other outstanding figures such as the biologists Grigore Antipa and Emil Racovitza, and the physicians Henri Coandă and Hermann Oberth. Some were friends of GMC's: the politicians Georges Bratiano, Constantin Argetoiano, Grégoire Gafenco, and Viorel Tilea; the musicians Georges Enesco and Dinu Lipatti; the writers Tudor Arghezi, Wolf von Aichelburg, Rainer Biemel, Lucian Blaga, Eugen Lovinescu, Camil Petrescu, Ion Pillat, and Mihail Sebastian; artists such as Balasha Cantacuzino, Henri Catargi, Oscar Han, Ion Jalea, Theodor Pallady, Militza Pătrașcu, Wladimir Siegfried and Jean Al. Steriadi; and architects like Horia Creangă, Octav Doicescu, Henriette Delavrancea, Marcel Janco, Horia Teodoru and many others.

In 1965, Biemel (known as Jean Rounault in France), Georges Pingusson (one of GMC's old friends from the École des Beaux-Arts), Ionel Schein (who studied under GMC in the 1940s) and Siegfried, honoured GMC with a commemorative event at the Bookshop Vincent Fréal et Cie in Paris.

118 GMC's Carlton Building in Bucharest (destroyed in the 1940 earthquake). Period photograph by Willy Pragher. © Landesarchiv Baden-Württemberg, Staatsarchiv Freiburg.

119 Advertising sign on Calea Victoriei, based on the portrait of Josephine Baker. Photograph by Willy Pragher. © Landesarchiv Baden-Württemberg, Staatsarchiv Freiburg.

Political attitude

Which hopes did GMC himself have in the Restoration[1]? Undoubtedly a hope for settling the political crisis; for spreading a pro-Western atmosphere across the country; for a liberal economic policy along with substantial commercial exchange, thus paving the way for the modernization of the country. Certainly he also hoped that Carol II would launch a liberal and metropolitan cultural policy, giving a fresh impetus to architecture and urban planning, in favour of a moderate Modernism. Furthermore, GMC could have thought of Carol II, whom he possibly met in Paris in the 1920s and who was just six years his senior, as a prospective client. In his articles and broadcast lectures GMC reminded that architecture and urban planning are in the public interest. He argued for "harmonizing constructive techniques with social organisation"[2] and called for serious state encouragement in regards to urban planning and architecture:

• official buildings should embody the durability and trustworthiness of state institutions, or, to put it in the words of Tony Judt: official buildings should be "visual representations of collective identity"[3].

• a long-term urban masterplan for Bucharest should combat deficiencies like planning improvisation, building speculation, and demagogy. He called for the slum belt to be replaced by proper districts, and the entire city to be furnished with a robust infrastructure. The traffic network should be improved according to street aesthetics, and hospitals, kindergardens, parks, public baths and public markets should be erected.[4]

• the architectural heritage of old cities like Jassy should be named areas of conservation and be protected from the pressures of development and insensitive planning.[5]

120 Horia Teodoru, *Apartment building*, Magheru Blvd, Bucharest (1934). Photograph W. Weiss.

121 Mihail Sebastian (1907-1945), Romanian writer and friend of GMC's.
Detail from a period photograph showing Sebastian in Paris in the 1930s.

Some of these hopes came true, as will be seen soon, and GMC made his contribution to them.

And what about GMC's political commitment? Being a Carlist himself, he, in 1930 joined the new party of the Young Liberals founded by his friend Georges Bratiano, and went campaigning for the general elections in his constituencies in Bucharest and Dolj county in western Wallachia, where both the Bibescos and Ştirbeys had properties.[6]

The policy of the Young Liberals boasted an impressive blend of conservative, liberal and social-democratic reformist features. They called for a "moral renewal"[7] of the country and a return to veritable liberalism. As GMC reported, the Young Liberals also desired to "reinforce the elements of the regional life, particularly where they can secure the economic development and protect cultural traditions."[8]

In Bucharest GMC's constituency was situated on the poor outskirts, at the *mahala*. In a letter to Marthe Bibesco he mentionned that he founded a medical cabinet for those in need and organized open university courses.[9]

At times the election campaigns were indignant, but occasionaly they did not lack humour. According to Paul-Emil Miclesco (1901-1994), the architect and friend of GMC's,[10] he was once being accused by his political adversaries of not being Romanian-born and therefore not capable of speaking a correct form of Romanian. During the political campaign, GMC, however, responded to his political adversaries in the most elegant Romanian language, much to the pleasure of the audience.[11]

There were other difficulties too. But because he was convinced of the urgency of rooting aesthetics in ethics, GMC believed he had a mission to carry on. On 29th December 1931 he wrote in his diary:

"There are moments when I feel like leaving public life behind me. Art itself claims an entire life, which, regardless of its length, is, in fact, always too short. One day you have to choose. But you don't choose. You don't go to war because you want it. War takes you in. And I am at war."[12]

122 Grigore Gafencu (1892-1957), the Romanian Foreign Minister from 1938-1940 (*first from the left*), in conversation with Winston Churchill, in 1939, at 1 Belgrave Square, then the Romanian Legation in London. Clement Attlee (*first from right*) and Lord Robert Vansittard converse on the right side of the image. Gafencu, *Europas letzte Tage*. Zurich 1946.

Subsequently GMC's joining with the Young Liberals contributed to limiting the influence of the extremist parties, both the Iron Guard and the underground Communist Party. In 1935 Mihail Sebastian commented that "at the moment, the reformist movement is represented by young liberals".[13] The election results of 1931, 1932, and 1933 show that the PNL led by Georges Bratiano had many loyal voters, slightly outnumbering the Iron Guard:[14]

Elections	*Young Liberals*	*Iron Guard*
June 1931	12 Seats (5.93 %)	8 Seats (3.89 %)
July 1932	14 Seats (6.53 %)	11 Seats (5.32 %)
November 1933	10 Seats (5.11 %)	9 Seats (4.47 %)
December 1937	16 Seats (3.89 %)	66 Seats (15.6 %)

But after the Iron Guard's overwhelming success in the last democratic general elections in late 1937, the Young Liberals joined the old Liberal Party. GMC was desillusioned. Subsequently he supported Carol II's authoritarian policy of protecting civic order against the political demagogy and crimes of the Iron Guard. He joined the *Front of the National Renaissance*.[15]

123 Constantin Argetoianu (1871-1955) (*left*), Romanian diplomat, politician and freemason, in conversation with Georges V. Bibesco (1880-1941), GMC's uncle and chairman of the *International Aeronautical Federation* (1930-1940). Period photograph.

In 1930 GMC was also invited to join the Freemason Lodge Liberty in Bucharest.[16] This commitment was in harmony with his reformist liberalism.

We can summarize that together with the Young Liberals around Georges Bratiano, and pro-Western politicians such as Constantin Argetoianu, Armand Călinescu, Grigore Gafencu, Viorel Tilea, Nicolae Titulesco, and writers like Tudor Arghezi, Mihai Ralea, Mihail Sebastian and Tudor Vianu, GMC was one of the few voices who defended democracy in Romania against the attacks from both left und ring wing extremism, thus calling for a truly democratic revision of the political system. In regards to the crimes of the Iron Guard GMC wrote to his wife Sanda on the 7th December 1938:

"But how sad. It is the eternal war of the people against order. It is easy to be against things, to oppose and to plot and to imagine there is something romantic about plotting. It is easy to complain and moan about injustice and all the other things, but what is difficult ist to govern, to act within the law, to defend the law and to take personal responsibility. To build something that will endure. In short, to be civilised. Romanians refuse to recognise this. In their sentimental as well as in their social life all they want is a sense of adventure. Never in my life have I felt more at odds with this odious society than now."[17]

GMC's commentary is reminiscent of, in the words of Betrand Russell, the "Roman [...] virtue of devotion to the impersonal state".[18] In his essay *Western Civilization* published in the anthology *In Praise of Idleness* (1935) Russell pointed out that "[t]he Romans seems to have invented the virtue of devotion to the impersonal state as opposed to loyalty to the person of the ruler. [...] The Roman conception of devotion to the state has been an essential element in the production of stable government in the West."[19]

124 Viorel Tilea (*left*) in conversation with Lord Halifax in London. (Ileana Tilea-Troiano, 1998).

O.N.T.

Contributions to modernizing Romania

In view of this troubled political and social background, GMC was grateful for the opportunity to work on outstanding tasks, and to pursue in material security his desire to be a "cavalier seul"[1] – in the public letter to Marcel Janco in 1931 GMC stylized himself as a deliberate outsider. All through his life he offered society fruits of his intense *vita contemplativa*, in the belief that "culture begins beyond the sufficient"[2]. He was deeply concerned with the "destiny [...] of this country, so steeped in sacrifice and patience"[3]. He wanted to contribute to set the anchor for durable and reliable social and political structures. "Romania ... a country of great charm and little virtue. The only way to improve this country is to love it dearly."[4]

GMC acted as a sort of "Cicerone accredited to all the celebreties visiting Bucharest"[5], showing around guests such as Charles Diehl, the French historian; Paul Morand, the French writer and diplomat; Derek Patmore, the English writer; Lord Lloyd of Dolobran, the chairman of the British Council (1937-41), or Herbert M. Gutmann, the art lover and banker chairman of the Dresdner Bank, who in 1929 led the German economic mission, which was to have talks on financial aid with the Romanian government.[6]

Obviously GMC built on the tradition of Enlightenment and aristocratic philantropy as fostered by some of his ancestors and other historic leaders such as Prince Demeter Cantemir in Moldavia and Governor Samuel von Brukenthal in Transylvania.

Greater Romania, "that country in the making"[7] invited to being creative and to contribute to determining the course for the future. For GMC, the 1920s and 30s were something of a Renaissance, a period "of youthful enthusiasm [...] and [...] full of expectation"[8]. Like some of his contemporaries including George Enesco and Marcel Janco, GMC set a wide range of activities against the bleak present. He was active as an architect, draughtsman, painter, curator, art and architectural historian and theorist, critic, translator, professor at three institutions of higher education and as a politician. Looking back on his career he commented in 1959:

"Not being a poet, yet being an admirer of poetry, aware that its harmony would never find a place in the strict rhythm of architectural space, I turned to painting to find new ways of expression. At the same time, I went on building according to the austere laws of architecture. Thus I was able to live in a paradise which, already in early childhood, my moments of idleness had allowed me to discover. If, to these activities, I added writing – painting having been the first one – I did so because of my desire to participate in life as much as possible. When I look back now, I realise that all three activities were part of a single, essential need. Many people have accused me of having too many interests. In none of my work was I ever a dilettante. I always felt an absolute need to build, to paint and to write. I did not choose. Choosing any form of art without profound conviction is the beginning of dilettantism. You are an artist only when art imposes itself on you as a vital need. To become an artist, that is to say a creator of harmony and to accept the necessary discipline you must have some firmly rooted fundamental ideas – all important to your work."[9]

126 GMC, *Cereals stock exchange and apartment building*, Bucharest (W 54), destroyed in the 1977 earthquake. Perspective drawing, c. 1934 (AGMC-PM).

125 Opposite:
GMC/V. Arion, *Hotel Rex*, Mamaia (W 61). Photograph W. Weiss, 1938 (AGMC-PM).

Architecture and Urbanism

Projects

Shortly after he became *Architecte Diplômé par le Gouvernement Français* in February 1929, GMC opened his own architectural office.[1] The next decade, which coincided with the reign of Carol II, proved to be the most prosperous time of GMC's career. With his former partner Schmiedigen he remained befriended and collaborated occasionally, as for example on the pavilion at the 1939 New York World's Fair.

In the 1930s GMC realized about seventy of the some one hundred projects in total of his architectural work. They cover the whole range of tasks he already experienced as a student: new buildings, transformation and modernisation of old buildings, conservation of historic monuments, landscape and urban design. The building typologies range from villas and apartment blocks, via commercial, office, industrial, and cultural buildings to churches and hotels.

Some of his projects stand out as major contributions to the country's economic and social development, including the first purpose-built stations of the Romanian Broadcasting Company in Bucharest and Bod/Brenndorf near Brașov/Kronstadt, the IAR aircraft factory at Brașov/Kronstadt, and the tourism projects at Eforie and Mamaia.

Convinced as he was of the necessity to harmonize architecture and urban design with state authority, infrastructure, and the social question, GMC embarked on urban planning too. To begin with, in 1929-30 he designed the masterplan for the seaside resort Eforie on the Black Sea Coast. In 1934-35 he contributed to the Bucharest Masterplan: he co-authored the substantial introduction; then he elaborated the chapter on urban technical infrastructure.[2] And in 1940 he worked on the urban masterplan for Constantza.[3]

Regarding the relationship between architectural objects and urban texture, some of GMC's Bucharest projects can be considered, in the sense of Colin Rowe and Fred Koetter, stabilizers[4] of the traditional amorphous urban fabric of the Romanian capital. Some, for instance, help define the public space of squares: this is true for the Soutzo buildings at University Square; the Bragadiru apartment block at Lahovary Square; the Kretzulesco apartment block at Amzei Square; the Kretzulesco office building opposite the Royal Palace at Royal Square, further providing an appropriate background for the Kretzulesco Church. On Bratianu Blvd, one of Europe's most splendid modernist urban avenues, the Carlton Building was, if only for five short years, Romania's highest building and a symbol of modernity.

This confident decade culminated in the design of the Romanian Pavilion at the 1939 New York World's Fair and in the project for the British Institute in Bucharest (1939-40).

128 GMC, *third Soutzo building* (W 54). Period photograph, c. 1960 (AGMC-PM).

129 Sitemap of the *Soutzo buildings*, Bucharest (ADT).

130 GMC's *Industrial Credit building*, Bucharest (second Soutzo building W 53). Period postcard (ADT).

127 Opposite: View of Magheru Blvd (formerly Bratiano Blvd), in Bucharest, with GMC's *Carlton Building*. Period postcard (ADT).

131 Advertisement of the Malaxa Factory. *Guide de la Roumanie*, Bucharest 1938.

132 GMC/V. Arion, *Carlton cinema*, c. 1932-1936. Destroyed in the 1940 earthquake. Period photograph W. Weiss (AGMC-PM).

133 GMC, *Aircraft Factoy IAR* in Brașov/Kronstadt, W 34 (c. 1931-1933). Period photograph W. Weiss (AGMC-PM).

Clients

The vast spectrum of GMC's clients involved private and state patrons as well as public-private-partnerships. The private clients included aristocrats like Marthe Bibesco, Marina Brancovan, Anne-Marie Callimachi, Radu and Sarmisza Cretzianu, Nicolas Kretzulesco, Nicolas Mavrocordato, Alice Rosetti-Tescanu, Alice Sturdza, Pulcheria and Demeter Sturdza, and the bourgeois such as composer Mihail Andricu[1] and writer Tudor Arghezi[2], professor Nae Ionescu, Angela Mornand, diplomat Viorel Tilea, as well as magnates like the Bragadiru family and Nicolae Malaxa, and bankers like Aristide Blank and Nicky Chrissoveloni.

In addition to these, GMC was commissioned by public institutions: the Ministry of Defence commissioned the design of the Military Casino at Mamaia on the Black Sea Coast; CFR and the Department of Tourism the Hotel Rex also at Mamaia; the Department of Cultural Affairs on behalf of King Carol II the official pavilion at the New York World's Fair; and the British Government the British Council Institute in Bucharest. Furthermore there were private companies like the aircraft factory IAR, the Romanian Credit Bank, the Romanian Broadcasting Society, the Society of War Invalids and the Techirghiol Ltd.

134 GMC/V. Arion, *Bragadiru apartment building*, Bucharest, W 47 (c. 1934-1935). Main entrance (ADT).

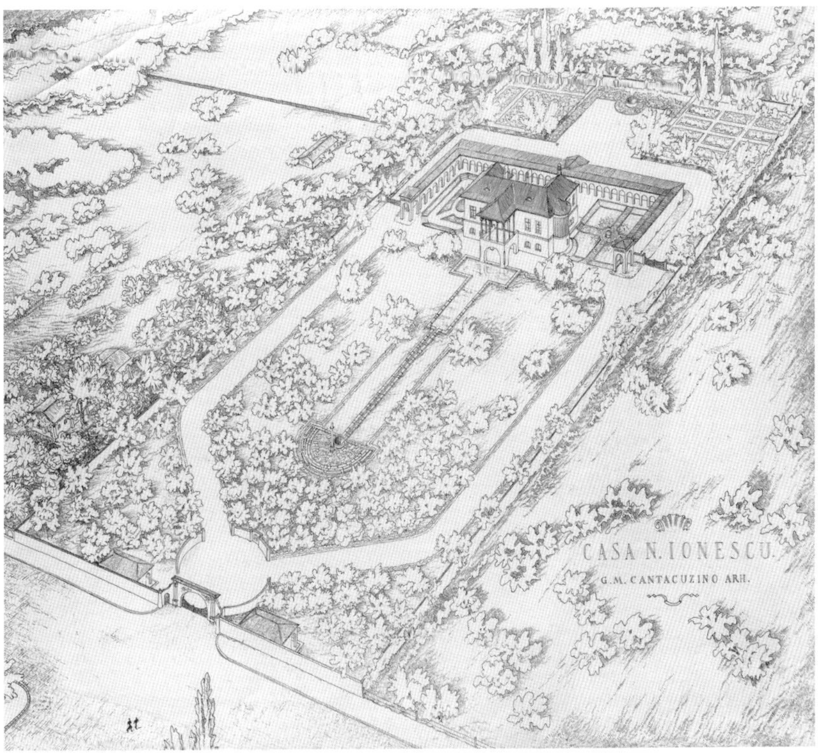

135 GMC, *Villa Nae Ionescu*, Bucharest (c. 1936-1937), W 64. Perspective drawing (AGMC-PM).

136 Advertisement of the *Bragadiru Brewery*. *Guide de la Roumanie*, Bucharest 1938.

137 GMC, *Hotel Neptun*, Eforie Nord, Black Sea Coast (c. 1929-1932), W 14. Period photograph W. Weiss (AGMC-PM).

Eforie

Techirghiol Ltd was active in the Black Sea resort of the same name, some 15 km south of Constantza. For hundreds of years, a modest village gathered around inland lakes boasting an abundance of mud that was found to have curing effects. The story, in fact, started back in 1894, as the Eforia (Charity Foundation of Public Hospitals in Bucharest) saw a profit in the mud as a medical cure and founded in Techirghiol a health spa for treating rheumatism.[1]

Techirghiol Ltd was principally financed by the Romanian-Jewish banker and philantropist Aristide Blank (1883-1960), chief of Marmorosch, Blank & Co. Bank.[2] Blank also sponsored the Literary Prize Techirghiol-Eforie, which in 1933 was awarded to Mircea Eliade, the novelist and later historian of religions.[3] The Board of Trustees of Techirghiol Ltd involved, among others, Aristide Blank and Viorel Tilea.[4] For both, GMC designed villas on the coast promenade overlooking the Black Sea.

From 1926 to 1940 Techirghiol Ltd co-operated with the Romanian National Bank and National Tourism Agency ONEF (Oficiul Național de Turism) to expand the traditional inland village up to the coast and turn it into a modern seaside resort, to the effect that in 1933 the village and new district were united to the town of Eforie. In 1937, Eforie offered three hotels, sixty villas for rent, two youth camps, along with the necessary urban infrastructure (mud baths, sea promenade, restaurants and bars, railroad station and so forth). Also, Carol II had his summer residence built at Eforie – the so-called *Sand Castle*,[5] which seems to have vanished in the meantime.

GMC's projects at Eforie mark him as the third exceptional modernist in Romania beside Marcel Janco and Horia Creangă. Here, the Techirghiol Ltd commissioned GMC with a truly unique project. In a sense, Eforie meant to GMC what Vicenza meant to Palladio. Next to Bucharest, Eforie is the place where GMC could realize the greatest number of projects. Not only did he

138 GMC, *Wooden pergola on Grand Blvd* (now Ovid Blvd), Eforie Nord, (c. 1929-32), W 29-30. Demolished around 1960. Period photograph W. Weiss (AGMC-PM).

lay out the masterplan of the seaside resort, he also contributed at least two hotels and numerous villas in the first phase of realisation. On this project he wrote to Marthe Bibesco on the 30th September 1929:

"I will inform you in detail of how a small white and blue town, near Tekir-Ghiol, rises on my designs. This miracle is due to our friend Aristide [Blank]."[6]

And in the letter from the 11th march 1930 he continued: "[M]y little city on the Pont-Euxin is at the moment my chief preoccupation".[7] In this respect, Derek Patmore observed in *Invitation to Romania* (1939):

"George Cantacuzène has executed several ambitious modern projects. He had laid out all the town-planning of Eforia, a seaside resort on the Black Sea, and his rows of simple modern white plaster villas with blue windwos and doors are very pleasing."[8]

Today, only few of these buildings are known to have been designed by GMC, like the Hotel Bellona on the headland and some villas on the coast promenade, including Villa Lilly next to Hotel Bellona, then Villa Aviana for Aristide Blank, Villa Bibesco, and Villa Tilea-Martaloglu. Research in some private archives and the archive of the city of Constantza revealed further projects, some congenially photographed by W. Weiss.

A few have been demolished, others are in a very poor condition. It may suffice here to mention the corner building on the coast promenade and Ovid Blvd (formerly Grand Blvd), destroyed around 1960. That Loos-like simple two-storey building with a powerful tower on a stepped terrace perhaps housed the former railway station, with a restaurant and guest house. A villa, smaller in size but of similar simple and refined architectural language, survives, if even in a derelict state, some fifty meters westwards on Ovid Blvd). Close to it are another two fine modernist villas prey to decay, which were commissioned by the Tilea family: Villa Flora and Villa Blue (Albastră).[9]

139 GMC, *Villa Flora*, Eforie Nord, Black Sea Coast (c. 1932-35), W 38, built for Mrs Tilea-Russo. South-east view (Photograph ADT).

140 View of Grand Blvd (now Ovid Blvd), Eforie, with the wooden pergola, Villa 8a (*first from right*; W 27) and the *Villa Tower* in the background centre (W 13). Period postcard (ADT).

141 GMC, *Villa Tower* (*left*; W 13), *pharmacy pavilion* and *pergola* (W 29-30), Eforie. All demolished c. 1960. Photograph W. Weiss (AGMC-PM).

142 *Villa Z* (W 37), Eforie Nord. Attributed to GMC on aesthetic grounds. Front façade (Photograph ADT).

143 *Villa Z* (W 37), Eforie Nord. Staircase to the terrace. (Photograph ADT).

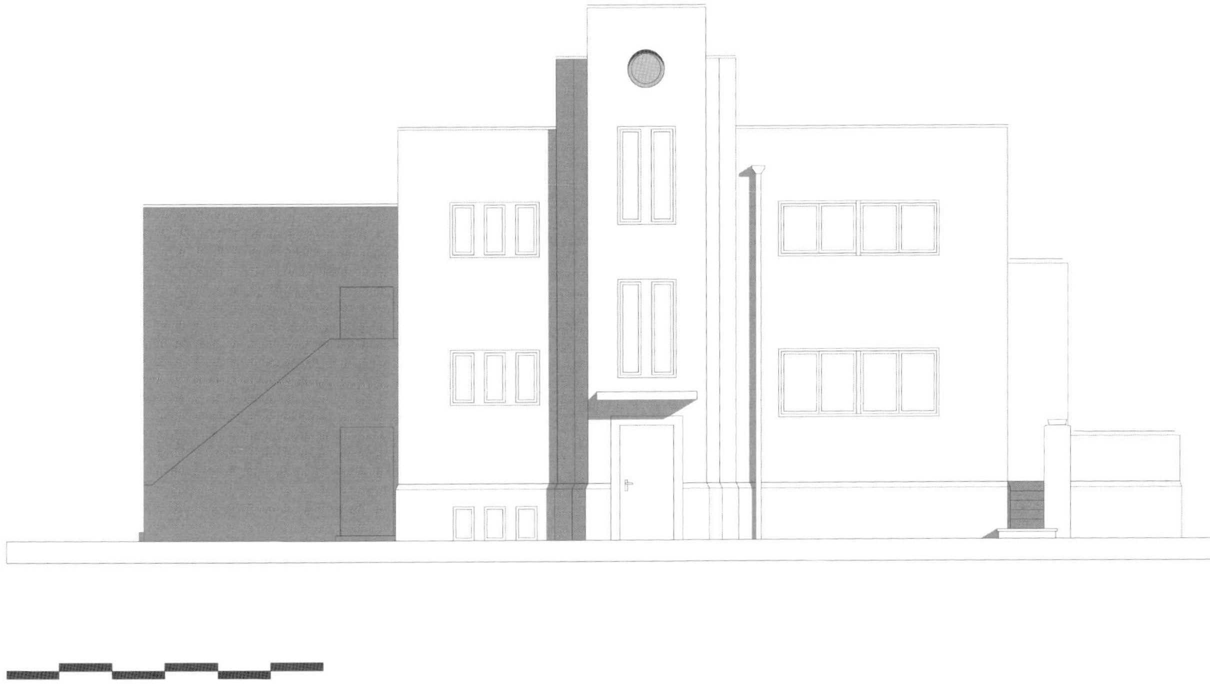

144 *Villa Z* (W 37), Eforie Nord. Attributed to GMC on aesthetic grounds. Reconstruction of the front elevation (ADT).

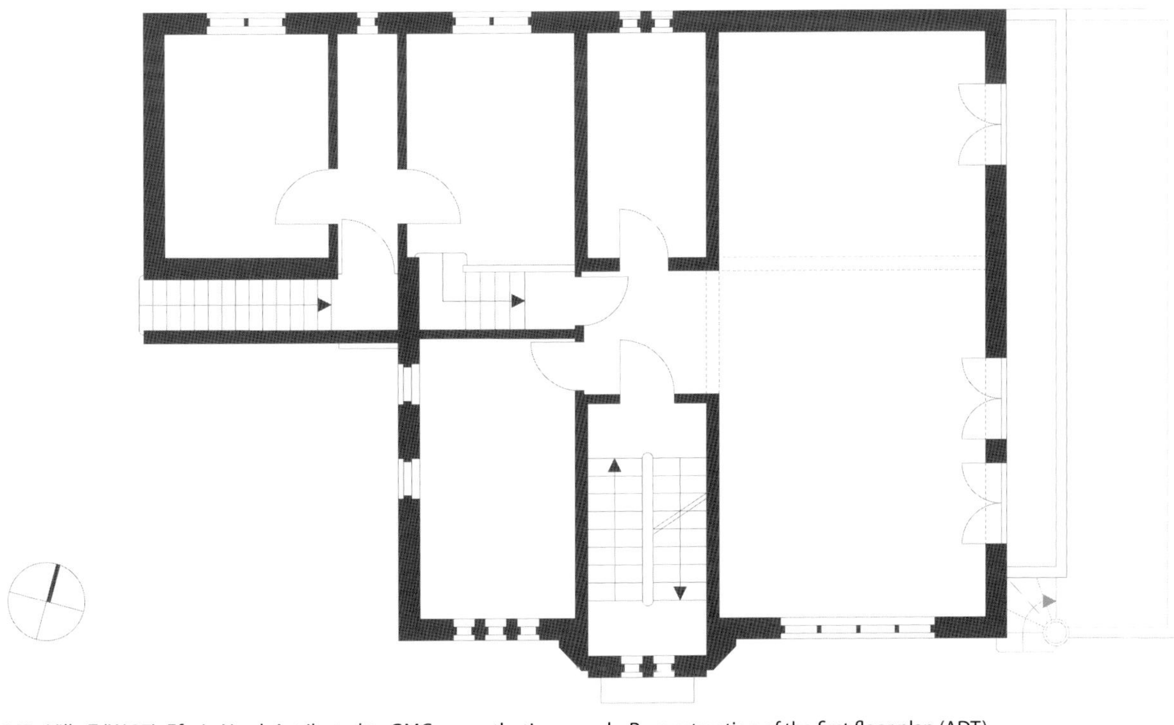

145 *Villa Z* (W 37), Eforie Nord. Attributed to GMC on aesthetic grounds. Reconstruction of the first floor plan (ADT).

146 GMC, *Design project for a Military Casino* Mamaia (c. 1930-31; W 22). Gouache drawing (AGMC-PM).

Mamaia

Mamaia was the second city on the Black Sea Coast for which GMC designed important projects. He started with the impressive Military Casino in 1930. Whether it was destroyed or remains still in its original design is uncertain.

Around 1934-37 GMC, together with Vasile Arion, his partner at the time, probably continued with two equally impressive projects: first, the extension of the tourist casino including a vast terrace and bathing infrastructure;[1] and secondly, the *Salvamar* (Sea Rescue Service) Casino on the shore of the Siutghol Lake, a building demolished by the Communist authorities in 1960.[2] The so-called *Ship House* beared witness to the same *architecture parlante* spirit as the Hotel Bellona. The two buildings had the same length and a similar typological disposition, if for different functional reasons: whereas Bellona initially had a sort of a courtyard to mark the entrance and welcome guests, the *Ship House* had on its eastern side, that is opposite of the Siutghiol Lake, a compact one-storey service close to the Constantza railroad line. For CFR (Romanian Railways) and ONT (National Tourism Department) GMC designed, again together with Arion, the Hotel Rex (1936-38).[3] The hotel was named after King Carol II, who felt a deep interest in its completion.[4] Derek Patmore remembered his visit in 1939:

"A vast luxury hotel, built with arcades and terraces leading down to the sea, it stands alone on a magnificent stretch of golden sand overlooking the Black Sea. Designed to become the Romanian Lido, the arrangement of this hotel, with its elegant modernity and carefully thought-out luxury, is typical of Cantacuzene's work, and it provides another example of the modern Romania's desire to compete with the West in every standard of contemporary efficiency and comfort."[5]

Meanwhile, the hotel does not stand alone any more. Its grand unity has been amputated, with the northern arcades wing having been demolished in favour of a new hotel a few years ago.

147 Advertisment of the National Tourism Department ONT for the *Hotel Rex*. *Guide de la Roumanie*, Bucharest 1938.

148 GMC/V. Arion, *Hotel Rex* (W 61), Mamaia. Perspective drawing, seaside view (AGMC-PM).

149 GMC/V. Arion, *Hotel Rex* (W 61), Mamaia. Seaside view, c. 1960. Period postcard (ADT).

150 GMC's three close collaborators in the 1930s: Kaller (*left*), Paul Marinescu (*centre*) and Eugen Eppler, c. 1935. On the wall in the background are two interior perspectives of the Carlton cinema and a front elevation of an unknown project (AGMC-PM).

Architectural Office

In his office GMC chiefly relied upon a team of three close collaborators: Paul Marinescu, his chief assistant, along with Kaller and Eugen Eppler.[1] Thanks to them he could engage in other activities too. GMC usually developed the *esquisse* and relevant details of the design. He also loved to elaborate on axonometric and perspective views – in pencil, black ink, as well as watercolours or gouache. He profited abundantly from his travel sketch books and photographies, as well as from his impressive library, which he constantly increased. Until 1940 it included some international architectural reviews, to which GMC had subscribed.[2] The library was also the place for jour fixes and meetings. For the construction design and constant supervision of construction sites he largely relied upon his employees or co-operated with builders or colleagues, especially with local architects in the case of remote projects. At Eforie, for example, he worked with architect Ferencz,[3] and at Mamaia he possibly co-operated with Gospodin, the chief architect of Constantza.[4] GMC particularly enjoyed intense moments of team work before submitting a design project: "I very much love this atmosphere of work late at night and this disciplined cohesion of my collaborators in such circumstances. These are indeed precious moments in the life of my atelier."[5]

151 GMC, *Villa Policrat*, Bucharest (W 58). Plaque on the wall facing the Calea Floreasca (Photograph Emil-Dinu Popa).

152 GMC and August Schmiedigen with workmen on the construction site of the *Flămânda church* (The Hungry One) in Câmpulung-Muscel in the Southern Carpathians (1937-1942; W 76), on 22nd August 1938 (AMLSC).

„At that time", the Romanian architect Anghel Marcu, one of GMC's former students, wrote in 1993, GMC "was at the top of his profession with an enormous work load"[6], overwhelmed by commissions and requests. Early on in 1938, for instance, his office designed five projects and supervised twelve construction sites located at least at nine different places.

Construction sites he found particularly moving. At meetings with engineers and builders, by contrast, he often missed imagination and open-mindedness.[7] Some profited from him, even to his detriment, as we shall see later. He preferred the intense and straightforward co-operation with craftsmen.

When it came to stonemasonry, he was thrilled, as suggested by this passage from a letter to Marietta Stern-Guetta on the building of *Flămânda Church* in Câmpulung-Muscel at the foot of the Southern Carpathians:

"I am so pleased to be back here. At some places the walls are already five meters high. Working with stone is magnificent. I drew on site the details of the capitals and cornice. You just can't imagine what a delight it is for the mind to think in stone. My construction site is most picturesque with my stonemasons dressed in their peasant costumes, and the stone setting recalling antiquity."[8]

153 GMC's architectural office stamp in the 1930s (PBM).

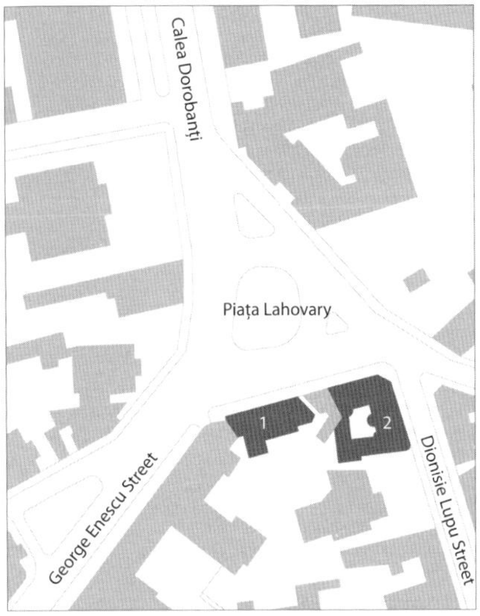

154 Site map of Lahovary Square in Bucharest with the apartment buildings by Horia Creangă (1) and GMC (2) (ADT).

155 The apartment buildings by GMC (*left;* W 47) and Horia Creangă at Lahovary Square, Bucharest (Photograph Marius Voica).

156 Marcel Janco, *Portrait of Horia Creangă*, c. 1935. © VG Bild-Kunst, Bonn, 2014.

Ethos, Friendship and Romanian Modernism

On some projects GMC co-operated with colleagues like Vasile Arion and Duiliu Marcu (1885-1966). His longest and most fruitful collaboration, however, was with Octav Doicescu (1902-1981). It culminated in their projects for the New York World's Fair and the British Council headquarters in Bucharest. In 1939, Doicescu also joined GMC as steady co-editor of the annual periodical *Simetria*, and they became friends. GMC was a co-author of the 1935 Bucharest Masterplan together with Roger Bolomey, Ion Davidescu, Duiliu Marcu and Teodor Rădulescu. With Davidescu, one of his former study colleagues, he worked on a masterplan for Constantza in 1940.

Horia Creangă, another leading figure of Romanian Modernism, was a close friend of GMC's since their study years in Paris. On the night before New Year's Eve, they used to invite other colleagues such as Horia Teodoru, Haralamb Georgescu or Nicolae Nedelescu to a restaurant to celebrate and talk about architecture and urbanism, and how to improve them in Romania. Obviously they shared a common professional outlook. This shows, for example, in Creangă's and GMC's moderate modernist buildings on the Lahovary Square in Bucharest, and in Eforie. Whereas in Bucharest their two eight-storey appartment buildings define the southern end of the square, which otherwise remains quite amorphous to date, Creangă's villa for the Crown Prince Michael marks the northern end of the Eforie's sea promenade. Creangă was a co-editor of *Simetria IV*, up to his untimely death. GMC paid homage to him with an obituary in *Simetria V*.

As regards Marcel Janco, it seems that GMC did not meet him not until the spring of 1931. GMC took the initiative and wrote him a public letter on the contemporary architectural scene in Romania. Janco immediately published it in his avant-garde review *Contimporanul*, which he co-edited with the artist Ion Vinea (1895-1964). GMC expressed his deep respect and congratulated Janco for being the pioneer of Modernism in Romania:

157 Bucharest, Tache Ionescu Blvd (now Magheru Blvd) with Horia Creangă's *ARO Credit building and cinema* (1929-31). Period postcard (ADT).

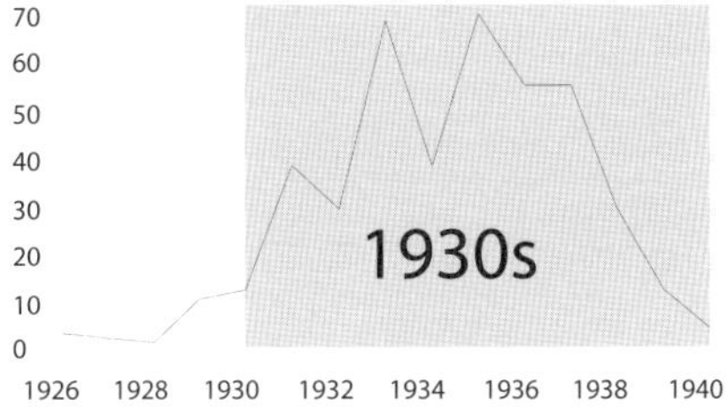

158 Diagramme of the development of Modernism in Romania according to the number of modernist buildings constructed from 1926 to 1940. Without being exhaustive, the survey is based on the monographs on H. Creangă, M. Janco, O. Doicescu, D. Marcu, GMC, on the standard work of L. Machedon/E. Scoffham, *Romanian Modernism*. Cambridge, Mass./London 1999, and on GMC's updated list of works.

"My firm conviction is, that you have been the first in this country to turn his back on its tired and sterile mentality."[1]

At the same time, GMC called for a collective reformist ethos. He suggested that this ethos could be the *classical attitude*, which drew on the position of the Parisian *Groupe des Architectes Modernes* around Perret and Expert. For GMC, the "critical spirit of permanent classicism"[2] had acknowledged some "essential moments" of the new architecture. GMC conceived of Classicism as the "embodiment of the steady efforts [...] to maintain architecture in a balance defined by the human scale"[3].

Janco's reply appeared in the next *Contimporanul* issue in the autumn of 1931. There he remarked, that within a few months Modernism had almost advanced to a mainstream movement, but also critized the stylish superficiality of a great part of the new buildings.[4]

The public dialogue between two leading figures of the Romanian architectural scene, seemed to have stimulated in no small part younger or more prudent architects, to embrace modernism and to try to link it to both classical and Romanian traditional principles. As pointed out by Ilinca Manaila in her study on Marcel Janco at the ETH Zurich, the year 1931 appears to have "marked a turning point not only for *Contimporanul* but for Modernism in Romania on the whole"[5].

Despite their differences in architecture, leading architects in Romania further committed themselves to this outlook.[6] Horia Creangă, like the group of Italian Modernists around Giuseppe Terragni, insisted on the basic familiarity between vernacular architecture and Modernism, in particular as regards the immaculate simplicity of Wallachian *culas*.[7] GMC's *classical attitude* and the culture of dialogue or, in the words of French philosopher Edgar Morin, the "dialogic"[8] seemed to have become a corner-stone of Romanian Modernism. Its breakthrough occurred at the beginning of Carol's II reign, who, as we have seen, greatly encouraged the arts and architecture.

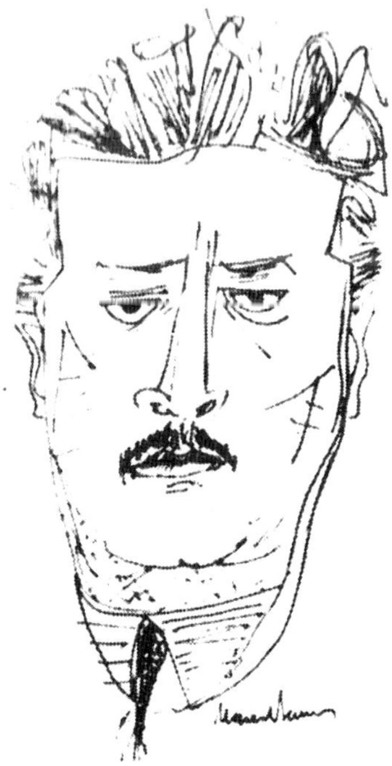

159 Marcel Janco, *Self-portrait*, c. 1935. © VG Bild-Kunst, Bonn, 2014.

160 Horia Teodoru, *Dalles Foundation Building*, Magheru Blvd (now N. Bălcescu Blvd), Bucharest, 1932 (Photograph W. Weiss, *L'Architecture d'Aujourd'hui* 5/1934).

Indeed, the friendship and culture of dialogue fostered by leading personalities is one phenomenon which contributes to explaining the power and creative coherence of this original variation on Modernism.

As reported by Radu Patrulius, Marcel Janco argued that "the encounters and conversations with Horia Creangă, G. M. Cantacuzino and other colleagues were undoubtedly essential for the ideas and experiments at the time. Despite the unfavourable general atmosphere in Romania, they promoted the evolution of a new and revolutionary art."[9] Patrulius added: "We have to concede that the 1930s were decisively marked by the initiatives of forceful characters".[10]

Wih respect to the role of dialogue and friendship in this effervescent and creative period, one might be tempted to think of similar periods in cultural history. Érik Orsenna, for instance, commented on the importance of friendship to French Classicism, highlighting the closeness between André Le Nôtre (1613-1700), the landscape architect; Louis Le Vau (1612-1670), the architect; Charles Le Brun (1619-1690), the painter, art-history theorist and interior designer; and Jean-Baptiste de La Quintinie (1624-1688), the Botanist:

"Perhaps the key to the Golden Age is to be found in friendship. These artists had bonds of affection going back to their youth, feelings that were a refuge for them, the answer to an instant need."[11]

We find something similar in England in the early eighteenth century and one century later in Germany. In England, that creative circle included Richard Boyle, 3rd Earl of Lord Burlington (1694-1753), William Kent, the architect; J. M. Rysbrack, the sculptor; Sebastiano Ricci, the fresco painter; and Alexander Pope, the poet; Sir Hans Sloane, the Botanist.[12] Then the "Golden Age of the German spirit"[13], as Rüdiger Safranski observed, culminated in the friendship between Goethe and Schiller.

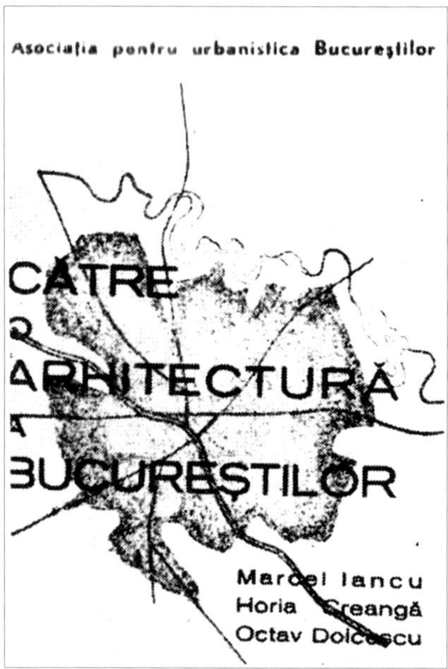

161 M.Janco/H. Creangă/O. Doicescu, *Către o arhitectură a Bucureștilor* (Towards a new Bucharest architecture). Bucharest 1935. Front cover.

In 1935 Creangă, Doicescu and Janco published the pamphlet *Towards a new Bucharest architecture* (Către o arhitectură a Bucureștilor). This passionate essay in favour of modernist architecture complemented, so to speak, the Bucharest Masterplan. The essay was published on behalf of *The Association for the Promotion of Urbanism in Bucharest*, which included personalities from various disciplines – architects like Petre Antonescu, Horia Creangă, Octav Doicescu, Marcel Janco, Duiliu Marcu, GMC, urbanists like Ion Davidescu and Cincinat Sfințescu, politicians like Constantin Argetoianu, art historians like Alexander Tzigara-Samurcaș and writers like Emanoil Bucuță.[14] The association was founded by Dem Dobrescu (1871-1948), who just retired from his post as mayor of Bucharest (1929-1934).[15] The goal was to sensitize the government and public to the urban planning concerns in general, and the Bucharest Masterplan in particular.[16] The looseness of this association emphasizes the informal character of Romanian Modernism, which relied on a vivid culture of conversation. This form of dialogic was unmistakbly rooted in Bucharest's vibrant café scene.

Indeed, Bucharest boasted a long tradition of cafés, of which two were outstanding in the interwar-period: Corso and Capșa. Capșa was strategically situated on the famous Calea Victoriei in the heart of the capital.

At Capşa GMC himself used to celebrate his exhibitions and to have dinner with family, friends or international guests. The French writer and diplomat Paul Morand was one of them, and in his 1935 travel book *Bucarest* he offered a breathtaking description of Capşa:

"Bucharest, hot spot Capşa. Capşa, that's the heart of the city, in terms of topography and morale. Capşa, that's four institutions at once: a hotel, a confiserie, a restaurant, and a café. Imagine, in a house of quite modest appearance, four European glories united: the restaurant Foyaut, confiserie Rumpelmayer, café Florian of Venise, and hotel Sacher of Vienna. Capşa, that's a style of its own, a living tradition and habit, a railroad station hall, a true monument and coat of arms."[17]

Furthermore, there were fruitful collaborations between architects and artists. Creangă, for instance, designed a villa and workshop for sculptor Cornel Medrea;[18] Janco did the same for sculptor Militza Pătraşcu;[19] Pătraşcu, on her part, portraited Janco and Vinea for *Contimporanul*.[20]

GMC himself collaborated with a number of artists both on *Simetria* – as we shall see later in this chapter – and on some architectural projects: Paul Miracovici (1906-1973) painted a fresco in the hall of the hotel Rex at Mamaia;[21] Oscar Han, Mac Constantinescu, and Militza Pătraşcu provided sculptures for the official pavilion at the New York World's Fair, whose opening event included a concert directed by Georges Enesco.[22]

W. Weiss was GMC's favourite architectural photographer. His archives seem to be irretrievably lost. Some of his photographs, still unknown to the wider public until now, have survived in GMC's dispersed archives. Weiss documented a great number of GMC's buildings, some of which vanished. Weiss also contributed the photographs for GMC's *Petits Édifices*, published by Vincent, Fréal et Cie in Paris in 1931.

Militza Pătraşcu (1892-1976), a disciple of Constantin Brancusi,[23] was particularly close to GMC. She made bronze busts of his family and him, and contributed with a title drawing to his book *Evasion*, the manuscript of which seems to be lost; they also worked together on the memorial house of the late poet Octavian Goga.[24]

162 Marcel Janco, *Portrait of Octav Doicescu*, 1935. © VG Bild-Kunst, Bonn, 2014.

163 Advertisement of the Bucharest photographer W. Weiss. *Arhitectura* No. 2/1941, Bucharest

164 Horia Creangă, Entrance to the *Malaxa Factory*, Bucharest, c. 1930 (demolished).

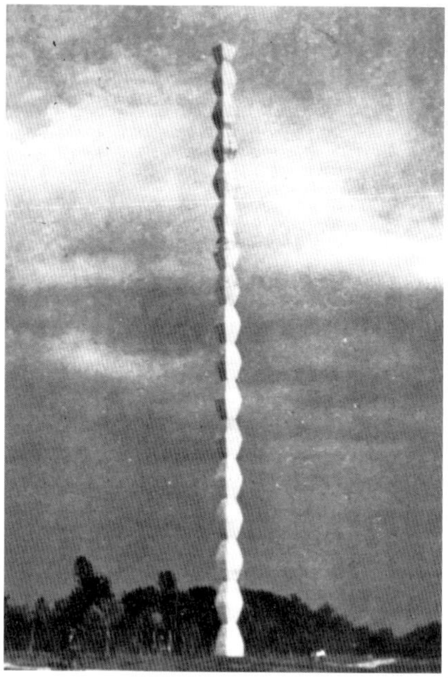

165 Constantin Brancusi, *The endless column*. Târgu-Jiu, photograph Brancusi, c. 1938. © VG Bild-Kunst, Bonn, 2014.

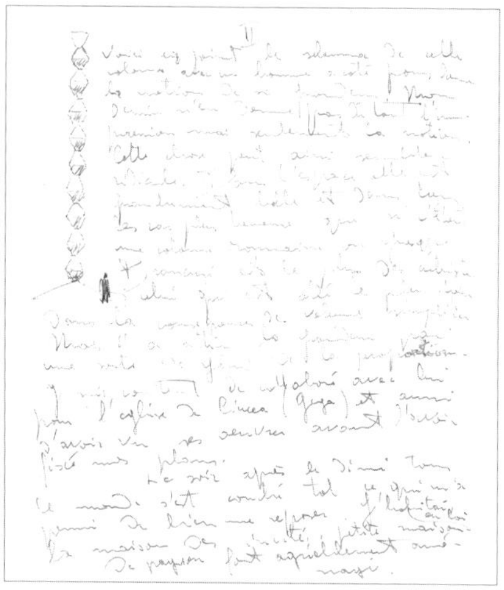

166 GMC, Letter to Marietta Stern-Guetta, 21st August 1938 (in French). Page containing the description of Brancusi's *Endless Column* (AMLSC).

At first, Brancusi was supposed to contribute sculptures to both the Goga project and the New York pavilion. However, he left these projects to Militza Pătraşcu. Brancusi possibly did so because Pătraşcu arranged for him to get the Târgu-Jiu project. In addition, he was busy with the *Temple of Meditation*, a project commissioned by the Maharaja of Indore. Eventually this project never materialized.[25]

When GMC met Brancusi in 1938, he was literally captured by his charisma, being deeply moved by the newly completed land-art trilogy in Târgu Jiu in south-eastern Wallachia. There Brancusi laid out a War Memorial – an urban axis consisting of three monuments: the *Table of Silence* and the *Gate of the Kiss* in the Central Park, and the *Endless Column*.[26] At that time, Brancusi was less accepted in Romania. GMC was one of the few who instantly appreciated Brancusi's genius. Sanda Tattarescu-Negropontes, the client's daughter, remembered that "[t]he architect Cantacuzino [...], upon seeing the column, fell to his knees with tears rolling down his cheeks."[27] In a letter to Marietta Stern-Guetta GMC commented on this event:

"Having arrived yesterday [...at] Târgu-Jiu [...], I, in company with Militza Pătraşcu, Mme Tatarescu and her daughter, immediately went to visit the works of Brancusi, which was a tremendous delight. The most peculiar thing is the endless column which Brancusi errected on a hill over the city. It is indescribable and consists of a series of identical volumes which are placed on top of each other in the same rhythm and seem to end somewhere in the sky. Here is a sketch of this column with a man close to it, so as to convey an idea of its height. My sketch doesn't give but an idea of it. In its setting the column is truly beautiful and definitely better than any traditional Romanian or even ancient Greek column would have been. Of all cubists, Brancusi is the one who ventured farthest into simplifying volumes. He achieved his mastery by a genius of proportions. I am glad to collaborate with him on the Ciucea church (Goga), and to have seen his works before fixing my plans."[28]

GMC was indeed fascinated by Brancusi: "Yesterday I dined with the old Brancusi. What a long spiritual delight it was! We stayed until two o'clock in the morning in a *cârciumă* [pub], and laughed and philosophied a lot. He relies upon a deep common sense and a great heart. His work seems to be closer to magic than to what we use to call art."[29]

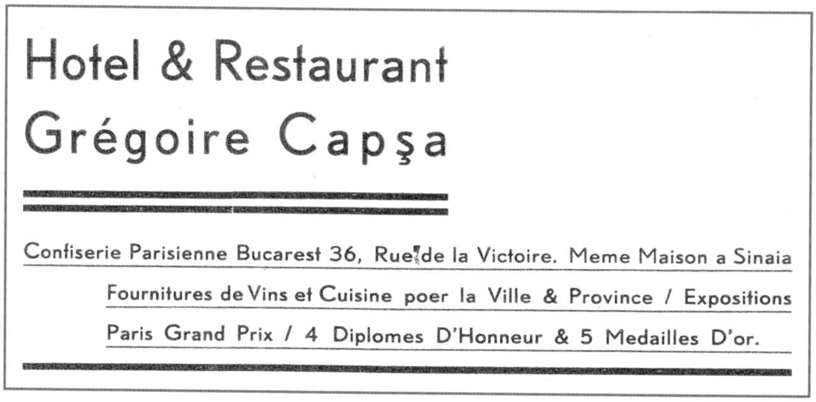

167 Advertisement of the Capşa Hotel and Restaurant. *Guide de la Roumanie*, Bucharest 1938.

Painting and Drawing

GMC's first solo exhibition took place in the Ileana Hall at the Cartea Romaneasca Bookshop on the 15th January 1931.[1] During the 1930s there followed three further solo shows along with participations in group exhibitions. One of these was the group exhibition involving Nina Arbore, Mac Constantinesco, Marcel Janco und Militza Pătraşcu (November 1939 to January 1940).[2] Rated as the country's best exhibition of the year 1940, it was also Janco's farewell exhibition before leaving for Palestine.[3]

All of this contributed to firmly establishing GMC within the cultural life of Romania. Around 1938 the Academy of Fine Arts in Bucharest, where Oscar Han, Paul Miracovici and Jean Al. Steriadi were professors, appointed GMC as honorary professor for graphic arts, that is analytical geometry, freehand drawing and calligraphy.[4]

He was active as a curator too, especially in the late 1930s, as far as we know. In the spring of 1938 he curated the exhibition of the Venetian artist Guido Cadorin (1892-1976) at the Italian Cultural Institute in Bucharest.[5] Together with Nicolae Nedelescu he in 1939 staged an exhibition on the wide range of activities pursued by CFR;[6] and in the spring of 1940 he collaborated with Octav Doicescu on the exhibition of popular art commissioned by Aretia Tattarescu.[7]

In hours of leisure GMC loved to paint, for instance at the family country retreats at Băileşti in south-western Wallachia or Dărmaneşti in south-western Moldavia.[8] After dinner, he often retreated to his atelier. Architectural projects and their settings also inspired him to draw and paint. This was particularly true of Moldavian sceneries or the Black Sea Coast. Being a great swimmer, he also very much enjoyed the sea:

"After such a sporting morning [...and] a long inspection of my construction sites [...] I will paint one of my favourite landscapes: wild grass, the sea and the sky."[9]

On travels he drew and painted too. The works which came down to us concentrate especially on landscapes and cityscapes in Romania, Italy, New York, and the Middle East.

168 Guido Cadorin, *Venice*. Pencil drawing, 1937. *Simetria III* (1940-1941).

169 Moldavian landscape at the Dărmăneşti country retreat of GMC's family (AMLSC).

170 GMC painting (detail), 1930s (AMLSC).

171 Ancient ruins of the Sasanian Imperial Palace of Ctesiphon on the Tigris, near Baghdad. Photograph GMC, c. 1935 (AGMC-IP).

L'ARCHITECTURE D'AUJOURD'HUI

5, RUE BARTHOLDI, BOULOGNE (SEINE) — TÉLÉPHONE: MOLITOR 19-90 et 19-91

COMITÉ DE PATRONAGE: MM. POL ABRAHAM, ALF. AGACHE, L. BAZIN, EUGÈNE BEAUDOUIN, LOUIS BOILEAU, DJO BOURGEOIS, VICTOR BOURGEOIS, URBAIN CASSAN, PIERRE CHAREAU, JACQUES DEBAT-PONSAN, JEAN DÉMARET, ADOLPHE DERVAUX, JEAN DESBOUIS, ANDRÉ DUBREUIL, W. M. DUDOK, FÉLIX DUMAIL, ROGER EXPERT, LOUIS FAURE-DUJARRIC, RAYMOND FISCHER, TONY GARNIER, JEAN GINSBERG, HECTOR GUIMARD, MARCEL HENNEQUET, ROGER HUMMEL, FRANCIS JOURDAIN, ALBERT LAPRADE, H. LE MÊME, MARCEL LODS, BERTHOLD LUBETKIN, ANDRE LURÇAT, ROB. MALLET-STEVENS, LOUIS MADELINE, J. B. MATHON, J. C. MOREUX, HENRI PACON, PIERRE PATOUT, AUGUSTE PERRET, G. H. PINGUSSON, HENRI PROST, MICHEL ROUX-SPITZ, HENRI SELLIER, CHARLES SICLIS, PAUL SIRVIN, MARCEL TEMPORAL, JOSEPH VAGO, ANDRÉ VENTRE, VETTER

ANDRÉ BLOC, DIRECTEUR

COMITÉ DE RÉDACTION

PIERRE VAGO, RÉDACTEUR EN CHEF

HISTORIQUE: ALBERT LAPRADE
URBANISME: EUGÈNE BEAUDOUIN
ARCHITECTURE: JOSÉ IMBERT
TECHNIQUE: G. H. PINGUSSON
INTÉRIEURS: J. P. SABATOU
EXPOSITIONS: RENÉ DROUIN
CHANTIERS: ANDRÉ HERMANT

JULES POSENER
SECRÉTAIRE DE LA RÉDACTION

CORRESPONDANTS: ALLEMAGNE: JUERGEN SCHWEIZER — ANGLETERRE: E. GOLDFINGER — AUTRICHE: EGON RISS — BELGIQUE: DE KONINCK — BULGARIE: LUBAIN TONEFF — DANEMARK: HANJEN — ESPAGNE: GUITIERREZ SOTO — ÉTATS-UNIS: DEXTER MORAND — EXTRÊME-ORIENT: HARRY LITVAK — GRÈCE: GEORGES KALYVAVS — HONGRIE: GEORGES MASIREVICH — ITALIE: P. M. BARDI — JAPON: BRUNO TAUT — PALESTINE: J. BARKAI — PAYS-BAS: J. P. KLOOS — PORTUGAL: PARDAL MONTEIRO — ROUMANIE: G. CANTACUZÈNE — SUÈDE: VIKING GOERANSSON — SUISSE: H. ZWEIGENTHAL — TCHÉCOSLOVAQUIE: JEAN SOKOL — U. R. S. S.: PROF. ARKINE — YOUGOSLAVIE: L. ILITCH ET S. PLANITCH

Mme M. E. CAHEN, SECRÉTAIRE GÉNÉRAL

DÉPOSITAIRES GÉNÉRAUX DE « L'ARCHITECTURE D'AUJOURD'HUI » A L'ÉTRANGER BELGIQUE: LIBRAIRIE DIETRICH, 10, PLACE DU MUSÉE A BRUXELLES. — ROUMANIE: LIBRAIRIE « HASEFER », RUE EUGEN CARADA, BUCAREST. — ESPAGNE: ÉDITIONS INCHAUSTI, ALCALA 63, MADRID. — ARGENTINE: ACME AGENCY, CASILLA CORREO 1136, BUENOS-AYRES. — BRÉSIL: PUBLICACOES INTERNACIONAES, AVENIDA RIO BRANCO, 117, RIO-DE-JANEIRO ET HARRIS, CAIXA POSTAL 2286, RIO-DE JANEIRO — COLOMBIE: LIBR. COSMOS, CALLE 14, N° 127, APARTADO 543, BOGOTA

5me ANNÉE - 4me SÉRIE - N° 8 - OCTOBRE-NOVEMBRE 1934

ABONNEMENTS (12 NUMÉROS) FRANCE: 150 FRS. — ETRANGER: PAYS A 1/2 TARIF POSTAL: 230 FRS. — PAYS A PLEIN TARIF POSTAL: 250 FRS. — PRIX DU NUMÉRO: FRANCE: 18 FRS. — ÉTRANGER: PAYS A 1/2 TARIF POSTAL: 22 FRS — PAYS A PLEIN TARIF POSTAL: 25 FRS.

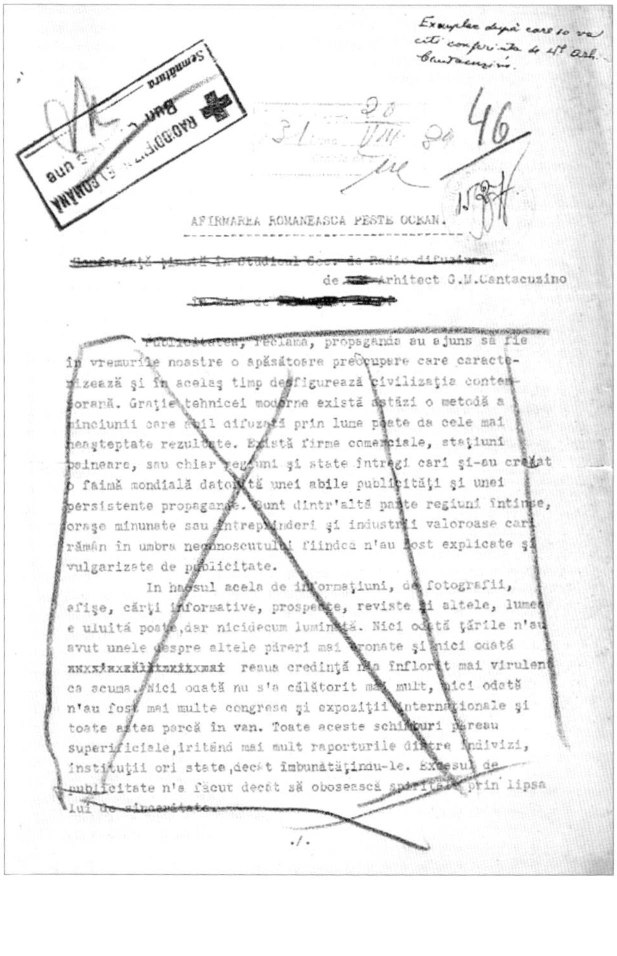

AFIRMAREA ROMANEASCA PESTE OCEAN.

de Arhitect G.M.Cantacuzino

Publicitatea, reclama, propaganda au ajuns să fie in vremurile noastre o apăsătoare preocupare care caracterizează şi în acelaş timp desfigurează civilizaţia contemporană. Graţie tehnicei moderne există astăzi o metodă a minciunii care abil difuzată prin lume poate da cele mai neaşteptate rezultate. Există firme comerciale, staţiuni balneare, sau chiar regiuni şi state întregi cari şi-au creiat o faimă mondială datorită unei abile publicităţi şi unei persistente propagande. Sunt dintr'altă parte regiuni întinse, oraşe minunate sau întreprinderi şi industrii valoroase cari rămân în umbra necunoscutului fiindcă n'au fost explicate şi vulgarizate de publicitate.

In haosul acela de informaţiuni, de fotografii, afişe, cărţi informative, prospecte, reviste şi altele, lumea e uluită poate, dar nicidecum luminată. Nici odată ţările n'au avut unele despre altele păreri mai eronate şi nici odată reaua credinţă n'a înflorit mai virulent ca acuma. Nici odată nu s'a călătorit mai mult, nici odată n'au fost mai multe congrese şi expoziţii internaţionale şi toate acestea parcă în van. Toate aceste schimburi păreau superficiale, iritând mai mult raporturile dintre indivizi, instituţii ori state, decât îmbunătăţindu-le. Excesul de publicitate n'a făcut decât să obosească spiritele prin lipsa lui de sinceritate.

./.

Journalism, criticism and study travels

Throughout the 1930s GMC pursued a busy schedule of lecturing, travelling, and writing. He was a valued and prolific contributor to daily newspapers and cultural reviews, including *Revista Fundaţiilor Regale* (The Royal Foundations Review)[1] and *Viaţa Românească* (The Romanian Life)[2], with over thirty articles published. In 1931, GMC co-founded and co-edited *Revista Istorică Română* (The Romanian Review of History) together with the young historians Georges Bratiano, N. Cartojan, C. C. Giurescu, S. Lambrino, P. P. Panaitescu and the linguist Al. Rosetti.[3]

He also gave public lectures, especially in Bucharest, Craiova and Jassy. With great pleasure, he accepted in 1930, the invitation on behalf of the Romanian Broadcasting Company SRR to deliver broadcast lectures on cultural and architectural subjects in a fifteen-days rhythm.[4] Most lectures were part of the programme called *Radio University*, a sort of Open University radio programme. From 1930 to 1940, GMC gave eighty-seven radio talks; his last three radio essays were broadcasted in 1942 and 1944.

The SRR (Societatea Română de Radio) was founded in 1927, some eight years after the pioneering British Broadcasting Corporation. The BBC was soon followed by the USA (1920); France (1922); Belgium, Germany, Spain, and Czechoslovakia (1923); Soviet Union (1924). Initially, SRR was a public-private-partnership, three fifths of it financed by the Romanian state, and the rest by private investors. The technical equipment of the first two broadcasting stations at Bucharest-Băneasa and Bod near Braşov/Kronstadt, which were largely built to designs of GMC, was provided by Marconi's Wireless Telegraph Company Ltd. Given its status as company, SRR rested upon long-term subscriptions. The number of subscribers increased from 14,587 in 1928 to 162,132 in 1936. Still, these numbers were small in view of the total population of c. 19 million inhabitants.[5]

From 1930 to 1944, a great number of public personalities influenced the character and development of SRR. Among them were Nicolae Iorga, Grigore Antipa, Dimitrie Gusti, Tudor Arghezi, Nichifor Crainic, Eugen Lovinescu, Mircea Eliade and Constantin Noica. GMC himself seems to have been the only architect to have talked on the radio at the time.[6]

As an independent institution, SRR refused political propaganda – but onyl until 1938, when it was taken over and exploited by the state, which was virtually until 1989. Not unsurprinsingly, some passages of GMC's post-1937 broadcast lectures were subjected to censorship. The essay *Romania's Appearance in the USA* (Afirmarea românească peste ocean) is a notable example. On the first page of the manuscript, GMC criticised political propaganda and its exploitation of publicity, including tourism publicity. In fact, the entire page was censored (*see fig. 173*).[7]

With his notion of a vivid tradition in mind, GMC, in his essays, reflected upon Romanian art and architectural history. He didn't hesitate to address the deplorable way in which the state dealt with some historic monuments. One of them was the Văcăreşti Monastery, the largest monastery in South-Eastern Europe, erected in the early nineteenth century. Văcăreşti was misused as a penitentiary, and GMC contested this.[8]

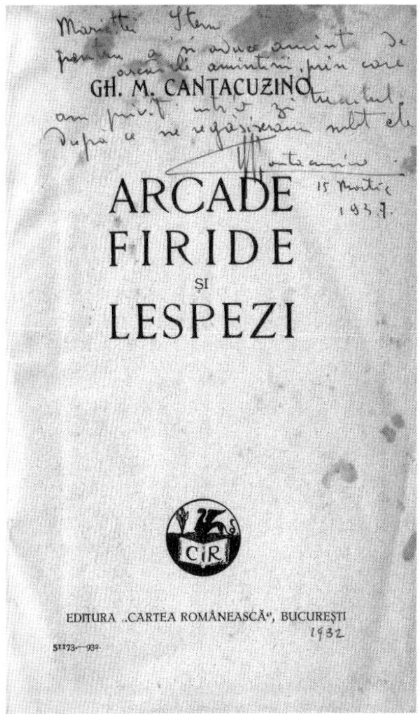

174 GMC, *Arcade, firide şi lespezi* (Arcades, Niches and Flagstones). Bucharest 1932. Front page with dedication to Marietta Stern (AMLSC).

Opposite:

172 Left: *L'Architecture d'aujourd'hui*, No. 8/1934, Paris, October 1934. First issue of this periodical with GMC as correspondent for Romania.

173 GMC, *Afirmarea românească peste ocean* (Romania's Appearance in the USA). Broadcast lecture, 1st September 1939.

175 GMC, *Pătrar de veghe* (Moonwatch). Bucharest 1938. Front cover.

In further broadcast lectures, GMC introduced into art and the architectural history of the Early Civilizations, and Greek antiquity; presented his own designs; commented on current cultural issues; related the Romanian architectural scene to international Modernism; and championned his *classical attitude*. He seems to have presented only the buildings that he experienced at first hand. A passionate traveller, he kept travelling through his Arcadian Romania, then further into the Near and Middle East, via the Dacia steamliner, from Constantza into the Mediterranean: via Turkey, Greece, and Crete to Egypt, further to the Lebanon and Palestine, Syrian, Irak and Iran; back in Europe, he travelled to France, Germany, England, and time and again to his beloved Italy. Sometimes he travelled by car, sometimes by the Orient Express or Simplon Orient Express.[9] Before the decade was out, he found himself aboard the *Normandie* crossing the Atlantic in order to work and live for four months in the USA.[10]

Of GMC's broadcast lectures, two selected volumes appeared: *Arcades, Niches and Flagstones* (Arcade, firide și lespezi) (1932) and *Sources and Stopovers* (Izvoare și popasuri) (1934). They complemented, so to speak, the photographic documentation *Petits Édifices* (1931), one of the first comprehensive monographs on traditional vernacular and religious architecture of Romania published in Europe.

During the 1930s GMC undertook four travels to the Middle and Near East.[11] He was particularly fascinated by Palmyra, Gerasa, Baghdad, Ctesiphon, Isphahan and Persepolis. His experiences were distilled into *Moonwatch* (Pătrar de Veghe, 1938). On his voyages he met various archaelogists and befriended Friedrich Krefter (1898-1995), the German architect and archaeologist, who took over the excavations at Persepolis from Professor Ernst Herzfeld in 1934.[12] GMC's books received excellent reviews, for instance by George Călinescu and Mihail Sebastian.[13] In 1938, aboard the *Normandie*, he started a travel book meant to be the Western sequel to *Moonwatch* – the manuscript seems to be lost.[14]

176 Friedrich Krefter's discovery of the Foundation Tablets of Apadana/ Persepolis, 19th September 1933. © Dr Heiko Krefter.

Early in 1934 GMC published *Tendances dans l'architecture roumaine* in *L'Architecture d'Aujourd'hui*.[15] Later that year, he became correspondent of this French periodical, a post he held until the end of 1936 (from No. 8/1934 to No. 11/1936).[16] In this period *L'Architecture d'Aujourd'hui* published three notes on Romanian topics, including an article on a building by Marcel Janco: *Sanatorium à Prédéal, Roumanie. Architectes: Marcel et Jules Jancu et P. Feldman*. Although not signed, it seems plausible to attribute them to GMC.[17] At the close of 1936 GMC retired from his commitment to *L'Architecture d'aujourd'hui*, possibly because of the prospect of becoming chief architect of CFR the next year.[18]

In the spring of 1939 GMC founded the annual periodical *Simetria. Notebooks for art and criticism*. The title was programmatic, as was the motto reminding of the antique significance of symmetry: "Symmetry in its original sense means feliticious proportion or commensurability."[19]

The close circle of permanent *Simetria* co-editors consisted of Octav Doicescu, Matila Ghyka and Paul-Emil Miclescu, with Paul Marinescu as illustrator. Contributions were made by a great number of architects, artists and intellectuals.[20] They included the English poet Derek Patmore (1908-1972) and French writer Michel Dard (1908-1979). Patmore contributed *Notes from Turkey* (Note din Turcia)[21], which GMC translated into Romanian.[22] Dard wrote one of the three obituaries with which *Simetria VII* commemorated the late Paul Valéry, *Paul Valéry or the creative form* (Paul Valéry sau forma creatoare).[23] GMC himself wrote *Paul Valéry or the architect* (Paul Valéry sau arhitectul).

Simetria was published by *Cartea Românească* (The Romanian Book), of which GMC was a shareholder. The graphic lay-out was simple: an unusual but practical size (19 by 25 cm) with a Roman type on solid yellowish paper. There were no photographs at all, "on principle"[24], as GMC wrote to his wife Sanda, but just black and white reproductions of drawings, engravings, paintings and watercolours. The contents were organised according to the classical tripartite division: the introduction consisted of an editorial; the main part comprised essays on subjects from various disciplines, along with articles from an architectural and cultural dictionary; the concluding part contained miscellanies: reviews, replies to articles from other press, announcements, translations, and brief and concise statements to topical questions. In total, there were eight *Simetria* editions from 1939 to 1947.

Cartea Românească published three other books of GMC's: *Palladio* (1928), *Arcades, Niches and Flagstones* (1932), and *Moonwatch* (1938). The publishing house was founded in the early 1920s by Ion Athanasiu, dean of the University of Bucharest, and professor Ion Simionescu. Their goal was to provide the wider public with an affordable access to culture. *Cartea Românească* can be compared to similar projects in Europe, including *Reclam* of Stuttgart (est. 1828), *Everyman's Library* of London (est. 1906), or *Livre de poche* of Paris (est. 1953). *Cartea Românească* soon became one of the leading publishing houses in Romania with many bookshops and a popular exhibition hall at the main bookshop in Bucharest.[25]

The variety of the *Simetria* articles ranged from aesthetic questions via subjects of architectural criticism and history; civil engineering; landscape architecture; urban plannig; sociology; typography; music; literature to interdisciplinary articles. GMC himself wrote seventy-four of the entire one hundred eighty-three essays: he co-authored all editorials (seven of them with Octav Doicescu, and the last one with Titu Evolceanu), numerous studies, and the best part of the dictionary articles and miscellanies.[26]

Eventually *Simetria* bears witness to the "Europe of the mind"[27] highlighted, for instance, by Ernst Robert Curtius, the German cultural historian and friend of T. S. Eliot. This concept was also illustrated by Eliot's cultural periodical *Criterion*, which championed the belief in a common European tradition and the invitation "to analyse its constituents in the various nations of Europe; and proceed finally to the further formation of such a tradition."[28]

Simetria can be indeed considered a substantial contribution to this process of reinforcing and updating the common cultural tradition of Europe based on the Roman Empire and, in the words of T. S. Eliot, on "the continuity of the impulse of Rome to the present day. [...] It is in fact the European idea – the idea of a common culture of Western Europe."[29]

Egypte. Village arabe.

177 Egyptian village. Photograph GMC, 1932. (AGMC-IP).

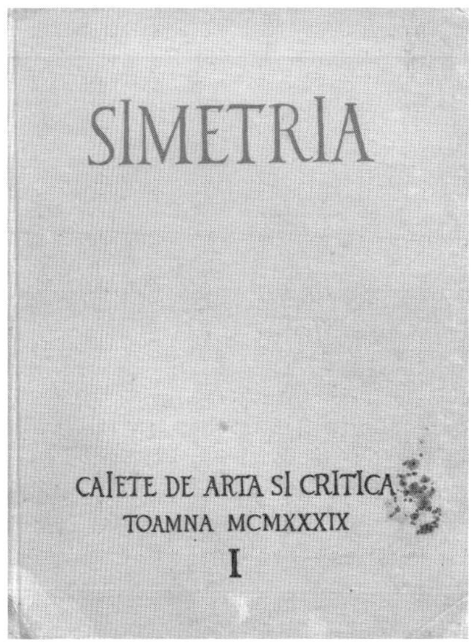

178 *Simetria I* (1939), front cover.
After 1990 the spirit of GMC's periodical is revived by leading Romanian architects. Today *Simetria* is the most important architecture and design publishing house in that country.

ANGLO ROVMANIAN SOCIETY
ARHITECTS.
G.M. CANTACVZINO O. DOICESCU

Diplomatic Architecture

The British Institute in Bucharest

After Carol II had successfully established his authoritarian regime early in 1938, Romania sighed with relief for a while and pursued its tradition of neutrality. This foreign policy involved the reinforcement of her diplomatic, economic and cultural ties to Great Britain.[1]

One of the cultural cornerstones of this policy was the Anglo-Romanian Society, founded by anglophile Romanians in London in 1917. Its first Romanian branch was established by Viorel Tilea in Cluj in 1923, followed by the Bucharest branch in 1927. Since 1937 the Anglo-Romanian Society was under the patronage of Queen Mary and her son King Carol II.[2]

This enriched Romania's diversified cultural life. The Press scene of the 1920s and 30s, for instance, boasted some four hundred and fifty newspapers and periodicals in several languages in addition to Romanian, including Armenian, French, German, Greek, Hungarian and Russian.[3]

Of the minorities, it may suffice here to mention the Germans. Before World War II some 560,000 Germans lived in Romania. The Transylvanian Saxons, whose ancestors settled there chiefly in the thirteenth century, formed the largest part aside from the Banat, Danube and Sathmar Swabians. The Saxons fostered a comprehensive education system, which withstood the official Romanisation policy. Up to 1945, the Saxons, backed by their Protestant Church, had no less than 263 primary schools, 18 high schools, 40 kindergartens and 10 trade schools. Naturally, most schools were in Transylvania, but there were some in other cities too, including Bucharest. These schools enjoyed a high reputation and were open to all.[4] GMC and his wife themselves had their children attend the German school in Bucharest.

On 1st April 1938, the Romanian Broadcast Company launched a news programme in English, initiated by the Anglo-Romanian Society.[5] A month later a Romanian National Exhibition opened at 41 Grosvenor Square in London. With its contents *The Country. The Peasants. The Royal Endowments for Culture and Education* the show was a rehearsal for the New York World's Fair the following year.[6]

These events were preceded by the Anglo-Romanian cultural festival held at the Atheneum, Bucharest's most famous concert hall. Being organised by Carol II himself, the festival stood under the patronage of Queen Mary.[7] The honorary guests included Sir Reginald Hoare (1882-1954), the British Ambassador to Bucharest from 1935 to 1941.[8]

On this occasion the idea was born to establish a branch of the British Council in Bucharest. This seemed especially appropriate given the highly positive experience of the English Language Course for Adults organised by the Anglo-Romanian Society – in 1938 the requests increased from 300 to some 2,300.[9] Subsequently, the ARS and the British Council co-founded the British Institute in Bucharest. It was preceded by other cultural institutes: the Institut Français (est. 1924, with Henri Focillon as one of the honorary guests)[10]; the Society of the Friends of the United States, with GMC being a member of it (est. 1925 under the patronage of the leading liberal politician

180 King Carol II and Crown Prince Michael of Romania arrived at Victoria Station, London on 15th November 1938 for a state visit and were welcomed by King George. Britain's King George VI, back to the camera, shaking hands with King Carol II of Romania.
© picture alliance/ AP Images, Image No. 43220782.

181 Group photograph in front of the Bibesco residence at Posada in the Prahova Valley. From left to right: Valentine Bibesco; her mother, authoress Marthe Bibesco; Charles M. Palairet, British diplomat in charge of the British legion in Bucharest; Lord Lloyd of Dolobran, British Council Chairman and George V. Bibesco.
Period photograph.

179 Opposite:
GMC/O. Doicescu, *Design project for the British Institute in Bucharest* (1939-40).
Pencil perspective drawing, © UAR-AOD.

182 Lord Lloyd of Dolobran (1879-1941), British Council Chairman from 1937-1941.

I. G. Duca, a friend of Marthe Bibesco)[11], and the Istituto Italiano di Cultura, which was established in 1933 in the Neo-Romanian villa Disescu.[12] A Romanian-German Saxon Cultural Institute was founded in the early 1930s with branches at Brașov/Kronstadt, Bucharest and Sibiu/Hermannstadt, followed in 1940 by the German Cultural Institute in Bucharest.[13]

The British Institute was opened on 12th October 1938 by George Ambrose Lloyd, 1st Baron Lloyd of Dolobran (1879-1941), the "very energetic chairman"[14] of the British Council from 1937 to 1941.

"I would mention in this connection", wrote Lord Lloyd of Dolobran to Lord Halifax on 29th December 1939, "the dramatic and indeed embarrassing success of the Institutes of English Studies in Athens and Bucharest, in which places the over-worked teaching staff whom the Council have sent out are literally unable to deal with the thousands of enthusiasts clamouring for admittance."[15]

However, the first headquarters of the British Institute were provisional. After his official visit to England and King George VI in November 1938,[16] King Carol II asked the Mayor of Bucharest to grant a suitable site to the British Institute, which duly happened on 23rd November 1938.[17]

The site lay on the famous Calea Victoriei, just south of the former villa of Queen Elisabeth of Greece. At about that time GMC was approached to design the headquarters of the British Institute. Perhaps he was recommended for it by Carol II himself, given the fact that he had already appointed him as the architect of the official pavilion for the 1939 New York World's Fair. Also the Anglo-Romanian Society included a number of friends of GMC's, such as Nicky Chrissoveloni, Nicholas Mavrocordato, and Viorel Tilea.

In fact, GMC met Sir Reginald Hoare already early in March 1938:

"Yesterday, during the dinner at the British Embassy, I had a highly interesting conversation with Sir Reginald Hoare [who] just announced that he and an English writer would come and see my paintings of the Middle East."[18] Later, he was to meet Lord Lloyd of Dolobran too.

As reported by *The Times*, the RIBA appointed GMC as Honorary Corresponding Member on 16th May 1938, probably at the suggestion of Sir Reginald Hoare and Lord Lloyd of Dolobran. On the same day the RIBA elected two other Honorary Corresponding Members – Gio Ponti from Milan and F. Schuster from Vienna – along with new RIBA Fellows such as Wells Coates.[19]

On 28th October 1938, Charles Bridge, the secretary of the British Council, wrote to Lord Lloyd: "I have also suggested [...] that as soon as possible, probably after Rex Hoare's return, a local architect, perhaps Prince Cantacuzino, should be asked to prepare plans of a future *Maison Anglaise* and submit them to us with estimates of costs."[20]

183 Sir Edwin Lutyens, *Britannic House*, London (1924-1927). (Photograph ADT).

GMC invited Octav Doicescu to cooperate on the project. They elaborated a monumental three-storey block with a courtyard and an open and arched civic loggia beneath the wing facing the Calea Victoriei. Its entrance was via the imposing three-bay corner on the Calea Victoriei in the vicinity of the former estate of Queen Elisabeth of Greece. Conceived as a triumphal arch with four giant columns and sculptural figures above a rusticated basement, it brings to mind two buildings of Palladio in Vicenza: the *Loggia del Capitaniato* and the *Palazzo Porto-Breganze* or *Ca`del Diavolo*, the gem fragment on the Piazza Castello. On 15th October GMC wrote to his wife:

"[T]he project is well conceived and presented in a Palladian spirit. I have sought to express British dignity through architectural forms."[21]

At the same time, GMC could have been inspired by English architecture too, notably by Palladian and modern classicist examples. On his visit to London in March 1939, he stayed at the Royal Court Hotel at Sloane Square, and had "a most pleasant week"[22] there. He "visited many museums, attended several theatre performances, strolled a great deal and even visited some surroundings of the city."[23]

His vivid interest in English architecture was also reflected by his public lecture on *The Spread of the Gothic Style across England*, given in Bucharest on 29th November 1939.[24]

For one thing, he could have been stimulated by Sir John Soane's Pitzhangor Manor House, particularly by the majestic Palladian main entrance; or by buildings of Sir Edwin Lutyens, the "master of classicism"[25], including his Britannic House (1924-27); or, more recently, by the impressive RIBA headquarters by George Grey Wonurm at 66 Portland Place.

As for Lutyens, GMC could have learned more about him thanks to Antoine Bibesco, one his cousins and former Romanian Ambassador in Washington D. C. (1920-1926).[26] In 1919 Antoine Bibesco married Elisabeth Asquith, daughter of Margot and Herbert Henry Asquith, the British Prime Minister from 1908-1916. Lutyens received several commissions from the Asquith family and their circle of friends. Particularly involved was Reginald MacKenna, a son-in-law of the Asquiths, and trustee of the Midland Bank built to the designs of Sir Edwin Lutyens from 1924-1939.[27]

On 15th October 1939 GMC and Doicescu submitted their design with an explanatory note and estimates of costs of forty thousand pounds (fifty millions Lei in 1939).[28]

Already in January 1939 Marthe Bibesco together with other anglophile Romanians offered Lord Lloyd of Dolobran a support of four millions Lei, that is to say, some eight per cent of the later estimate: "To sum it up: this is a contribution from Romanians who like the idea of a British Institute in Bucharest."[29]

In November 1939 Sir Reginald Hoare and Lord Lloyd travelled to Bucharest for the presentation of the design of the British Institute. They were delighted, as GMC noted in a letter to Sanda:

"I have seen Lord Lloyd. The project of the British Institute was a success. We have been commissioned and are waiting for the Royal Treasury to settle the financing. The last week was completely full of official receptions and dinners at Capşa […]. Yesterday I was invited to dinner at the English Embassy where I had the opportunity to talk at considerable length to Sir Reginald [Hoare] and Lord Lloyd."[30]

Early in 1941, unfortunately, it so happened that the British diplomatic mission was withdrawn from Romania[31] and the project remained unfinished.

184 *Sloane Square Hotel* (formerly Royal Court Hotel), Sloane Square, London. (Photograph ADT).

185 Sir Edwin Lutyens, *Midland Bank Headquarters*, London (1924-1939). (Photograph ADT).

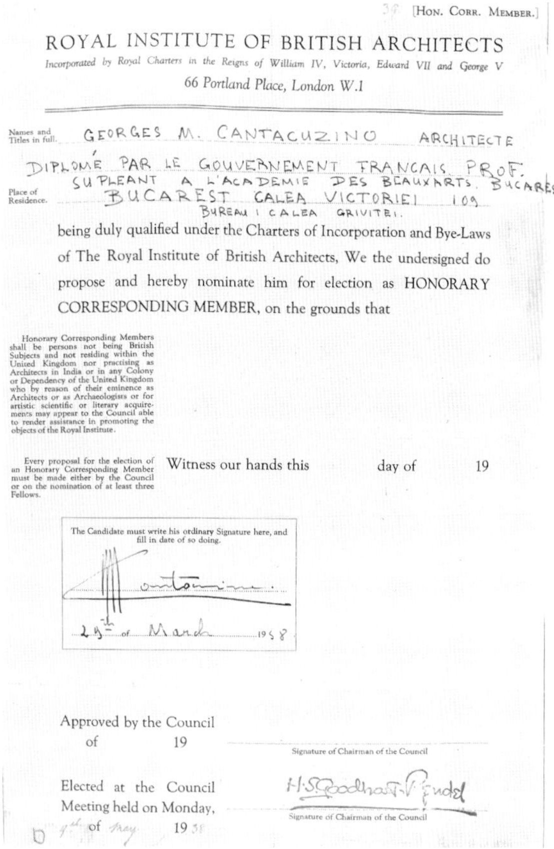
[Hon. Corr. Member.]

ROYAL INSTITUTE OF BRITISH ARCHITECTS

Incorporated by Royal Charters in the Reigns of William IV, Victoria, Edward VII and George V

66 Portland Place, London W.1

Names and Titles in full. GEORGES M. CANTACUZINO ARCHITECTE DIPLOMÉ PAR LE GOUVERNEMENT FRANCAIS. PROF. SUPLEANT A L'ACADEMIE DES BEAUXARTS. BUCAREST

Place of Residence. BUCAREST CALEA VICTORIEI 109 BUREAU I CALEA GRIVITEI.

being duly qualified under the Charters of Incorporation and Bye-Laws of The Royal Institute of British Architects, We the undersigned do propose and hereby nominate him for election as HONORARY CORRESPONDING MEMBER, on the grounds that

Honorary Corresponding Members shall be persons not being British Subjects and not residing within the United Kingdom nor practising as Architects in India or in any Colony or Dependency of the United Kingdom who by reason of their eminence as Architects or as Archaeologists or for artistic scientific or literary acquirements may appear to the Council able to render assistance in promoting the objects of the Royal Institute.

Every proposal for the election of an Honorary Corresponding Member must be made either by the Council or on the nomination of at least three Fellows.

Witness our hands this day of 19

The Candidate must write his ordinary Signature here, and fill in date of so doing.

Cantacuzino

29th of March 1938

Approved by the Council of 19

Signature of Chairman of the Council

Elected at the Council Meeting held on Monday, 9th of May 1938

H.S. Goodhart-Rendel

Signature of Chairman of the Council

186 Nomination Papers of GMC as RIBA Honorary Corresponding Member, 1938.
© RIBA Library Drawings & Archives Collections, London.

187 GMC, Palladio's Palazzo Porto Breganze *(Ca` del Diavolo)* (1570s), Piazza Castello, Vicenza. Watercolour (GMC, *Palladio* 1928).

188 Sir John Soane, *Pitzhangor Manor House*, Ealing, London (1800-1802). Main entrance (Photograph ADT).

189 Andrea Palladio, *Loggia del Capitaniato* (c.1565/71-1572), Piazza dei Signori, Vicenza (Photograph ADT).

190 GMC/O. Doicescu, *Design project for the British Institute in Bucharest* (1939-40). Pencil perspective drawing. © UAR-AOD.

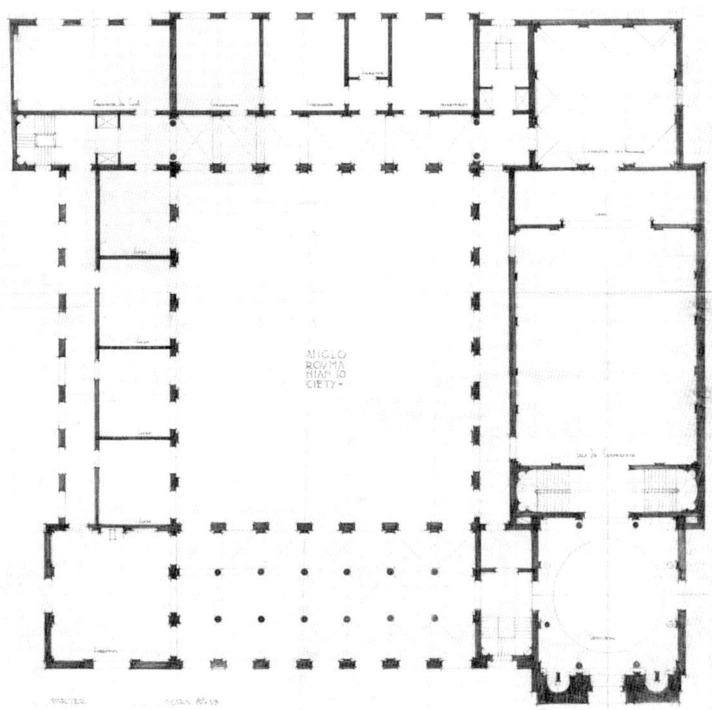

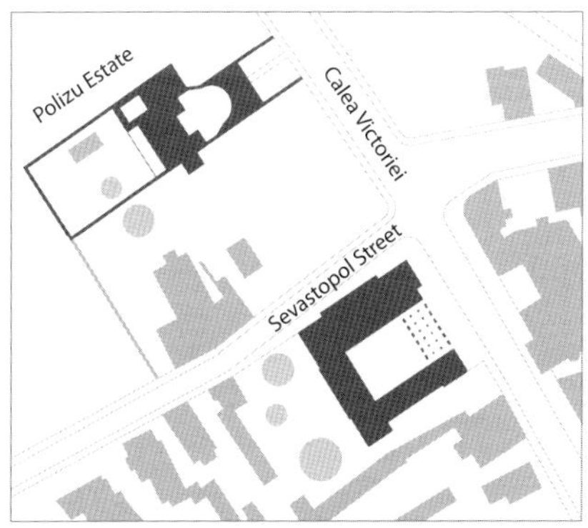

191 Reconstruction of the site map of the *British Institute* in Bucharest (ADT).

192 GMC/O. Doicescu, *Design project for the British Institute in Bucharest* (1939-40). Ground floor plan. Pencil drawing. © UAR-AOD.

THE TRAINING OF THE YOUTH
AT ATHLETE
MANIANS
IV· PATRONS OF CVLTVRE: PRINCES NEAGOE AND MATTHEW BESSARABA, BASIL LVPV, CANTEMIR, BRANCOVAN
BVILD CH RCHES PAINT BOOKS· PRINCE CVZA ACHIEVES THE LASTING VNION OF MOLDAVIA AND WALLACHIA
CAROL I ACHIEVES INDEPENDENCE OF HI
THE COUNTRY THROUGH EDUCATION
TOBACCO
THE INSTITUTE OF AGR NOMIC RESEARC

The 1939 New York World's Fair

On 25th May 1938 GMC and Doicescu went aboard the *Normandie*. Their destination: New York. The City of New York accommodated them in a spacious apartment at the Savoy Plaza Hotel. There they improvised an architectural office in order to continue the work on their projects and to co-ordinate them with the Board of Design of the World's Fair.[1] All seemed to work very smoothly: "The Board of Design has sent the King a telegram of congratulations on the choice of his architects!"[2]

While Doicescu designed the so-called Romanian House, GMC pondered over the plans for the official Romanian Pavilion. The Romanian Pavilion was located by the Board of Design on the main axis from the Theme Centre to the United States Federal Building. Together with the France Overseas Pavilion, its symmetrical pendant to the north, it marked the place where the Lagoon of Nations met the Court of Peace. At the Lagoon of Nations the Romanian Pavilion was facing the Belgian Pavilion and the French Pavilion in the west, the latter being built to the designs of Roger-Henri Expert.[3]

194 GMC, *Onboard the Normandie*, 10th March 1939. Watercolour (AMLSC)

The motto of the New York World's Fair, "Building the World of Tomorrow"[4], was interpreted by the Romanian team under Professor Dr Dimitrie Gusti in a spirit dear to GMC. Doicescu and GMC tried to show that "the respect for tradition and age-old harmonies is not incompatible with technical progress".[5] Indeed, the Romanian Pavilion encapsulated GMC's *classical attitude*. He presented this synthesis in several essays and broadcast lectures.[6]

The building volume laid out by the Board of Design consisted of a compact block on a square ground plan of c. 30 by 30 meters. GMC very much appreciated its "classical lines and modern simplicity"[7], and worked on the façades and interior design of the double-height, single cube galleried hall (the building was sadly demolished along with the best part of the World's Fair in late 1940). People entered the pavilion from the public square facing the France Overseas Pavilion via the asymmetrical monumental portico with three pillars. GMC sought to enliven the simple volume and clad its steel frame structure "with noble and durable materials"[8].

The materials included marble, alabaster and rock salt plates, as well as light and bronze nails. The façades had the classical tripartite elevation and marble-cladding with stone from the Transylvanian Ruschiţa quarry[9], as did the portico pillars and windows of the main façade.[10]

Above the pink pedestal rose the main part, "sometimes white, sometimes bluish-purple"[11]. The marble-clad cornice was punctuated with gold leaf circular medallions. The height of the cornice corresponded to the width of the portico pillars. Beside the portico three grand vertical windows were set into the main façade. Their mashrabiya-like marble-cladding drew on two Brancovan motives: sunflower and tulip.[12] This may also have been reflective of GMC's travels to the Middle East, during which he learned to appreciate common features of traditional Islamic, Persian and Romanian architecture.[13] The portico pillars were covered with bas-relief texture modelled on a Scythic sword. The entrance from the portico was topped by an ogee arch, "the sole obviously archaic element of the little pavilion".[14]

193 Opposite:
GMC, interior view of the Official Pavilion of Romania at the 1939 New York World's Fair. Photograph Underwood & Underwood (AGMC-PM).

195 Stamp of the Romanian House (architect Octav Doicescu) issued by the Romanian Post on the occasion of the participation at the 1939 New York World's Fair (ADT).

196 New York World's Fair, 1939, Lagoon of Nations with Hall of Nations, U. S. Gov't Bldg. (in background) and Romanian Pavilion (right). Period postcard A. Mainzer, New York (ADT).

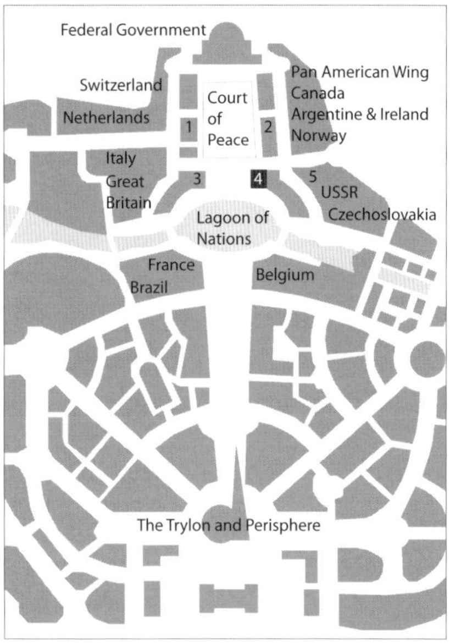

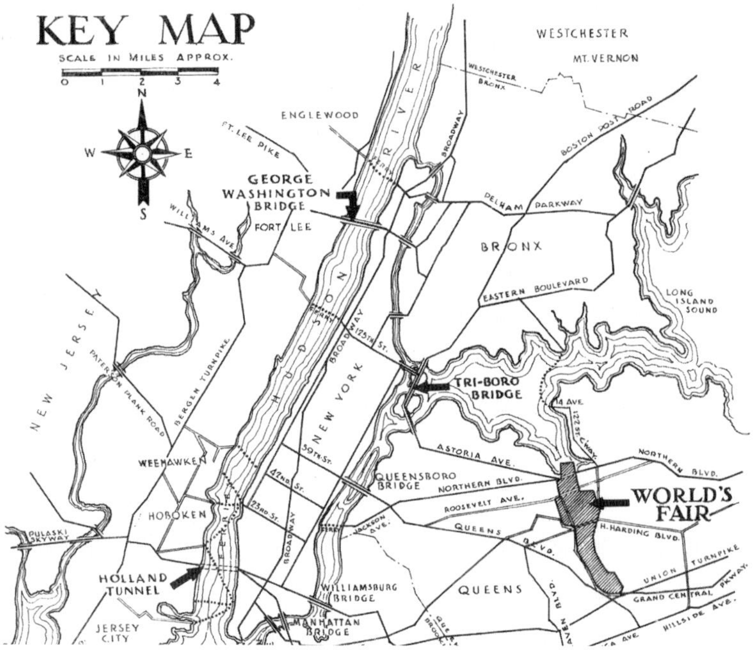

197 Above:
Detail of the site map of the 1939 New York World's Fair (ADT).
1 Hall of Nations North
2 Hall of Nations South
2 France Overseas Pavilion
4 Romanian Pavilion (GMC's project)
5 Romanian House (O. Doicescu's project)

198 Centre:
Key Map of New York with the location of the 1939 World's Fair (detail).
© UAR-AOD.

199 Right:
Roger-Henri Expert/Pierre Patout, *Official Pavilion of France* at the 1939 New York World's Fair, as seen from the Romanian Pavilion. Photograph John A. Davis. Period postcard (ADT)

200 GMC, New York Skyline (*Simetria III* 1940-1941).

201 Stamp of the Official Romanian Pavilion issued by the Romanian Post on the occasion of the participation at the 1939 New York World's Fair (ADT).

202 Above:
Window detail with sun-flower motif of the *Official Pavilion of Romania* at the 1939 New York World's Fair. Photograph Underwood & Underwood (AGMC-PM).

203 Centre:
The Official Pavilion of Romania at the 1939 New York World's Fair, as seen from the Lagoon of Nations. Photograph Underwood & Underwood (AGMC-PM).

204 Left:
Interior view of the *Official Pavilion of Romania* at the 1939 New York World's Fair. Period postcard by Foto Seal Co. New York (ADT).

205 Monastery Church of Voronetz, Bucovina. (Photograph ADT).

The pavilion's airy interior was conceived as a centralised and sky-lit hall with an U-shaped circular gallery. The gallery embraced and welcomed the visitor in front of the iconographic map of Romania displayed on the entire rear wall. Behind that wall two symmetric stair-flights led up to the gallery, which rested on six alabaster-clad pillars lit from behind. The inter-pillar spaces were also alabaster-clad "in the powerful rhythm of round arches".[15]

Between the walls and ceiling there was a subtle joint of mirror glass. The suspended ceiling itself consisted of thin sky-lit native salt plates, and the texture of the marble floors echoed the wall claddings and ceiling.

GMC's design matched the exhibition concept of Dr Gusti and his team of "inviting the visitor to get an impression of Romania while strolling along at his ease"[16]. This intention reflected, as it were, Palladio's advice to build "handsome and well adorned places to walk in, that their clients may remain there without inconvenience"[17]. The visitor was being informed about the then contemporary Romanian society by information panels, diorams, bas-reliefs, sculptures, a few photographs, and maps, including a map of crystal. The gallery balustrades, for instance, bore a bronze fries by sculptor Mac Constantinescu depicting scenes from Romanian history, and on the interior pillars aphorism-like phrases made of large bronze letters pointed to landmarks of Romanian culture.[18]

The interior was literally bathed in a golden light from the sky-lit rock salt ceiling and blue light from the alabaster-clad pillars, all of which were reflected by the marble floor. The soothing effect of this wealth of colours complemented and perfected the tendency to de-materialisation announced by the discreet and precious textures of the external façades. In fact, the outward cladding consisted of three layers: the marble cladding as basic layer; then a juxtaposing delicate net of bronze nails, intarsings, gold leaf covers, and perforations; and finally the soft shading produced by the moving sun. On the two main external façades, monumental sculptures by Oscar Han[19] emphasized the pavilion's elegant simplicity, in a vivid contrast to the delicacy of the texture and chromatic play of the marble cladding. All these features added to the architectural effect aesthetics which GMC, a passionate visual man, extracted from the forms and materiality of his design. The stonemasonry was provided by August Schmiedigen Associates. Schmiedigen, who already worked on the 1937 Paris World's Fair became the impressario of the 1949 Haiti International Exposition.[20]

In GMC's design, we can also discern some Roman and Byzantine motives, including the central space, basilical scheme, and round arches. The superposition of central and longitudinal space recalled the Hagia Sophia in Constantinople, on which many Orthodox churches in Russia and South-Eastern Europe are modelled. The ogee arch above the main entrance reminded, not just of Brancovan but also of Islamic and Gothic architecture. The latter includes in Romania the so-called Black Church in Brașov/Kronstadt, the largest Gothic hall church in South-Eastern Europe.[21]

206 Salt mine, Slănic, Romania. *Guide de la Roumanie*, Bucharest 1938.

Then we can connote GMC's building with the diaphanous moment of Byzantine churches both in regard to interiors and mural paintings, including the late-Byzantine Wallachian and Moldavian churches with their unique fusion of architecture and frescos. They provided further themes for GMC's subtle and discrete decoration designs: for instance, the spiralled columns of monastery churches such as Horez or Văcărești; the loggia balustrades with vegetable and animal ornaments; and the plaster decoration of the Brancovan palace at Potlogi and Fundenii Doamnei church.

The most renowned pavilions of the New York World's Fair included two variations of the open plan: Alvar Aalto's Finish pavilion, and the Brazilian pavilion, designed by Lucio Costa and Oscar Niemeyer in the wake of their master Le Corbusier. GMC, for his part, pursued his experiments in stone. In doing so, he championed the "ethics and aesthetics of masking"[22] continuing the tradition line of Semper, Wagner, and Loos. In addition, the diaphanous moment of GMC's building could point at some more recent projects, including translucent marble walls at the Beinecke Rare Book and Manuscript Library at Yale University/New Haven, Connecticut by SOM (1963), and the St Pius church at Meggen/Luzern by Franz Füeg (1966); or the onyx ceiling in the new entrance hall to the Rietberg Museum in Zurich by Alfred Grazioli and Adolf Krischanitz (2007). Eventually, GMC's little pavilion, of which only a few photographs and drawings have survived, must have conveyed the impression of a precious box welcoming the visitor in its centre.

207 GMC, *New York*, 16th March 1939. Watercolour (AMLSC).

New York

In 1938 GMC lived and worked in New York for four months. "A city without dreams and tenderness, New York is the most nostalgic monument built for ambition and will."[1] The virile architecture of the city inspired him to a great deal of drawings and watercolours, but after all he felt "irretrievably European"[2]. During his stay he also visited Washington D. C. and met several American officials, including Fiorello La Guardia (1882-1947)[3], "[r]eformer and perhaps the most outstanding mayor in U. S. history"[4], then the mayor of New York (1935-1945).

GMC knew he had a mission to perform both architectural and diplomatic.[5] In a letter to his wife he stated: "I believe Romania could make a strong impression over here. She truly needs it. The other day an American told me: Romania is judged here like the champagne: good and sparkling, but lightweight."[6]

The inauguration of the oficial Romanian Pavilion took place on Friday, 5th May 1939, with Georges Enesco directing the New York Philharmonic Orchestra.[7] It was a success. GMC and Doicescu were appointed Honorary Citizens of New York.[8] As reported on the following day by *The New York Times* in *Rumanian Ideals are Praised at Dedication of Fair Pavilion*, Fiorella La Guardia in his inaugural speech called on "Romanians to play their historic role in Europe and 'resist tha barbarians'".[9]

But GMC was aware that "the great enemies of Romania's destiny are, in the first place, Romanians themselves with their lack of civic conscience."[10] On 21st September the Iron Guard assassinated the brilliant Prime-Minister Armand Călinescu.[11] In a letter to his wife GMC wrote on 29th October 1939:

"What happened some six weeks ago will not be easily forgotten. Every conscious Romanian has an open wound that cannot heal but hardly."[12]

208 Marble quarry, Ruschița, Romania. Photograph by Willy Pragher, 1942. © Landesarchiv Baden-Württemberg, Staatsarchiv Freiburg.

209 GMC, Interior perspective drawing of the Official Pavilion of Romania at the 1939 New York World's Fair (AGMC-PM).

210 Interior view of the Official Pavilion of Romania at the 1939 New York World's Fair. Photograph Underwood & Underwood (AGMC-PM).

The late 1930s

In view of the spiritual smog, spread across the country by the Iron Guard through the revolutionary mystique of their assassination attempts,[1] GMC and his wife Sanda decided that their children ought to be educated in a true civic society. As they had English friends, they opted for Great Britain, a country they highly appreciated. GMC believed that "the great ethic health of England makes her superior to all the Slav and Latin paradises"[2].

Sanda and Şerban Cantacuzino moved to England in spring 1939, while Marie-Lyse stayed with GMC in Bucharest. At the close of December 1939 GMC flew to London as a diplomatic courier of the Romanian Foreign Minister Grigore Gafencu. He stayed for a couple of weeks and celebrated Christmas and New Year's Eve together with his wife and son.[3] In spring 1940 Sanda returned to Bucharest to take Marie-Lyse to England.[4]

The English friends of the Cantacuzinos included Lady Beryl Charnwood, Carola Cochran, Colonel Eddie Boxshall, Derek Patmore and the young Patrick Leigh Fermor. GMC and Fermor knew each other through Balasha Cantacuzino, "the first great love of his life"[5]. During the four years he spent in Romania from 1936 to 1940, Fermor "learnt Romanian, studied its history, and read as much as he could in that language and French. Above all"[6], he was grateful for the "sense of family"[7] Balasha and the Cantacuzinos had given him. Later in England, Fermor befriended GMC's family.[8] He wrote a great deal about Romania, including the preface to Matila Ghyka's memoirs, *The World Mine Oyster* (1961) and the best part of *Between the Woods and the Water* (1986).

As an important architect and public intellectual, GMC stayed in Romania. Until 1947 he managed his wife's estate and regularly sent money to his

212 GMC, San Geremia, *Venice*. Ink drawing. *Simetria II* (1940).

213 Giorgio de Chirico, *Mercurio volante*. Ink drawing. *Simetria II* (1940). © VG Bild-Kunst, Bonn, 2014.

211 Opposite: GMC, *Mogoşoaia*. View of the front façade with balcony. Pencil drawing. *Simetria II* (1940).

214 Nina Ruwisch (*centre*) with Marina (*left*) and Sanda Ştirbey, 1919 (AMLSC).

family. After the war, so GMC hoped, there would be the chance for a new democratic beginning, and his family could return to Romania. Never was GMC to see his family again.

The beginning of the Second World War disillusioned GMC:

"What is so serious is that this catastrophe casts doubt on the very principle of civilisation. This period of hyperactivity will be followed by nights of doubt and discouragement. [...] We are, at the moment, paying for two centuries of philosophical diletantism. [...]. At least I am so relieved to know that you and the children are safe and that you are living in a country that still has a sense of order and dignity."[9]

His work, his father and antique philosophy gave him strength to carry on: "My daily companions are Plotinus and Plutarch."[10] Painting was also fundamental to him: "I paint every day discovering the problems of painting while Pallady hurls criticism at me and Henry C.[atargi] gives me advice."[11]

In autumn 1939 his home on 109 Calea Victoriei was also a welcoming refuge for a renowned Polish Count and businessman on his way into the British exile.[12]

In August 1940, still chief-architect of the Romanian Railroads CFR, GMC was sent on a delegation to Berlin, probably with regard to the Bucharest CFR headquarter project.[13] On this travel GMC possibly met the German architect Hans Hertlein (1881-1963), then chief-architect of Siemens, who could have shown GMC his Siemensstadt projects.

GMC mentioned a number of contemporary architects in his writings, including Le Corbusier and Auguste Perret. But GMC usually wrote about subjects he knew from first-hand experience. Hertlein was in fact the only contemporary architect to whom GMC dedicated an entire essay, as he did in *Simetria III* (1940/1941)[14] a few months after his visit to Berlin. GMC could have known Hertlein from the opening of the Siemens headquarters in Bucharest in 1929, which were built to the designs of Hertlein.[15]

In Berlin, GMC visited some family friends, including the journalist Mrs Nöllenburg, and Nina Ruwisch, the former favourite nanny of Sanda Cantacuzino. Mrs Ruwisch, originating from Lippstadt in Westphalia, was trained as a nanny at the Prussian von Tresckow family before moving to the Ştirbeys in Bucharest in 1914. There Mrs Ruwisch accompanied Sanda from the age of six, and later managed the family's estate at Dărmăneşti. Early in 1940 she returned to Gerd von Tresckow, but GMC succeeded in convincing her to come back to Romania. Later on Gerd von Tresckow, who was engaged in the plot against Hitler on 24th July 1944 together with his brother, visited Mrs Ruwisch and GMC in Bucharest.[16]

This was GMC's last official task as CFR chief-architect. On 6th September 1940 King Carol II was forced to abdicate and leave Romania for his exile in Portugal. General Antonescu invited the Iron Guard to join him and declared Romania a national legionary state. This pushed the country to the wall, and was a heavy blow for all democrats to take who still had some faith that the country could maintain its neutrality. The forced abdication of Carol II hit GMC's career too. And worse was soon to follow.

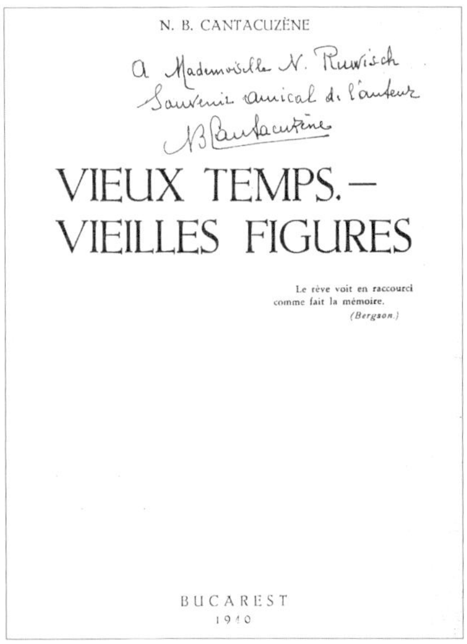

N. B. CANTACUZÈNE

a Mademoiselle N. Ruwisch
Souvenir amical de l'auteur
N B Cantacuzène

VIEUX TEMPS. –
VIEILLES FIGURES

Le rêve voit en raccourci
comme fait la mémoire.
(Bergson)

BUCAREST
1940

215 N. B. Cantacuzino, *Vieux Temps – Vieilles Figures*. Bucharest 1940. Front page with dedication to Nina Ruwisch (AMLSC).

216 Hans Hertlein, *Schaltwerk-Hochhaus*, Siemensstadt Berlin (1927). South-east view. Hertlein (Wasmuth) 1927.

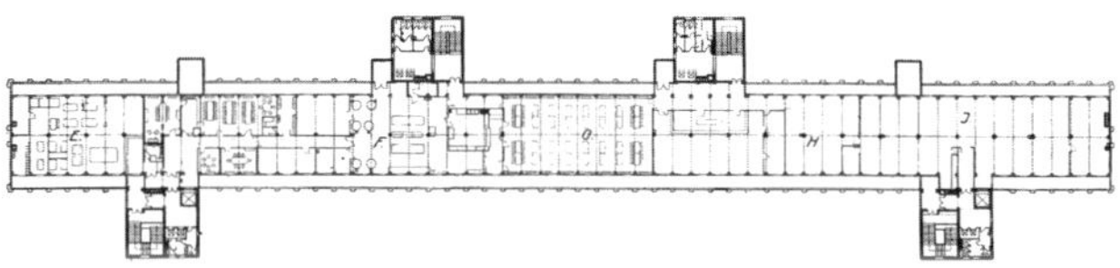

217 Hans Hertlein, *Schaltwerk-Hochhaus*, Siemensstadt Berlin (1927). First floor plan. Hertlein (Wasmuth) 1927.

218 Hans Hertlein, Schaltwerk-Hochhaus, Siemensstadt Berlin (1927). West view. Hertlein (Wasmuth) 1931.

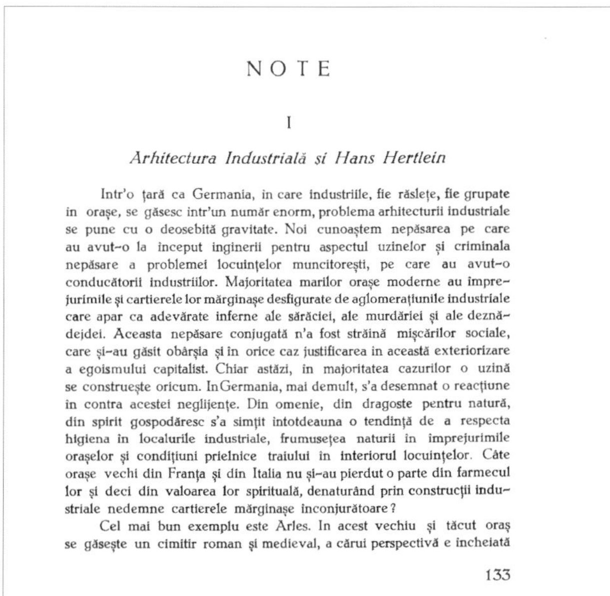

NOTE

I

Arhitectura Industrială şi Hans Hertlein

Intr'o ţară ca Germania, in care industriile, fie răsleţe, fie grupate in oraşe, se găsesc intr'un număr enorm, problema arhitecturii industriale se pune cu o deosebită gravitate. Noi cunoaştem nepăsarea pe care au avut-o la inceput inginerii pentru aspectul uzinelor şi criminala nepăsare a problemei locuinţelor muncitoreşti, pe care au avut-o conducătorii industriilor. Majoritatea marilor oraşe moderne au imprejurimile şi cartierele lor mărginaşe desfigurate de aglomeraţiunile industriale care apar ca adevărate inferne ale sărăciei, ale murdăriei şi ale deznădejdei. Aceasta nepăsare conjugată n'a fost străină mişcărilor sociale, care şi-au găsit obârşia şi in orice caz justificarea in această exteriorizare a egoismului capitalist. Chiar astăzi, in majoritatea cazurilor o uzină se construeşte oricum. In Germania, mai demult, s'a desemnat o reacţiune in contra acestei neglijenţe. Din omenie, din dragoste pentru natură, din spirit gospodăresc s'a simţit intotdeauna o tendinţă de a respecta higiena in localurile industriale, frumuseţea naturii in imprejurimile oraşelor şi condiţiuni prielnice traiului in interiorul locuinţelor. Câte oraşe vechi din Franţa şi din Italia nu şi-au pierdut o parte din farmecul lor şi deci din valoarea lor spirituală, denaturând prin construcţii industriale nedemne cartierele mărginaşe inconjurătoare?

Cel mai bun exemplu este Arles. In acest vechiu şi tăcut oraş se găseşte un cimitir roman şi medieval, a cărui perspectivă e incheiată

133

219 GMC, *Note. Arhitectura industrială si Hans Hertlein* (Notes. Industrial Architecture and Hans Hertlein). First page of the essay. *Simetria III* (1940-1941), pp. 133-135.

Hans Hertlein (1881-1963), the German architect, studied in Dresden, Berlin-Charlottenburg and Munich, especially under Richard Riemerschmid, Friedrich von Thiersch, and Fritz Schumacher. Hertlein worked for Siemens from 1912 to 1951, being the chief-architect for some 36 years. Hertlein designed numerous Siemens buildings in Berlin Siemensstadt, as well as in other German cities like Mannheim (1923), Hannover (1924), Essen (1930), Dresden (1937), Nuremberg (1940), Erlangen (1951). In addition he projected Siemens branches' headquarters around the world, including Den Haag (1922), Buenos Aires (1925), Bucharest (1929), Vienna (1929) and Milan (c. 1940). Hertlein was a member of the Prussian Academy of Architecture and Civil Engineering; Academy of Fine Arts (c. 1929); honorary doctor of the Technical University of Hannover (1931); professor of construction design and industrial architecture at the Technical University of (West) Berlin (1946-c.1957); member of the Academy of Fine Arts in West Berlin (1955), honorary senator of the Technical University of (West) Berlin (1957).

The fact that Hertlein received honours both during the Weimarer Republic and after the Second World War, points to the fact that he managed to survive the Nazi period with a certain degree of dignity. In the standard books on German architects during the Nazi-time and their later careers in either of the two German states Hertlein is not mentioned.

On Hertlein cf. W. Ribbe/W. Schäche, *Die Siemensstadt. Geschichte und Architektur eines Industriestandortes*. Berlin 1985, pp. 177-179, 182, 667-668; *Wasmuths Lexikon der Baukunst*, Vol. 3, Berlin 1931, pp. 94-95.

Under three dictatorships (1940-60)

Fascism, Carlton collapse, imprisonment and war

The political disaster of September 1940 was followed by a severe earthquake in South-Eastern Romania in the night of 9th to 10th November the same year. Many buildings collapsed, including the Carlton, with some one hundred and forty people having lost their lives.[1]

As a liberal politician and cosmopolitan architect, GMC was likely to be easy prey for his political enemies, now in power. Both General Antonescu and Iron Guardists indeed put the blame on GMC and took him to court. After a summary political show trial, he was locked up at Văcărești prison.[2] At the same time, other liberal and conservative politicians and intellectuals were arrested. At the close of November 1940 the Iron Guard unleashed a public massacre among its political enemies both free and imprisoned.[3]

With the help of some fellow prisoners, who hid him in the bell tower of the monastery church, GMC survived. Of this formidable situation we possess a picture as reported by Alice Magheru, the doctor and close friend of GMC's:

"For a long time GMC was a happy artist, a happy man. Then came the Earthquake and the crash of the Carlton. He was in no way to blame. The seven weeks he spent in Văcărești changed him, changed his outlook on life. Never again was he the cheerful man he had been. There, at Văcărești, something very touching happened. On that dreadful day when that awful drama took place and the Iron Guard killed so many politicians, a lot of prisoners were in the courtyard, GMC among them.

He told us that, suddenly, he was surrounded by six fellow prisoners who were pushing him on, ahead, completely in silence – he had no idea what they were up to. As there was a lot of ugly noise, he feared for the worst. The men pushed him towards the church and up into the Bell tower. They locked him in, and went away. When the noise subsided, he went to sleep. Some indefinite time later the men returned and unlocked the door, saying: 'Come on, Prince, it's over.' When he asked them who they were and why they had protected him, they answered: 'Don't you recognize us? We worked for you on several building sites.' I expect he had treated them very well and that is why they looked after him."[4]

Marina Brancovan, GMC's sister-in-law, personally vouched for him at Antonescu. After seven weeks GMC was released on the condition to keep himself available both for the ensuing case and re-entering the army.[5] For GMC it was a bitter blow to take:

"The prison, the rebellion, and the sadness of the times give life a sort of sinister depth. My life has changed since November. I have had to exert myself just to survive. Even now I am like a man who has lost a great deal of blood, sometimes I feel totally disoriented and cannot take in my misfortune. Luckily my health did not let me down. Your mother and Marina particularly were very helpful. Marina's devotion went as far as heroism. It was she who got me out of prison. [...] Sad at heart, I have started wor king again, especially painting. It often upsets me to think of the impending

221 GMC/V. Arion, *Carlton building*, Bucharest (c. 1932-36), W 44. Destroyed in the 1940 earthquake. Period postcard (ADT).

222 *Archangel Gabriel*, fresco detail from the naos of the Văcărești Monastery's Church, Bucharest (1716-36), rescued from destruction in 1987. Exhibited at the Mogoșoaia Gallery in April 2013 (ADT).

220 Opposite:
GMC, *Office building*, Vasile Lascăr Street, Bucharest (1945-47), W 94. Branch of the Institute of Hydro-Electrical Research and Design/ISPHE (Photograph ADT).

223 GMC, *Cherson*, Russia. Watercolour, 16th August 1942 (AMLSC).

224 GMC, *Stalingrad*, Russia. Watercolour, 28th September 1942 (AMLSC).

court case. I will have to prepare for it and it will be the source of endless trouble. Thank goodness that recently things have changed a bit for better and the mob will not be judging my case. You cannot imagine what it was like and just how horrifying a crowd can be – literally, criminals of all sort – and when they are out of control it is like a vision of hell."[6]

Not until 1943 did his pending case come to an end, when he was finally freed of all charges. The fault obviously lay with the Schindl builder company, which had partly stolen materials and partly used poor ones instead of proper materials.[7] This affected especially the reinforced concrete structure, including the main corner pillar, which proved to be worthless in static terms.[8]

One might be tempted to think that high-rise steel frame structure could have been more appropriate for a high-rise building in a region affected by earthquakes. The first high-rise building in Bucharest, the Telephone Company Headquarters on the Calea Victoriei close to the National Theatre, for instance, withstood the earth-quakes of 1940 and 1977 also on account of its steel frame structure. The building was constructed to the designs of the American architects Walter Froy, Louis Weeks and E. van Saanen-Algy from 1929-1934. Certainly the comprehensive knowledge which exists today on the matter was not at disposal in the 1930s. Also civil engineers in Romania applied the German construction standards, which were famous for their precision and strictness already at that time.

In fact, GMC himself suggested why steel had possibly not been used with the Carlton. In his article *Tendances de l'architecture roumaine* in *L'Architecture d'aujourd'hui* (1934), written at the time when he designed the Carlton, he made it clear that in Romania architects had to face serious economic and structural problems regarding construction materials and even their quality. Then he pointed out that the "construction with steel-frames is equally impossible thanks to a steel monopoly which maintains the steel price twenty per cent higher than that of reinforced concrete".[9] In doing so, GMC actually hinted at the magnates Auschnitt and Malaxa, who virtually excluded the use of steel in construction.

In March 1941 GMC was called up into the army. First he was active as an artillery officer, then as war correspondent, and stayed for some two years in Crimea. During all these campaigns he made many sketches and watercolours, including of Stalingrad.[10]

In August 1944 another grief awaited him. Soon after King Michael I had Antonescu arrested on 23rd August 1944, Bucharest suffered some heavy bombardments. GMC's home and his office were being largely destroyed in such an air raid. It possibly targeted the adjoining Știrbey Palace, the home of Prince Barbu Știrbey, who was involved in secret peace treaties with the Alllies in Cairo in spring 1944. At any event, only a small fragment of GMC's archive and library survived.[11]

Professional activity 1942-1948

Architecture

From 1941 to 1944 GMC realized only few projects. In spring 1942 Antonescu demanded him to transform his new headquarters, the villa he virtually confiscated from the descendants of the late Professor Nae Ionescu.[1] This villa, built on the designs of GMC from 1936-37, was particularly attractive for the dictator: for one thing, it was the largest private estate in Bucharest next to the royal premises; secondly, it was surrounded by vast grounds; and lastly, it happened to be strategically well located in northern Bucharest in close proximity to the Băneasa airport and railway station. After the war both the villa and its grounds were given over to agricultural research.[2]

In addition GMC completed some buildings begun in 1937: the Kretzulesco palace, in collaboration with Duiliu Marcu; and the Flămânda Church near Câmpulung at the foot of the Southern Carpathians.

225 GMC/D. Marcu, *Kretzulesco office and commercial building*, 45 Calea Victoriei, Bucharest (1937-1942), W 75. Photograph Dan Teodorovici.

The project which enthused him most was the transformation of a country manor dating from the eighteenth century Brancovan period.[3] It was located in the village of Drugănești, some 30 kilometres south of Bucharest, and belonged to Marina Brancovan. When he was commissioned by her in 1939, the building was practically a ruin. Originally, the manor consisted of a central block with a grand balcony to the south, and a smaller lateral wing dating from the nineteenth century.

He approached Drugănești in the same creative spirit as Mogoșoaia some fifteen years ago. From GMC's standpoint "the restoration of a monument [...] could never be a matter of building science and history alone."[4] Rather, he revived the Brancovan spirit and adjusted it to a new life. He transformed the manor according to the building type of the suburban Palladian villa: basement, piano nobile, and mezzanine. These storeys are usually contained in the central block, with a columned portico on the front façade, a loggia on the rear façade, and subordinate lateral wings. GMC could have found examples in the work of Palladio or Schinkel, for instance in Palladio's Villa Cornaro, Schinkel's Landhaus Behrend at Charlottenhof (sad to say, demolished in 1905) or Schinkel's Schauspielhaus on the Gendarmenmarkt in Berlin.

As for Schinkel, GMC did not mention him at all in his writings. But some of his statements and projects invite us to read between the lines. From GMC's only documented visit to Berlin as chief architect of CFR in 1940, only one postcard photograph has survived.[5] This photograph could not be more expressive. It shows GMC in an elegant three-piece suit, with walking stick and hat, looking self-confidently into the camera of the street photographer, and walking down Unter den Linden, the eastern corner of the Humboldt University to his right, and the Neue Wache of Schinkel in the background – as if GMC would have said: with Schinkel behind you, you can devote yourself to architecture with great confidence. On that voyage he might have visited various buildings by Schinkel in Berlin and Potsdam along with the Schinkel Museum, which opened in 1931 in the former Princesses's Palais Unter den Linden.[6]

226 GMC on Unter den Linden, on his trip to Berlin as chief-architect of the Romanian Railways CFR (Căile Ferate Române), in August 1940 (AMLSC).

227 *Drugănești manor*, interior view of the balcony with main entrance (CLADRA).

228 GMC, Modernisation of the eighteenth-century *Drugănești manor*, rear façade with loggia (1939-46; W 88). Drugănești, c. 30 km south of Bucharest (Photograph CLADRA).

229 *Drugănești manor*, front façade with side-view of the balcony (CLADRA).

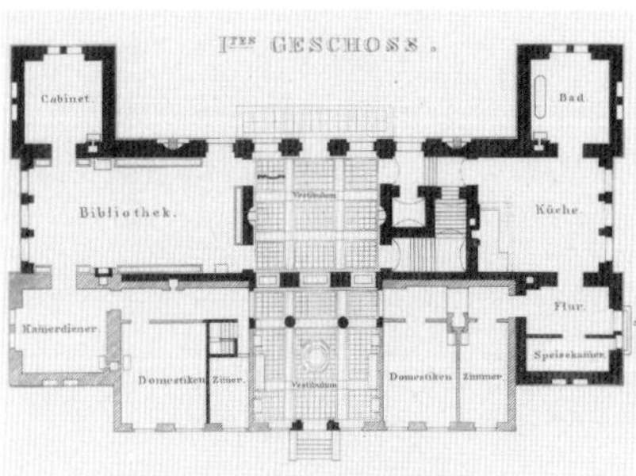

230 K. F. Schinkel, *Tegel Palace*, Berlin (1820-1824), ground floor plan. WLB Stuttgart, Sch. K. Fol. 1063, 1-12.

Another project by Schinkel could have inspired GMC, both in an operative sense and regarding its character: the palace of Wilhelm von Humboldt in Tegel north-west of Berlin. The original building dated from the sixteenth century and consisted of a modest two-storey rectangular block with a tower on one side. Schinkel extended and transformed the manor on the model of Greek antiquity into a representative building with a symmetrical disposition and a total of four towers.[7] The palace is of a gentle and intimate monumentality which could have appealed to GMC.

GMC himself extended the Drugănești manor and turned it into a regular villa of axial symmetrical composition. He added a lateral wing to the west, and enriched the central block with a loggia on the rear façade overlooking a vast field. Then he built a slate roof and freed the façades from the few remaining plaster surfaces in favour of the vivid red brick texture. The southern rooms of the lateral wings serve to protect the northern side from the heat in summer time. Whereas Schinkel had no use for a loggia at the Schauspielhaus but monumentalized the portico according to the need for representation, GMC maintained both architectural forms. Unlike the Villa Cornaro, where the portico and loggia have the same size in plan and elevation, GMC designed the loggia at Drugănești as an aesthetic counterweight of the compact balcony. The balcony serves as the main entrance but also as a shady outdoor retreat in summer days. The loggia, by contrast, is designed as a narrow room running the whole length of the southern façade of the piano nobile. In addition GMC designed the building to such proportions that it can be placed both in plan and elevation into concentric circles, according to the proportional arrangement of parallel lines drawn diagonally to the central axis of the building. The project was completed in 1946 and presented by GMC in the *Simetria* edition of the same year.[8]

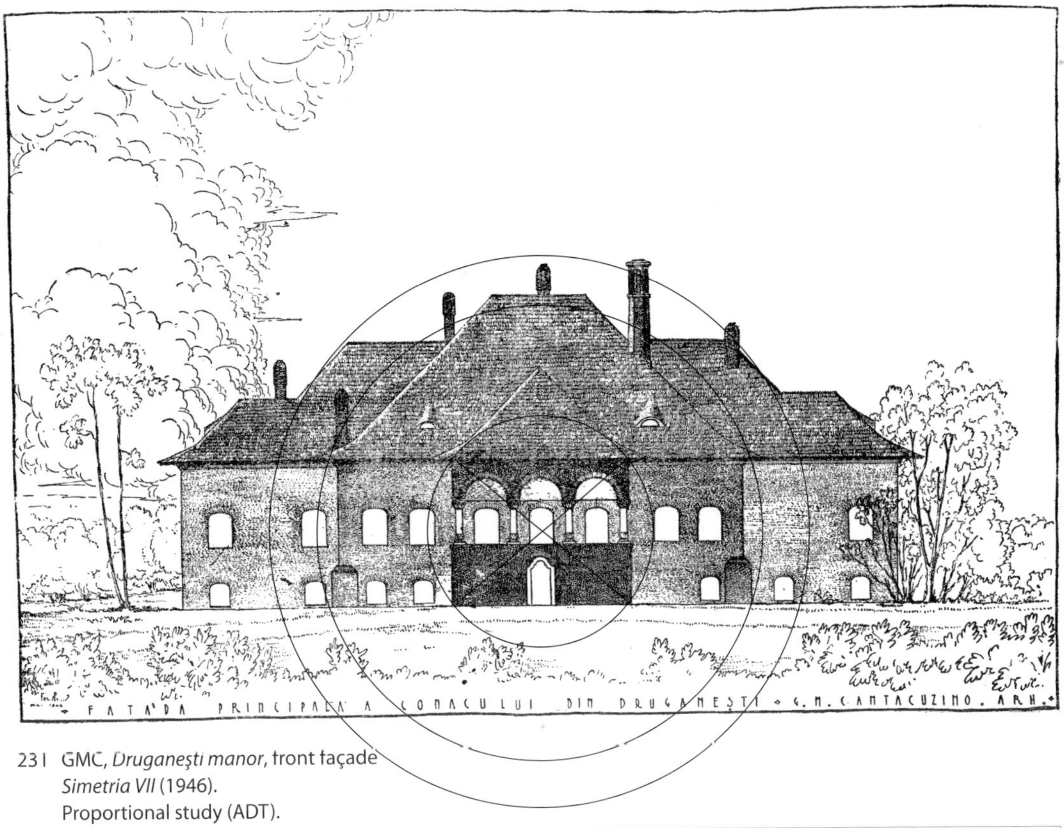

231 | GMC, *Druganeşti manor*, front façade *Simetria VII* (1946).
Proportional study (ADT).

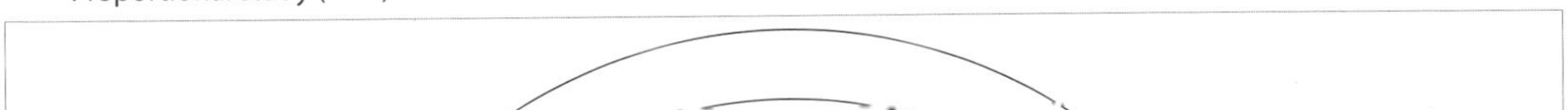

232 GMC, *Drugăneşti manor*, piano nobile plan, *Simetria VII* (1946). Proportional study (ADT).

233 GMC, *Office building*, now Institute of Hydro-Electrical Research and Design/ISPHE (W 94), Vasile Lascăr Street, Bucharest (1945-47). South view (ADT).

234 GMC, *Office building*, now Institute of Hydro-Electrical Research and Design/ISPHE (W 94), Vasile Lascăr Street, Bucharest (1945-47). North view (ADT).

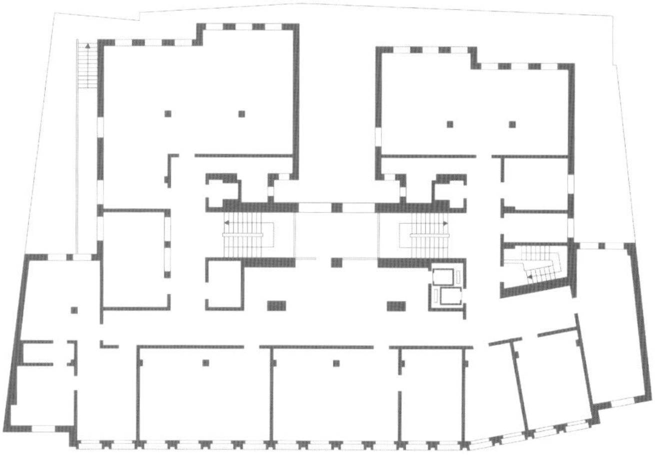

235 Institute of Hydro-Electrical Research and Design/ISPHE (W 94), Vasile Lascăr Street, Bucharest (1945-47). First floor plan (ADT).

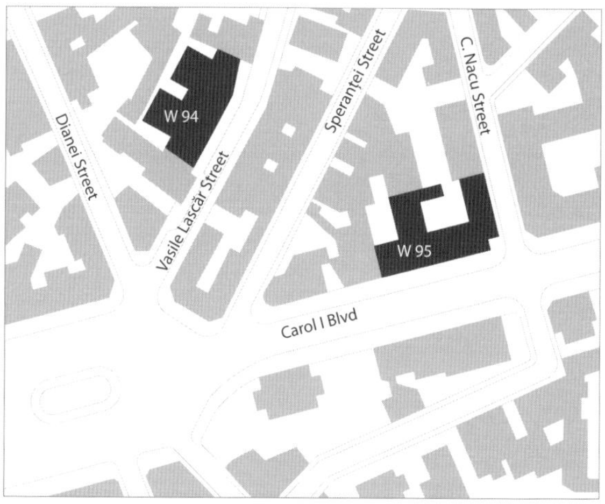

236 Site map of the two office buildings W 94 and W 95, Bucharest (1945-47) (ADT).

Of the projects GMC realized from 1945 to 1947 two office buildings in Bucharest are noteworthy: purpose-built for the Gas Electric Company, they now house the Institute of Hydro-Electrical Research and Design (on 29 Carol I Boulevard and on 5-7 Vasile Lascăr Street). They are located in close proximity to each other, fit in well with the urban texture and show a similar aesthetic approach by GMC.

This is particularly true for the building on Vasile Lascăr Street. The main façade is basically clad with red bricks. You enter the building from Vasile Lascăr Street through a limestone porch. The three-storey central part projects above the basement with its limestone panels proportioned according to the Golden Section. The three upper storeys are successively recessed to the effect that the building should not overshadow the adjacent buildings and street, according to the Bucharest Masterplan of 1935.[9]

The simple main façade with sash-windows follows the Vasile Lascăr Street with an elegant curve, recalling buildings by Hans Hertlein or Baldassare Peruzzi's Palazzo Massimo alle Colonne in Rome (c.1533-1536), a building which GMC must have known both from first-hand experience and the monograph *Palais Massimi à Rome* (1818) by F. T. Suys and L. P. Haudebourt.

237 GMC, *Office building*, Carol I Blvd, Bucharest (1945-47; W 95) (ADT).

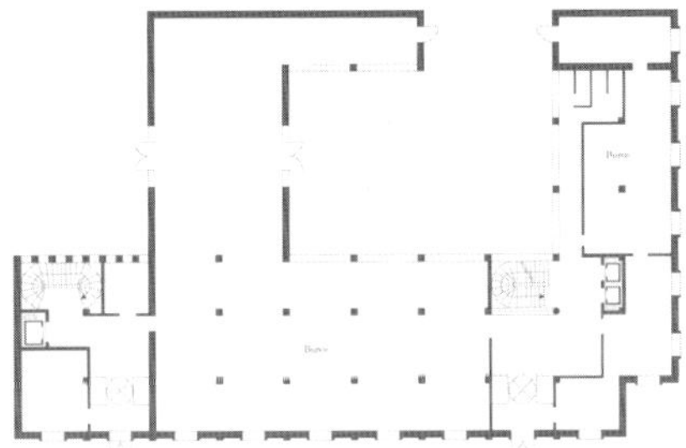

238 GMC, *Office building* (1945-47; W 95). Ground floor plan (ADT).

Lecturing in Bucharest

In spring 1942 the School of Architecture in Bucharest appointed GMC as honorary professor for the history and theory of architecture, and in summer he became professor for analytical geometry at the Academy of Fine Arts. Then the Polytechnic University of Bucharest appointed him as honorary professor for landscape architecture at the Institute of Urban Planning.[1]

239 Baldassare Peruzzi, *Palazzo Massimo alle Colonne*, Rome (c. 1533-1536), view from St Pantaleo Street. Letarouilly 1857, vol. 3. WLB Stuttgart, Sch. K. F. A 22g165.

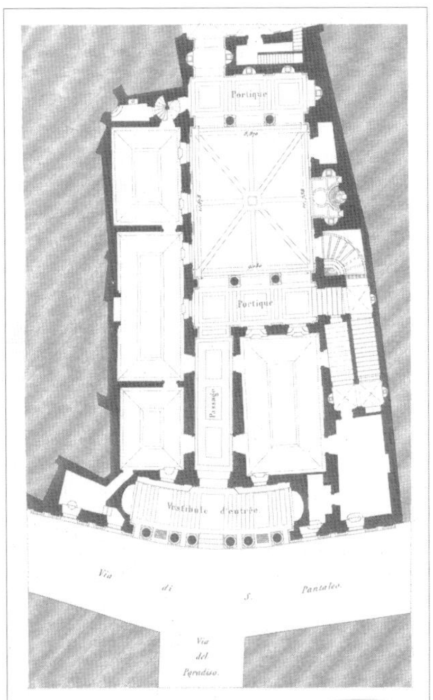

240 Baldassare Peruzzi, *Palazzo Massimo alle Colonne in Rome*, ground floor plan.

241 GMC, *St George Church*, Hârlau, Moldavia (1492). Drawing, *Simetria VII* (1946).

To his students he used to recommend drawing and painting, for "[d]rawing is thought, painting is dream: it is a way of dreaming with your eyes open, always keeping watch. Beauty is born out of this watchfulness".[2]

In his first lecture at the School of Architecture he presented an outline of architectural history from Ancient Egypt to Vitruvius.[3] At about the same time he began to work on the very first translation of Vitruvius's writings into Romanian, probably from a French version, and completed it in 1947. In the same year, GMC gave a copy to the Library of the Romanian Academy, consisting of three carefully handcrafted files:[4] firstly, the actual translation; secondly, a substantial introduction; and finally, a great number of illustrations, possibly provided by Paul Marinescu, his chief collaborator in the architectural office and *Simetria* illustrator. GMC made at least two other copies: he gave one to Professor Grigore Ionescu, his colleague at the Department of History and Theory of Architecture,[5] the other he kept for himself.

His lectures rested on three corner-stones: in the first place, he gave an overview of the subject; then he focused on landmarks, which he illustrated from memory on the blackboard with rough yet concise chalk sketches of buildings, city maps or skylines. The lecture was further enriched with cultural historical commentaries, geographical annotations, and suggested readings. Occasionally he discarded the chronological exposition, comparing buildings, artists and events from different periods.[6] In doing so, he made his students aware of how close the relations can be even between distant historic events, figures or streams of thought. GMC's attitude as a "deperiodizer"[7], to use the term coined by Erwin Panofsky, was novel in Romania at the time and welcomed by his students.

His outstanding personality, stupendous erudition and *classical attitude* commanded respect. The *classical attitude* he summed up in the sound view that "tradition does not mean being reactionary but getting the right balance".[8] His manners too seemed to have been exemplary: "He had the rare gift of making the people whom he met feel at ease"[9] Dr Radu Patrulius remembered him as a "magician of the word and drawing".[10] There was no need for notes, information leaflets, slides, or films. Seemingly effortless, GMC spoke from memory, and what a good memory he must have had.[11] Yet he prepared every lecture accurately and industriously, as Patrulius learned to know during his traineeship in GMC's architectural office. The lectures were, in the words of Patrulius, "cultural baths"[12]; Dan Corneliu, architect in Constantza, spoke to the author of "hours of gliding, it would appear, on a flying carpet"[13]; Stephan Eleutheriadis, architect and painter in Rio de Janeiro/Brazil, wrote in a letter to the author about a "time of dreams, in which we forgot the bitter reality surrounding us"[14]; Dr Eugenia Greceanu, who became an expert in conservation, confirmed this in a conversation with the author.[15] She noted that GMC with his aristocratic appearance and classical attitude acted in defiance of the then emerging "sovietisation of architectural education"[16] as well as of education in general. Those who passionately embraced, to say it in the words of Paul Zucker, the "functionalism as concept of style"[17], very much stylish in post-war Romania, rejected GMC as old-fashioned traditionalist.[18]

Journalism and criticism

From 1942 to 1947 GMC contributed to the reformist liberal periodical *Romanian Life* (Viaţa Românească) and continued to edit *Simetria*. Although a target of ridicule in the beginning,[1] by 1945 *Simetria* was at the forefront of the promotion of architectural and cultural criticism.[2]

But *Simetria* also reveals GMC's humanitarian commitment during the Second World War. He intervened on the behalf of Jews at the City of Bucharest that they should be freed from forced labour.[3] GMC also protected his Jewish friends such as Simon Bayer, Mihail Sebastian, or Tudor Vianu. Vianu co-edited *Simetria* from 1943 to 1947, and contributed many articles to it.[4] Sebastian, in his posthumously published internationally acclaimed *Journal 1933-1944*, recalled a notable dinner at GMC on Sunday, 16th March 1941:

"An amicable supper yesterday at Cantacuzino's. I had a strange feeling of being in a different city, with books, paintings, and friendly people, instead of war, Germans, and Hitler."[5]

242 GMC, *Despre o estetică a reconstrucţiei* (On the aesthetics of reconstruction), Bucharest 1947. Front cover.

At the same time GMC outlined in lectures and essays a long-term strategy of reconstruction. His volume of selected essays *On the aesthetics of reconstruction* (Despre o estetică a reconstrucţiei) was even being printed in 1947, but the Communist authorities forbade its selling.[6] In February 1946 he gave a public lecture on *The Fine Arts in the USA*, on the invitation of The Society of the Friends of the USA in Bucharest. On the surface, this event was inconspicuous. Nevertheless, the Secret Police considered it as an effort to unite the Romanian Intellectuals against the Communist regime.[7]

In view of the Antonescu dictatorship and the following Communism in post-war Romania, GMC's liberal attitude and some of his writings had an underlying subversiveness. Like Ryszard Kapuściński noted in his *Travels with Herodotus*, at that time "an obsession with allusion"[8] spread across Eastern Europe. It was to mark the intellectual opposition to Communism well until 1989. Watched from this perspective, we could identify in *Simetria* moments of protest both quiet and open. A quiet protest could be discerned in *Simetria VII* (1946). Herein GMC published a few selected aphorisms by Plotinus, probably translated by himself from a French or German edition of *The Enneads*. One maxim is particularly noteworthy:

"[T]o exalt ourselves above the Intellectual-Principle is to fall from it."[9]

This maxim appears like a call to resist "the slavery of the mind in totalitarian countries"[10], as Karl Jaspers observed in his preface to the German edition of Czeslaw Milosz's *Captive Mind* (1953). Bertrand Russell also disapproved of the anti-intellectual outlook promoted by Communism:

"There is in Marx, and in current Communist thought, an undue glorification of manual against brain workers."[11]

The year 1948 indeed marked the climax of the "agony of cultural life in Romania"[12]. Apart from other monstrosities, it included the banning of Western languages from education both in high schools and universities; the closing down of the Istituto Italiano di Cultura; and the arrest of guests in the Institut Français and American Library.[13] Roland Barthes, cultural attaché at the French Legation in Bucharest in the late 1940s, witnessed this phenomenon:

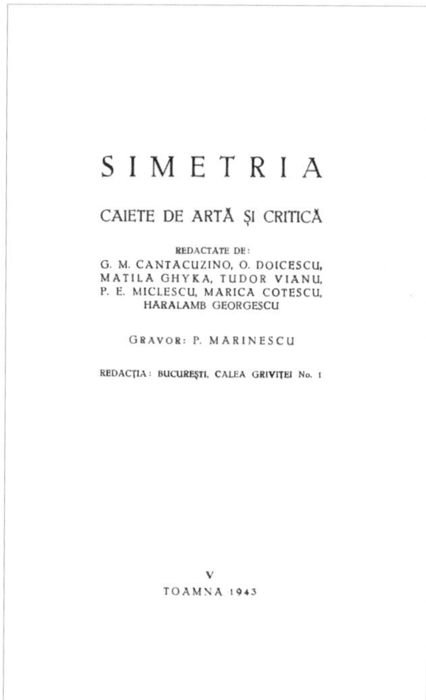

SIMETRIA

CAIETE DE ARTĂ ŞI CRITICĂ

REDACTATE DE:
G. M. CANTACUZINO, O. DOICESCU,
MATILA GHYKA, TUDOR VIANU,
P. E. MICLESCU, MARICA COTESCU,
HARALAMB GEORGESCU

GRAVOR: P. MARINESCU

REDACŢIA: BUCUREŞTI, CALEA GRIVIŢEI No. 1

V

TOAMNA 1943

243 GMC *et al*, *Simetria V*. Bucharest 1943. Title page listing all co-editors and the engraver Paul Marinescu.

"The Stalinist propaganda proceeds with a theme embodied by a key-word. This is to be inserted, by all means possible, into the minds of the people. [...] The massive campaign unleashed against cosmopolitism in the sciences will sooner or later affect a great deal of Romanian scientists."[14]

As though in defiance of this savage policy, GMC included in what was to be the last edition of *Simetria* in 1947 a great number of French drawings and etchings. In the same edition he published the essay *The Artist and the Freedom* (Artistul şi libertatea). It was a dignified protest against the Communist limitation of civil freedom and humanity.[15]

In 1942 GMC completed another "book called *Evasion* [...] about an imaginary journey into contradictory thoughts and ideas.[...] It has two chapters: 1) *The Journey*, and 2) *The Feast at Malcontenta*. It will appear with a drawing on the front cover by Militza [Pătraşcu]."[16] This book is unknown today, and it is uncertain if it was published at all.

In retrospect GMC's criticism from 1942 to 1947 appears as an attempt in times of existential insecurity to establish some kind of order based on the classical foundations of Europe, involving particularly Vitruvius, Plotinus, Goethe, Gide and Valéry. On the European scale we can find similar approaches. As, for instance, Ryszard Kapuściński recalls, in the mid 1940s the Warsaw historian Professor Seweryn Hammer provided the very first translation of Herodotus's *The Histories* into Polish. It was published in 1954, right after Stalin's death.[17] Notable too is the series of twelve lectures given by José Ortega y Gasset in 1948 and 1949 to accompany the creation of his Institudo de Humanidades in Madrid. Ortega y Gasset called his lectures *An Interpretation of Universal History. Exposition and Examination of A. J. Toynbee's work, A Study of History*. Well beyond the horizon suggested by the title, Ortega y Gasset presented a radical "analysis of life established in illegitimacy [...] of which the two gigantic examples are the declining days of the Roman Empire and the period in which we ourselves are living". [18]

244 GMC, Valentina Bibesco (Marthe Bibesco's daughter) and Demeter Ghyka, posing in front of the southern entrance of the Mogoşoaia gardens in 1942 (AMB-JG).

Hopes of democratisation

At the same time GMC kept in close touch with Western artists, diplomats and journalists who ventured to Romania. They included "Colonel Eddy Boxshall, senior member of SOE"[1] and son-in-law of Prince Barbu Ştirbey;[2] Mr Chollerton, the correspondent of the *Morning Post* for Romania;[3] Sir John Helier Rougetel (1894-1975), the English Ambassador in Bucharest from 1939-1940 and 1944-1946;[4] and René de Weck (1887-1950), the Swiss Ambassador in Bucharest in 1945. De Weck and GMC met at Mogoşoaia, where the Swiss Embassy was evacuated during the war. De Weck was a close friend of Marthe Bibesco and Grigore Gafencu.[5]

Furthermore, GMC made some friends among the intellectuals of the Institut Français in Bucharest, such as Jean Mouton, the director from 1940-1946;[6] Philippe Rebeyrol, the director from 1946 to 1949;[7] and Michel Dard, who contributed to *Simetria*.

Then he befriended Monique de la Bruchollerie (1915-1972), the great French musician and one of the finest European concert pianists of her day. Her concert co-operations involved directors such as Sergiu Celibidache and Herbert von Karajan.[8] De la Bruchollerie was on several concert tours in Romania, and instrumental in securing a part of the correspondence between GMC and his family in London.

As in 1947 the political and economic situation was becoming worse than ever, the hopes of a new democratic beginning on the Western model faded away. Like in other countries unofficially annexed by the Soviet Union, the Romanian economy suffered from the heavy reparations. They included the large dismantling of factories and production equipment and their relocation in the USSR, like was the case of the IAR (Romanian Aircraft Industry) factory in Braşov/Kronstadt, designed by GMC in the early 1930s. Forced collectivization, nationalization, and disorganization of the liberal professions finally destroyed the free market.

On the other hand, the extensive development of heavy industries following the Soviet model neglected agriculture to the effect that the food supply almost collapsed. It was not until after Stalin's death in 1953 that the pressure exerted by the Soviet Union lessened considerably, so that the economic situation could improve. For instance, the Sovrom companies, which exploited Romania's mineral resources, were dissolved in 1954; two years lates the war debts were being cancelled.[9]

"Until the Moscow conference we still had a bit of hope", stated GMC in a letter to his wife in spring 1946. "We now know that the Atlantic Charter is just a piece of literature signed in a moment of confusion. We also know that Romania as well as the whole of Central and Eastern Europe will remain as good as annexed to the USSR. [...]. Romania is going through fierce and carefully planned sabotage, it is being deliberately impoverished – lately this has got much worse, its institutions are suppressed or curtailed one after the other, and the dictatorship of the proletariat [...] is putting out, one after the other, the lights of the spirit – the few that dare to burn."[10]

GMC himself felt more and more like a stranger in his own country. In these circumstances the contact with his students was of great help:

245 Pierre Puvis de Chavannes, Study of the first painting of the triptych *The Childhood of Sainte Geneviève* (Panthéon, Paris, 1893-98). Drawing taken from the collection of Matei B. Cantacuzino when published by GMC in *Simetria VI* (1945).

246 Monique de la Bruchollerie (1915-1972). French pianist and friend of GMC's. © Diane de la Bruchollerie, Paris.

247 Albrecht Dürer, *Melancholy*.
First figure in GMC *et al*, *Simetria VIII* (1947).

"The only thing that keeps me going amidst all this is my teaching. Being in touch with the younger generation does me good. But for how long can I go on lecturing without becoming suspect? I am surrounded by suspicion."[11]

The Communist authorities knew he firmly believed in the Western values and was a convinced anglo- and francophile; they also knew he was highly respected as a leading architect and public intellectual. But GMC himself had not the slightest intention of playing the role designed for him, as for all leading intellectuals, by the Communists.

"I struggle and I defend my position from day to day. But I know full well that the citadel I am living in will fall if things don't change. And I can't see any change. I would find it very hard to leave this country. But I am incapable of dancing to the Marxist tune and I can't serve the Russians and hang onto my freedom. Being free is the greatest risk of all. They do not want us here anymore."[12]

Balasha Cantacuzene, the painter and great friend of Patrick Leigh Fermor, saw it likewise. On the back of a photograph sent to him in 1946, she wrote: "They do not want us, our education or culture anymore."[13]

The government headed by Dr Petru Groza won the parliamentary elections on 19th November 1946 thanks to a massive vote rigging. According to the Moscow Allies' Conference in 1945, those elections were supposed to be the first free elections in Romania since 1937. Already before election day, Groza informed the speechless US American representative in Romania that "the Anglo-Americans [...] [at the Moscow Conference] thought of free elections in the sense of the English or American model. The Russians, by contrast, thought of free elections in the sense of the Russian model. In view of the Red Army's presence in Romania the coming elections will probably follow the Russian interpretation of free and unhindered elections".[14]

248 GMC painting in his Bucharest studio, c. 1958 (AMLSC).

Imprisonments (1948-1954)

Nevertheless, to leave one's country is often a momentous decision. "It is always sad to break with a tradition of some five centuries"[1], wrote GMC in a letter to his wife. He continued: "Romania was created by a very liberal elite: *We* were that elite. We and all those we trained. That part of Romania has disappeared. What remains is just a ghetto serving the Soviets. Because we represent culture and wealth and individualism they mean to get rid of us."[2]

His official attempt to visit his family in England failed. In summer 1946 he obtained the Romanian passport and the British visa, but was denied the Soviet one.[3] Some months later, he tried again. This time Emil Bodnăraş himself, the Romanian Minister of the Armed Forces,[4] refused GMC's application for an exit visa.[5]

"Catastrophes are not conducive to meditation", wrote GMC to his wife in those days. "Unable to deny anything or to give up anything, I stand aloof and become a monk who carries the cloister within him rather than being surrounded and protected by it. For the time being I look after my solitude like a secret garden."[6]

For a while there was still some hope of freedom, symbolized by King Michael I: "The nation is almost unanimously united around King Michael. The minority of those who are not longing for freedom, but fight against it and aim at an unconditioned subjugation through the Slavs, is grouped in the Communist Party. This minority is unpopular, but armed and supported by the Russians."[7] But at the close of December 1947 the Communist government forced King Michael I into exile.[8]

Early in 1948 GMC was interrogated several times by the Secret Police.[9] Then he decided to take action. He had a boat prepared at Agigea near Constantza to sail to Constantinople together with some relatives and friends. The plan being betrayed, the entire group was arrested *in situ* – save GMC,

249 Theodor Pallady, *Church*. Watercolour. *Simetria IV* (1941-42).

250 GMC, *Boat on the beach*. Watercolour (AMLSC).

251 John VI Cantacuzino (c. 1295-1383) as monk, detail from the double portrait of him as Byzantine emperor and monk, taken from the *Recueil des traités théologiques de l'empereur Jean VI Cantacuzène* (Greek, c. 1347-1354).
© Bibliothèque Nationale de France, Paris.

who was an excellent swimmer and reacted at considerable speed. It was a hair-breadth escape. He possibly took temporary refuge in one of the villas he designed in Eforie in the 1930s or in Mangalia, with his "great friend the painter Miracovici who live[d] there six months a year in a little Turkish house".[10]

Then he struggled on alone to Posada in the Prahova valley in the Southern Carpathians. His goal: to find shelter and perhaps political asylum at the French Legation in the Posada manor. The Posada manor was originally a country retreat of Marthe Bibesco, who left Romania in 1946 thanks to English diplomats. Confiscated after 1945, the manor was being rented by the Romanian state to the French Legation. GMC succeeded in getting to Posada and hid in the attic. But he was again betrayed and handed over to the police on the 26th April 1948.[11] Obviously, not even the French Legation protected him.

In the light of this bitter experience he might have remembered an appropriate aphorism of one of his distant ancestors, the Byzantine Emperor John VI Cantacuzino:

"The example of the infidelity of men is like a mirror that shows that there is nothing stable nor safe in this world."[12]

In a show trial on the16th December 1948 GMC was sentenced to a five year imprisonment.[13] First he was sent to the Jilava prison near Bucharest. On 22nd January 1952 he was transferred to the Aiud prison in Transylvania. The first nine months he was kept in solitary confinement. Thereafter he worked in the metal workshop of the prison, where he manufactured together with fellow prisoners cots for selling and swings for children's playgrounds. Thanks to his incredible memory he gave lectures in architecture to his fellow prisoners. One of them was the architect Virgil Antonescu, who reported that GMC's sketches must still be hidden in a metal box somewhere in a cell.[14] His sentence expired on 24th April 1953, but on the very next day it seemed to have been extended for one more year.[15]

Given the slight respite after Stalin's death in March 1953, many political prisoners were freed in the whole of Eastern Europe. This is why GMC might have been released from Aiud prison on probation on 29th July 1953.

"I have returned from my voyage",[16] he wrote in the first letter to his family in England on 15th August 1953. A few days later, however, he was again arrested.[17] This happened because of another betrayal. GMC entrusted a further letter to his family to a Romanian-born British citizen who was on visit in Romania during the International Youth Festival. The letter was handed over to the Securitate.[18]

First, GMC was sentenced to forced labour at the Danube-Black Sea-Canal.[19] Whilst working in a quarry he got hit by a rock his legs being severely injured.[20] On the 26th September 1953 he was transferred to the Pitești Penitentiary some one hundred kilometres north-west of Bucharest.[21] There the Communist regime had established between 1949 and 1952 a monstrous system of re-education in order to shape the new socialist man.[22] Although GMC was sentenced to an imprisonment of one year only, it was not until the 21st June 1954 that he was released from Pitești prison.[23]

252 GMC, *Self-portrait*, 1955 (AMLSC).

Inspector at the Department of Historic Monuments

In late summer 1954 GMC got a job as an inspector at the Department of Historic Monuments in Bucharest.[1] Dubbed "the cemetery of elephants"[2], this office accommodated former aristocrats and intellectuals whom the Communist authorities regarded as inconvenient but inoffensive.

To begin with, he worked in Bucharest and its surroundings. For one thing, GMC supervised the restoration of the Soutzo Palace in Bucharest.[3] Then, according to Radu Patrulius, he prepared "hundreds of files"[4] with analytical drawings, photographs and information about historic monuments: "churches, monasteries, *hans* [large traditional guest houses consisting of four two- or three-storey wings enclosing a vast courtyard], apartment blocks, villas, wells, statues, parks and private gardens"[5].

All of this was compiled in *Cultural Monuments in Bucharest*, a manuscript found by Radu Patrulius in GMC's estate,[6] but obviously lost since then.

The close of 1954 saw GMC being sent as an inspector of the Department of Historic Monuments to "Moldavia, [...] everything I love in this sphere".[7] He was charged with the supervision of the restoration of a number of buildings including the Sf Sava Church in Jassy and the Sucevitza Monastery.[8] On the way to Sucevitza he once had a grave car accident, which caused him to limp.[9] During his convalescence from late December 1954 to late March 1955 he "had the opportunity to read a great deal"[10], focusing upon *Port Royal*, Sainte-Beuve's masterpiece, and rereading Proust's *À la Recherche du Temps Perdue*.[11]

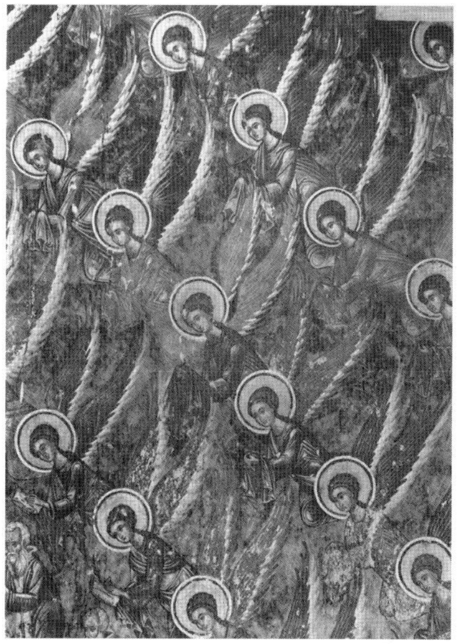

253 *The Divine Staircase with the Choir of Angels*. Sucevitza Monastery's Church, exterior wall painting. (Photograph c. 1962).

Once recovered from the operation, he started again to give public lectures, some of which have been posthumously published in 1993, including *On the influences in Romanian art* (Consideraţiuni asupra influenţelor în arta românească), *What is a historic monument?* (Ce este un monument istoric?), *On landscape* (Consideraţii despre peisaj), *The painted churches in Moldavia* (Bisericile pictate din Moldova), *Mogoşoaia: a palace, a garden, a landscape* (Mogoşoaia: un palat, o grădină, un peisaj), *Brancovan palaces and mansions* (Palatele şi casele brâncoveneşti).[12]

Again according to Dr Patrulius GMC in this period completed two manuscripts ready for publishing, which, again, seem to be lost. They highlighted GMC's constant need for reinforcing practical activity with a critical and theoretical backbone: *Cities and historic monuments in Northern Moldavia* (Oraşe şi monumente din Moldova de Nord) and *Guiding Principles for the Restoration and Maintenance of Historic Monuments* (Directive pentru restaurarea şi întreţinerea monumentelor istorice).[13] The concluding phrases of the latter manuscript were as follows:

"The historic monuments and their surroundings are cultural artefacts and landmarks of time, in which societies had condensed their accomplishments. The restoration of a cultural monument is a cultural act, its protection a civic duty."[14]

Simultaneously GMC was concerned with protecting both historic monuments and the landscapes where they were standing.[15] A case in point is the safe translocation and resettlement of the historic monuments situated in the area of the Bicaz reservoir in the Moldavian Carpathians; another one,

254 Sucevitza Monastery's Church, photograph W. Weiss. GMC, *Petits édifices*. Paris 1931.

255 GMC painting in his Bucharest studio, c. 1958 (AMLSC).

the protection of the Neamtz monastery and stronghold, along with their grounds. GMC personally supervised the actions.[16]

But the daily life remained a constant source of unease. In a letter to his wife in 1955 he noted that "the way they [the Communists] want *I cannot* and the way I can they don't want. In the realm of the spirit, I make no concessions."[17] In the same letter he commented on his visit to Eforie in summer 1955: "Nothing new has been erected there. My buildings are still the chief attraction in spite of all that has been done to have me sunk into oblivion."[18]

256 Tudor Arghezi (1880-1967). Romanian writer and friend of GMC's.

It was in painting that he found some consolation and strength. Since his last exhibition in 1947 he had produced a great number of pencil drawings, water-colours and oil paintings. "I work every day on my paintings and drawings, making up for the years when I was not able to paint or draw."[19] Then the sculptor Theodora Kitzulescu, one of his former students at the Academy of Fine Arts in Bucharest, convinced him to face the public again. She curated what was to be his last exhibition.[20] The show opened on 3rd October 1956, with Tudor Arghezi, the writer and friend of GMC's, speaking the welcoming address:

"I came to see what the architect might have achieved after so many years of silence. I came away from his paintings each one compact like a sonnet, purer and rejuvenated. Each one of these poems in colour around

257 GMC at the opening of his last exhibition in Bucharest, 3rd October 1956 (AMLSC).

us smiles on our sensibility and pronounces as if in a whisper the magic of Romania."[21]

The exhibition was a tremendous success. With GMC being an aristocrat and dissident, the authorities feared the exhibition could become a starting point of civil protest. Subsequently Lydia Macovei, the director of the Department of Cultural Affairs in Bucharest, had the exhibition closed down on the third day:[22]

"My former pupils organised an exhibition last autumn for me, but it was very quickly shot down – too successful and too non-conformist."[23]

All this happened shortly before the anti-Communist upheavals that started at the student demonstration in Budapest on 23rd October 1956, and soon spread across the whole country. The Romanian authorities feared that the revolutionary climate would radiate into Romania. Indeed, student demonstrations occurred first in Timişoara, then in Cluj and Bucharest. The demonstrations were cracked down hard, a great number of students being arrested and excluded from university.[24] GMC himself at one point expressed his solidarity with the demonstrations both in Hungary and Romania. On this account, he was being sacked from the Department of Historic Monuments early in 1957, declared an enemy of the people and subject to permanent surveillance by the Securitate.[25]

258 GMC, *Cetăţuia Monastery*, Jassy, c. 1958. Watercolour (AMLSC).

259 GMC, *The twin pavilions of the Metropolitan church in Jassy*, c. 1960. Oil on cardboard (AMLSC)

Informal diocesan architect in Jassy (1957-1960)

With no way of staying and earning his living in Bucharest, GMC moved to his beloved Jassy. Thanks to the Moldavian bishop Justin Moisescu, and tolerated by the authorities, GMC was employed as an unofficial diocesan architect by the Orthodox Church. To be sure, the bishop treated him as a subaltern, and GMC, in return, referred to him ironically as "His Highness [Înaltul]".[1] He lived as a monk and designed the extension of the Metropolitan church. On week-ends he returned to his little studio in Bucharest where he drew and painted.[2] He managed to send some paintings to his family in England, some were made gifts to relatives and friends in Romania. Of particular interest are the ninety-nine watercolours he donated to the University Library in Jassy in September 1960. In fact, "[f]or more than thirty years they lay forgotten in a cupboard"[3] were re-discovered by chance and then published in an album in 2006.[4]

In 1958 GMC designed a little church in the Ceahlău valley in the Moldavian Carpathians (still unknown), wrote an essay on Giotto and found a publisher for his translation of Vitruvius,[5] but nothing happened. The book was in fact published in 1964 by Professor Grigore Ionescu, to whom GMC gave a copy of the work. Ionescu, who edited the book together with the Romanian Latinist Traian Costa, pretended that GMC had not finished the translation. He also omitted GMC's introduction.[6] As for the introduction, it was not published until 1993, when Zamfira Mihail, GMC's former disciple in Jassy, edited a volume of previously unpublished essays by GMC.[7] Zamfira was the daughter of the priest Paul Mihail, and his family was one of the few friendly places GMC found in those days.

Although forced to live on the fringe of society he refused to be a victim. Rather, he took to heart the lesson of Baudelaire, that

"When once our hearts have gathered in their fruit,
To live is a curse! a secret known to all".[8]

On the project in Jassy he wrote to his wife on 9th November 1958:

"My work in Jassy consists of improving the city landscape. An ensemble of buildings, terraces with the Cathedral in the middle [...]. A bit like Trinità dei Monte."[9]

260 GMC with a workman on the construction site of one of the twin pavilions in Jassy, c. 1960 (AMLSC).

The three-storey massive twin pavilions with a partly rusticated, partly diamond basement, are built to screen the Orthodox cathedral, and form a square with terraces, ramps and stairs in front of it. This intimate public square overlooks the valley of the Bahlui river and is located at the south-western end of a strip of urban grounds that extends from the Cathedral to the north-east via a vast green park to the Jassy theatre. One of the pavilions houses a library which GMC "particularly cherish[ed]".[10]

GMC's love for Palladianism and especially its historical version were given free rein in Jassy. It is a response to the baroque cathedral and echoes the Chrissoveloni Bank back in the 1920s. Furthermore, GMC regarded the Palladianism as a contribution to reinforce the Latin character of Jassy.[11] Herein he may have been encouraged by Henri Focillon, who "in 1919 interpreted the revival of Latin culture in art according to the Enlightenment in a universal manner [with] 'the spirit of Renaissance, the classical forms of thinking and the Graeco-Roman principles being invented not for a particular nation, but for the entire humanity'"[12].

His design, wrote GMC to his friend Jean David, would also reflect "that Moldavian style of the nineteenth century, sobre and yet discreetly ornamental"[13] GMC recalled the notes of prince Charles de Ligne (1735-1814) on Moldavia written at the close of the eighteenth century.[14] He pointed out that de Ligne, who "knew the whole of Europe like his own garden"[15], in his *Coup d'œil sur Belœil et sur une grande partie des jardins de l'Europe* (1795) had greatly admired Moldavian country retreats and city palaces in Jassy for their version of the "Palladian branch of Late Renaissance"[16].

GMC held the view that Jassy was a city of great architectural, historical and symbolic importance, similar to the role played, for instance, in Romania, by Sibiu/Hermannstadt, Sighişoara/Schässburg, or Braşov/Kronstadt in Transylvania, and elsewhere for example by Rome in Italy, Warsaw in Poland, Heidelberg in Germany, or Oxford and Cambridge in England.

On Jassy he gave a passionate and erudite lecture, *Jassy, an urban landscape* (Oraşul Iaşi, un peisagiu). He delivered the lecture first in Bucharest on 2nd October 1955,[17] and then, in an updated version, on behalf of the Union of Romanian Architects at the University of Jassy on 21st March 1958. Given his status of an enemy of the people, the invitation of both the Union of Romanian Architects and the University of Jassy was indeed an act of civilian courage. It was not until 1981 that the text was published, thanks to Dr Eugenia Greceanu.[18] She concluded her substantial introduction noting that "the integral publication of the text of GMC's lecture would help to save, not only what is left of Jassy's historic urban fabric, but also the surviving historic centres elsewhere in the country"[19]. But GMC was ignored, "and in due course Jassy was torn apart and systematised",[20] as were many other towns and cities throughout Romania. In 1990 Dinu C. Giurescu, the great Romanian historian, published on behalf of the World Monuments' Funds and US/ICOMOS an impressive report on the destructions carried out by the Ceausescu regime, *The Razing of Romania's Past*.[21]

Jassy, capital of the former principality of Moldavia, was, for GMC, the only major Romanian city with an unbroken historical continuity in the course of the short five hundred years of architectural tradition of the Danubian Principalities. Yet since Jassy became a provincial city in the aftermath of the unification of Wallachia and Moldavia in 1859, a great part of the historic fabric was replaced, which resulted in a considerable architectural and urbanistic loss.[22] On this tendency he observed in his lecture at the University of Jassy in 1958:

"Urban planners often turn to the pick axe as a conclusive argument and final solution. But such a sporting activity should be resolutely avoided, for the organization and rearrangement of an old city is a matter of common sense, sensitivity and taste."[23]

But Jassy still boasted a proud university along with important monuments set in a unique city landscape. Therefore, GMC urged the Romanian authorities to classify the historic centre of Jassy as a Heritage Protection Area.[24]

261 GMC, *The northern twin pavilion of the Metropolitan church in Jassy* (ADT).

262 Portrait of *Charles Joseph de Ligne* (1735-1814), taken from. C.-A. Cantacuzène, *Prince de Ligne*. Paris 1934.

263 GMC, *Twin pavilions of the Metropolitan church in Jassy* (ADT).

264 GMC, *Sketch of the twin pavilions and public square in front of the Metropolitan church in Jassy* (AMLSC).

On 26th and 27th October 1960 the University of Jassy celebrated its centennial festivity. GMC's project for the Metropolitan Church was one of the principal attractions. Many visitors, including guests from European universities, enjoyed GMC's guiding tour of the construction site with one completed pavilion. The priest Paul Mihail remembered the dean of the University of Padua to have been delighted at the porticos and Florentine conference hall. Two days later GMC suddenly suffered a severe internal bleeding. The doctors in the Spiridon Hospital of Jassy were powerless. In the night on 1st November 1960 GMC died. He was laid to rest in the Eternitatea cemetery in Jassy.[25] To his family he left some drawings, watercolours, oil paintings, memories and a handful of letters:

"That in black ink my love may still shine bright."[26]

265 GMC, *Moldavian tree* (detail), c. 1958. Oil on cardboard (AMLSC).

266 GMC, *Flowers for Sanda*, c. 1956. Oil on cardboard (AMLSC).

G.M. CANTACUZINO MCMXLV

Part II: On the *classical attitude*

268 GMC *et al*, *Simetria VIII* (1947). Frontispiece.

Explanatory Note

In his 1940 article on classicism, written for the *Simetria Dictionary* GMC states, "Classicism is a term we do not find in philosophical dictionaries. In principle it does not have a philosophical meaning."[1] Nonetheless, this is precisely what GMC intends to do – infuse Classicism with a philosophical note. For him, "classicism is an ethical attitude"[2] and coins it "classical attitude"[3]. This approach might seem unusual.

For this reason, and without attempting to be exhaustive, I shall try to rethink GMC's intellectual world by sketching his version of a *classical attitude* and thereby revealing some of the corner-stones to this approach. In addition to discussing GMC's concept of architecture and of being an architect, I shall discuss history, tradition, and modernism. Finally I shall try to place him within the contemporary European context as well as within his artistic and intellectual background.

For GMC a *classical attitude* is an ethical attitude, which in regard to architecture stems from a deep and complex cultural relationship between ethics and aesthetics. This concept is based on the assumption that traditions and modernism are mutually compatible. GMC takes advantage of two kinds of differentiation extensively used by the French philosopher Henri Bergson: In his *Creative Evolution* of 1907 Bergson distinguishes between differences in nature and differences in degree. Secondly he distinguishes between closed systems and movements or streams of thought.

In addition the *classical attitude* could be regarded as a cultural strategy with which GMC tries to establish himself within contemporary Romania and Europe. This strategy is influenced by the debate on call to order launched by Jean Cocteau in 1926 in his *Rappel à l'ordre*. Also under consideration is a current theory on the relationship between the Old and New: in his essay *Über das Neue. Versuch einer Kulturökonomie* (2004) the philosopher Boris Groys explores strategies of innovation as a development of cultural exchange. This theoretical discussion could help examining the *classical attitude* in terms of cultural policy and history.

267 Opposite:
GMC, *Andrea Palladio's Villa Foscari on the Brenta (La Malcontenta)*.
Ink drawing (1945), *Simetria VII* (1946).

269 *The foundation*, after Vignola. GMC *et al*, *Simetria II* (1940).

Attempt at explaining the classical attitude

GMC's understanding of the classical attitude

The *classical attitude*, pursued by GMC with indefatigable persistance, runs through his writings like Ariadne's thread: from his very first essay *Introduction to the Study of Architecture* (1926), via *Palladio. Un essai critique* (1928, 1931); the public letter to Marcel Janco (1931) and other articles from the 1930s like the programmatic broadcast lecture *Traditionalism and Modernism* (1932) and the manifesto-like *Declaration* which introduces the cultural magazine *Simetria* (1939), through to the essay *Opinions* (1947) and his last conferences in the late 1950s.

The terms *classical* and *classicism* show that GMC values architectural and cultural history. He stresses the importance of choice inherent to the two terms: choice with regard to "old and tried and customary things"[1]. At the same time he discovers that the "conventional understanding of the term classical is rather restrictive, as it generally only labels the Graeco-Roman architectural movement and its successors. We think this definition is wrong."[2] GMC liberates the aesthetic notion of classicism from a purely stylistic perspective and binds it to ethics: "To be classical, I think, embraces a certain state of mind and does not imply a doctrine based on style."[3] This attitude denotes a "mental balance between knowledge and feeling; between individuality and tradition; between a cheerful present and a studied past and an intuitively prepared and instigated future."[4]

Notion of history and tradition

This conceptual approach relies on the notion of history as process, which GMC shares with Georges Bratiano and the group of young historians of the *Romanian Review of History*. Striving for authenticity, this notion of history is expressed in a "social, economic, and cultural orientation"[1], whilst rejecting ideological or political abuse. Any attempt at reconstructing the complexity of historical events must be based on facts and an awareness of that particular epoch. Marc Bloch and Henri Focillon make a similar point. As Natalie Adamson notes in *The Burlington Magazine* (May 2008), "Focillon [...] conceive[s] of tradition as an open and synthesising force permitting both classical heritage and a more spontaneous conception of art to be assimilated within the French esprit."[2] In an undogmatic way he advocates a "process-like notion of history [...] [and] liquifies tradition."[3] Bloch, on his part, favours of the concept of the "critical science of historical change [...] in the age of the theory of relativity and quantum mechanics".[4]

GMC belongs to the same school of thought, as he makes clear in his *Introduction to Vitruvius* (1947): "True historiography is not judgemental, it only detects facts and relates a story. At any rate an objective historiography worth of its name must neither be tendentious nor manipulative."[5] And in his *Letters to Simon* he comments on the same subject: "To judge, examineing our past with the eyes of the present, constitutes the same error that passionate historians make when they condemn whole centuries of civilisation that are found wanting by the present. In this exploration we shall enter, at least in appearance, into conflict with morality, out of the fear of complacency. But in the exploration of facts, images and feelings, it is not a question of complacency towards the self, but only of lucid attention. What was good or evil, what seems to us blameworthy or praiseworthy, must be viewed in the totality of its valences."[6]

This approach recalls a maxim by Montesquieu:

"To apply the ideas of the present time to distant ages is the most fruitful source of error."[7]

GMC's attempt at reviving the antique notion of tradition is also a contribution to updating the critical tradition of Enlightenment, which itself is derived from the critical antique concept of tradition. Indeed, GMC regards "tradition [as] a restlessness which keeps the spirit awake"[8] with respect to both the Old and New. To him "tradition is a critical equilibrum and not a reaction".[9] Certainly he refuses to idealize tradition, and draws upon Catullus:

"'Every man has his vanity assigned him,
But no one sees the pack that's strapped behind him'"[10].

Citing Catullus, a classic Roman poet, GMC subscribes to the view that Graeco-Roman antiquity was the first European classic period in which a critical consciousness was the principal corner-stone of the philosophical approach.

For GMC, this critical consciousness emerged from "certainties"[11] which were fruits of "a wealth of experiences preserved in the memory of mankind"[12]. And harmony, as perceived by antique thinkers, springs from a critical consciousness based on a close relationship between aesthetics and ethics. "This restlessness of tradition is imbued with an incurable nostalgia for the Golden Age when man strove to perfection and the highest idealised version of himself. This version can only be found in the past."[13]

GMC's nostalgia for the past, however, is a disciplined and sceptical one. Most of all, he aims to discern from the past some guiding architectural and philosophical principles. A true Bergsonian, GMC is sceptical of replacing the past with the future in terms of worship.[14] In fact he proves himself a true conservative, very much like T. S. Eliot, another one of his favourite authors. For Eliot tradition is also, as Roger Scruton notes in *The Aesthetics of Architecture* (1980), "an ideal to be rediscovered by the modern consciousness"[15]:

"Tradition [...] cannot be inherited, and if you want it you must obtain it by great labour. It involves, in the first place, the historical sense, which [...] compels a man to write not merely with his own generation in his bones, but with a feeling that the whole of the literature of Europe from Homer and within it the whole of the literature of his own country has a simultaneous existence and composes a simultaneous order. This historical sense, which is a sense of the timeless as well as of the temporal together, is what makes a writer traditional. And it is at the same time what makes a writer most acutely conscious of his place in time, of his own contemporaneity."[16]

This spirit, which applies to architecture as well, is reinforced in Eliot's essay *Tradition* (1934): "We are always in danger, in clinging to an old tradition, or attempting to re-establish one, of confusing the vital and the unessential, the real and the sentimental. Our second danger is to associate tradition

270 *Urbanism*, after Vignola.
GMC *et al*, *Simetria II* (1940).

271 GMC, *Villa Foscari (La Malcontenta)*. Chalk drawing, *Palladio*. Bucharest 1932.

with the immovable [...], instead of aiming to stimulate the life which produced that condition in its time. [...] What we can do is to use our minds, remembering that a tradition without intelligence is not worth having, to discover what is the best life for us not as a political abstraction, but as a particular people in a particular place; what in the past is worth preserving and what should be rejected; and what conditions, within our power to bring about, would foster the society that we desire."[17]

Like Henri Berson GMC updates the metaphysical aspect of the antique notion of tradition "in opposition to the structural crisis of tradition or its absence in contemporary civilization".[18]

Bergon's *Creative Evolution* (1907), for instance, "is regarded as a work of natural philosophy that combines physics and metaphysics; it is a fresh version of Plato's Timeus and reasoned by a modern man who read the Genesis. It is the continued creation of the world."[19]

In my view, GMC interprets the "nostalgia for the origins"[20] as an expression of the transcendental ethics as seen, for instance, by Wittgenstein[21] and relates it to the artistic matrix of classicism. So the "tradition of the antique notion of harmony"[22] is still of tremendous significance to us. Writing in the same spirit as Sir Ernst Gombrich, who in his influential *The Story of Art* referred to the early sixteenth century Italian Renaissance as "[h]armony attained"[23], GMC maintains in his entry to the *Simetria Dictionary* (1940):

"Harmony and critical consciousness acknowledge a postulate which to creative minds is a certainty: In art there are perfect harmonies (or: in art harmony has been achieved); in thought, truth is bound to remain for ever relative, whereas in beauty perfection has been accomplished."[24]

The classical attitude, the Aristotelian theory of the mean state and Palladio

In his essay on classicism GMC undertakes a structural tour de force through the history of architecture, well beyond Graeco-Roman antiquity and Europe. He explores how the notion of classicism, once freed from the historical sequence of styles and then grounded on ethics, materialized over time.

"Having looked at the past and having analysed some historical moments, we aim to relieve the notion of classicism of that of style."[1] In doing so, "we soon realized that this balanced and cheerful outlook never ceases to exist, but instead overcomes time and again the archaic prejudices, the naturalistic reactions, the romantic crises and the principles of positivism."[2]

Actually GMC argues for a modern notion of the aesthetic prime examples of architectural history, thus for the modern notion of classics. He also seems to question how that "perfection in beauty"[3] might have been achieved. In fact, he presumes that the birth of the classics could have been stimulated by an outstanding ethical typology. GMC believes that the classicism would express the Aristotelian and humanist ideal of "moral virtue"[4] as a "mean state"[5].

The *classical attitude*, then, would be nothing less than a strategy to transpose this philosophical approach into art and architecture. There may be other authorities on the subject of classicism GMC could have considered. Gottfried Semper, for instance, in his 1869 Zurich lecture *On styles in architecture* suggests "how the 'cosmopolitan architecture of the future' could develop from Roman antiquity"[6].

GMC mentions Semper only once, praising his Dresden opera house on which the Odessa concert hall was modelled.[7] Nonetheless Semper's work was part of the basic artistic knowledge of GMC and the *Simetria* circle. Tudor Vianu, for instance, in his *Simetria* essay *The aesthetics of building materials*, reviews Semper's cladding theory.[8] GMC himself defends the belief in the polychromy of Antique and Byzantine architecture in his contribution on Byzantium to the *Simetria Dictionary* in 1943.[9]

In his study *From Palladio to Schinkel* (1911) the German architectural historian Paul Klopfer aims, very much like Semper, to formulate the "characteristics of a classicist architecture as derived from the Palladian school"[10]. In addition, GMC could have been inspired by Henri Focillon's view on classicism, put forward in his *The Life of Forms in Art* (1934):

"But classicism is not the result of conformism. On the contrary, it has been created out of one final, ultimate experience, the audacity and vitality of which it has never lost. How good it would be could we rejuvenate this venerable word – a word that has today lost all meaning through so much careless and indeed illegitimate usage! Classicism: not a slow and monotonous application of 'rules', but a pure, quick delight, [...] so delicate that the pointer of the scale scarcely trembles."[11]

Of all architects, GMC finds Andrea Palladio the supreme embodiment of the dynamic equilibrum as suggested by Aristotle's *mean state* or Chamfort's "[e]st in medio verum"[12]. For GMC Palladio is indeed "the prototype of the Palladian artist, who introduces hellenic subtlety into the noisy Renaissance. In architecture he stands for what Mozart represents in music: *Tiefe aus Oberflächlichkeit* (depth out of superficiality), is how Goethe used to put it."[13]

Goethe himself presents Raphael as such a model: "Raphael [...] worked all his life with constant and ever-growing ease. His mental vigor and his physical energies were in such complete harmony that it we feel safe in saying that no modern artist has conceived his works so purely and effectively, and expressed himself so lucidly as did Raphael. He was one of those talents who present us with the freshest water from the purest source."[14]

In a similar vein, GMC when standing in front of Palladio's villa Foscari "is tempted to passionately meditate upon the secrets of so graceful a fulfilment ... like all true fulfilments. [...] Here proportion appears to be the one and only measure: after all foundations have been laid by the individual rhythm, the module would be nothing else than an attribute, instrument of control and the last collaborator in establishing harmony. [...] [L]a Malcontenta has led us to this double conclusion: first there is a balance between knowledge and emotion and secondly a balance between the two of them and the act of design."[15]

GMC's question brings to mind a paradox aphorism of Brancusi, an aphorism chosen by the Dutch architect Herman Hertzberger as motto for his *Lessons for students in architecture* (1995):

272 John Michael Rysbrack, *Andrea Palladio*. Statue at Lord Burlington's Chiswick House (1726-29), London. (Photograph ADT).

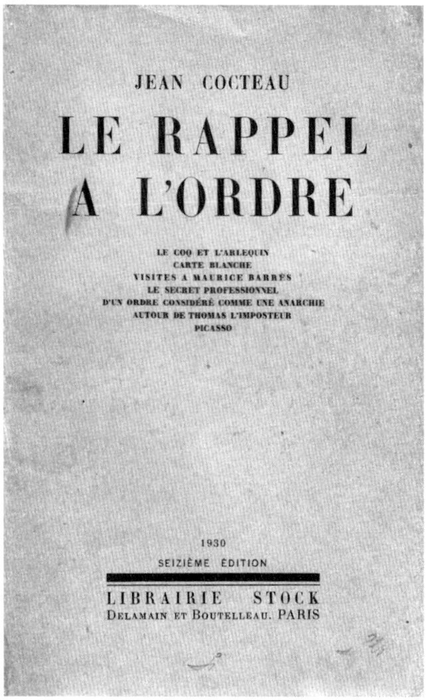

273 Jean Cocteau, *Le Rappel à l'ordre*. Paris 1930. Front cover. © Éditions Stock, Paris.

"Things are not difficult to perform.
What is truly difficult is to place oneself
In the proper mood for performing them."[16]

GMC's *classical attitude* and his reading of Palladio's work can be regarded as a contribution to the European debate on the "importance of Classicism"[17] in the first half of the twentieth century. In 1899 this debate was greatly influenced by *The classical art*, Heinrich Wölfflin's treatise on "the great masters of Central Italy"[18].

Like GMC in his *Palladio* (1928 & 1932), Wölfflin in 1931 will appreciate "Palladio beyond the formula of the 'Great and Simple' as a witness of human depth"[19]. In the same line as Heinrich Wölfflin and later Werner Oechslin, GMC highlights Goethe's reception of Palladio:

"*The Four Books of Architecture* radiate an integrity and modesty which fully justify Goethe's opinion of Palladio as the prototype of the great man."[20]

The recourse to antiquity

Parallel to his declared belief in the Graeco-Roman Classic GMC follows a tradition of the Parisian École des Beaux-Arts, that, in the words of Werner Oechslin, "only classic art would not run out and hence claim an enduring importance"[1].

As we have seen, this outlook is backed up by leading art historians and architects of the day. Especially "[i]n the first decade of the twentieth century",[2] as Ákos Morávanszky notes, "different kinds of classicism coexisted."[3] Classicism has been momentous for leading European architects suchs as Auguste Perret, Sir Edwin Lutyens, Otto Wagner and his disciples including Max Fabiani, Josef Hoffmann, and Jozé Plečnik; it was "also the style of choice of the reform movement"[4], involving "leading Werkbund architects"[5] like the German Fritz Schumacher and Hungarian József Vágó.[6]

The Viennese master Adolf Loos also comes out in favour of Classicism. In *Der Architekt* (1898) he recommends that he who aspires to rejuvenate architecture should try to become a classicist like Schinkel and Semper, since "the great architect of the future will be a classicist. One who does not follow the works of his predecessors, but who makes a direct connection to classical antiquity"[7].

In the manifesto-like preface of the inaugural *Simetria* issue of 1939, GMC and Octav Doicescu advocate similarly to Loos: "Vitruvian symmetry is eternal."[8] What at first sight could seem to be a reactionary step back towards a return to order will prove to be a vital pillar of a call to order as championed by Adolf Loos or Jean Cocteau in *Rappel à l'ordre* (1926). Both the return to order and call to order detect the lack of a present order and imply the existence of an established order in the past, like in Antiquity. The return to order is a mere retrospective attempt at reimposing that past order, whereas the call to order is quite the contrary: it asserts the necessity of clarifying the premises of a present order, to which the past might give helpful hints. The call to order is open "towards both directions, to the past as well as to the future"[9]. GMC makes this clear in the motto of his cultural review, a motto which also embodies his *classical attitude*:

"Symmetry, in its original sense, means felicitous proportion or commensurability."[10]

GMC's revival of the antique notion of symmetry is certainly not a recommendation to imitate antiquity in the sense of merely copying. Rather, GMC's approach bears comparison with José Ortega y Gasset's concept of studying history. It is a question of tracking down, bringing back and updating notions and principles for present tasks:

"History is so difficult a task for the very reason that because it is repetition [...] and etymologically Wiederholung means to 'go back to take something that has been left more or less at a distance'; hence 'to search it'."[11]

This idea goes back to Kierkegaard and was renewed by Heidegger "in talking of Wiederholung, a word which in modern German means in fact 'repetition'. But Heidegger, like every genuinely great thinker– and beyond question he is one – on saying a word does not have in mind merely its present meaning, but also its whole human past".[12]

GMC seems to be conscious of such an approach, as he recognizes the Vitruvian or antique notion of symmetry as a theme on which innumerable variations can be produced. In the chapter *Les Lois Antiques* (The Rules of Antiquity) of his essay on *Palladio* (1928) he writes:

274 Corner detail of the Parthenon, Athens. Photograph GMC 1933 (AGMC-IP).

"Life spins and unravels its threads in the course of events and deeds of man and its purpose remains unknown to us. Art forever recommences an eternal theme on infinite variations. The variations are our own matter. The theme, by contrast, is given to us. So it is the theme which we should try to discern among the works we have inherited from the past."[13]

Wittgenstein, in his *Tractatus* of 1922 sees it similarly:

"2.024 Substance is what exists independently of what is the case.

2.025 It is form and content.

2.0251 Space, time and colour (colouredness) are forms of objects. [...]

2.0271 The object is the fixed, the existent; the configuration is the changing, the variable."[14]

Naturally GMC follows the authority of Palladio, who, as Oechslin notes in *Palladianismus* (2008), studied antiquity with "thoughtfulness and method"[15]. In his *Palladio* (1928), GMC observes:

"Times differ in their notions of tradition and science since every epoch pursues ideals of its own. Sometimes it projects them into the future, sometimes into the past. The mystery of creation will forever slip away from us. To confine architecture to an intellectualised and symbolic geometry, to Vitruvian rules or to expose it to a sentimental and thus arbitrary approach – all these ideas are misguided, for it is natural that man imparts the rhythms of life to his creations."[16]

At the same time this thought could be seen in the wake of the Aristotelian mimesis. Plotinus, whose philosophy is essential for GMC, also approves of it: one should not imitate external nature, but an ideal one – eventually, resembling a construct of antique Greek philosophy. Mimesis is a basic term of Aristotelian poetics. In essence "mimesis means an artist does not create out of nothing, but with reference."[17] One aspect of this referential character could be a metaphysical one as suggested, for instance, by Plotinus.

275 The Propylaea, Athens.
Photograph GMC 1933 (AGMC-IP).

The legitimacy of imitation as instrumental in the development of art and architecture is certainly contested by Modernist art and architectural criticism. It is only recently that original approaches are being rediscovered, like Gabriel Tarde's *Les Lois de l'imitation* (1890), a book mentioned in the surviving inventory of GMC's library.

Referring to the way imitation is dealt with by writers, Cees Nooteboom finds Aristotelian mimesis often mistaken for an imitation of external nature:

"Writers are people [...] who do not imitate the reality based on misunderstanding the Aristotelian receipt. On the contrary, they profit from the endless possibilities of art, in order to violate it, to undermine it, to turn it upside down, or to aggrandize it – for without art life is unbearable. Therefore writers do the only job they truly master: they fabricate lies and practise witchcraft. The rest is done by television, politicians, and sociologists – the adequate or inadequate administrators of true reality. Their lies, to be sure, hardly constitute art."[18]

Already Plotinus seems to think it necessary to identify this misunderstanding: "Still the arts are not to be slighted on the ground that they create by imitation of natural objects; for, to begin with, these natural objects are themselves imitations; then, we must recognize that they give no bare reproduction of the thing seen but go back to the Ideas from which Nature itself derives, and, furthermore, that much of their work is all their own; they are holders of beauty and add when nature is lacking. Thus Pheidias wrought the Zeus upon no model among things of sense but by apprehending what form Zeus must take if he chose to become manifest at sight."[19]

Undoubtedly GMC's understanding of history as a process and of tradition as a critical consciousness significantly influences his concept of architecture. Although he admires the concern for classicism on behalf of the Viennese School for Art History led by Wölfflin and Burckhardt, he has not at all embraced its Hegelian frame of reference – the frame of reference that history is divided into distinct consecutive epochs, each of them with its own "'spirit'" or 'Lebensgefühl'"[20], and that true architecture must show the underlying spirit of its particular age.

Similar to Ernst Gombrich, GMC rejects a compartmentalized view on architecture: for him discontinuities and ruptures alone are not decisive. Gombrich, on his part disapproves of "the naïve misinterpretation of the constant change in art as a continuous progress"[21].

Likewise GMC perceives architecture as an ongoing phenomenon, a continuity in which tradition and modernism perpetually coexist and interweave with each other. In an explanatory note in *Simetria VII* (1946) he makes himself clear:

"The contemporaneity we are concerned with is rather relative. Starting from the presumption that in art there are permanent values, we have set out to seek these values both in the present and remote past. Relevant, to us, will be everything embraced by our initial frame of mind, that is to free ourselves of the burdensome archaisms and obsessive innovations alike, in favour of self-imposed principles which spring from a lucid and rigorous critical spirit."[22]

This is why GMC is concerned with common bonds, which might offer starting points for a critical and fertile transformational strategy for interweaving tradition with modernism. Eventually this is key to GMC's approach:

"It is not the varieties of style that we are concerned with, but rather the thread running through them. Considering the fluidity between disciplines, any attempt at a rigid classification based on style is illusory as the essentials of architecture do not consist in the individual nor in the particular."[23]

276 GMC, *The Spanish Steps,* Rome. Ink drawing, 1936 (AMLSC).

Concept of architecture and its invariants

Thus GMC aims to scrape principles of composition in humanist architecture off the historic languages of classicism, in order to rescue them from the formalistic and reductionist "sterility of the sleepy academies of fine arts"[1].

Georges Gromort also complains about academies inclining to compromise not only classicism and its principles as an architecture of humanism, but also the study of history and classics. On the latter he writes in his *Essai sur la Théorie de l'Architecture* (1946):

"I should never stop recommending, as regards the study of a work of art, to take […], not the preconceived point of view of contemporary man, but of the artist who created that work of art. First in line we should ask ourselves if he achieved the result he had aimed at […]. [W]e could say that every monument contains something timeless."[2]

And "Heinrich Wölfflin", as Ákos Morávanszky notes, "has [also] studied, like Semper and Riegel, the transformation of forms throughout history in order to find general principles of interpretation."[3]

In addition GMC argues "the term classic […] must not evoke the image of a gable or of a colonnade".[4] Other architects argue in the same spirit as GMC. Josef Frank, for instance, states:

"By antique tradition I do not mean the use of columns, cornices or other architectural forms of particular periods – which, by the way, will never completely disappear – but striving towards the organic shaping of inanimate matter. This is the true tradition which will back up our civilization as long as man stays the measure of all things."[5]

Subsequently GMC, in the wake of Gromort, and maybe of Wölfflin, defends the study of history. For "neither the forms nor the styles should captivate our attention, but the spirit, discipline and method which gave birth to them! The study of history will not become fecund unless the concern with style is limited to a reasonable measure, so that we will be free to turn our attention to the great and noble issues which preoccupied our predecessors!"[6]

But he does not aim to establish a closed system of architectural theory. Like Vitruvius, Alberti, Palladio, Schinkel and Loos GMC pursues the "search for a contemporary discipline, […] for 'the greatest liberty is born of the of the greatest rigour' (Paul Valéry)".[7] He only seeks for "some guiding principles"[8]. These guiding principles, in his view, are closely interlocked and anthropologically rooted. This involves a pragmatic approach to the relationship between theory and practice. In the *Introduction to the Masterplan of Bucharest* of 1935, for instance, GMC and his colleagues declare:

277 GMC, *Bench of Cippolino marble in the entrance hall of the Bragadiru apartment building*, Bucharest (1934-1935; W 54). A quiet homage to Loos (Photograph Marius Voica.)

"A theoretical scheme is usually rigid, whereas its practical application is elastic. Therefore we should not confuse theory with practice."[9]

GMC's approach is in the same line with Bergson:

"The free act is incommensurable with the idea, and its 'rationality' must be defined by this very incommensurability, which admits the discovery of as much intelligibility within it as we will."[10]

Gide is another pivotal reference for GMC:

"'A theory is good if it provides not the greatest calm, but the greatest efficiency. A theory is good if it enables you to surpass it'(661). In short, theory is only a tool at the disposal of the artist. An object of art cannot be the visualization of a particular theory, since the creative process always slips away from criticism. [...] We must differentiate between rules and theories. Rules represent a consciously and deliberately undertaken act to discipline the creative process. Theories, by contrast, are merely subsequent explanations or justifications."[11]

Likewise, Paul Valéry's figure of Socrates declares in *Eupalinos*:

"The project is separate from the act, and the act from the result."[12]
Eventually, GMC's understanding of the relationship between theory and practice turns out to be pragmatic in a contemporary sense; or, as Ákos Moravánszky observes: "The practical application of a theory has never produced notable architecture. Many architectural theories had been subsequent explanations to certain architectural movements. Theory, in this sense, is a discipline of reflecting and teaching architecture." [13]

As regards the nature of architecture, GMC is reluctant to define it: he believes architecture is an art. Yet he insists on a basic distinction between architecture and the fine arts. For him, architecture is rather a practical art which echoes the antique or Vitruvian concept of architecture, that is, the earliest codification of architecture that came down to us.

This concept reflects Aristotelian philosophy, as pointed out by Colin St John Wilson in *The ethics of architecture*.[14] He also notes that „[o]rder, proportionality and clarity [...] were metaphysical ideas before they were translated into optical facts. They were held to be properties of the work, not subjective sensations in the eye of the beholder; all that was communicable to the eye was answerable first to the mind."[15]

Aristotle himself states that "[t]he rationally practical state of mind then is different from the rationally productive state. Accordingly neither of them is included in the other; for action is not production, and production is not action. But as architecture e.g. is an art, and as it may be defined to be a rationally productive state of mind, and there is no art which is not a rationally productive state of mind, nor any such state of mind which is not an art, it follows that art must be the same thing as a productive state of mind under the guidance of true reason.

Again all art has to do with creation, i.e. it has to contrive and consider how to create some one or other of the things whose existence is contingent rather than necessary, and whose original cause lies in the producer, and not in the production itself. For art does not apply to things which exist or come into existence by necessity or by nature, as the original cause of these things lies in themselves. Production and action being different, it necessarily follows that the end of art is production and not action. There is a sense too in which chance and art have the same sphere, as Agathon says: 'Art fosters Fortune, Fortune fosters Arts.'"[16]

In other words, architecture is an evolving practical art; it shapes form and space and relies on a close relationship between ethics and aesthetics. GMC's concept of architecture combines the Vitruvian opening of antique architecture with a process-like understanding of history. He is convinced that a creative mind can proceed only from its own experience, for there are "no absolute fix points, but only points of comparison and control"[17].

It is the critical consciousness which distills such points of comparison and control from a liquefied concept of history: guiding principles and classics. As a result, GMC recommends, in the words of Jacques François Blondel, "the comparative study of the work of the great masters"[18]. For GMC, classics, that is, outstanding personalities, works of art and buildings play a key role in education.

First of all, the study of classics is beneficial in the education of taste.

"There is plenty to learn about architecture in the same way there is from music: the classics serve first and foremost as a means of education; after that, as a guide in life; and lastly, to teach one to judge and to create. That of course does not mean that one has to spend one's life drawing columns."[19]

And the taste, that is, the sense of beauty, is, so GMC argues, perhaps in the wake of Alexander Baumgarten, an intelligence of its own: "An artist needs above all talent and 'le sens artistique', a sense of beauty and form and that is, in fact, a type of intelligence."[20]

Secondly, the classics are instrumental in searching a spiritual family. This might encourage self-knowledge as, in the words of Gide and quoted by GMC, "'[t]he best way to learn to know oneself is to try to understand others'"[21]. And GMC adds: "This is true for individuals in particular, and for civilisations in general, as well as for nations in their relations to each other."[22] And finally, classics perform a vital role in developing "[c]ritical faculties [...] – these age old friends of liberty"[23].

Based on the human module, "architecture is perhaps the last expression, in a chronological order, of the human inclination to organize and harmonize forms"[24].

And GMC continues: "For we should not be mistaken: In the beginning, men fled under a roof in order to escape the forces of nature, but also the endlessness of the sky. To build means to harmonize the universe with the scale of human emotions."[25]

Then GMC welcomes the encyclopedic nature of architecture, which involves different techniques from thinking via conversing, organizing, supervising, sketching, drawing, construction design, material knowledge, through to craftsmanship and many more. Basically "art and technology are interdependent"[26].

At the same time, architecture would imitate nature only in so far as it obeys the laws of nature and tries to make them intelligible, as in the case of tectonic culture. Palladio advocates in the same line:

278 Adolf Loos, *Bench at the entrance of the Villa Müller*, Prague (1928-1930). Photograph 1930.

279 Colin St John Wilson, *Marble bench in the elevator niche of the British Library*, St Pancras, London (1974-1998). Another quiet homage to Loos (Photograph ADT).

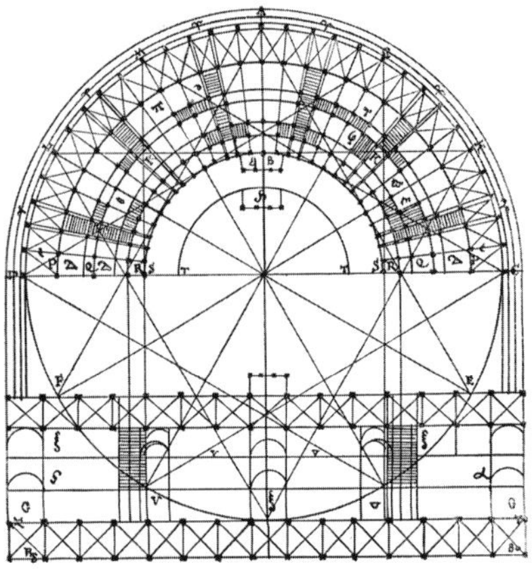

280 *Theatre*, after Vitruvius. GMC *et al*, *Simetria IV* (1942).

"I say therefore, that architecture, as well as all the other arts, being an imitatrix of nature, can suffer nothing that either alienates or deviates from that which is agreeable to nature; from whence we see, that the ancient architects, who made their edifices of wood, when they began to make them of stone, instituted that the columns should be less thicker at the top than at the bottom, taking example from the trees, all which are thinner at the top than in the trunk, or near the root. And because it is very probable, that those things are depressed upon which some great weight is put, bases were placed under the columns, which, with their bastoni and cavetti, seem to be crushed with the burden laid upon them."[27]

Relying upon mathematics and utility in a comprehensive sense, architecture would be a second nature, or counter-nature, with the power to ennoble the natural landscape. Being committed to tradition, society and the *genius loci* of landscape or urban texture, architecture translates social needs and cultural values into shaped matter and is one of the supreme expressions of a civilization.

GMC regards architectural design as a composition rooted in the triad of proportion, rhythm and harmony. Following a humanistic approach, this aesthetic triad is based on the human scale. Man himself has not changed throughout history: his physical, spiritual and intellectual constitution remained the same. Consequently the aforementioned principle contains three meanings: practical, spiritual and intellectual – all of which are different in kind, but nevertheless inseparably interrelated within man.

As GMC unfolds his maxim, he suggests pairs of mutually compatible concepts based on terms different in kind, but not in intensity. According to the intelligible antique sense of order, that is, to the dynamic equilibrium of antique harmony, these terms are not exclusive but complementary – such as art and technique, objectivity and subjectivity, tradition and modernism, utility and symbol. So GMC highlights that the "secret lying at the core of architecture is how to recognize the symbol of the features of utility, and the features of utility in life."[28] After all, "architecture comes into being only if the bare necessities are surpassed."[29]

This perspective recalls Goethe's frame of mind who relates "necessity and usefulness"[30] to sensual harmony, which might have inspired Schinkel to link the historical and the poetic realm. It is, as Moravánszky notes, in the face of "the rigid doctrine of moralising functionalism"[31] that Schinkel gains this insight: "Quite soon I slipped into the error of pure abstraction. Whenever I designed a project merely on the ground of its trivial aspects of function and construction, there emerged a dry and rigid building that lacked all freedom of spirit and excluded two essential features: the historical and the poetical."[32] Simultaneously one could think of two motifs used by Semper: "the symbolism of construction"[33] and the "postulate of necessity"[34]. Otto Wagner's verdict "Artis sola domina necessitas"[35] mirrors these ideas, as does the maxime of Jean Mignot, a French architect of the Middle Ages: "Ars sine scientia nihil est."[36]

But usefulness and symbol fulfill another function in GMC's thinking. When he suggests that they "recall the Vitruvian method of conceiving architectural forms and spaces"[37], he reminds, as it were, of the evocative role played by "the written word [...] in the Graeco-Roman world"[38]. This had been emphasized, for instance, by Charles-Auguste de Sainte-Beuve in his *Cahiers*, André Gide in his *Journal*, and Arnold Toynbee in his *Civilization on Trial*. GMC's reading of Vitruvius shows, not that he would deplore the lack of a closed system of architectural theory, but that he understands the *Ten Books on Architecture* according to "the Greek line of approach"[39] as pointed out by Toynbee: "to study books not just for their own sake, but also because they are the key to the life of the people who wrote them."[40]

281 *Theatre*, Segesta, Sicily.
Photograph GMC, 1930s (AGMC-IP).

Drawing on the explanations of Gilbert Murray, late professor of Greek Studies at Oxford University, Arnold Toynbee highlights the special meaning of text in the Graeco-Roman world. "Like the present-day broadcaster's typescript, the Graeco-Roman 'book' was really a system of mnemonics for conjuring up winged words, and not a book in our sense of something intended for reading to oneself, like the ordinary printed volume that is produced nowadays by publishers."[41]

According to Tonybee, the present Western way of studying texts is a Christian-Jewish Rabbinical method. It was handed down to us by the Greeks and Romans, but goes back to "the Syrian world"[42] and "the Rabbinical method"[43] which treats a book as "the revealed word of God"[44]. The advantages of this method are obvious: "closeness and thoroughness"[45].

However it "has two vices. It inclines one to think of a book as a thing in itself – something static and dead – instead of seeing it, for what it is, as the material track or echo or débris of human action (for intellectual acts are as authentic a form of action as exertions of will power or physical energy). The second vice is really the same thing stated in more general or philosophical terms. The Rabbinical method of study makes one inclined to think of life in terms of books instead of vice versa. The opposite method – which is the Greek line of approach – is to study books not just for their own sake, but also because they are the key to the life of the people who wrote them."[46]

In his *Journal* entry of 8th June 1921 Gide advocates a similar position and cites a phrase from Sainte-Beuve's *Cahiers*. GMC reviewed Gide's *Journal* in Simetria. The essay shows GMC's high regard for Gide.

Indeed GMC very much appreciates the power of order or balance of the "Vitruvian spirit, which symbolizes the ancient virtues and the enduring hellenism"[47]. And he adds:

"By Vitruvian spirit I do not refer to the obscure character of Vitruvius, which is difficult to grasp. Instead I address the huge anonymous potential contained in his treatise [...] [including] the Roman integrity, the Etruscan constructivism and the Greek subtlety."[48] Vitruvius "codified a number of enduring principles conceived by the Greeks: the principle of equilibrium, of measure and of symmetry."[49] These principles lead to "form and commensurability [...] – two notions that lie at the heart of architecture."[50]

282 *Bust of a philosopher, perhaps Plotinus* (c. 205-270 AD), Ostia Museum inv. no. 68. c. 250 AD.

Ethics and Aesthetics

Features of the relationship between Aesthetics and transcendental Ethics
The terms ethics and aesthetics seem to have two meanings for GMC: ethics is transcendental or practical, whereas aesthetics denotes the architectural form or a critical reflection upon architecture.

With his *classical attitude* GMC proposes a late Enlightenment humanistic approach: he maintains man's place at the heart of life, but denies him any claim to omnipotence. Like Gide, GMC argues for transforming the antique concept of harmony according to contemporary needs. Invoking the spirit of Matila Ghyka's "speculative aesthetics of Neo-platonic roots"[1], GMC accepts the validity of harmony. There are two kinds of harmony which are to be constructed: first, the harmony of conception, from which different branches may spring; and second, the harmony of the architectural object. In view of the classic ideal of perfection, GMC frees the anthropological core of harmony from the ties of antique metaphysics and declares the human scale as the basis for a modern conception of harmony.

GMC's commitment to the legitimacy of metaphysics recalls Wittgenstein's concept of transcendental ethics:

"6.421 It is clear that ethics cannot be expressed.

Ethics are transcendental.

(Ethics and aesthetics are one)."[2]

As this approach implies, in the words of Camus, to "recognize the limits of reason, [...] this middle path where the intelligence can remain clear"[3] could be perceived as a sort of safety mechanism to protect man from hubris. In *The Myth of Sisyphus* (1942) Camus notes: "It is always wrongly thought that the notion of reason is a one-way notion. [...] Reason bears a quite human aspect, but it also is able to turn towards the divine. Since Plotinus, who was the first to reconcile it with the eternal climate, it has learned to turn away from the most cherished of its principles, which is contradiction, in order to integrate into it the strangest, the magic one of participation. It is an in-strument of thought and not thought itself. Above all, a man's thought is his nostalgia. Just as reason was able to soothe the melancholy of Plotinus, it provides modern anguish the means of calming itself in the familiar setting of the eternal. The absurd mind has less luck. [...] The absurd on the contrary establishes its limits since it is powerless to calm its anguish. [...] The absurd is lucid reason noting its limits."[4]

Wittgenstein, in his turn, maintains: "Ethics and aesthetics are one".[5]

Only a form of aesthetics, which includes architecture, is in the position to express ethics – by way of showing it: "6.522 There is indeed the inexpressible. This shows itself; it is the mythical."[6] GMC holds the same belief: "The forms art uses, give special meaning to mystery".[7] In the end the topic of aesthetic limitation suggests a correlation with virtues and thus between ethics and aesthetics. Alluded to by Wittgenstein, updated by Camus in his essay on the absurd, this leitmotif was formulated by Plotinus. In *Simetria VII* (1946) GMC publishes a few aphorisms by Plotinus. One phrase is particularly trenchant:

"A being gets better by limiting itself."[8] Here GMC seems to have compressed into his own translation of a French or German version of the *Enneads* the following passage on a maxim: "What, then, precisely is Virtue, collectively and in the particular? [...] The Civic Virtues, on which we have touched above, are a principle or order and beauty in us as long as we remain passing our life here: they ennoble us by setting bound and measure to our desires and to our entire sensibility, and [by] dispelling false judgement – and this by sheer efficacy of the better, by the very setting of the bounds, by the fact that the measured is lifted outside of the sphere of the unmeasured and lawless."[9]

In his *Nicomachean Ethics* Aristotle puts forward the same belief, "for evil is in its nature infinite, to use a Pythagorean figure, but good is finite".[10]

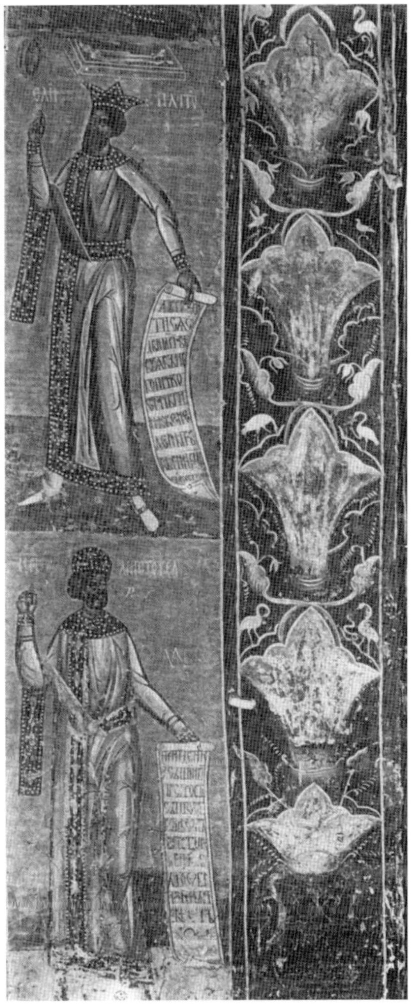

283 *The figures of Plato and Aristotle* (below). Fresco painting on the exterior walls of the Voronetz Monastery's Church, Moldavia, 16th century (Ştefănescu 1928, plate 66).

Features of the relationship between Aesthetics and practical Ethics

The relation between aesthetics and ethics is one of practical ethics. In the case of GMC, what appears particularly interesting, is the moral reflection on two dimensions: his understanding of architecture and his concept of being an architect. GMC believes that human scale is an authentic and universal standard. This includes:

- the aesthetic triad of proportion, rhythm and harmony,
- the social responsibility of architecture, and
- the symbolism of architecture.

By rooting proportion, rhythm and harmony in the human scale – that is, in body, soul and spirit – , GMC, like Rudolf Wittkower in his *Architectural principles in the age of humanism* (1949), vigorously opposed those advocates of the arbitrary nature of proportion, such as Julien Guadet or Kurt Bauch. Guadet, the pre-eminent architectural historian and theorist in Paris around 1900, maintains in "the *Éléments et théorie de l'architecture*, the often re-printed handbook of the students of the École des Beaux-Arts in Paris"[1], that he would find it impossible to make any binding statements on proportion: "The proportions, they are infinite."[2] And the influential German art historian Kurt Bauch, for instance, in his 1932 inaugural lecture at the University of Frankfurt argued that „[s]ymmetry, rhythm and proportion are nothing but mere frameworks, relations with no substance".[3]

In fact GMC's conception of proportion is flexible, or, better: elastic. Proportion oscillates within a certain dimensional span, the limits of which are determined by man, the master of human scale by means of a rigorous approximity. However, "geometry cannot create proportion, it can only check and control it."[4] This also points at geometrical design devices such as the *tracés régulateurs* and Golden Section, which have been championed by many modernists, aestheticians like Matila Ghyka and architects such as Le Corbusier. Le Corbusier, for instance, draws heavily on Ghyka's writings, including *Le Nombre d'Or. Rites et rythmes pythagoriciens dans le développement de la civilisation occidentale* (1931).[5]

GMC's call for an "osmosis between objectivity and subjectivity"[6] also reminds of Palladio's approach, who, as Erik Forssman notes, "regarded the ideal proportions as a theoretic guide. [...] In his designs, however, he often

284 Alberto Giacometti, *Medium Figure III*, c. 1948-49, Bronze, 125 x 20 x 34 cm.
© ADAGP, Paris.
© Alberto Giacometti Estate (Fondation Alberto et Annette Giacometti, Paris).
© Staatsgalerie Stuttgart, 2014.

subtly altered the ideal proportions according to his professional experience, aesthetic judgement and the practical necessity."[7]

With Vitruvius "we find the two leitmotifs of antique aesthetics: first, the Pythagorean-Platonic rational idea of beauty, which is based on numbers and proportions [...]; and second, the Hellenic sensual conception of beauty, which relies on individual taste and can be perceived by the senses. In short: the harmony of symmetria and the harmony of eurythmia."[8]

Such "leitmotifs of antique aesthetics"[9] mark the antique notion of beauty – venustas. According to Vitruvius, beauty can be achieved through ordinatio, a synthesis between the harmony of symmetria, the harmony of eurythmia, and décor. Symmetria "means the harmony of the parts in relation to the whole"[10]. Being related to objectivity, which is based on geometry, symmetria is, mathematically speaking, the necessary element of eurythmia. Subjectivity is the sufficient part of eurhytmia, that is the creative freedom of the architect, imbued as it is with experience and taste. Décor, in its turn, points at effect aesthetics, that is the relationship between ethics and aesthetics: "the appropriateness of form and content".[11]

There is another aesthetic notion which GMC relates to human scale: monumentality. Just as he aims to revive the antique conception of symmetry, he asserts that monumentality is determined, not principally by large dimensions, but by proportion and the upright carriage of man. Consequently he conceives the seemingly paradoxical maxim of an "intimate monumentality"[12] and maintains:

"If man did not have an upright carriage, our aesthetics would be completely different. Proportion therefore concerns a space shaped in harmony with us. [...] Reason has created several geometries, all of which are valid. Proportion can take on a great number of forms, but, unlike geometry, it cannot disregard the human body. This is the reason why a proportion and a building – regardless of their size – can be monumental, not in abstract terms with regard to a plant or mountain, but only with respect to man. There are huge buildings, which do not produce the effect worth of their masses. Such buildings are simply unable to accommodate man, since there is nothing at or in them to remind of his presence."[13]

One of his Parisian fellow-artists, Alberto Giacometti, holds a similar view on monumentality, as magnificently illustrated in his small-sized sculptures, including versions of *Femme Debout* (Medium Figure). In his essay *The Dream, the Sphinx, and the Death of T.*, Giacometti writes about a visit at St Peter in Rome in 1921:

"Inside St Peter, a man who suddenly shows up beside a column becomes a giant, but the temple does not diminish, the metrical size is still valid. On photographs by contrast, the empty interior of this church appears rather small, and men look like ants, but St Peter does not grow, it is just the metrical dimension that acts."[14]

On top of that, the human scale in architecture implies its social commitment which GMC firmly believes in. Not only does he welcome the Modernist demand for architecture and urban planning to contribute to solving social problems, but he bases it on the Roman concept of *Civitas*:

"The antique city was laid out on earth and the horizon constructed by strong and firm lines. Its laws were the fruit of a deep reflection upon an internal balance and an external beauty. [...] Rome was a permanent representation of fame, fortune, and power. Rome was the great stage of the world. [...] The Romans considered architecture an ethical stimulation to translate their history into spatial forms. [...] The collective effort to keep alive that colossus of Roman Empire was at least as magnificent and heroic as the struggle to raise it. Herein architecture played a key role."[15]

Then the *Civitas* was revived in Italian Renaissance:

"In Italian Renaissance building oneself a house meant a social act. For someone who built himself a house or a palace did not only do it to satisfy his own needs. He added to the beauty of his city. That need for beauty, that collective care for harmony, inseparably linking ornamental fantasy to the civil spirit of the urban ensemble – they are nowhere more strongly felt than in Venice. There the traces of all ages combine in one single moment. Since the available space is highly scarce, the Venetians used it with the greatest care. As everything is created according to the human scale, it attracts onlookers and leads them from one pleasant impression to another, in a continuous file of joy and marvel."[16]

285 *Villa Z*, Eforie Nord, Black Sea Coast, c. 1932-1935 (W 37), attributed to GMC by the author (Photograph ADT).

Because Western democracy has reinvigoured the *Civitas*, GMC prefers it to all other forms of government. Together with his colleague Doicescu he eventually declares: "We have opted for the Western civilization."[17] Or: "Civis Romanus sum."[18]

Similar to Semper's commitment to a "republican political attitude"[19], as manifested in his theory of cladding, GMC's classical attitude is marked by a reformist liberal political conviction. Modern democracy usually is – and certainly was in inter-war Romania – marked by both cultural, ethnic and regional pluralism and by increasing social homogeneity.

In the first place, GMC suggests that a capital like Bucharest should embody the *Civitas*. At the same time a capital should be the dignified symbol of the entire country. GMC was inspired by Michel de Montaigne, who adored Paris precisely because Paris is a civic symbol of the whole of France and adds to the beauty of the world: "I am only French", writes Montaigne, "by this great city, great in people, great in the felicity of her situation; but, above all, great and incomparable in variety and diversity of commodities: the glory of France, and one of the most noble ornaments of the world."[20]

Secondly GMC calls for a "unitarian thinking, from which different architectural forms could harmoniously evolve"[21]. Also, their external appearance should be tempered by aesthetic sobriety. He makes it clear that his call does not aim at a formal standardization, but at a qualitative standardization of construction materials of both industrial and vernacular. This call is an integral part of GMC's belief in a close relation between tradition and Modernism as well as an element of practical architectural ethics.

While emphasizing the inseparability of usefulness and symbol, GMC also points at the two meanings of architectural theory and criticism. First, the architectural tractistic bears its value in itself, as it exemplifies the happiness and joy of the antique figure of *bios theôretikos* so conclusively cham-

286 K. F. Schinkel, *The profile of Vitruvius* cast into the surviving bronze porch of the Bauakademie in Berlin, 1831-36 (Photograph Thorsten Stelter).

pioned by Aristotle. Second, tractistic is important as a means of reflection upon architecture. In architectural practice the "intellectual virtue"[22] of the "intelligence of life (phronêsis)"[23] serves "to reify the ethical orientation in particular situations".[24]

At the same time, through usefulness and symbol GMC suggests considering "architecture as a subject of thought"[25]. This evokes, for instance, the symbolic aspect in Semper's theory of cladding, Mies van der Rohe's call for the "spiritual in architecture"[26] or Fritz Schumacher's treatise *Der Geist der Baukunst* (The Spirit of Architecture) of 1938. At the Viennese Congress of the German Werkbund in 1930, Mies recommends fostering the spiritual in architecture and "foresees that technical progress will bring with it a loss of the meaning of building. Mies van der Rohe speaks of the 'value-blind' of progress of events, which will lead to the elimination of meaning and hence to a lack of standards and to chaos in the establishment of values."[27]

In fact, Mies is another great contemporary whom GMC does not mention. However, it is still possible that he read Mies's articles in *Die Form* (1930 and 1932)[28], or even attended the congress on his way from Bucharest to Paris or *vice versa*. *Der Geist der Baukunst* received a very positive review by Romanian architect Marica Cotescu in *Simetria*, who praised Schumacher's "impeccable erudition, great sensitivity, clear and well organized mind"[29].

For GMC the concern for philosophy is an inner need, as witnessed in his reading of Vitruvius: "To Vitruvius, architecture meant building in a harmonious and gentle way. 'As long as we have bodies we must inhabit the dwellings prepared for us by our good sister the Soul in her vast power of labourless creation.' (Plotinus)"[30]. Searching for the innate links between aesthetics and ethics in antique architecture, GMC reads Vitruvius's *On Architecture* through the perspective of Plotinus's *Enneads*. He suggests that "beyond the pale and impersonal text of Vitruvius"[31] there lies the philosophy of his time. Vitruvius himself recommends that philosophy ought to play an important role in architectural education:

"Philosophy in fact makes the architect high-minded and ensures that he will not be arrogant, but rather flexible, fair, and trustworthy without greed, which is the most important quality, since no work can be carried out satisfactorily without loyalty or integrity".[32]

Undoubtedly the "heavy metaphysical orientation"[33] of Neo-platonism appeals to GMC. "If today we seek to at any cost release architecture from every metaphysical bond," writes GMC in his *Introduction to Vitruvius* (1947), "in order to again confine it to technology, this hardly means that the situation in Athens must have been the same. In Athens culture was rather homogeneous and indivisible. We, on our turn, deliberately incline to the rudimentary. Much too easily do we forget that the Greeks were more rational than us. They introduced the sophisticated dialectic into mathematics, in order to more precisely build a sentence, to improve their thinking, and eventually to formulate an idea as good as possible. Therefore it is unacceptable to assume that this notion or concept of carefully shaping words should have escaped architects. For them carving a precise form in stone was the supreme expression."[34]

Perhaps GMC is aware of the fact that the "Neo-platonism of late Antiquity is a conclusive synthesis of the entire philosophy of Greek antiquity – a synthesis, of course, in which everything is subordinate to the basic platonic ideas."[35] Perhaps he also realizes that Plotinus's philosophical project could be seen as a parallel to Vitruvius's treatise. About two hundred years before Plotinus, Vitruvius set off to synthesize the architectural knowledge of the Roman Empire. Plotinus himself could have known Vitruvius's treatise. For instance, he wished "to found an ideal philosophical city called Platanopolis in Campagna in Southern Italy".[36] Although Plotinus was a friend of emperor Gallienus and his wife, his plan finally fell prey to an intrigue.[37]

287 *Urban design of a city*, after Vitruvius. GMC *et al*, *Simetria IV* (1942).

Naturally Vitruvius focuses on architecture and Plotinus on philosophy. But it is notable indeed that both touch on the other's main topic: Vitruvius on philosophy and Plotinus on architecture. Obviously in Graeco-Roman antiquity the conceptions of architecture and philosophy were closely connected and pervaded each other. It is this very relationship GMC is so delighted about, and which he would like to revive, particularly in the face of the contemporary qualification of values:

"For someone who reflects upon architecture, Vitruvius's treatise represents the sum of architectural experiences of a civilisation which believed firmly in its durability, in the highest magnanimity of man and in his virtues and his creative ability to design harmonies worthy of their gods. Through geometry, music, and architecture, man created for himself a harmony founded on numbers, the constancy of which helped him face his fate uprightly. *De Architectura* reveals a deep ethical security and firm conviction (Vitruvius's hesitation is only verbal). [...] We, by contrast, live in a time, when every notion, every form is questioned on behalf of progress"[38].

In GMC's view, there would be nothing left to do but "to look back sceptically and ironically at antique joyfulness. Nevertheless we should first reconquer joyfulness and then master matter. We shall not forget that permanence and invariants of architecture do lie within us, and not within the materials we are using. The difference between the man of antiquity and us consists in his ability to foresee the consequences of his inventions." [39]

Wittgenstein holds a similar view: "Today the difference between a good architect and a poor architect is that the poor architect succumbs to every temptation and the good one resists."[40]

These statements recall Günther Anders's famous diagnosis of the "promethean difference between what we can produce and what we can use."[41] Eventually, GMC invites his fellow architects to refresh themselves in the antique striving for perfection:

"The sensibility of the antique concept of equilibrum expresses deep passions. It is the most lucid effort ever to stay within the framework of the possible. It demonstrates with utmost simplicity the urge for perfection which awakens within man, as soon as he is given the opportunity to act in a civilized society. Progress is ceaseless change. Always searching for inventions progress leaves behind innumerable débris. Striving towards perfection in search of spiritual fulfilment requires calmness and depth of thought. Perfection does not care about time. Antiquity opts for perfection."[42]

288 Engraving of the equestrian statue of Marcus Aurelius on the Capitol in Rome. Giovanni Cavalieri, *Antiquarium Statuarum Urbis Romae*. Rome c. 1609. WLB Stuttgart, Altert. Fol. 168.

A noble banality and GMC's concept of being an architect

With regard to his *classical attitude* GMC draws also on the antique concept of civic virtues. According to Plotinus civic virtues supplement the human soul. Man can acquire them through insight, habituation and practice, thus by striving to equal God:

"[T]he Civic Virtues [consist of] the Prudence which belongs to the reasoning faculty; the Fortitude which conducts the emotional and passionate nature; the Sophrosyne which consists in a certain pact, in a concord between the passionate faculty and the reason; or Rectitude which is the due application of all the other virtues as each in turn they themselves should command or obey."[1]

In general the notion of concord is key to the classical attitude. Especially GMC's call for "a balance between knowledge and emotion"[2] appears to be consistent with the Sophrosyne, one of the civic virtues. These were regarded as imitations or images of the so-called higher virtues. The higher virtues were ideals inherent to the higher world or the higher being. However, the higher being itself will not require any virtues. Plotinus asserts that "in fact virtue is one thing, the source of virtue quite another. The material house is not identical with the house conceived in the intellect, and yet stands in its likeness: the material house has distribution and order while the pure idea is not constituted by any such elements; distribution, order, symmetry are not parts of an idea. So with us: it is from the Supreme that we derive order and distribution and harmony, which are virtues in this sphere; the Existences there, having no need of harmony, order or distribution, have nothing to do with virtue; and, none the less, it is by our possession of virtue that we become like to Them."[3]

Picking up the antique thread of civic virtues GMC encourages his fellow-architects to connect the striving for perfection to an ethical and aesthetical moderation: "Isolation is indeed no spacial, but a moral question. The isolation demonstrates a determined attitude, a spiritual pride and privilege."[4]

T. S. Eliot holds a similar belief: "Art, as Goethe said, is in limitation; and a great poet is one who makes the most of the language that is given to him: The truly great poet makes his language a great language."[5]

This outlook radiates a stoic character. Apart from GMC's natural inclinations towards stoicism, he is probably aware that it lay at the core of the *Civitas*, especially during the four centuries of the *Pax Romana*. As José Ortega y Gasset, one of GMC's favourite contemporary philosophers, points out:

"One must note – and do not see, in this, specific praise for my speciality – that the only philosophy of truth influential in Rome was Stoicism, and this was not produced until four centuries after the common Roman belief began to disintegrate, precisely in the period of what we call the 'Spanish emperors' – Trajan, Adrian, and, following them, Marcus Aurelius – who were themselves Stoics. Stoicism, extended throughout all the nobility and the bourgeoise of the Empire, gave the world one of its periods of best government and sweetest happiness. It is an incontrovertible fact that when philosophy is effectively influential it is not isolated in this or that individual but prevails in broad and profound social groups – therefore, in the collective soul of Rome; there it achieves, even if temporarily, what seemed impossible; namely, that a people which had lost all vigorous common belief would recover, thanks to Stoicism, something like a collective faith which held them together for some time; and as it could be no less, it would promote the only period of something like legitimacy which the Roman Empire enjoyed in its five centuries of slow and dragging life."[6]

We could further associate GMC's approach with the ethics of humility of René Descartes established in his *Traité des Passions* of 1649 – even more so as it was compulsory reading for architecture students at the École des Beaux-Arts in Paris. Descartes's treatise on passions, now almost sunk into oblivion, made a conclusive impact on the development of the notion of caractère.[7]

GMC in fact champions a concept of banality, which one might call, not a positive banality in the sense of Robert Venturi, but a noble banality:

"One is tempted to wish architects the courage to be banal. Such a banality, which is shown in resisting obsessions with decoration and outbursts of bad temper, could grow into a virtue."[8]

Here GMC seems to make use of the beneficial nuance of banality: every-day life. Every-day life implies duration, continuity, and intimacy; it suggests conventions, that is, rules agreed upon; it encourages the development of identity; and it reverts to perfection. As for duration, in *his Introduction to the Method of Leonardo da Vinci* Paul Valéry maintains that duration stands for rigour and double-value:

"'Duration' comes from the same root as dur, 'hard'. All this amounts to giving certain visual, tactile, and motor images – or their combinations – a double value."[9] And Valéry continues: "Once rigour is established a positive liberty becomes possible. Apparent liberty being no more than a liberty to surrender to every chance impulse."[10]

Cioran argues in the same spirit when he notes that there is "[n]o true art without a strong dose of banality. The constant employment of the unaccustomed readily wearies us, nothing being more unendurable than the uniformity of the exceptional."[11]

In the wake of Adolf Loos one might describe this noble banality a tasteful monotony: "Are we afraid of uniformity? But were the old buildings within one period and one country also not uniform? So uniform that it is possible for us to place them in order according to the styles of countries, peoples and towns. Nervous vanity was alien to the old masters. [...]

Who can show me something bad in taste from past, cultivated times? The houses by a minor bricklayer in a provincial town were in good taste. But there were certainly great and minor masters. The great works were reserved for the great masters. The great masters had a more intimate contact with the spirit of the world, thanks to their outstanding education."[12]

With his call for tempering "the hypertrophy of self-centred personality"[13], GMC takes the same line as Loos and appreciates the "implicit antiindividualism of [Classicism]"[14] as part of the call to order: a means to protect the aesthetic triad of proportion, rhythm, and harmony, from being discredited and abused. Again, GMC finds a suitable backing in Andrea Palladio:

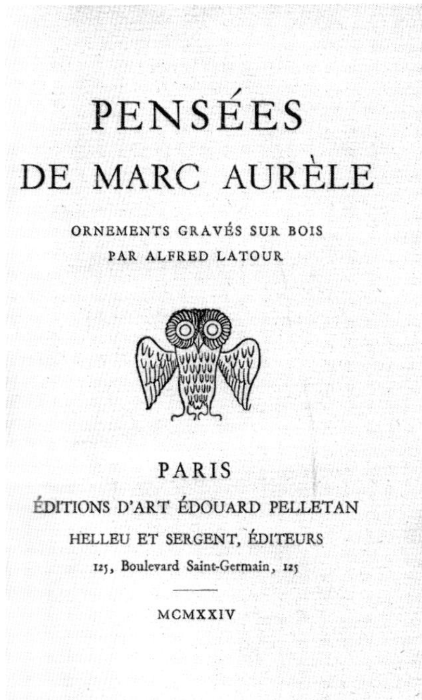
PENSÉES
DE MARC AURÈLE
ORNEMENTS GRAVÉS SUR BOIS
PAR ALFRED LATOUR
PARIS
ÉDITIONS D'ART ÉDOUARD PELLETAN
HELLEU ET SERGENT, ÉDITEURS
125, Boulevard Saint-Germain, 125
MCMXXIV

289 Marcus Aurelius, *Pensées*. Paris 1924. From GMC's library (AGMC-IP).

290 GMC, Palladio's *Villa Rotonda*, Vicenza. GMC, *Palladio*. Paris 1928.

"In this view, Palladio is an astonishing example. Kepler used to say he had witchcrafted the stars by formulating the celestial mechanics. But neither had Kepler invented his stars, nor had Palladio invented his architectural elements. He had only formulated and applied certain principles, which are in fact primary truths for those who intend to organize the space for human life! Nothing else is architecture after all. The principles of proportion, rhythm and harmony underlie every style; they are common to the architecture of all civilizations and of all times. This is true on account of their common module: man, this unchanging phenomenon, who reverts all problems to the same starting point."[15]

Then GMC concludes: "Palladio seems to transcend individualism and passions, as if he were meant to guide us by his incorruptible lucidity."[16]

In his view GMC could have been influenced by Paul Valéry's portrait of Leonardo da Vinci: "The most exalted figure is never 'an original'. With him what is merely personal becomes as insignificant as possible. No unevennesses; no intellectual superstitions."[17]

T. S. Eliot argues in the same spirit: "The process of an artist is a continual self-sacrifice, a continual extention of personality. [...] It is in this depersonalization that art may be said to approach the condition of science."[18]

GMC was convinced that an architect with such an attitude, if it was reflected in his work, could exert an ethical influence upon his contemporaries, both colleagues and the public. Such an approach is characteristic of the late Enlightenment and recalls, for instance, the position championed by Schinkel in regards to his Altes Museum in Berlin. According to Jörg Trempler, "Schinkel follows Schiller's idealistic concept that aesthetic education ennobles a man to being a citizen, a full member of the *Civitas*"[19].

We can sense GMC's pedagogical urge in his Loos-like combat of both the ornamental excesses of the Romanian Heimatstil and its ideological exploitation through archconservative politics. Although GMC does not mention him at all, GMC was very possibly influenced by the Viennese master, who himself fought against the ornamental excesses of historicism and those of Jugendstil in Vienna. As for Loos's material ethics, it too seems to have been dear to GMC. In his Principle of cladding Loos objects to the inappropriate treatment of wooden surfaces and cites good examples from the past:

"The law goes like this: we must work in such a way that a confusion of the material clad with its cladding is impossible. [...] The Middle Ages painted wood bright red for the most part, the Renaissance blue; the Baroque and Rococo painted interiors white, exteriors green."[20]

It is possible that GMC has known of such details. For instance, the windows and doors of his Black Sea villas, as reported by Derek Patmore, were initially painted blue – another plausible sign that he was passionate about Renaissance.[21]

As for ornament, GMC is open to it – when used to add nuances and human scale to the bare architectural mass aesthetics. His concept of discreet ornament is marked by a reduction in quantity, a typological abstraction and a substantial and symbolic density. In his architecture, we can discern a prominent ornamental feature: the tulip. It is worth noting that GMC infuses this simple floral motif with a subversive power to undermine chauvinist prejudices, as exemplified in an Art column essay for *The Royal Foundations Review* in 1934.[22] Also, GMC connects his notion of the ideal Architect with the modesty demonstrated by anonymous building masters, for instance in the former Danubian Principalities. Relying on his professional authority and humanist education, GMC himself appears to embody this ideal, which operates beyond the constraints of self-centred originality. In his view, one of the essential features of practical ethics for an architect is to show true empathy towards his clients, to discern their inner needs and wishes, and to translate them into well organized urban space. Perhaps GMC was inspired by one of his favourite Antique philosophers – Plotinus. Cioran points out that "Plotinus, Porphyrius tells us, had the gift of reading men's souls. [...] It has been a long time since philosophers have read men's souls. It is not their task, we are told. But we must not be surprised if they no longer matter much to us."[23] As a matter of fact, the architect should pay enough attention to the client. The architect's foremost duty is to enable the client to identify with his house as closely as possible:

291 GMC, *Andrea Palladio's Basilica and Loggia del Capitaniato*, Vicenza. Chalk drawing, 1937 (AMLSC).

"As soon as the house is finished, right after the last carpenter, electrician or painter has gone, I will leave too, softly, long before anyone could miss me or remember that I had ever been there."[24]

To be sure, the architect must not be a vicarious agent of the client. Instead he must act in full consciousness of his civic responsibility. Therefore, a house should represent an aesthetically disciplined materialization of the client's desires and needs. GMC believes that a "house [...] is only in the beginning an architect's child. Once the house is completed, the architect has to break with it and even entirely forget it. With time the house can become an ideogram of its client and thus enrich the city."[25]

In his Beaux-Arts mentor Gromort, GMC's approach certainly finds proper endorsement: "In architecture, it is the climate which counts: the spirit in which, according to our affinities and momentous humour, we study a programme. But if there is an art, which shall be freed from the tyrannies of fashion, then architecture is certainly the first and foremost one. And the very reason for this being that the buildings we erect are supposed to outlast us. Who cares for last year's hat? We want a change because it is worn out, and maybe we decide to not use it anymore at all. In contrast though, even the most modest building should last for at least one century!"[26]

Loos sees it likewise: "The house has to please everyone, contrary to the work of art, which does not. The work of art is a private matter of the artist. The house is not. The work of art is brought into the world without there being a need for it. The house satisfies a requirement. The work of art is responsible to none; the house is responsible to everyone. The work of art wants to draw people out of their state of comfort. The house has to serve comfort. The work of art is revolutionary; the house is conservative. The work of art shows people new directions and thinks of the future. The house thinks of the present."[27]

In GMC's image of the Architect we can find clear traces of two notions: the architect as a magician – as fostered by the Ecole des Beaux-Arts –; and

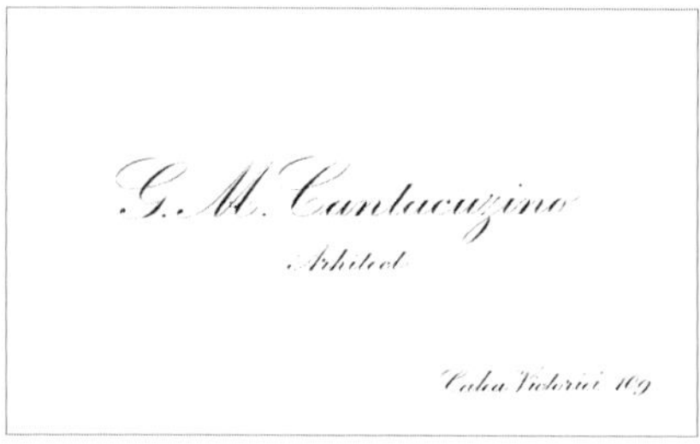

292 GMC, *Business card*, 1930s (AGMC-IP).

the architect as a surgeon – as promoted by Modernism. Apart from these divergent influences, there is the idea of an architect with a strong ethical and aesthetic backbone who plays different roles: the practical architect, who is, at the same time, a technician and a craftsman; the urban designer; the landscape architect; the philosopher; the diplomat and the public intellectual. As a public intellectual, GMC also binds aesthetics to ethics. This outlook claims wide assent amongst colleagues of the *The Romanian History Review*, *The Romanian Life* and *Simetria*. It is expressed by an appropriate and fair criticism, which does tend, not to polarize but to argue as objectively as possible; to answer questions of the day; and to sustain the public dialogue in the wake of the Antique culture of dialogue. This is indeed a duty of the architect, for his expertise lies in the translation of civic values into shaped matter. Or, as Colin St John Wilson expressed it:

"Nevertheless, what is unique to the kind of play here, is that it must be the translation of a set of needs in society, which is perhaps the nearest that the art of architecture will ever come to the classical condition of mimesis."[28]

In short, GMC is convinced that, as a public intellectual, the architect is to watch over the critical flame of public life – "'per non dormire', as D'Annunzio put it".[29]

293 GMC/Schmiedigen, *Porte aux tulips* (Tulip porch). The Chrissoveloni Bank rear entrance, Bucharest (1923-28). Photograph W. Weiss. GMC/Schmiedigen 1929.

Tradition and Modernism

On the motivation to formulate a classical attitude

Why have a *classical attitude* after all? In my view, GMC tries to establish himself, by means of the *classical attitude*, at the crossroad of the "competing visions"[1] of the avant-garde; the return to order; the call to order, and the wide romantic Romanian Heimatstil. The latter, in GMC's view, produced a number of excesses provoking a disregard for classicism.[2]

Against the setting of the Romanian version of the "drama of modernity"[3], GMC employs the *classical attitude* to develop a strategy for contributing to the renewal of Romanian architecture. But why, after all, does GMC rely so heavily upon the issue of ethics? This is all the more striking especially as he is fully aware of the fact that a strong relationship between ethics and aesthetics is neither natural nor universally acknowledged: "This assumption is a simplification which is only partly valid of a particular time."[4]

But GMC is convinced to be living in a time of radical change. Being marked by a "breathtaking lack of preconditions"[5], times obviously need an ethical re-adjustment. This is true for Romania as well, especially as the Heimatstil proved to be a cultural and political dead end.[6] Along with the right wing political radicalization, it counter-attacks the optimistic mood which initially propelled Romania after 1919. In these circumstances, GMC shares with his reformist fellow politicians of the Young Liberals the call for an ethical renewal of the country. But he goes a step further and calls for an ethical renewal, which should precede and prepare an aesthetic renewal. He models his approach on the Italian Renaissance – especially on its idea of freedom, its idealistic and sensitive orientation and on the view held by scholars like Henri Focillon, that the Renaissance was preceded by an ethical renewal of society inspired by St Francis of Assisi. The seventh centenary of his death was commemorated by publications like *L'influence de saint Francois d'Assise sur la civilisation italienne* (1926), of which Focillon was a co-author.[7]

294 GMC, *Villa Mornand*, Bucharest (c. 1936-40; W 63). Photograph ADT.

The classical attitude as a means for Cantacuzino to establish himself within the Romanian architectural scene

When in 1926 GMC comes to prominence, thanks to his essay *Introduction to the study of architecture* and first project successes such as Mogoşoaia and Polizu estate, he was aged twenty-seven and still a student in Paris.

At that time, the Romanian Heimatstil has been practised for some forty years mostly thanks to the culturally and politically influential Bucharest school of architecture, which fervently promoted the Heimatstil as the official architectural style of the country.

On the other hand, the European architectural landscape of Modernism is rich and varied. Its pre-eminent figures are internationally acknowledged, but controversially regarded by conservative circles. In Romania, especially Marcel Janco and his circle of the *Contimporanul* periodical strive to establish avant-garde and Modernism. In the late 1920s, some friends and student colleagues of GMC, including Horla and Lucia Creangă, return to Bucharest and join Janco in his striving.

295 Former entrance tower of the Homor Monastery's Church, Moldavia (17th century). Photograph W. Weiss. GMC, *Petits Édifices*. Paris 1931, plate 39.

As a matter of fact, the leading positions in Romania at the time were well established by both Traditionalists and Modernists. Naturally, GMC could easily and most comfortably have adhered to either position, but apparently he was far from being satisfied with them. Aside from that, neither party could have offered him a leading position, so that there seemed to be only one course open for him: classicism. At the same time classicism was the cornerstone in GMC's education.

His childhood in Vienna, his aristocratic background, his humanistic education in Montreux, Lausanne and Bucharest, supplied him with a cosmopolitan knowledge of languages, landscapes, architecture, art, literature, music, and history. His training in Paris provided him with a deep passion for architectural and art history, particularaly for antiquity and Renaissance. Additionally, the one contemporary architectural stream which possibly marked him most was the temperate modernist *Groupe des Architectes Modernes* in Paris. On account of his familiarity with German civilization in general, and Vienna in particular, he was probably also inspired by the treatises of leading art historians like Burckhardt, Wölfflin and Worringer, and by the work and critical attitude of Semper, Otto Wagner and Loos.

Hence we could say, GMC is the right man, at the right time, in the right place. Indeed he is to champion classicism and particularly the classicist branch of Palladianism. But he does not confine to classicism at all. He partly leaves this trotten way and pursues a new path, which eventually turns out to be the most difficult one. He transforms classicism it by creating the *classical attitude* as a strategy of architectural renewal: a connection between traditions and modernism which is deeply rooted in classical principles.

In the open letter to Marcel Janco in 1931 he somewhat romantically stylizes himself as a *cavalier seul* of the *classical attitude*. This clearly underlines his ambition to both staying independent and becoming a leader, through formulating and developping a position of his own.

This strategy resembles the contemporary theory on the innovative cultural and economic exchange developed by philosopher Boris Groys. In his theory Groys analyzes the manifold relationship between the Old and New, and makes the conclusive proposal that the Old and New should be judged as relating to a certain time but otherwise being of neutral content. Groys regards the Old as the "valued culture"[1], and the New, which is a reaction to the Old, as the "profane realm"[2]. For Groys the border between the Old and New is for ever fluctuating. The Old, the New, and strategies of cultural renewal were determined by the respective borderline position between high-grade and profane values.[3] According to Groys, the New is only new with regard to the "cultural archives"[4].

GMC's *classical attitude* is indeed new in Romania at that time. Consequently GMC tries to convince his fellow architects and the public in Romania, that tradition and modernism are, not at all exclusive, but rather complementary and capable of a fruitful co-operation. By contrast, only extreme forms of tradition and modernism would oppose and thus exclude each other: the ideologically and aesthetically incrusted extrems of arch-traditionalism and arch-modernism.

Arch-traditionalism and arch-modernism

In his view, both arch-traditionalism and arch-modernism will hinder a creative evolution of architecture, since they would pretend to have developed the irrevocable architectural canon. But GMC is convinced that "[w]e do not need to canonize a certain choice of objects and forms. We do rather need comprehensive ethics, which are capable of producing true aesthetics."[1]

As for arch-modernism, GMC first reproaches it for overestimating the principle of reduction. This principle would mean reducing architecture "to a mere social function and an applied technique".[2]

Second, arch-modernism would mistake "usefulness for a symbol, and volumes for architectural forms".[3]

Third, in conjunction with poor materials, it would lead to monotony.[4]

Fourth, it would deny the legitimacy of both history and criticism,[5] which is unacceptable.

Fifth, the Modernist call for sincerity in architecture would be simplistic:

"The Functionalists focus attention on material usefulness at the expense of dwelling intimacy. They are doing this on behalf of doubtful transcendental principles. But what of the true spiritual necessities? It is them which would deserve priority. Today it is said time and again: 'We have to express the construction.' Which construction? If the construction in question is the spiritual one, I fully agree; if expressing the construction means to externalise the resisting moments of concrete, I do not see the point of this apparent discipline."[6]

Finally, arch-modernism would lack empathy for the *Genius loci*:

"To put architecture, in the name of internationalism, on a solely abstract and intellectual scale, and cutting every bond to local emotions, is a superfluous as well as dangerous a game."[7]

As for the Romanian Heimatstil, GMC recognizes its concern with establishing an ornamental order of its own. Nonetheless, he disapproves of its predominant orientation, which has been thoroughly inapt at finding solutions for contemporary problems. What is more, the Heimatstil tends to abuse the architectural heritage both in a quantitative and in a nationalist way, hence showing an ignorance of the *Genius loci* very much similar, albeit with opposite signs, to arch-modernism. On the contrary, GMC's writings, broadcast lectures and his volume *Petits édifices* of 1931 show his deep knowledge of and respect for the rich variety of vernacular architecture of all regions in Romania. Subsequently he rejects the idea of a national style based on the Heimatstil:

"To proclaim, on the other hand, a local style, limited to historical forms which are more or less successfully adapted to contemporary needs, leads us straight into a dead-end."[8]

Since such an exploitation would prematurely drain the inspiring source traditional forms offer, GMC suggests to only use them with caution and discretion. On the other hand he recognizes the historical importance of the national romantic movement of the Heimatstil, since it contributed to endowing the young Romanian kingdom from 1866 on, with an architectural element of national identity.[9]

296 GMC, *Izvoare şi popasuri* (Sources and Stopovers). Bucharest 1934.

297 *The Fountain of Master Manole*, Curtea de Argeş, Wallachia (17th century). Photograph W. Weiss. GMC, *Petits Édifices*. Paris 1931, plate 56.

At the same time the Romanian Heimatstil was part of a European movement. However, even then it drew mainly upon the Wallachian Brancovan style of around 1700,[10] rather ignoring the Moldavian legacy particularly of the eighteenth century late Palladian architecture. In addition, after the Great War, Romania emerged almost double in size and as a multi-ethnic state, including Transylvania, which until 1918 was decisively marked by a Hungarian, Saxon and Austrian influence. In these circumstances, a type of Heimatstil based upon the Brancovan epoch could be even less suitable for providing a national architectural style – unless, one would see it as a more than questionable means of cultural centralization and inner colonization directed from Bucharest. But was there a true need for a national style?

In fact, GMC himself considers both the common features and the varieties of Romanian regions. In the course of time, it was only natural that a steady commercial and cultural exchange should have developed between the three main historical principalities. However, despite the strong connections, they established their own focal points of cultural identity, with some notable features in smaller regions such as Banat, Bucovina, Dobrugea or Maramureş.

Some of GMC's articles or radio talks could have encouraged other scholars to explore aspects of the architectural and cultural heritage of Romania. His broadcast lecture *Wells, lever arms and stops* (Fântani, cumpene şi popasuri) of 1932 included a substantial comment on the fountain of master Manole in Curtea de Argeş.[11] This essay, published two years later in the much acclaimed volume of selected essays *Sources and stopovers* (1934), possibly inspired Mircea Eliade (1907-1986), the historian of religions, to deal more in depth with this subject in his lectures at the University of Bucharest in 1937 and then publish his *Commentaries on the Legend of master Manole* (1943).[12]

Eventually GMC is convinced that to "give a country a coherent appearance, does not at all mean that a state should opt for standardizing forms thus creating monotony. If we use local materials and take into consideration the aspects of regional climate and customs then both domestic and public buildings would fit more neatly into a given landscape or urban fabric and even enhance it with a special meaning."[13]

Seen through such a perspective, GMC's classical attitude could be regarded as a visionary attempt to give an architectural shape to the actual historic and "cultural pluralism of Romania"[14].

Arguments for a synthesis between Tradition and Modernism

But how could there emerge a friendship between tradition and modernism? At least in respect to the architectural scene of Bucharest, GMC states:

"One can find these two styles and their extremes in Bucharest as well. At first sight, a synthesis between them appears impossible and unsolvable, since a style usually implies the entire aesthetic and constructive elements typical of a certain age."[1]

For his part, GMC suggests a break and opens a dialogue on the possible connection between tradition and modernism. Then he bids farewell to the term of style and opts for the notion of an architectural strand or tendency.

298 Brașov/Kronstadt, the former *City Hall* (now City Museum) (1770-74). Photograph W. Weiss. GMC, *Petits Édifices*. Paris 1931, plate 54.

He thus argues: "Neither the modern style nor the so-called Romanian style are really firmly established and even less mature. Both of them represent a tendency open to a long-term evolution or perfection. Both of them are based on a sum of experiences and await being judged by usage and time."[2] GMC, a true Bergsonian, regards the future as open. In his *Creative Evolution* (1907) Bergson observes that "to foresee consists of projecting into the future what has been perceived in the past, or of imagining for a later time a new grouping, in a new order, of elements already perceived. But that which has never been perceived, and which is at the same time simple, is necessarily unforeseeable."[3]

So GMC argues that architecture is in the becoming and should not be too hastily labelled with a certain style.[4] Henceforth one should continue with making architecture in the given circumstances and premises, and, above all, be patient with the evolution of architecture in Romania. For one thing, GMC's recommendations recalls Cocteau's verdict that "[s]tyle can never be a starting-point; it is a result";[5] for another, it reminds of Rilke's advice to a young poet:

"You are so young, all still lies ahead of you, and I should like to ask you, as best as I can, dear Sir, to be patient towards all that is unresolved in your heart and to try to love the questions themselves [...]. Do not now strive to uncover answers: they cannot be given you because you have not been able to live them. And what matters is to live everything. Live the questions now. Perhaps then you will gradually, without noticing it, live your way into the answer, one distant day in the future."[6]

As regards the premises of current architecture GMC's talks about – of what do they consist? Modernism, for GMC, is firstly a method of design and of construction.[7] It faces social challenge by means of technical progress, new materials, new tasks, a sober mass aesthetic and the young discipline of urbanism.[8] The Romanian Heimatstil for its part, especially through traditional Wallachian forms, seeks to express a certain need for feeling at home. Apart from this legitimate aspiration to defining originality in decoration, it rather avoids resolving imminent contemporary problems.[9] However, GMC argues that the two strands of architectural Romanian tradition – vernacular and religious – could well be used. At the same time, he reminds that these strands are not at all "purely autochthonous"[10], but are part of larger architectural movements. While religious architecture is one of the latest branches of Byzantine architecture, vernacular architecture and folkore are related to Oriental, Persian and Mediterranean civilisations.[11] As religious architecture died out due to historical developments, it is unlikely to give further substantial inspirations.[12] Vernacular architecture before the Second World War, on the contrary, was still as vital as it was some centuries ago. Therefore it could still inspire architects in terms of typology and formal simplicity and sobriety.[13]

Referring to Béla Bartók (1881-1945), who pioneered the study of folk music in Romania, GMC emphasizes the possibility of extracting from vernacular architecture "examples of balance and taste"[14], if carefully observed. Horia Creangă argued in the same vein with a special emphasis on *cula* buil-

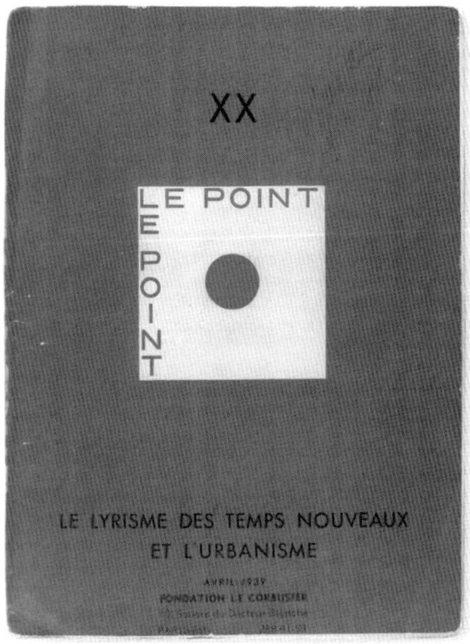

299 Le Corbusier, *Le Lyrisme des Temps Nouveaux et l'Urbanisme*. Paris 1939. © VG Bild-Kunst, Bonn, 2014.

dings: "The simplicity of these *culas* does not deny the modern architectural principles which I feel obliged to obey. Conceived in such a way, Modernism would not break with tradition but continue it."[15]

Similarly, the Italian rationalists around Giuseppe Terragni refused to reject the legacy of the Italian tradition, believing that their past and their present were indeed reconcilable with each other.[16]

Then GMC continues his exposition: "Seen through the prism of such an analysis, the apparent incompatibility between Modernist tendencies, in general, and our own in particular, vanishes."[17]

Eventually, Tradition, Heimatstil and Modernism prove to be phenomenon different in kind. As such, they are perfectly compatible with each other. All the same time, there is no need to develop from history an image of enmity.[18] GMC invites his colleagues and readers to be open both to each other and to modernity. Such an open-mindedness might contribute to activating both one's own potential and the emancipating potential of modernity:

"Modern architecture seeks its principles at the sources of utility, construction and social issues. Modern architecture in no way contradicts the aspirations of our own architecture, but only offers an amazing repertoire of new possibilities. If we open our curiosity and our spirit to these tasks, which are common to all people in the world, we surely will enter the constructive circle of modern life and enable our natural abilities to grow and evolve on a grander scale."[19]

In his study *Histoire et Vérité* Paul Ricœur, the French historian, forwards a similar approach in more general terms: "Only a civilisation capable of integrating the scientific rationality will survive and redefine itself time and again. The question is, not merely to repete the past, but to incessantly create something new whilst being anchored in the past."[20]

Such an emancipation of one's own creativity would promote a firm integration into the modern community of nations, since European identities share collective cultural features. At the same time, one's own cultural identity would be strengthened. A major feature of this identity is, for GMC, the *Civitas*. The *Civitas* is embedded in a cosmopolitan ease and openness towards the world, the globality of both modernity and history:[21]

"Our cities, without becoming banal, will adopt something of the civil pride of historic cities. Certainly we will live in greater harmony with our past instead of getting stuck in a retrospective attitude. Today we cannot reject the great questions of humanity, no less than we did in the past. For humanity comes first – regionalism second."[22]

GMC's self-confident conclusion is as follows:

"Our problem is not to reduce general tendencies to regional aesthetics; on the contrary, we have to appreciate our old regional heritage as a cultural value of general interest, that we transfer into the great realm of the eternal artworks of humanity."[23]

In recent years, GMC's estimation has been confirmed, at least in regard to the outstanding relevance of Moldavian monasteries, on the restorations of which he worked himself and which have recently been classified as UNESCO world heritage.[24]

Thoughts on the classical attitude

Cantacuzino's architecture, Romania and Critical Regionalism

With the *classical attitude* GMC appears to have formulated the ethos of the leading architects of the moderate and richly varied Romanian Modernism. GMC himself becomes at once a "chronicler of Romanian spirituality"[1] (Virgil Ierunca) and the "uncontested chief of the young Romanian architecture"[2], as observes Paul Morand in his portrait of Bucharest (1935).

A chief he may have been, but rather different in character than some leading figures of avant-garde or Modernist strands. For GMC also insists, as mentioned before, on being a *cavalier seul*, refusing the self-complacent autocracy of prophetic figures such as André Breton or Le Corbusier. "I have never liked prophets", notes GMC in one of his letters to Simon Bayer, "not even the more reliable ones."[3]

300 GMC, *Villa Bibesco*, Eforie Nord, Black Sea Coast (c. 1929-1932; W 17). Period photograph W. Weiss (AGMC-PM).

As for Le Corbusier, GMC could have met him, for example through Georges Pingusson or the *L'Architecture d'aujourd'hui* circle. But this is uncertain. In *Simetria VII* (1946) GMC has a sympathetic yet critical article on Le Corbusier published by the Romanian architect Nicolae Nedelescu. In his own writings GMC mentions Le Corbusier a few times, as a reference, with respect.

Nonetheless, in a letter to his wife Sanda, GMC contends that for him "Le Corbusier [...] remains a bit of a fraud with maybe a few brilliant ideas, but a fraud all the same. [...] [T]o approach Architecture (with a capital A) through Le Corbusier is to approach the easy way – which one is not allowed to do when approaching art."[4] Furthermore, in an explanatory note in *Simetria VII* (1946) GMC makes clear on behalf of the *Simetria* editors that "we consider the writings of Le Corbusier to be prey to caducity to a far greater extent than Alberti's commentaries on Architecture. Hence we do not believe in publicity acrobatics through which since a quarter of a century the basic notions of architecture are being undermined in favour of false ones."[5] And in the essay *The Artist and the Freedom* published in last *Simetria* edition GMC maintains that "[a]rchitecture is an art wherein dreams and lyricism are out of place"[6], as if he commented on Le Corbusier's book *Le Lyrisme des Temps Nouveaux et L'Urbanisme* (1939).

GMC's insistance on being a *cavalier seul* is clearly manifest in his architecture. Not only does he attempt to sythesize modernism, vernacular and classical traditions – throughout his career he also fostered the historical strand of Palladianism, and, according to Matila Ghyka, even developed a personal neo-classicism.[7]

From the viewpoint of Modernism, GMC's fondness of the historical Palladianism certainly appears retarded. But for him, the historical Palladianism has a European dimension. In Transylvania, it has a longer historic continuity, whereas in Wallachia and Moldavia Palladianism was introduced only in the late eighteenth century. Of such buildings only few survive. This is also why GMC pursues the historical Palladianism, which he regards as another way to reinforce the integration of Romanian architecture into Europe. GMC's commitment to the historical Palladianism can be seen as a sequel to the late Byzantine tradition in the Danubian Principalities, since they both

301 *Histria*, Marble ruins of the first Greek city on the Romanian Black Sea Coast (7th century BC).
Photograph Astrid von Lutitz, 1966.

represent late branches of European architectural movements. Or, as GMC notes in his essay on Palladio (1928): "The province is always a late developer as regards fashion and style."[8]

Eventually GMC's classical attitude and commitment to contributing to the integration of Romanian architecture into the European and international scene show, he was indeed a cosmopolitan European.

Perhaps GMC's importance for Romanian architecture might be compared to Georges Enesco's relevance for Romanian music. Enesco, the father of modern Romanian music, has striven for an original synthesis of classical music and Romanian folk-music, as demonstrated by compositions like the *Romanian Poem* (1897), and the two *Romanian Rhapsodies* (1902, 1903).[9]

The *classical attitude* can also be related to Kenneth "Frampton's almost quixotic task to unify vitality with calm, in order to 'create a still yet vital point within the whirlwind'".[10] GMCs closeness to Frampton's *Critical Regionalism* has already been pointed out by Romanian architectural historians such as Mirela Duculescu.[11] Indeed, some of the premises which Frampton puts forward as essential to the emergence of critical regional schools can be discerned in Romania of the 1930s as well – "a certain prosperity but also [...] an aspiration at least to some form of cultural, economic and political independence."[12] Although objectional of regionalism, GMC welcomes, as we have seen, the critical consciousness.

Features of *Critical Regionalism* can be seen, for instance, in the Villa Aviana, the Villa Bibesco and the Bellona Hotel in Eforie on the Black Sea Coast, the villa of the Romanian Broadcasting in Bod/Brenndorf, the Hotel Rex in Mamaia or the official Romanian Pavilion at the 1939 New York World's Fair.

In the case of the Villa Aviana a necklace-like footpath of irregular polygonal stone plates wraps itself around the building – similar to the well known design by Dimitris Pikionis of the "park paving on the Philopappus Hill"[13] in Athens (1957).

The Bellona Hotel is clearly modelled on the ship metaphor, so characteristic of Modernism. At the same time, the Black Sea Coast appears to be more suited to accommodating this kind of *architecture parlante* than many places in cities or other landscapes. At the same time, the Bellona Hotel is notable for some details that do not seem too modern at all. For instance, the hotel lies upon a sturdy base and its bow-like head is surrounded by a grand staircase, terraces and ramps. With its steep walls clad with large hexagonal rough stone plates, the base seems to grow out of the wild configuration of rocks, which marks the southern end of the Eforie promenade. Therefore the building creates the impression of an earth-bound fortress.

Such an explicit non-modernist feature recalls the historical fortifications along the western coastline of the Black Sea, starting with the Greek colonial cities of Histria (seventh century BC), Tomis (mid-seventh century BC, now Constantza) and Kallatis (sixth century BC, now Mangalia), up to the Renaissance fortresses of Akkerman and Hotin, erected by Stephen the Great, the Moldavian reigning prince, at the end of the fifteenth century. The blind round arches, which adorn the steep walls of the base, remind the onlooker of the Roman legacy of the Black Sea Coast – Tomis and the monument at

Tropaeum Trajani. Tomis was the capital of the *Moesia inferior* province, but might be best remembered as the place of exile of Ovid, the poet. The monument *Tropaeum Trajani* (now Adamklissi) in the Dobrudgea (108/109 AD) commemorates in addition to Trajan's column in Rome (113 AD) the final victory of Rome over the Dacians of the Carpathians and the Danube.

Then the villa in Bod/Brenndorf can be interpreted as a synthesis of Palladianism and local traditions. For instance, the mighty two-storey roof relates to snowy winters typical of Transylvania. The compact body of the house, calm and symmetrically disposed around a central portico with two twin-columns, a frontal staircase, two porthole windows, and two loggias, very much expresses the intimate monumentality advocated by GMC.

On the other hand, the Hotel Rex and the New York Pavilion can be considered in terms of the "monumental order"[14], typical of many buildings of the 1930s. However, the term monumental order, coined by the renowned architectural historian Franco Borsi, can easily be misunderstood as referring to an architecture lacking human scale. In his much acclaimed book *The Monumental Era. European Architecture and Design 1929-1939* (1987), Borsi deals with some architectural strands of 1920-40 until then virtually neglected by official architectural criticism and historiography. This impressive study includes the discussion of cases as disparate as the works of Asplund, Expert, Lewerentz, and Perret for one thing, and buildings of the totalitarian regimes of the day (fascist Germany and Italy, and communist Russia) on the other. Now, many official buildings errected by totalitariam regimes, do share in collective a feature: the tendency to step out of human scale in favour of megalomany. In architecture on the contrary, monumentality, has always been clearly defined by proportions indisputably related to the human scale. Therefore I think, the term monumental order when applied to all architectural strands discussed by Borsi, can easily lead to a momentuous misunderstanding – a misunderstanding to the effect that monumentality is made equal to megalomany, and is hence discredited.

Against this setting, GMC's works, like those of, for instance Lewerentz and Perret, were always committed to human scale. Not only does human scale mark GMC's notion of an intimate monumentality, but also his idea of the aesthetic triad of proportion, rhythm, and harmony. His recourse to both Greek and Roman antiquity and Renaissance, can well be related to Paul Ricœur's conviction of the necessity of knowing one's own cultural roots:

"Only a vibrant civilisation, which is at once committed to its own origins and creative in the arts, literature, and philosophy, is capable of truly meeting other civilisations, that is, of contributing to these meetings with real significance. Only if the participants in the encounter are creative, the encounter itself becomes creative [...]. For Europeans the question is not a matter of partaking in a vague collective belief, which they could even make the whole world accept. Instead we must first of all recall our cultural and civil beginnings, that means, our Greek, Hebrew, and Christian beginnings. Only in this case will we Europeans be a reasonable partner within the great contemporary dialogue of civilisations. You can only enter a partnership with a consciousness of self."[15]

302 GMC/V. Arion, *Hotel Rex*, Mamaia, Black Sea Coast (c. 1936-38; W 61). Postcard 1965 (ADT).

303 GMC, *Villa Aviana*, Eforie Nord (W 11). Period photograph W. Weiss (AGMC-PM).

304 GMC, *Villa Aviana (Villa Aristide Blank)*, Eforie Nord, Black Sea Coast (c. 1929-31; W 11). Seaside view. Period photograph W. Weiss (AGMC-PM).

305 GMC, *Villa Aviana*, Eforie Nord (W 11). Period photograph W. Weiss (AGMC-PM).

306 GMC, *Villa Aviana (Villa Aristide Blank)*, Eforie Nord, Black Sea Coast (c. 1929-31; W 11). Street view. Photograph W. Weiss (AGMC-PM). *L'Architecture d'aujourd'hui* No. 5/1934.

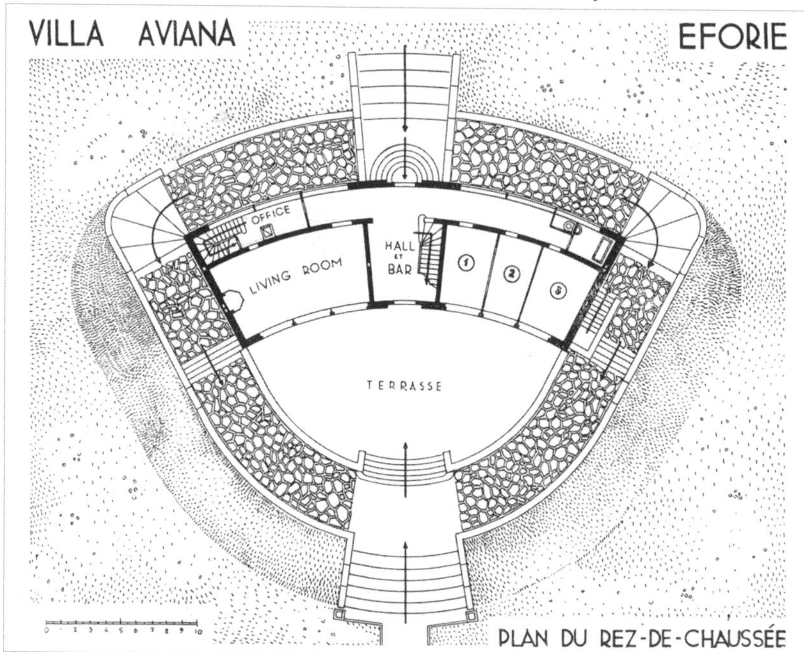

307 GMC, *Villa Aviana*, Eforie Nord (W 11). Ground floor plan. *L'Architecture d'aujourd'hui* No. 5/1934.

308 GMC, *Hotel Bellona*, Eforie Nord (c. 1932-1934; W 36). Aerial south view. Period postcard (ADT).

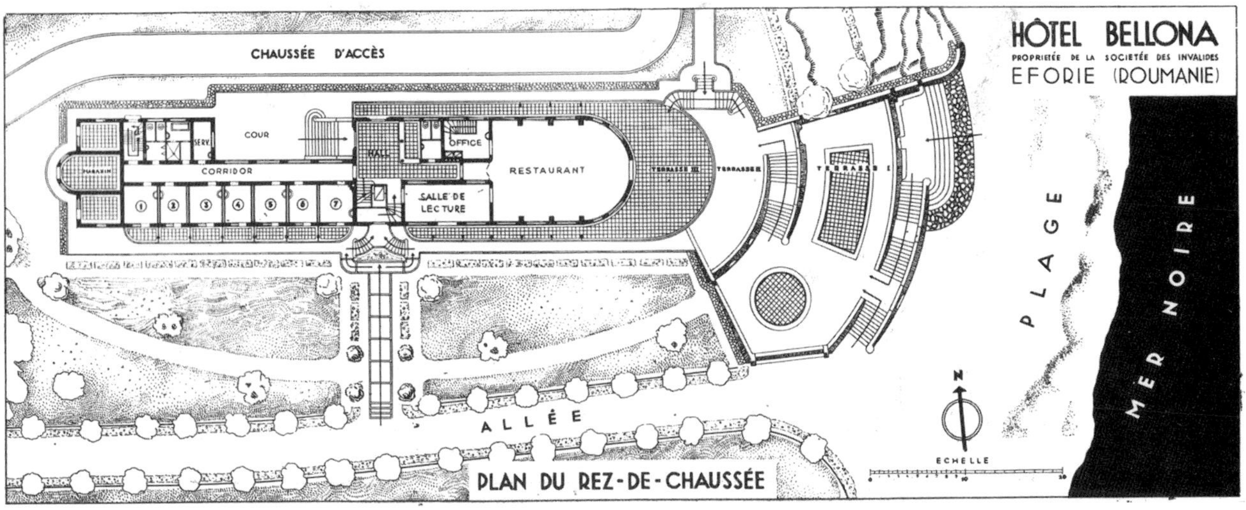

309 GMC, *Hotel Bellona*, Eforie Nord (c. 1932-1934; W 36).
Ground floor and site plan.
L'Architecture d'aujourd'hui No. 5/1934.

310 John Michael Rysbrack, *Inigo Jones*. Statue at Lord Burlington's *Chiswick House* (1726-29), London. Photograph ADT.

Further connotations to the classical attitude

With the classical attitude GMC contributes to the debates on classicism and on the call to order initiated by Jean Cocteau around 1920. Eventually, it offers a strategy for architectural renewal, which, starting from some guiding principles based on human scale, allows for a morphological variety. For this approach GMC draws especially upon Bergson's notion of *élan vital* and Plotinus's emanation system – which in its turn is updated by Bergson. It might be more appropriate to think of a consensus over some guiding principles in the antique Roman sense than of a holistic concept. The Roman notion of consensus is beautifully summed up by José Ortega y Gasset:

"The unity of Roman life, which was the most solid ever known, was in no way an inert and subsidized unity, but one that was won and achieved by the constant intershock of the formidable dynamism and quarrelsome spirit of those social groups; it was a unity of the equilibrum of forces – therefore a unity of compromise. It is clear that what gave the most solidity to this unity of rivals was the consensus, that total common belief in a certain conception of life and of the world; and in addition, the resolution agreed by all of them that whatever happened in their own quarrels and discussions, Rome would always exist, Rome would always win, and they would always go on being Romans. Unless one recognizes these assumptions, which appear to be contradictory, one cannot understand Roman history very well."[1]

This approach leads us to another contemporary of GMC's intellectual family: Marc Bloch. In the wake of Bloch's historiographic concept, we can think of the *classical attitude* as an architectural and cultural "minimal theory"[2]. Such a minimal theory might prove highly topical in view of the contemporary cultural complexity, social diversification and globalization.

The passion for Renaissance, with which the *classical attitude* is imbued, makes one think of Kees Christiaanse's concept of design as navigation:

"As urban planning organizes public affairs, it must keep a certain distance to architecture, so that architecture is able to let her thousand flowers blossom."[3] This idea is again consistent with Bergson, who in *Creative Evolution* (1907) points out that "[h]armony, or rather 'complementarity', is revealed only in the mass, in tendencies rather than in states. Especially (and this is the point on which finalism has been most seriously mistaken) harmony is rather behind than before. It is due to an identity of impulsion and not a common aspiration."[4]

Between tradition and modernism there have always been connections. One of the early eminent figures of this architectural filiation, is undoubtedly Andrea Palladio on account of his *usanza nuova*. He was followed by such figures as Inigo Jones, Karl Friedrich Schinkel and Auguste Perret.

As for Inigo Jones, for instance, Vaughan Hart highlights "the subtlety of his integration of new with old"[5]. Jones blended "all'antica and medieval motifs. In this marriage of the unfamiliar and foreign with the familiar and native, Jones introduced the all'antica style to his countrymen in a way that was calculated to maximise the acceptability of the architectural Orders"[6].

In Schinkel's theory of fusing Gothic and classical architecture we can discern a sequel to Jones's approach. Schinkel noted:

"The Historical does not only consist in drawing back upon or merely repeating the Old, for such an approach would ultimately destroy history. Rather, it is a question about inventing something new, which at the same time continues history. But how this should be put into practice, is a very delicate question, which requires the best education possible. An appropriate prototype could be offered by the fine arts, especially if they treat their subjects with measure and calm."[7] In a similar vein the contemporary German architectural critic Gerd De Bruyn states "classicism was the first strategy for modernizing architecture. [...] Until today, it is an essential part of architecture. [...] Therefore I am not really interested in the art historian's differentiation between classicism, neo-classicism, romantical classicism [...] since classicism remains a strategy for perpetual renewal of architecture."[8]

GMC himself pragmatically acknowledges the legitimacy of arch-traditionalism and arch-modernism. Nevertheless he defends a third position:

"There are the traditionalists, the modernists and the others. The latter include those architects who believe that it is necessary to seek an equilibrum based on classical disciplines without rejecting modern themes and without turning one's back on tradition."[9]

311 GMC, Palladio's *Basilica*, Vicenza. Chalk drawing (GMC, *Palladio* 1928).

For this path GMC again could have found endorsement in Schinkel and Perret. Schinkel states: "This new style will not emerge from history as an incomprehensible fantasy, which invades all contexts. On the contrary, one will hardly notice the new style, its greatest merit being the consequent application of a number of innovations that have been acknowledged in the course of time."[10] Perret confirms this approach: "He who, without denying the modern principles and building materials, creates a work which gives the impression to have always been there, he could indeed be satisfied."[11]

With respect to architectural theory, some of GMC's writings are outstanding: *Introduction to the Study of Architecture* (1926), *Palladio. Un essai critique* (1928) and the articles for the *Simetria Dictionary*. There he very precisely and eloquently comments on vital terms of architecture – among them, tradition, proportion, rhythm, harmony and composition.

In this regard it appears remarkable that GMC shares an intellectual bond with Rudof Wittkower. In his legendary work, *Architectural Principles in the Age of Humanism* (1949), Wittkower similarly draws attention to the basic elements of Renaissance architecture: proportion, tradition and the hierarchy of values. As Oechslin points out, Wittkower's treatise "was to become a saving anchor for a great number of architects right after 1945 when architecture had lost compass and substance"[12], and which was to enjoy "ground-breaking success beyond the academic realm"[13]. The architects greatly influenced by Wittkower include Colin Rowe and Fred Koetter. Through the "theory of contending powers"[14] presented in *Collage City* (1978), they unfold a strategy of synthesis of Tradition and Modernism. Similar to GMC, they suggest "to recognize the complementary relationship which is fundamental to the processes of anticipation and retrospection. [...] We may receive strength from the novelty of prophetic declamation; but the degree of this potency must be strictly related to the known, perhaps mundane and, necessarily, memory-laden context from which it emerges".[15]

312 John Michael Rysbrack, *Andrea Palladio.* Statue at Lord Burlington's *Chiswick House* (1726-29), London. Photograph ADT.

Palladio's *usanza nuova*, Jones's practise of blending Roman classicism and English medieval aspects, Schinkel's theory of fusing together Greek Antiquity and the Gothic, Perret's *structural classicism*, GMC's *classical attitude*, Rowe's and Koetter's *theory of contending powers*, Frampton's *Critical Regionalism*, de Bruyn's positive notion of classicism, are all strategies of architectural and cultural innovation. According to Boris Groys, such strategies "connect a positive and a negative continuation of tradition in such a way that both the continuation and breaking with tradition are expressed with the greatest clarity and intensity."[16]

Actually, these strategies do aim, not at completely reconciling and disolving oppositions and differences, but rather at linking them to each other. Also, these strategies can bear differences and inner tensions within a certain generously elastic framework. These strategies seem to continue the tradition of the "coincidentia oppositorum"[17], a philosophical and religious theme championed by Nicholas of Cues and Blaise Pascal. In his *Pensées*, Pascal included the following maxim which Camus used as the motto of his *Letters to a German Friend*: "We do not display greatness by going to one extreme, but in touching both at once, and filling all the intervening space".[18]

Albert Camus, Mircea Eliade and Massimo Cacciari are contemporary thinkers who have updated this approach. Cacciari, for instance, referring to Elias Canetti's essay on Karl Kraus and the critical modernism in Vienna, writes about the *complexio oppositorum* which can be instrumental in developing a "'school of resistance' [...] in the age of Nietzschean nihilism fulfilled".[19]

The *classical attitude* can be regarded as a substantial contribution to this attempt, with GMC talking about a "structural harmony"[20]. Continually threatened, this delicate construction has to be renewed and pursued, with what Camus called, the absurd and patient endurance of Sisyphus. Consequently GMC asserts: "Nothing is frailer than harmony and its corrolary,

Invitation	Association des Amis de Georges M. Cantacuzène
	Un homme de la Renaissance au XXe siècle **G. M. Cantacuzène, 1899-1960**
Carrefour	Avec les témoignages de G.H. Pingusson, architecte, professeur à l'Ecole des Beaux-Arts; Rainer Biemel, professeur; Siegfried, peintre; I. Schein
Lundi 12 avril 1965 à 21 heures	chez Messieurs Vincent et Fréal, libraires-éditeurs, 4 rue des Beaux-Arts, Paris 6

313 Invitation card to GMC's commemoration by the *Association des Amis de Georges M. Cantacuzène* at the Paris bookshop Vincent, Fréal et Cie, 12th April 1965.

beauty, ever contested, ever in danger of growing dim. Man possesses in himself so much potential for destruction, and the seeds of death are always in us."[21] The delicate yet elastic framework of this structural harmony is symbolized by the antique notion of symmetry: "Symmetry, in its original sense, means feliticious proportion or commensurability."[22]

GMC extends the meaning of symmetry into a dynamic proportional balance both culturally and politically. This approach remarkably parallels Rowe and Koetter, who see the theory of contending powers as an expression of democracy in architecture and urban planning:

"[I]f democracy is compounded of libertarian enthusiasm and legalistic doubt, and if it is, inherently, a collision of points of view and acceptable as such, then why not allow a theory of contending powers (all of them visible) as likely to establish a more ideally comprehensive city of the mind than any which has, as yet, been invented."[23]

GMC's approach, in its turn, may be considered an architectural and cultural attempt at designing the vision of a pluricultural Romania.

We can find this idea of a dynamic and complex balance as a symbol of democracy in other thinkers, including Julien Benda and Edgar Morin, too.

In his introduction to the 1946 edition of *The Great Betrayal* Benda, for instance, asserts that "[d]emocracy is based on an idea which is most likely to appeal to aesthetic sensitivity: the idea of balance, [...] an indescribably more complex notion than that of order."[24] Morin in his *Penser l'Europe* (1988), finds the term "dialogic"[25] and assigns it a distinctly European cultural feature – the culture of dialogue meaning the concept of an ongoing dialogue, which in spite of all historical shifts, discontinuities and conflicts, succeeds in rejuvenating itself with "obstinate rigour" (Paul Valéry)[26].

This idea also reflects in a most topical way the antique notion of symmetry: the understanding of harmony as a dynamic balance, as revived by GMC with his *classical attitude*: "Europe symmetrisizes".[27]

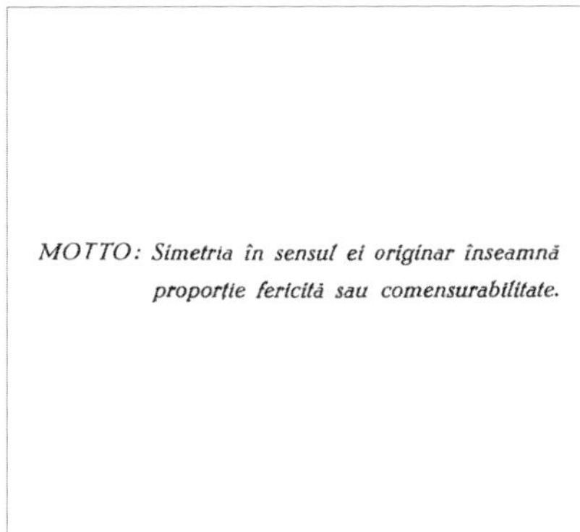
MOTTO: Simetria în sensul ei originar înseamnă proporție fericită sau comensurabilitate.

314 GMC *et al*, Motto of the cultural periodical *Simetria I-VIII*. Bucharest (1939-1947): "Symmetry, in its original sense, means feliticious proportion or commensurability."

315 GMC, *Hotel Bellona*, Eforie Nord (c. 1932-1934; W 36). Seaside view. Postcard 1960 (ADT).

Part III: Addendum (1)
List of architectural works

317 GMC, *Unknown villa project* (AGMC-PM).

With GMC's estate having been dispersed, the inventory presented here is only provisional. It relies on the basic writings by Radu Patrulius, Adrian Anghelescu and Mirela Duculescu. In addition to the known projects, this list incorporates references from other publications, from archives both public and private and from interviews with and letters by time witnesses. The best part of these references consist of the works mentioned by GMC himself in his private correspondance. Finally, this list includes works attributed to GMC by other sources or by the author on aesthetic grounds.

W 1-n indicates the name of a particular work, whereas * denotes works attributed to GMC. The detail site maps of Bucharest are drawn by the same scale, 1:2,500.

318 Overview of GMC's works in Romania, Bulgaria (Balcic) and the USA (New York). Drawing ADT.

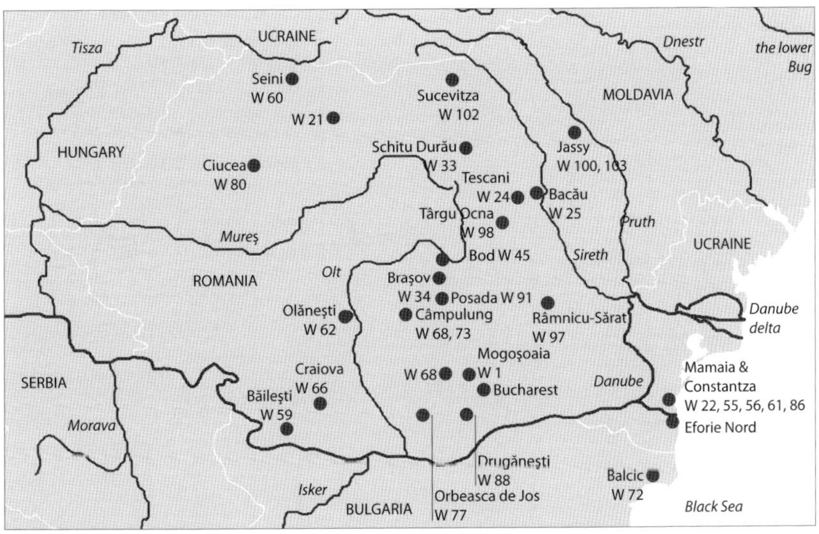

319 Map of Romania, overview of works designed by GMC or attributed to him. Drawing ADT.

316 Opposite: GMC/V. Arion, Detail of a perspective drawing of the *Carlton Building* (c. 1932-34; W 44) (AGMC-PM).

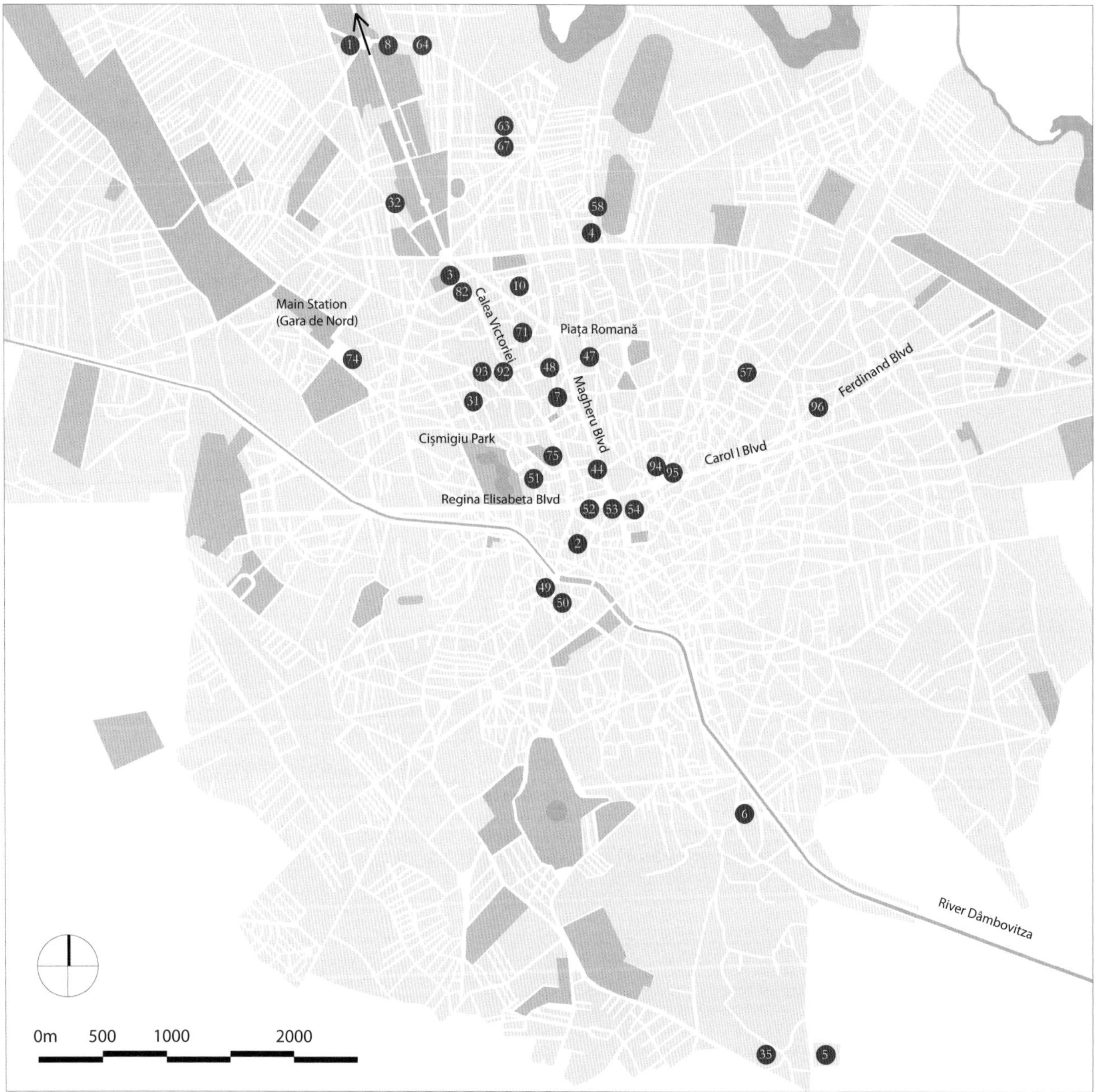

320 Map of Bucharest showing all works designed by or attributed to GMC based on the official map of Bucharest of 1938 (drawing ADT).

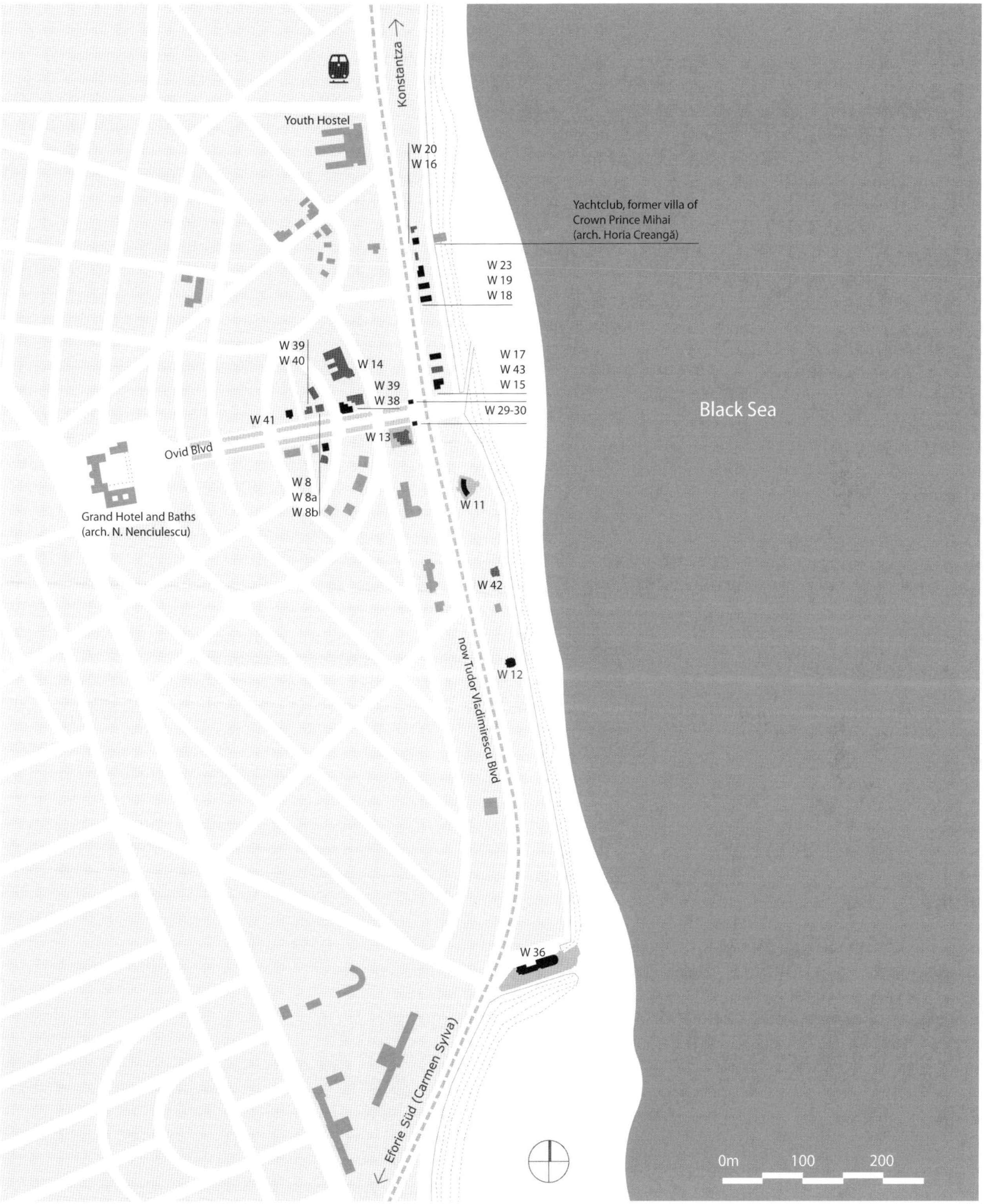

321 Map of Eforie Nord, Black Sea Coast, overview of works designed by or attributed to GMC. Reconstruction of the urban layout of Eforie (drawing ADT).

W 1

W 1 Mogoşoaia estate
NW of Bucharest, c. 12 km to the centre of Bucharest
1920-1931

Modernisation and extension of the Mogosoaia estate and gardens, commissioned by Marthe Bibesco; initially in collaboration with Domenico Rupolo

Lit.
Primary sources: GMC, *Mogoşoaia* 1932, pp. 209-223; *Mogoşoaia.* Radio talk, 11th May 1942, provenance: SRR; *Mogoşoaia: un palat, o grădină, un peisaj* 1993, pp. 146-160, c.1955, provenance: INMI/FDMI, Dos. No. 6499
Secondary sources: Patmore 1939, p. 39; Popa 1962; Ş. Cantacuzino 1999, p. XVII; Celac/Carabela/Marcu-Lăpădat 2005, p. 159; Narcis 2007, pp. 227-233; Duculescu 2010.

W 2

W 2 Chrissoveloni Bank
Bucharest, 16 Lipscani Street/Stavropoleos Street
1923-1928

Headquarters of the Chrissoveloni Bank from 1928-1933, commissioned by Jean Chrissoveloni (1880-1926), the president of the Chrissoveloni Bank Ltd.; designed in collaboration with August Schmiedigen; nationalized in 1948. The building is at present a branch of the National Bank of Romania and was restored in 1996-1998 by architects Gabriel Tureanu and Constantin Rulea.

Lit.
Primary sources: GMC, *L´architecture roumaine*, 1927, pp. 351-357; GMC/Schmiedigen 1929
Secondary sources: Gr. Ionescu 1938, p. 18; Patmore 1939, p. 39; Patrulius 1975a, p. 58; Ş. Cantacuzino 1999, p. XIII; Kirson 2001; Celac/Carabela/Marcu-Lăpădat 2005, p. 29; Duculescu 2010

W 3

W 3 Polizu Estate/Villa of Queen Elisabeth of Greece
Bucharest, 163 Calea Victoriei
c. 1923-1925, 1928-1929

Around 1923 Jean Chrissoveloni commissioned GMC to design a villa for Marie-Angèle Massart, the banker's mistress. On Chrissoveloni's death she sold the estate to the Queen Elisabeth of Greece, who asked GMC and Schmiedigen to extend the villa.

Lit.
Secondary sources: PMB, inventory 1927-35/1928, p. 46, Nr. 367; Morand 1990 [1935], pp. 180-181; Cicio Pop 1932, pp. 137-138; Gr. Ionescu 1938, pp. 84-85; Ghyka c. 1961, AMLSC; Patrulius 1975 a, p. 61; Patrulius 1982, p. 90; Crutzescu 1987 [1943], pp. 261, 337; letter by Olympia Zamfirescot† to the author, Cannes, 24th March 2008; Duculescu 2010, p. 147

W 4 Chrissoveloni Bank, housing block*
Bucharest, 9-11 Calea Floreasca
1925

A housing block for functionaries of the Chrissoveloni Bank, possibly designed in collaboration with A. Schmiedigen, commissioned by Jean Chrissoveloni (1880-1926).

Lit.
Secondary sources: Duculescu 2010, pp. 90-93, 147

W 5 **Monastery Church Văcăreşti***
Bucharest, 391 Calea Văcăreşti
c. 1923-1928

Possible restoration by GMC and Schmiedigen on behalf of the Department of Historical Monuments, Bucharest. The monastery was built from 1716-36, transformed into a prison in 1864 and demolished under the Ceauşescu's regime from 1985-87.

Lit.
Secondary sources: Alice Magheru, *G. M. Cantacuzino*. In: Dragu Dimitriu 2006, p. 23

W 5

W 6 **Casa Fraenkel, Capşa Café and Restaurant***
Bucharest, Calea Văcăreşti
c. 1926

Interior design of a Capşa branch, in collaboration with August Schmiedigen; commissioned by Capşa Ltd/Gregor Capşa; probably destroyed in the process of the vast demolition of a large part of the historic urban fabric of Bucharest in the 1980s.

Lit.
Secondary sources: Ioniţă 2000, p. 162

W 7 **Jockey Club**
Bucharest, 9 Episcopiei Street
c. 1927-1929

Co-operation with August Schmiedigen. HQ of the Jockey Clubs until 1947; later HQ of the Union of Romanian Architects; at present a restaurant and HQ of the new Jockey Club

Lit.
Secondary sources: Patrulius 1975a, p. 59; Patrulius 1982, p. 90; Duculescu 2010, list of works

W 7

W 8 **Romanian Broadcasting Institution**
Bucharest, Băneasa
c. 1928-1929

First purpose-built building of Romanian Broadcasting Company (Societatea Română de Radiodifuziune/SRR), inauguration on 1st September 1929.

Lit.
Secondary sources: Patrulius 1980, p. 153; Patrulius 1982, p. 90

W 8

W 9 **Eforie, Urban Masterplan**
Eforie Nord, Black Sea Coast
1929-1930

GMC layed out the urban masterplan for the modern seaside resort in Eforie and designed many buildings, of which only a few are known today; commissioned by Societatea Anonimă Techirghiolul/Banker Aristide Blank.

Lit.
Primary sources: GMC, letters to Marthe Bibesco, 30th September 1929, 11th March1930 and 17th August 1930, AMLSC
Secondary sources: Patmore 1939, p. 40

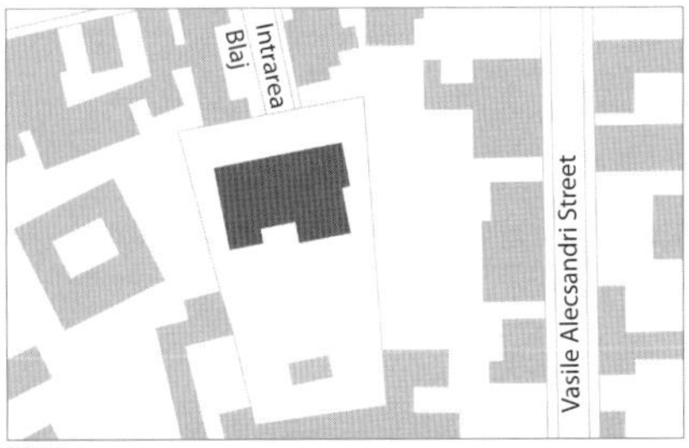

W 10

W 10 Villa Mavrocordato
Bucharest, 1 Intrarea Blaj (formely Fundătura Pietății)
c. 1929-1931

Villa and garden for Nicholas Mavrocordato; the estate was nationalized around 1945.

Lit.
Secondary sources: APM building permission 1929, PMB Inventory 1927-35, 1929, No. 169, p. 24 (no plans); Patrulius 1975b, p. 58; Patrulius 1982, p. 90; Celac/Carabela Marcu-Lăpădat 2005, p. 58; Duculescu 2010, p. 147

W 11

W 11 Villa Aviana
Eforie Nord, Tudor Vladimirescu Blvd
c. 1929-1931

Two-storey villa with terrace overlooking the Black Sea built for Aristide Blank, the banker, poet and president of Societatea Anonimă Techirghiolul.

Lit.
Primary sources: GMC in *L'Architecture d'aujourd'hui* 5/1934, pp. 60-6
Secondary sources: ANB/MMSOS, Dos. No. 277/1932, p. 108; Patrulius 1975a, p. 59; Machedon/Scoffham 1999, pp. 154, 256-259; Duculescu 2010, p. 147

W 12

W 12 Villa Lily (Vila Crinul)
Eforie Nord, Tudor Vladimirescu Blvd
c. 1929-1931

Two-storey villa with four apartments, possibly built for Societatea Anonimă Techirghiolul; restoration works in 2008.

Lit.
Secondary sources: Duculescu 2010, pp. 103, 147

W 13

W 13 Villa Tower
Eforie Nord, Ovid Blvd (formely Grand Blvd)
c. 1929-1932

Probably the former railway station of Eforie including a restaurant and guest house; possibly built for Societatea Anonimă Techirghiolul; demolished around 1960.

Lit.
Secondary sources: AGMC-PM, photograph by W. Weiss; ANB/MMSOS, Dos. No. 277/1932, p. 108 (the architect is not mentioned, but the building named *Villa Tower* could refer to W 13

W 14

W 14 Hotel Neptun
Eforie Nord, Black Sea Coast
c. 1929-1932

Hotel, at present in a derelict state; possibly built for Societatea Anonimă Techirghiolul.

Lit.
Primary sources: AGMC-PM, period photographs by W. Weiss
Secondary sources: ; ANB/MMSOS, Dos. No. 277/1932, Eforia-Tekirghiol-Agigea, Județul Constanța, p. 108

W 15 **Villa Violetta**
Eforie Nord, Tudor Vladimirescu Blvd
c. 1929-1932

Three-storey villa on the seaside promenade, now altered.

Lit.
Primary sources: GMC in *L'Architecture d'aujourd'hui* 5/1934, pp. 57, 61; letter to Sanda Cantacuzino, 11th August 1955, AMLSC; *Journal* 1964 [1931, 1932], pp. 149, 154, 158.
Secondary sources: Patrulius 1975a, p. 59; 1982, p. 90; Machedon/Scoffham 1999, pp. 154, 256-259

W 15

W 16 **Villa X**
Eforie Nord, Tudor Vladimirescu Blvd
c. 1929-1932

Two-storey villa on the seaside promenade, now altered; possibly built for Societatea Anonimă Techirghiolul.

Lit.
See W 13

W 16

W 17 **Villa Bibesco/First Villa Cula**
Eforie Nord, Tudor Vladimirescu Blvd
c. 1929-1932

Three storey villa on the seaside promenade, commissioned by Marthe and Georges V. Bibesco; now altered.

Lit.
Primary sources: GMC, *L'Architecture d'aujourd'hui* 5/1934, pp. 57, 61; AGMC-PM, period photographs by W. Weiss
Secondary sources: Duculescu 2010, pp. 102, 147; see W 14

W 17

W 18 **Villa Don/Second Villa Cula**
Eforie Nord, Tudor Vladimirescu Blvd
c. 1929-1932

Built for Mr Don, then mayor of Eforie; reported to the author by Mrs Ileana Tilea-Troiano, London, 28th November 2008
For further information see W 16

W 19 **Third Villa Cula**
Eforie Nord, Bd. Tudor Vladimirescu, ca. 1929-1932.

Possibly built for Societatea Anonimă Techirghiolul.
For further information see W 17

W 17-19 (from left to right)

W 20 **Villa Y***
Eforie Nord, Bd. Tudor Vladimirescu, ca. 1929-1932

Two-storey villa on the seaside promenade; demolished

Lit.
Secondary sources: Reported to the author by Mrs Ileana Tilea-Troiano, London, 28th November 2008

W 21 **Gravestone for Avram Ianco (17xy-18cv)**
Transylvania
c. 1930

Memorial slab for the peasant leader of the1848 revolution in Transylvania; possibly commissioned by the Romanian government.

Lit.
Secondary sources: Jean-Michel Cantacuzène 2011, fig. 12

W 22

W 22 **Military Casino**
Mamaia, Black Sea Coast
c. 1930-1931

Large estate with casino, hotel, open air theatre, terraces and gardens for the Guards' regiment *Mihai Viteazul* (Michael the Brave) of King Carol II; the project has not been located yet.

Lit.
Primary sources: AGMC-PM, period photographs by W. Weiss of GMC's design plans and two interior photographs but no exterior photographs

W 23

W 23 **Villa Tilea-Martaloglu**
Eforie Nord, Tudor Vladimirescu Blvd
c. 1930-1932

Two-storey villa, double house overlooking the Black Sea, built for the Martaloglu Family and for Viorel V. Tilea, politician and Romanian Ambassador to England in the 1930s; now altered.

Lit.
Secondary sources: Reported to the author by Mrs Ileana Tilea-Troiano, London, 28th November 2008; ANB/MMSOS, Dos. Nr. 277/1932, S. 108, Eforia-Tekirghiol-Agigea, Județul Constanța p. 108 (the clients are mentioned, the architect not); Tilea 1998, pp. 81, 148 (the architect is not mentioned)

W 24 **Church in Tescani**
Tescani, Neamtz County in the Eastern Carpathians, 20 km SW of Bacău
c. 1930-1940

Village Church, commissioned by Alice Rosetti-Tescanu.

Lit.
Primary sources: GMC, letter to Marthe Bibesco, 11th March 1930; letter to Sanda Cantacuzino, 8th April 1940, AMLSC.
Secondary sources: Patrulius 1975 a, p. 59; Duculescu 2010, p. 147

W 25

W 25 **City Hall**
Bacău, Moldavia
1931

Restoration and transformation of the city hall of Bacău.

Lit.
Primary sources: GMC, letter to Marthe Bibesco, 14th February 1931, AMLSC; AGMC-PM
Secondary sources: reported to the author by Matei Cantacuzino, Brussels, 27th November 2008

W 26 **Villa 8***
Eforie Nord, Ovid Blvd
c. 1931-1932

One-storey villa, possibly buitl for Societatea Anonimă Techirghiolul; attributed to GMC by the author on aesthetic grounds; now renovated.

W 27 **Villa No. 8a**/Villa Egreta
Eforie Nord, 4 Ovid Blvd
c. 1931-1932

One-storey villa, possibly built for Societatea Anonimă Techirghiolul; now altered.

Lit.
Primary sources: AGMC-PM, period photographs by W. Weiss
Secondary sources: ANDJC, Archive record *City Hall of Tekirghiol*, Dos. No. 49/1932, working plans scale 1:50 with the stamp of GMC´s office. Reported to the author by Gheorghe Vecerdea, Constantza, E-Mail message, 13th November 2007

W 27

W 28 **Villa No. 8b**/Villa Oiţa (The little Lamb)
Eforie Nord, Ovid Blvd, adjacent to W 27
c. 1931-1932

One-storey villa, possibly for the Societatea Anonimă Techirghiolul; now altered.

Lit.
Primary sources: AGMC-PM, period photographs by W. Weiss

W 29, 30 **Two Pavilions and Wooden Pergola**
Eforie Nord, Ovid Blvd
c. 1931-1932

Twin classicist one-storey pavilions at the intersection of Grand Blvd (now Ovid Blvd) and the coastline boulevard: a pharmacy to the south of the intersection and a hair-dresser to the north. In addition a wooden pergola on the southern side of the Grand Blvd. Both pavilions and the pergola were demolished around 1960.

Lit.
Primary sources: AGMC-PM, period photograph by W. Weiss
Secondary sources: ANDJC, Archive record *City Hall of Tekirghiol*, Dos. 49/1932: building proposal of the pharmacy pavilion scale 1:100.

W 29-30

W 31 **Concert studio of Romanian Broadcasting SRR**
Bucharest, 60 General Berthelot Street
1931-1932

First purpose-built concert studio of Romanian Broadcasting, adjacent to the nine-teenth-century villa which housed the Broadcasting Company. The entire complex was destroyed by bomb damage in WW II.

Lit.
Primary sources: AGMC-PM, period photograph of W. Weiss
Secondary sources: Radio-Fonia 1932, p. 19, photograph by W. Weiss; reported to the author by Dr Liliana Muşeţeanu, director of the SRR text archives; PMB Bucharest, archive record of the *City Hall IV Green*, Dos. No. 244/931

W 31

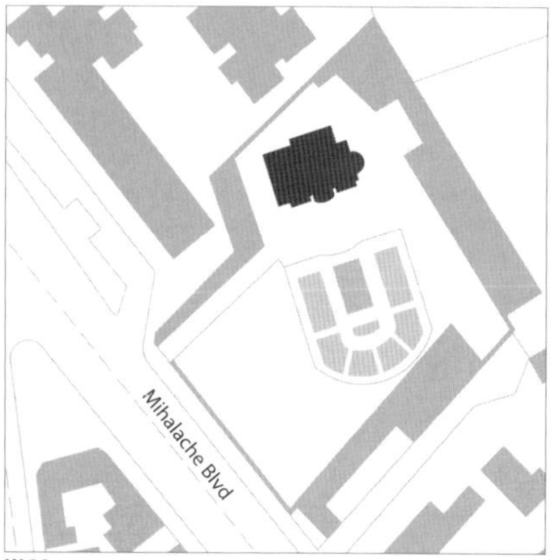

W 32

W 32 Villa D. Sturdza*
Bucharest, possibly 28-30 Mihalache Blvd (formely Col. Ion Ghica Blvd)
c. 1931-1935

Villa with garden and water-basin for Pulcheria and Demeter Sturdza; the villa was extended by a two-storey annex containing a garage and flat by the architect I. Bozianu in 1935.

Lit.
Primary sources: GMC in *Journal* 1962, p. 93, entry on 22nd November 1931 (without referring to the location of the house)
Secondary sources: Possibly Patmore 1939, p. 41; reported to the author by Prof Alexandru Beldiman, Bucharest, 21st September 2006; for Bozianu´s project see PMB Bucharest, Archive record of the City Hall I Yellow, Dos. No. 125/935, BG 12 N, 24th September 1935

W 33 Villa Guranda
Schitul Durău, Moldavia, Eastern Carpathians, at the foot of the Ceahlău Mountain
c. 1931-1935

The building in question was perhaps the country retreat *Mecaresco* of Demeter Sturdza.

Lit.
Secondary sources: Cicio Pop 1938, p. 416; Patrulius 1982, p. 90

W 34

W 34 Aircraft Factory IAR
Brasov/Kronstadt, Transylvania
c. 1931-1933, 1937-1938

First aircraft factory in Romanial (Întreprinderea de Avioane Română/IAR) , extended in collaboration with Octav Doicescu 1937-1938; now altered.

Lit.
Primary sources: GMC, *L'Architecture d'aujourd'hui* 5/1934, pp. 58-59
Secondary sources: ITB Brasov/Kronstadt, survey of the building; UAR/AOD Bucharest, Box 4/C; Patrulius 1975a, p. 59; Patrulius 1980, p. 56; Curinschi 1981, p. 300; Machedon/Scoffham 1999, p. 293; Stiller 2007, p. 50; Duculescu 2010, p. 147

W 35 Villa of the writer Tudor Arghezi
Bucharest, 26 Mărţişor Street

GMC helped his friend Arghezi with the design and construction of his residence.

Lit.
Secondary sources: Duculescu 2010, pp. 110-111, 147

W 36

W 36 Hotel Bellona
Eforie Nord, Tudor Vladimirescu Blvd, c. 1932-1934

A purpose-built sanatorium for The Society of War Invalids, the building was transformed into a hotel in the 1930s; construction supervisor architect Ferencz; now altered and renovated.

Lit.
Primary sources: GMC, *L´Architecture d´aujourd´hui* 5/1934, pp. 60-61; GMC *Journal* 1964 [1932], pp. 149, 154, 158; letter to Sanda Cantacuzino, 11th August 1955, AMLSC
Secondary sources: ANDJC, Archive record of the *City Hall of Tekirghiol*, Dos. No. 47/1932, building permission plans scale 1:100; Patrulius 1975a, p. 59; Patrulius 1980, p. 65; Patrulius 1982, p. 90; Machedon/Scoffham 1999, pp. 154, 256-259; Stiller 2007, p. 42; Duculescu 2010, pp. 104, 105, 147.

W 37 **Villa Z***
Eforie Nord, Ovid Blvd
c. 1932-1935

Possibly built for The Societatea Anonimă Techirghiolul; attributed to GMC by the author on aesthetic grounds, typological closeness to Villa Tower (W 14); urban composition unit together with Villa Flora; altered and derelict.

W 37

W 38 **Villa Flora**
Eforie Nord, Ovid Blvd
c. 1932-1935

Two-storey villa on the northern side of the Ovid Blvd (formerly Grand Blvd), initially with a shop on the ground floor and twelve rooms for renting, built for Mrs Tilea-Russo, grandmother of Ileana Tilea-Troiano; now altered and derelict.

Lit.
Secondary sources: Reported to the author by Mrs Ileana Tilea-Troiano, London, 28th November 2008;

W 38

W 39 **Villa Type 1a***
Eforie Nord, Ovid Blvd
c. 1932-1935

Attributed to GMC by the author on aesthetic grounds, typological closeness to Hotel Neptun, Villa Villa Tilea-Martaloglu, Villa 1b und Villa Hyacinth.

W 40 **Villa Type 1b***
Eforie Nord, nearby Ovid Blvd
c. 1932-1935

Attributed to GMC by the author on aesthetic grounds, typological closeness to Hotel Neptun, Villa Tilea-Martaloglu, Villa 1b und Villa Hyacinth.

W 41 **Blue Villa** (Villa Albastră)
Eforie Nord, Ovid Blvd
c. 1932-1935

Two-storey villa on the northern side of the boulevard, originally with a blue interior, built for Mrs Tilea-Russo, grandmother of Ileana-Tilea-Troiano; now altered and derelict.

Lit.
Secondary sources: Reported to the author by Mrs Ileana Tilea-Troiano, London, 28th November 2008; Cicio Pop 1940, p. 365 (reference to the Blue Villa without mentioning the architect)

W 41

W 42 **Villa Hyacinth*** (Villa Zambila)
Eforie Nord, Tudor Vladimirescu Blvd
c. 1932-1935

Attributed to GMC by the author on aesthetic grounds, typological closeness to Hotel Neptun, Villa Tilea-Martaloglu, Villa Type 1a and Villa Type 1b.

W 42

W 43 **Villa Anemone***
Eforie Nord, Tudor Vladimirescu Blvd
c. 1932-1935

Two-storey villa on the seaside promenade, adjacent to W 15; possibly for The Societatea Anonimă Techirghiolul; attributed to GMC by the author on aesthetic grounds.

W 44

W 45

W 47

W 44 Bragadiru-Callimachi Building
Carlton Building
Bucharest, Bratiano Blvd (now Nicolae Bălcescu Blvd)
c. 1932-1936

Apartment building commissioned by the Bragadiru and Callimachi families; the Carlton comprised the Carlton Cinema and the HQ of the Romanian Medical Association; in collaboration with Vasile Arion, civil engineer D. Mavrodin, builder Gebr. Karl & Leopold Schindl; design c. 1932-1935; construction c. 1935-1936; destroyed in the November 9th/10th, 1940 earthquake.

Lit.
Primary sources: AGMC-PM Bucharest
Secondary sources: Curentul 1940, p. 1; Beleş 1941, pp. 1172-1182; Sieberg 1941, pp. 32-33, 76-77; Patrulius 1975b, pp. 54-55; Willy Prager 1942, pp. 116-117; Prager 1979, pp. 451-453; Machedon/Scoffham 1999, pp. 177, 179; Pelin 2005, pp. 60-63; Duculescu 2010, p. 147

W 45 Romanian Broadcasting SRR
Bod/Brenndorf, c. 15 km N of Braşov/Kronstadt
1933-1935

First purpose-built broadcasting institution for nationwide transmission, in collaboration with Gh. Trifu. GMC layed out the urban and landscape composition, and he designed the porter's loge, the employees' apartment building and the engineers' villa (see fig. W45). Trifu designed the broadcasting institution building and the power station.

Lit.
Primary sources: GMC, radio talk, 16th October 1934, SRR Bucharest
Secondary sources: SRR, Dos. Nos. 23/1933, 33/1933; Gr. Ionescu 1943, fig. 30; Patrulius 1980, p. 153; Patrulius 1982, p. 90; Iordănescu/Georgescu 1986 (2), p. 157; Denize 1998, p. 313; Duculescu 2010, p. 147

W 46 Masterplan for Bucharest
21st February 1934-1st November 1934

GMC designed the technical infrastructure and was a co-author of the explanatory introduction (72 pages), in collaboration with the architects Roger Bolomey and Duiliu Marcu, urban planner Ion Davidescu and engineer Teodor Rădulescu; commissioned by the City of Bucharest, Mayor Dem Dobrescu and his successor Al. Donescu.

Lit.
Primary sources: Bolomey/Cantacuzino/Davidescu/Marcu/Rădulescu 1935; GMC, 1934 in: *Revista Fundaţiilor Regale*, I, No. 12, 1st December, pp. 580-591; GMC, 1935, broadcast lecture, 20th May 1935; GMC, 1935 in: *Revista Fundaţiilor Regale*, II, No. 10, 1st October, p. 210
Secondary sources: Patrulius 1975a, p. 59; Machedon/Scoffham 1999, pp. 75-100, 328.

W 47 Bragadiru apartment building
Bucharest, 65 Dionisie Lupu corner Lahovary Square
c. 1934-1935

Designed in collaboration with Vasile Arion for D. D. Bragadiru, brewery businessman.

Lit.
Secondary sources: PMB Bucharest, Archive record of the City Hall I Yellow 1930-1935, department of architecture, 1934, entry No. 235, p. 14, obviously no plans; Patrulius 1975a, pp. 59, 61; Machedon/Scoffham 1999, p. 205; Celac/Carabela/Marcu-Lăpădat 2005, p. 61. Duculescu 2010, p. 147

W 48 Kretzulesco apartment building
Bukarest, Amzeiplatz 11-15, ca. 1934-1935.

Designed in collaboration with Vasile Arion for Emmanuel Kretzulesco

Lit.
Secondary sources: PMB Bucharest, Archive record of the City Hall I Yellow 1930-1935, department of architecture, 1934, entry No. 518 A, p. 31, BG 32A7681/1934; Patrulius 1975a, pp. 59, 61; Machedon/Scoffham 1999, p. 203; Castello Branco dos Santos/Georgescu/Levy 2001, pp. 40-41; Celac/Carabela/Marcu-Lăpădat 2005, p. 60; Duculescu 2010, p. 147

W 48

W 49 Apartment building*
Bucharest, 1 and 1b Vânători Street
c. 1934-1935

Attributed to GMC by the author on aesthetic grounds, typological closeness to the following buildings: Carlton (W 44), Bragadiru (W 47), Kretzulesco (W 48) and the Soutzo Cereals Stock Exchange (W 54); now altered; there seem to be no plans in the PMB Archive of the City Hall of Bucharest.

W 49

W 50 Apartment buildings*
Bucharest, 4-10 Poenaru Bordea Street

Attributed to GMC by the author on aesthetic grounds, typological closeness to the following buildings: Carlton (W 44), Bragadiru (W 47), Kretzulesco (W 48) and the Soutzo Cereals Stock Exchange (W 54); now altered; there seem to be no plans in the PMB Archive of the City Hall of Bucharest.

W 51 Apartment building*
Bucharest, 29 Brezianu Street

Attributed to GMC by the author on aesthetic grounds, typological closeness to the following buildings: Carlton (W 44), Bragadiru (W 47), Kretzulesco (W 48) and the Soutzo Cereals Stock Exchange (W 54); there seem to be no plans in the PMB Archive of the City Hall of Bucharest.

W 51

W 52 Soutzo apartment building
Bucharest, Ion Nistor Street (formerly Ion Ghica Street)
c. 1934-1935

The first Soutzo building, the so called *Soutzo-Palace,* had 240 apartments; possibly commissioned by Demeter Soutzo but it is uncertain if it was built.

Lit.
Secondary sources: Leopold and Karol Schindl, *Un apartament pentru D-voastră?* Publicity catalogue, Bucharest 1934, in: AN Fond Familia Cantacuzino, inv. 1830, dos. 536, cited after Duculescu 2010, p. 112

W 53 Industrial Credit Office building
Bucharest, University Square
1934-1935

The second Soutzo building was erected for the Industrial Credit Office.

Lit.
Secondary sources: Arhitectura 1/1941, p. 199; Patrulius 1975b, p. 55; Anghelescu 1977, p. 508; Institutul de proiectare *Carpați*, architect V. Popa 1998; Ș. Cantacuzino 1999, p. XIII; Celac/Carabela/Marcu-Lăpădat 2005, p. 33; N. Ș. Noica 2006, p. 267; Duculescu 2011, p. 147

W 53

W 54

W 54 **Cereals Stock Exchange and Soutzo apartment and office building**
Bucharest, Toma Caragiu Street (formerly Ion Ghica Street), facing the Russian Church
c. 1934-1936

The third Soutzo building, the so called *Continental* building, housed the Cereals Stock Exchange from 1936 to 1947, afterwards a theatre and night-club, with apartments on the upper floors; destroyed in the 1977 earthquake.

Lit.
Primary sources: AGMC-PM Bucharest
Secondary sources: Constantin 1986, p. 65; Machedon/Scoffham 1999, p. 364; Duculescu 2010, p. 147

W 55

W 55 **Ships' house*** (Casa Bărcilor])
Mamaia, Black Sea Coast
On the eastern shore of the Siutghiol Lake opposite the Casino (W 56)
c. 1934-1936

Commissioned by the City of Constantza and the *Salvamar* Society (Sea Rescue Service); possibly designed in collaboration with Vasile Arion, Radu Dudescu and Gospodin, then chief architect of Constantza; aesthetic closeness to Hotel Bellona (W 36); demolished in 1960.

Lit.
Secondary sources: Reported to the author by architect Dan Corneliu and Gheorghe Vecerdea, then chief urban planner of Constantza, 11th September 2006; letter by Gheorghe Vecerdea to the author, 25th September 2008; A. Lăpuşan/Ş. Lăpuşan/Gh. Stănescu 2006, pp. 147-149 (Radu Dudescu is mentioned here as the architect)

W 56

W 56 **Casino and Baths***
Mamaia, Black Sea Coast
c. 1934-1937

Large building complex including a casino with café, restaurant, shops and baths as well as a landing stage leading to a sea platform with waterslides. The complex was built in two stages for the National Office of Tourism ONT and possibly the Romanian Railways CFR. The first stage, which included the central block, was designed either by Victor G. Ştephănescu (1877-1950) alone or by GMC in collaboration with Ştephănescu; for the second stage it is possible that GMC collaborated with Vasile Arion and the civil engineers Vermecher and Aurel Ioanovici. In 1937 GMC became the successor of Ştephănescu as chief architect of the Romanian Railways.

Lit.
Secondary sources: Prager 1979, pp. 284-286; the following sources mention Ştephănescu as the architect: *Arhitectura* 1935, No. 2, pp. 31, 33; 1941, No. 3-4, pp. 30-31; A. Lăpuşan/Ş. Lăpuşan/Gh. Stănescu 2006, p. 120; Machedon/Scoffham 1999, p. 387; M. Ştephănescu 2007

W 57 **Villa Andricu***
Bucharest, Silvestru Street
c. 1935-1937

Villa and garden for Mihai Andricu, the Romanian composer;
the exact address is unknown.

Lit.
Secondary source: Patrulius 1982, p. 90

W 58 **Villa Policrat**
Bucharest, 24 Calea Floreasca
1935-1936

Three-storey villa with garage, balcony and little courtyard for Florica Policrat.

Lit.
Primary source: AGMC-PM, probably photograph by Paul Marinescu; PMB Archive record *City Hall of Bucharest I Yellow 1935*, No. 258, p. 21, building permission plans
Secondary sources: ; Patrulius 1982, p. 90; Duculescu 2010, p. 147

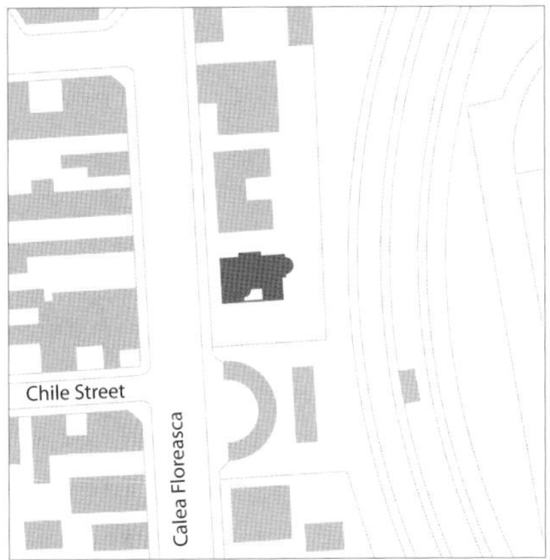

W 58

W 59 **Church in Băileşti**
Dolj County, Southh-West Romania, some 20 km north of the Danube
c. 1935-1937

Church of the village of Băileşti, where the Ştirbeys, the family of GMC's wife Sanda, had large estates.

Lit.
Secondary sources: Patrulius 1975a, p. 59; Patrulius 1982, p. 91; Duculescu 2010, p.1 47

W 60 **Church in Seini**
Maramuresch County, Western Carpathians, 20 km NW of Baia Mare (Nagybánya)
c. 1935-1937

Possibly commissioned by Veturia Goga, wife of Octavian Goga, the Romanian poet (see W 80); the church was destroyed during WW II.

Lit.
Secondary sources: Patrulius 1975a, p. 59; Patrulius 1982, p. 91; Duculescu 2010, p. 147

W 61 **Grand Hotel Rex**
Mamaia, Black Sea Coast
c. 1936-1938

Commissioned by the National Office of Tourism ONT and Romanian Railways CFR; designed in collaboration with Vasile Arion, the painter Paul Miracovici (frescos) and Marietta Stern-Guetta (interior design); civil engineers Vermecher and Aurel Ioanovici; southern pergola destroyed around 2011 because of the construction of another hotel.

Bibliography
Primary sources: GMC, letter to Marietta Stern-Guetta, Mamaia, 5th August 1937; AGMC-PM Bucharest
Secondary sources: Patmore 1939, pp. 40, 113-114; Prager 1979, pp. 284-286; Iordănescu/Georgescu 1986, vol. 1, p. 546; Duculescu 2010, p. 147

W 61

W 62 **Sanatorium**
Health spa in Olăneşti, 19 km N of Râmnicu Vâlcea, located in the Southern Carpathians between the monasteries of Cozia and Horez
c. 1936-1938

Lit.
Secondary sources: Patrulius 1975a, p. 59; Patrulius 1982, p. 91; Duculescu 2010, p. 147

W 63

W 63 Villa Mornand
Bucharest, 16 Muzeul Zambaccian Street (formerly Av. Cpt. Demetriade Street)
c. 1936-1940

Two-storey villa for Angela Mornand.

Lit.
Primary sources: PMB Bucharest Archive of the *City Hall I Yellow* 1939, No. 689/619, p. 52, building permission plans

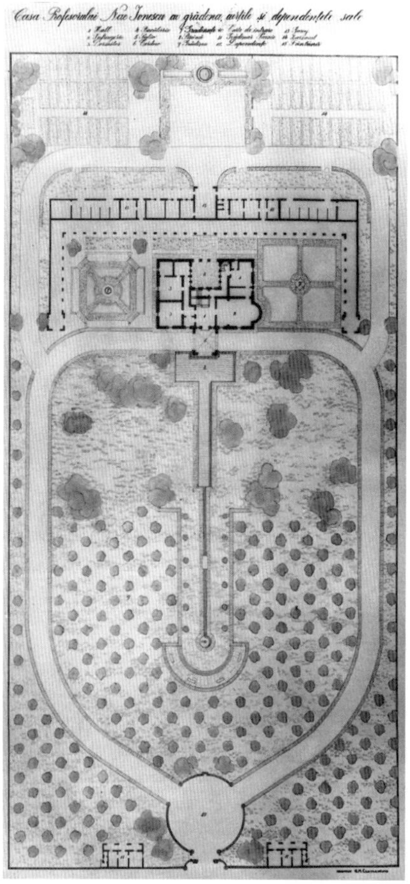

W 64

W 64 Villa Nae Ionescu
Bucharest, 4 Ion Ionescu de la Brad Street (formerly Carol II Boulevard)
c. 1936-1937, 1942

This estate for Professor Nae Ionescu was GMC's largest villa project with garden; designed in collaboration with Marietta Stern-Guetta (interior design); on Ionescu's death the estate was taken over by Marshall Ion Antonescu who commissioned GMC to extend the villa.

Lit.
Primary sources: GMC, letter to Marietta Stern-Guetta, 5th July 1937, AMLSC; GMC, letters to Sanda Cantacuzino, 19th March 1942, 7th May 1942, AMLSC; AGMC-PM Bucharest
Secondary sources: Patrulius 1975a, pp. 54, 55; Patrulius 1975b, p. 59; Patrulius 1982, p. 90; Vulcănescu 1992, pp. 136-137; Ș. Cantacuzino 1999, p. XV; Duculescu 2010, p. 147

W 65 Villa Malaxa
perhaps in Bucharest
c. 1937-1938

Villa for Nicolae Malaxa, the Romanian industrial magnate.

Lit.
Primary sources: GMC, letter to Marietta Stern-Guetta, 5th July 1937, AMLSC

W 66 Apartment building with Lux Cinema
Craiova (capital of Dolj County), c. 300 km W of Bucharest
3 Al. Cuza Street
c. 1937-1938

Five-storey apartment building including a cinema on the ground floor and first floor; commissioned by G. Negrețu, advocate in Craiova.

Lit.
Primary sources: GMC, letter to Marietta Stern-Guetta, 5th July 1937, AMLSC; ANDJD Dos. 79/1936 National Archive Craiova/Dolj, building premission plans

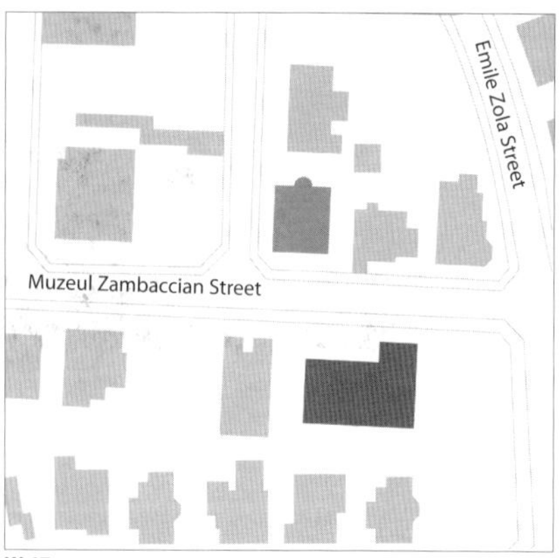

W 67

W 67 Villa Alice Sturdza
Bucharest, 18 Muzeul Zambaccian Street
(until1945 Av. Cpt. Gh. Demetriade Street)
c. 1937-1938

Villa for Alice Sturdza, née Cantacuzino.

Lit.
Primary sources: GMC, letter to Marietta Stern-Guetta, 5th July 1937, AMLSC
Secondary sources: Patrulius 1982, p. 90; letter by Olympia Zamfiresco to the author, Cannes, 24th March 2008; Pippidi in *Dilema Veche*, 26th February 2011

W 68 **Chapel**
On the route from Bucharest to Piteşti
c. 1937-1938

A family called Ştefănescu commissioned GMC to design a chapel in remembrance of their daughter killed in a car accident.

Lit.
Primary sources: GMC, letter to Marietta Stern-Guetta, 1st July 1937, AMLSC

W 69 **Villa Butculescu**
perhaps in Bucharest
c. 1937-1939

Villa for the Butculescu family.

Lit.
Primary sources: GMC, letter to Marietta Stern-Guetta, 5th July 1937, AMLSC

W 70 **Villa Grecescu**
perhaps in Bucharest
c. 1937-1939

Villa for the Grecescu family.

Lit.
Primary sources: GMC, letter to Marietta Stern-Guetta, 5th July 1937, AMLSC

W 71 **Villa Kretzulesco**
perhaps in Bucharest, Henri Coandă Street corner Dacia Blvd
c. 1937-1939

Villa for Nicholas Kretzulesco, friend of GMC's.

Lit.
Primary sources: GMC, letter to Marietta Stern-Guetta, 5th July 1937, AMLSC
Secondary sources: Alice Magheru in Dragu Dimitriu 2004, p. 26; Pippidi in *Dilema Veche*, 26th February 2011

W 72 **Villa Mavrocordato**
Balcic, Southern Dobrodgea (now in Bulgaria), Black Sea Coast
c. 1937-1938

Design of a villa suspended over the cliffs of Balcic
commissioned by Nicholas Mavrocordato.

Lit.
Primary sources: GMC, letter to Marietta Stern-Guetta, Bucharest, 24th June 1937, AMLSC.

W 73 **Sanatorium**
Câmpulung-Muscel, Argeş County, Southern Carpathians
c. 1937-1940

Commissioned by the Ştefănescu family (see W68)

Lit.
Primary sources: GMC, letter to Marietta Stern-Guetta, Bucharest, 1st July 1937

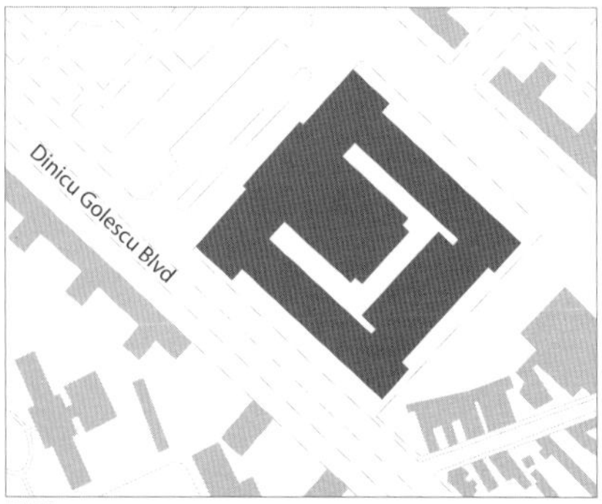

W 74

W 74 Headquarters of the Romanian Railways CFR
Bucharest, Dinicu Golescu Blvd/Gara de Nord
opposite to the Main Station
c. 1937-1940

The building was built to the designs of Duiliu Marcu in collaboration with Paul Smărandescu, Ernest Doneaud and Paul Emil Miclesco (1934-1937); as CFR chief architect GMC managed the project from 1937-1940, which was completed from 1946 to the late 1950s (without GMC).

Lit.
Primary source: GMC, letter to Sanda Cantacuzino, Posada, 3rd September 1939
Secondary source: Paul Emil Miclescu in Rădulescu 2005, p. 301

W 75

W 75 Kretzulesco Office and Commercial building
Bucharest, 45 Calea Victoriei
1937-1942

Commissioned by Nicholas Kretzulesco; designed in collaboration with Duiliu Marcu.

Lit.
Primary sources: GMC, letter to Marietta Stern-Guetta, 24th June 1937; GMC, letters to Sanda Cantacuzino, 30th January 1941, end of February 1941, 2nd January 1942; GMC, handwritten declaration, 3rd March1948, in: CNSAS, Dos. No. 7279, RPR, AV, MAI 549/33, 318 3/8A; AGMC-PM, Bucharest; AMLSC London; INMI/FDMI Bucharest; PMB Bucharest
Secondary sources: Radu Patrulius 1975b, pp. 54-55; Patrulius 1982, p. 91; Celac/Carabela/Marcu-Lăpădat 2005, p. 58; Duculescu 2010, pp. 130, 131, 147

W 76

W 76 Flămânda Church (the Hungry One)
Câmpulung-Muscel, Argesch County, Southern Carpathians
c. 200 km north-west of Bucharest, 100 km south-west of Braşov/Kronstadt,

1937-1942.

Commissioned by the Ştefănescu family (see W 68 and W 73).

Lit.
Primary sources: GMC, letter to Marietta Stern-Guetta, 1st July 1937; GMC, letters to Sanda Cantacuzino, 29th September 1940, 7th May 1942
Secondary sources: Patrulius 1975a, p. 59; Anghelescu 1977, p. 508; Patrulius 1982, p. 91; Ş. Cantacuzino 1999, p. XV; Duculescu 2010, pp. 132, 147

W 77 Villa Cretzeanu
Orbeasca de Jos, Teleorman County, 70 km SW of Bucharest
c. 1938-1939

Country retreat for Radu and Sarmiza Cretzeanu.

Lit.
Secondary source: Patrulius 1982, p. 91

W 78 Transformation of a Villa
c. 1938-1940

Commissioned by Nicholas Mavrocordato.

Lit.
Primary source: GMC, letter to Marietta Stern-Guetta, Bucharest, 5th March 1938, AMLSC

W 79 **Church in the Bucovina**
c. 1938

Possibly commissioned by Nicholas Mavrocordato.

Lit.
Primary source: GMC, letter to Marietta Stern-Guetta, Bucharest, 5th March 1938, AMLSC

W 80 **Mausoleum of the poet Octavian Goga**
Ciucea, Cluj County, Transylvania
1938-1939

Commissioned by Veturia Goga, the poet's widow;
designed in collaboration with sculptor Militza Pătraşcu.

Lit.
Primary sources: GMC, letters to Marietta Stern-Guetta, 21st August 1938, 27th August 1938, AMLSC; GMC, letter to Sanda Cantacuzino, 3rd September 1939, AMLSC.
Secondary sources: Patrulius 1975b, p. 58; Patrulius 1982, p. 90; Duculescu 2010, p. 147

W 81 **Official Pavilion of Romania at the New York World's Fair 1939**
New York, USA
1938-1939

GMC designed the official pavilion, whereas Octav Doicescu planned the Romanian House (Casa Românească); in collaboration with *August Schmiedigen Associates*; the director of the Romanian team was Professor Dimitrie Gusti, the sociologist.

Lit.
Primary sources: GMC, letter to Marietta Stern-Guetta, 10'h May 1938, AMLSC; GMC, letters to Sanda Cantacuzino, 1st, 2nd and 9th June1938, AMLSC; GMC, radio talks, 13th December 1938, 31st August 1939; GMC in *Arhitectura* No. 1/1941, pp. 166-169; AGMC-PM Bucharest; UAR/AOD Bucharest, Box 6/I AB
Secondary sources: Patrulius 1975a, p. 59; Anghelescu 1977, pp. 508-509; Wurts/Applebaum 1977, p. 118; Derer/Doicescu 1983, p. 11; Lerner/Rolfes/Zim 1988, p. 153; Machedon/Scoffham 1999, p. 302; Duculescu 2010, pp. 133, 147

W 81

W 82 **British Institute**
Bucharest, 151 Calea Victoriei corner Sevastopol Street
1939-1940

Commissioned by the British Council and British Government; designed in collaboration with Octav Doicescu; the project was stopped early in 1941 due to WW II; the site map is a reconstruction based on the plans from the archives of the Union of Romanian Architects.

Lit.
Primary sources: GMC, letters to Sanda Cantacuzino, 15th October 1939, 19th November 1939, AMLSC; UAR/AOD, Bucharest, Box 2-I, A: ARS; NA London, BW 53/1 and BW 53/2

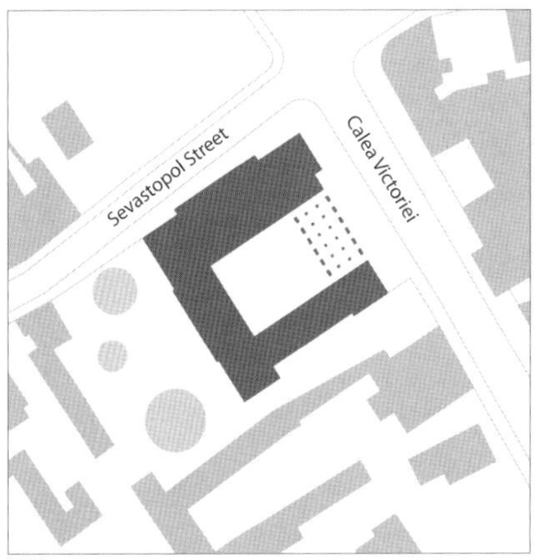

W 82

W 83 **Costandaky Project**
c. 1939-1940

Building for Georges Costandaky, perhaps in Bucharest.

Lit.
Primary source: GMC, letter to Sanda Cantacuzino, Bucharest, 2nd August 1939, AMLSC

W 84 **Callimachi Project**
c. 1939-1940

Building for Anne-Marie and Jean Callimachi, perhaps in Bucharest.

Lit.
Primary source: GMC, letter to Sanda Cantacuzino, Bucharest, 2nd August 1939, AMLSC

W 85 **Villa Chrissoveloni**
c. 1939-1940

Villa for Nicki Chrissoveloni, perhaps in Bucharest.

Lit.
Primary source: GMC, letter to Sanda Cantacuzino, Bucharest, 15th October 1939, AMLSC

W 86 **Urban Masterplan for Constantza**
1940

Urban masterplan including the design of a civic centre and of public squares; in collaboration with Ion Davidescu; the project was probably stopped on account of the radical change of government on the 6th September 1940.

Lit.
Primary source: GMC, letter to Sanda Cantacuzino, 28th March 1940, AMLSC

W 87 **Villa Cantacuzino**
c. 1940-1942

Intended as a country retreat for GMC's own family near Bucharest, the villa was not built.

Lit.
Primary source: GMC, letters to Sanda Cantacuzino, Bucharest, 8th April 1940, 2nd January 1942, 14th July 1942, AMLSC

W 88

W 88 **Drugăneşti Manor (Conac)**
Drugăneşti-Stoeneşti, Ilfov County, 30 km south of Bucharest
1939-1946

Transformation and extension of a derelict eighteenth-century manor; commissioned by Marina Brancovan-Ştirbey, sister-in-law of GMC's.

Lit.
Primary sources: GMC, letters to Sanda Cantacuzino, 8th May 1940, 30th January 1940, end of February 1940, 2nd January 1942, 7th May 1942, AMLSC; *Simetria VII* (1946)
Secondary sources: Patrulius 1975b, p. 59; Patrulius 1982, p. 90; Păcurariu/Pandele, DCCPCNG Doc. No. 437, 8th August 2005; CLADRA Architects, Bucharest

W 89 **Transformation of a manor house**
1942

Transformation and modernisation of a historical *Heiduc* manor, perhaps in the Carpathians.

Lit.
Primary sources: GMC, letters to Sanda Cantacuzino, 2nd January 1942; 11th June 1942, AMLSC

W 90 **Villa**
1942

Villa for an employee of Marshall Ion Antonescu, perhaps in Bucharest.

Lit.
Primary source: GMC, letter to Sanda Cantacuzino, 14th July 1942

W 91 **Church in Posada**
Posada, Prahova Valley, Southern Carpathians, 8 km SW of Sinaia
c. 1943

Commissioned by Marthe Bibesco.

Lit.
Primary sources: GMC, letter to Sanda Cantacuzino, 9th December 1943, AMLSC; reported to the author by Marie-Lyse Cantacuzino-Ruhemann, London, 30th November 2008

W 92 **Villa**
Bucharest, 109 Calea Victoriei corner 1 Calea Griviţei
c. 1945/1946-1955

Perhaps commissioned by the Ştirbey and Cantacuzino families, the villa was meant to be built on the site of the former *Corps-de-garde* building of the Ştirbey Palace, where GMC's family lived, and where he had his architectural office (the *Corps-de-garde* building was destroyed by bombing in 1944). The villa was never built; see also W 93.

Lit.
Primary source: GMC, letter to Sanda Cantacuzino, 4th March 1946, AMLSC

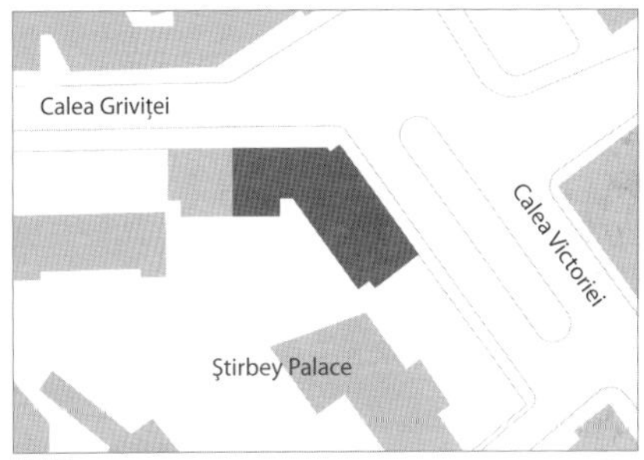

W 92

W 93 **Office building (originally with theatre)**
Bucharest, 1 Calea Griviţei
c. 1945/1946

Commissioned by the Romanian Pension Scheme, this multi-storey office building (initially with a theatre) was placed on a site which belonged to the Ştirbey family; designed in collaboration with O. Doicescu; after GMC's arrest in 1948 W 92 and W 93 were obviously altered to the effect that the designs were enlarged and fused into one massive office block, which turns its back on the Ştirbey Palace.

Lit.
Primary sources: GMC, letter to Sanda Cantacuzino, 4th March1946, AMLSC; GMC, handwritten declaration, 3rd March 1948, in: CNSAS, Dos. No. 7279, RPR, AV, MAI 549/33, 318 3/8A
Secondary sources: Celac/Carabela/Marcu-Lăpădat 2005, p. 64; Duculescu 2010, p. 147

W 93

W 94 **Office building**
Bucharest, 5-7 Vasile Lascăr Street,
1945-1947

Originally a building for the Gas and Electric Company, it now houses a branch of the Institute of Hydro-Electrical Research and Design (ISPHE).

Lit.
Primary sources: GMC, handwritten declaration, 3rd March 1948, in: CNSAS, Dos. No. 7279, RPR, AV, MAI 549/33, 318 3/8A
Secondary sources: Celac/Carabela/Marcu-Lăpădat 2005, p. 34; Duculescu 2010, p. 147; ISPHE Bucharest (drawings by the author based on ISPHE's survey of the building)

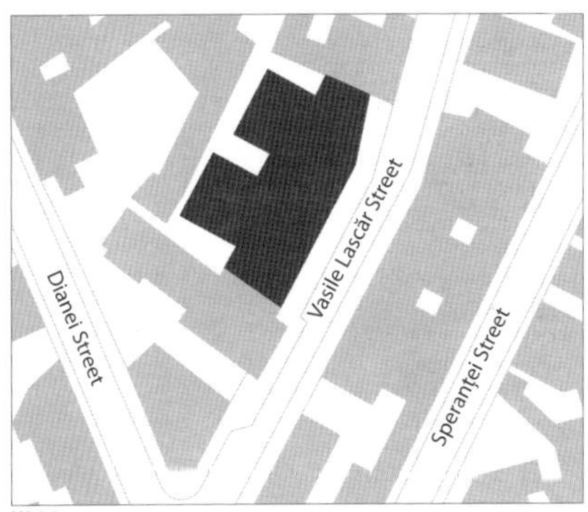

W 94

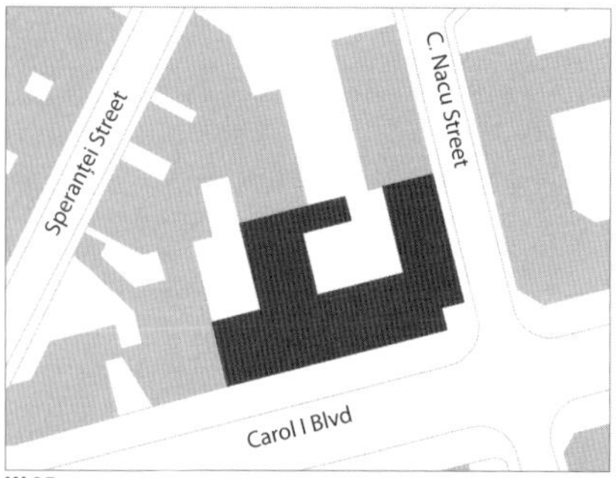

W 95

W 95 **Office building**
Bucharest, 29 Carol I Boulevard
1945-1947

Originally a building for the Gas and Electric Company, it now houses another part of the Institute of Hydro-Electrical Research and Design (ISPHE)

Lit.
Primary sources: See W 94
Secondary sources: Patrulius 1975a, p. 62; Patrulius 1975b, pp. 54, 55; Celac/Carabela/Marcu-Lăpădat 2005, p. 34; Duculescu 2010, p. 147; ISPHE Bucharest (drawings by the author based on ISPHE's survey of the building).

W 96

W 96 **Office building***
Bucharest, Ferdinand Blvd (Gh. Dimitrov Boulevard from 1945-1989)
1945-1947

The building at 51 Ferdinand Blvd could be attributed to GMC on aesthetic grounds, involving sober Palladianism applied to a multistorey block (now an apartment building) and the tulip motif of the wrought window grilles; there seem to be no plans in the PMB Archive of the City Hall of Bucharest.

Lit.
Secondary source: Patrulius 1982, p. 91

W 97 **Hotel**
Râmnicu-Sărat, 125 km NO of Bucharest
c. 1945-1947

Designed in collaboration with Nicolae Nedelescu.

Lit.
Secondary source: Patrulius 1975a, p. 59

W 98 **Sanatorium**
Târgu-Ocna, 200 km N of Bucharest
c. 1945-1947

Commissioned by the Romanian Pension Scheme for Civil Servants; designed in collaboration with Berindey and Nicolae Nedelescu.

Lit.
Primary source: GMC, handwritten declaration, 3rd March 1948, in: CNSAS, Dos. No. 7279, RPR, AV, MAI 549/33, 318 3/8A

W 99

W 99 **Restoration of the Soutzo Palace**
Bucharest, Bratiano Blvd
c. 1954-1956

The house was built for the Soutzo family to the designs of the German architect Konrad Schwing from 1832-1834; the building was used by the Chrissoveloni Bank during the 1930s until 1948. As an inspector of the Department of Historical Monuments (DMI), GMC supervised the restoration of the building, which had been transformed into the Bucharest Museum.

Lit.
Primary source: INMI/FDMI Bucharest, Dos. No. 2480

W 100 Restoration of St Sava Church
Jassy
c. 1954-1957

GMC's duty as an inspector of the Department of Historical Monuments (DMI) included the supervision of the restoration of this church.

Lit.
Secondary source: Patrulius 1975a, p. 59

W 100

W 101 Church
in a valley of the Ceahlău Mountain, Eastern Carpathians
c. 1958

Lit.
Primary source: GMC, letter to Sanda Cantacuzino, Bucharest, 13th September 1958

W 102 Restoration of the Sucevitza Monastery
Sucevitza/Bucovina, c. 40 km NW of Suceava
c. 1954-1957

One of GMC's duties as an inspector of the Department of Historical Monuments (DMI) was to supervise the restoration of this monastery.

Lit.
Primary sources: INMI/FDMI Bucharest, Dos. No. 8783; AMLSC
Secondary source: Reported to the author by Dan Corneliu, Constantza, 11th September 2006

W 102

W 103 Extension of the Metropolitan Church Complex in Jassy
Jassy
1957-1961

Commissioned by the Justin Moisescu, Moldavian Bishop of the Romanian Orthodox Church, GMC designed three pavilions and a public square with ramps, stairs and terraces to screen the Metropolitan Cathedral.

Lit.
Primary sources: GMC, letter to Sanda Cantacuzino, Bucharest, 13th September 1958, AMLSC; letter to Marie-Lyse Cantacuzino-Ruhemann, Jassy, 25th December 1958, AMLSC; letter to Jean David, Jassy, 2nd May 1960, AMLSC; AGMC-IP Bucharest; AMLSC London
Secondary sources: Patrulius 1975a, p. 62; Patrulius 1975b, p. 58; Patrulius 1982, p. 91; Anghelescu 1977, p. 511; Ş. Cantacuzino 1999, p. XIII; Duculescu 2010, pp. 140-143, 147

W 103

TRADITIONALISM şi MODERNISM.

Conferinţă ţinută în studioul Soc. de Difuziune Radiotelefonică din România, la 23 Iulie 1932 de Arhitect G. M. Cantacuzino.

Acum câteva decenii, din cauza vechimei sale, campanilul cel mare al Veneţiei îngenunchiă într'o bună dimineaţă şi pe urmă se culcă răpus de oboseală pe piaţa San Marcă.

Vigiile corăbiilor care sosiră în aceea zi se crezură rătăcite când văzură în zare umbra unui oraş al cărui semn distinctiv pierise, că nu Veneţia era aceea simfonie de turnuri şi cupole, dar cine ştie ce miraj mincinos născocit din jocul luminii! Aşa de întipărit era în amintirea tuturor navigatorilor hieroglifa verticală din orizont, de un albastru străveziu în orele dimineţii, opac şi metalic pela prânz, trandafiriu şi ireal la asfinţitul soarelui, galben ca ceara în nopţile de lună, încât pieirea lui desorienta pe toţi marinarii, care vedeau în acel turn care le arunca bunvenitul în lovituri de clopot, semnul sosirii, al odihnei şi al mândriei natale. Astăzi un campanil nou, edificat din materiale sănătoase ferita de igrasia fundaţiilor lacurtre şi-a substituit realitatea vechiului edificiu, iar pescarii adriatici ştiu să citească ora după culoarea pe care şi-o însuşeste gigantica clopotniţă.

In Italia fiecare oraş îşi desprinde pe cer mândria unei siluete care nu-i decât semnul viu al libertăţii cucerite. Natura a favorizat aceste aşezăminte astfel că între dânsa şi artă se face o deplină fuziune, iar stâncile par a fi opera unor sculptori ori arhitecţi.

Addendum (2): Selected Essays

The Romanian Review of History (1931)
GMC co-authored this editorial to the first edition of this periodical together with G. Bratiano, N. Cartojan, C. C. Giurescu, S. Lambrino, P. P. Panaitescu and Al. Rosetti.
Published in *The Romanian Review of History,* Vol. 1, Faks. 1.
Bucharest (Universitatea din Bucureşti), 1931, pp. 3-6. Excerpt.

Traditionalism and Modernism (1932)
This lecture in the series *Radio University* was broadcast by the Romanian Broadcasting Company on the 23rd July 1932.
Published in *Izvoare şi Popasuri* [Sources and Stopovers].
Bucharest 1934, pp. 13-19

In Praise of the Tulip* (1934)
Published in the series *Cronica plastică* [The art column] of *The Royal Foundations Review*, Vol. I, No. 12.
Bucharest, 1st December 1934, pp. 671-673.
Reprinted by Virgil Ierunca as *Prejudecăţi* [Prejudices] in:
GMC, *Scrieri* [Writings]. Paris 1966, pp. 61-64.

The "Mitocan" as a factor in Romanian civilisation (1941)
Published in *Simetria II*. Bucharest 1941, pp. 89-90.
Translated from the Romanian by Şerban Cantacuzino

Explanatory Note (1946)
Published in *Simetria VII*. Bucharest 1946, pp. 208-209

The Artist and the Freedom (1947)
Published in the last *Simetria* edition,
Simetria VIII. Bucharest 1947, pp. 101-107

Letter to Marie-Lyse Cantacuzino-Ruhemann,
Bucharest, 25th December 1958 (AMLSC).
Translated from the Romanian by Marie-Lyse Cantacuzino-Ruhemann

* This title has been suggested by the author.
[] Words shown in brackets are added by the author in clearness' sake.

322 Opposite:
Traditionalism and Modernism.
Radio broadcast, 23rd July 1932, Title page (SRR).

The Romanian Review of History (1931)
Excerpt from the first editorial

The Institute of Romanian History at the University of Bucharest is to start a new periodical publication – a review devoted to Romanian history. The need for such a review has been evident for a long time. [...]

The review's purpose is to study the past of the Romanian people, considering all aspects of life: history, politics, institutions, social and economic life, language, literature, art, religion and folklore. The study will consider these aspects, both in themselves and in the relations between them, as parts of an organic entity. This analysis will show what is specifically Romanian, what is borrowed from foreign civilisations and what Romanians have contributed to neighbouring civilisations.

The generation of historians before the Great War was concerned with the ideal of Romanian society: national unity. The present generation has experienced the fulfilment of this ideal and faces problems of a different kind: social, economic, cultural. [...] Therefore the social, economic and cultural orientation, if not exclusive, will be essential to our review. Besides, this coincides with the general tendency of contemporary historiography in Europe.

The reconstruction of our past was and still is the subject of innumerable controversies and disputes which are often due to particular political parties. Therefore the foremost duty of our review must be the strict respect of truth. History must not be abused by, nor be the servant of political and social disputes. Rather history should contribute to clarify the premiss of such disputes. Only a truly objective approach can produce incontestibly scientific results. Both from a national and individual point of view truth can never be wrong; it is, on the contrary, invariably useful. Between patriotism and truth there is no contradiction. [...] The quest for truth demands a profound study of detail. For him who knows how to look, merest detail may reveal general character. This is the only possible foundation for a true historical synthesis.

In Romania, in all sciences and especially in history, there is an acute need for a competent, sincere and serious critique, presented in an urbane manner. [...] As we pay particular attention to the relationships and exchanges with our neighbours, we have extracted from a number of foreign historians the promise of their precious collaboration.

The foremost requirement of a review is regularity, the very opposite of haphazardness. [...]

The Romanian Review of History publishes articles and commentaries in the following languages: Romanian, French, Italian, English and German. The articles published in Romanian will be accompanied by a summary of one of these four foreign languages.

Traditionalism and Modernism (1932)

Some decades ago, the great Campanile of Venice broke down on the San Marco Square. It was overpowered by fatigue and age. On that day, the sailors heading home thought they were lost. They were confused by the skyline of their city, which suddenly lacked its major symbol. They got so used to that upright hieroglyphic on the horizon that they believed not to have seen Venice, that symphony of domes and towers, but to have fallen prey of the deceptive blaze of lights. Indeed, the Campanile could take on many colours: a transparent blue at dawn, a dim metallic at high noon, an irreal bluish at dusk, and even a yellow of candle-wax at full moon. The Campanile welcomed the sailors with the ring of its bells. Its disappearance confused all sailors, for whom it was the symbol of home, calmness and local pride. Today, there is a new Campanile, built of more solid materials and well protected from the Sea. Meanwhile the sailors have learned to read the time by the colours of its new bell-tower.

In Italy, every city boasts a skyline which expresses its civic freedom. Here nature is friendly to man. Between nature and art there is a complete fusion, with the rocks and mountains seeming to be the work of some sculptors or architects.

We, on the contrary, have come to terms with the tempests of history. The trees on the seashore are usually smaller and take a forced shape in order to resist the whirling tempests. Likewise, our architecture grew harmoniously into the landscape, becoming rather discreet, calm and scarcely noticed. Our architecture only sketches the outline of a spirituality, some restrained emotions and almost silent witnesses.

But there were moments of triumph as well. There are more protected places, like, for example, Suceava.

Seen from the valley, with its towers and ruins, this city resembles an army camp of tents and lances: it is the vivid image of Stephen the Great and Peter Rareş. Jassy, on its hills, might be the best urban expression of our pride. The Moldavian City of Roman with its monastery, or the Wallachian cities of Târgovişte and Râmnicu-Vâlcea, are other attempts at leaving the valleys to charm the travellers, at least for a couple of moments. No matter how rare these examples are, they nonetheless invite us to reflect upon their successes.

For in our modern cities, we seem to have forgotten the art of the skyline, which embodies the civil pride much better than any social or patriotic theory. Indeed, our new cities reflect our instinctive laziness: we laid them out like oil-patches on pieces of paper, without any purpose, without any method, without any aesthetic concern. Our dull ignorance, our crude love of improvisation and transience, our megalomanic vanity have caused us to hastily embrace undignified appearances and to neglect time, without which nothing enduring can be created. As a result, our cities grew ordinary and our official representation got balkanised.

Today, as we are a free nation living within its natural borders, and as nothing hinders us from freely developing our abilities, it is even more unacceptable that, amongst other things, we were not able to create any satisfying urban programme to connect the main rail station with the high street which could express the respect for the citizen and public welfare.

I disapprove of mere retrospective approaches. But I believe that outstanding works of the past can provide suitable and safe places for dreaming of the future. As this safety proves so fertile for the imagination, I regard it as the essential feature of historical works. These are models, not to be slavishly copied, but to give us inspiration.

For we believe that being Romanian is not limited to identifying oneself with the present state. It implies too to accept in its entirety the past evolution with all its sufferings and successes. You cannot be Romanian just from now on, since you are a product of that past, regardless of your aspirations for the future.

To put architecture, in the name of internationalism, on a merely abstract and intellectual scale, and cut every bond of local emotions, is as superfluous as dangerous a game. To proclaim, on the other hand, a local style, limited to historical forms which are more or less successfully adapted to contemporary needs, leads us straight into a dead-end: Such an abuse would both prematurely dry out the inspiring source of traditional forms; on the other hand, it would compromise the further evolution of architecture. As a consequence, Romanian art, and especially architecture, is in an embarrassing situation.

Everywhere in the world a new architecture has come into being. An experimental architecture, which worships the light, tries to settle social problems, and which, above all, profits from the progresses and subtleties of mechanics. Something of the aesthetics of luxury cars, steamliners, locomotives and high speed trains, has entered into architecture.

All the features of speed seem to have pervaded the immobility of architecture, all the features of restlessness seem to have penetrated the protecting shelter of men, as if even in day-to-day life the bored humanity longed for the illusion of travelling. As a consequence, intimacy is often reduced to the neon light of a ship cabin, and apartments often resemble hotel rooms.

These facts cannot be neglected. In view of the new world, which rises before our eyes in Moscow as well as in New York, Prague, and Budapest, the Romanian hesitates between this strange and yet somehow seducing charm, and the nostalgia for a quiet parochial life that fills his soul.

One can find these two styles and their extremes in Bucharest as well. At first sight, a synthesis between them appears impossible and an unsolveble problem, since a style usually implies the entire aesthetic and constructive elements that stem from a common tendency of a certain age.

Neither the modern style nor the so-called Romanian style are really firmly established and even less mature. Both of them represent a tendency open to a long term evolution or perfection. Both of them are based on a sum of experiences and await the judgement of use and time.

Now which are the Romanian tendencies in respect to the modern one? Let us analyse them to see if they are really incompatible. Although our country grows more and more democratic, our established architecture, which is favoured by both the general public and the officials, usually consists of traditional elements taken from our religious or vernacular architecture.

The more we leave the time of monasteries, *conacs* [manor houses] with *cerdacs* [balconies] behind us, the more the public favours these elements. The arcade, the vault, the niche, the balcony, the roofs in picturesque outlines, exterior stairs, and rich ornaments occur time and again in our contemporary architecture.

These aesthetic externals reveal a laudable concern to define a certain originality by somehow harking back to the past. This need is quite acute. However, it has nothing to do with the more actual need to find solutions for contemporary problems. The general tendency of our architecture is basically ornamental. We are sincerely seeking for an original ornamental idiom. Since our cities for example are largely lacking in old buildings, new public buildings are required to remind us of the past to which we feel commited.

Seen through such a prism of analysis, the apparent incompatibility between the modern tendencies in general and ours in particular vanishes.

Modern architecture seeks its principles at the sources of utility, construction and social issue. In no way does it contradict the aspirations of our own archi-tecture. On the contrary, it launches amazing prospects. If we open our curiosity and our spirit to these tasks, which are common to all people in the world, we surely will enter the constructive circle of modern life and enable our natural abilities to develop on a larger scale.
Our cities, without becoming banal, will adopt something of the civic pride of historic cities. Certainly we will live in greater harmony with our past than if we got stuck in a retrospective attitude. Today we cannot reject the great questions of humanity, no less than we did in the past.

For humanity comes first, and regionalism only second. Our problem is not to reduce general tendencies to regional aesthetics; on the contrary, we have to appreciate our old regional heritage as a cultural value of general interest, that we transfer into the great realm of the eternal artworks of humanity.

In Praise of the Tulip* (1934)

Some months ago I was commissioned by the Director-General of a company to design a small art-object which was meant to be a gift for a high official. That object was to be crafted of silver and decorated with golden inlays.

This delicate task did not by all means meet the expertise of an architect, all the more so since the goldsmith's art has its own technique and rules. Nonetheless I tried to design the object in relation to our traditional goldsmiths' works and, at the same time, to conform with its purpose.

Now I must admit that I have always had a deep passion for tulips. In their vigorous, yet graceful lines, and in their colourful vivacity I recognize some essential ornamental qualities. When I design an architectural ornament, no matter if it should fit in a rigorous classical order or enrich the simple surface of a Modernist building, the image of the tulip almost instinctively occurs to me as a very suitable motif. In this particular case, I found her downright made for being hammered out by a goldsmith.

A few days after having presented my project to the Director-General, I happened to meet him in the company of an important member of the board of directors. On seeing me, he looked away. Feeling that my project had "deeply hurt" a hidden antenna of their aesthetic sensibility, I asked about my project. They tried to change the subject. As I insisted, the Director-General bid me into his office. After the heavy leather clad double door closed behind us, he told me: "Don't you know that the tulip is a Hungarian flower? We had the object done, but without the flower motif." He carefully produced the object from beneath a piece of paper, as if it were a precious item that had just escaped from a train accident. On doing so, he added amicably: "The board of directors was shocked; how could you, a prominent expert of Romanian art, do us such harm?"

While the Director-General kept talking, I remembered the smoky sky of the Netherlands, where spring and tulip fields emerge at the same time. I remembered the Garden of the Tuileries, in which at the end of April tulips embrace the ghostlike statues thus bringing to the grey Paris the first colour spots of spring. I remembered the flower-girls by the Seine, with their booths protected by huge sunshades, whilst others were pushing some drays full of bunches of tulips. I remembered the days before

Easter on the streets of Rome and in front of the stairs leading up to Trinità dei Monte, where thou-sands of tulips waited in earthen pots in the shade of the walls for pious hands to come and lay them on the altar of St Mary.

On the screen of my memories there glided other springtime impressions from other places. A long time ago I spent one whole month of May at Mogoşoaia, where tulips were blossoming to reach their stone colleagues from Brancovan times. At that time, the tulip inspired craftsmen to decorate stone facades with opulent carvings, silver covers of psalm-books, or marble gravestones of many a princess. Above the fresco of living memories I reviewed for a moment an encounter from the last autumn in Oltenia: three youths with flowers by their ears sang a song with an obsessive refrain:

"Green leaf and a tulip …"

These words I hurried to tell the Director-General as a reply to his refusal to re-naturalize the tulip. He was quite aghast at it.

But I have not yet finished with the tulip. Each time I used the tulip as a motif, people reminded me that this flower so dearly loved by Prince Brancovan (and, incidentally, by the whole Orient) would be through and through Hungarian. Does the lily belong to Florence or to royal France, now? Is the narcissus a Swiss possession? And the anemone, a Palastinian property? But what I am speaking of is far from being a singular case. From my memories I have just chosen an example.

The tulip does not grow better in Hungary than in Romania. The Dutch turned it into a commodity. However, all this here is of no importance – except of a negative one. The case I have dealt with at the beginning served as an example of the dangerous effects of the hypertrophic "Romanian idiosyncracy".

The chesnut, so the legend goes, came to us in the travel bag of St Nicodemus; the maize was introduced by Prince Şerban [Cantacuzino] some two centuries ago.

For our ornamentation, for our sculpture, neither the motif nor the object of design will be decisive. Decisive will be the spirit in which we will treat them. To some, this statement might appear banal or even simplistic … Nonetheless it is hardly known. We do need, not a canonising choice of objects and forms, but a comprehensive ethics which could give birth to true aesthetics. Therefore we must destroy the prejudices – and decidedly forget the whole monkey business performed on behalf of the Romanian tradition.

The "Mitocan" as a factor in Romanian civilisation (1941)

What is a *mitocan*? A *mitocan* does not represent a social category, but is found in abundance in the whole of Romanian society, takes on every aspect, exercises every function, is omniscient and forever present in everything to do with Romania. The *mitocan* is neither the loud suburbanite, the bourgeois happy to be alive, nor the high-hearted party lover. The *mitocan* is the vanity-inflated wag and sceptic who resolves any situation, any problem however serious in a vulgar way. The *mitocan* has a corrosive influence on our intellectual activity and especially on our working life.

The *mitocan* is born angry and against things. Against any generous initiative, against existing institutions, against optimism, against everything heroic. He makes a pretence at being a patriot while being essentially anti-patriotic, he is amoral but severe, impertinent and a coward.

What makes the *mitocan*, however, enemy number one of Romanian civilisation is his desire to chase illusions and ideals, and to destroy methodically all hope, discourage optimism, introduce inferiority complexes in clean and proud hearts, cultivate depreciation and try to maintain life in Romania in a hypostasis of self-irony, denigration and lack of trust.

Uncultured yet vehement, he is unfamiliar with Romanian history which he denies, and with the present state of Romania which he tries to destroy or at least belittle. He doesn't read, especially Romanian books, takes no part in the life of the country but sets himself up as a judge, raising his hand at every infraction, saying he had foreseen it. He shuns responsibility but expects to be given honours. He never travels but forever makes comparisons with foreign countries. He doesn´t bring up his children properly but declares them geniuses.

A post-war product of a confused Romania, he maintains the Romanian environment in a feverish state preventing any kind of open-handed activity and causing the loss of a large part of the nation's energy. Because of this, intellectuals and artists live a long way away from what we call our society.

Architects, who can't allow themselves the supreme luxury of isolation, have to a large extent been the victims of the *mitocan*. The confusion resulting from his lack of intellectuality, his inability to relate in any real sense to his country or to fit into any kind of discipline, has brought us towards this nihilism of forms and excess of elements in the architecture of our capital.

Informed only by the cinema, after long meals and empty days, the *mitocan* wants to apply in his house the décor of all the world's love tragedies in which Basque facades have Venetian windows or Mexican facades Brancovan-style elements, while Roman cupolas span bath houses and iconostaes serve as cocktail-bars. The *mitocan* is not a believer in the religious sense, though he owns a burial-vault of the most pompous kind at the Bellio Cemetry [in Bucharest] to enable him to face eternity serenely alongside kings and saints.

Absorbed in the pleasures of his vulgarity, he doesn't realise that times are changing and working imperceptibly against him. Today's much greater seriousness of life threatens him with extinction. His still weighty presence is felt especially in Bucharest. The provinces with their simpler form of life do not provide an environment favourable to this type. With the increasing control over life in Romania, the field of action of the *mitocan* (whose wife is often an aesthete) is reduced more and more. Nevertheless, long after the disappearance of the *mitocan* from today's scene, the ravages left by him will continue to be felt.

Explanatory Note (1946)

Some readers expressed their astonishment or even anger at our notes, on the account that we often discuss books published a long time ago instead of more recent publications. Obviously, these readers have failed to understand the concern of the periodical of art and criticism Simetria. The contemporaneity we are concerned with is rather relative.

Starting from the presumption that in art there are permanent values, we have set out to seek them both in the present and remotest past. Topical therefore will be everything embraced by our initial frame of mind, that is to free ourselves from the burdensome archaisms and obsessional innovations alike, in favour of self-imposed principles which spring from a lucid and rigorous critical spirit.

Fashion does not bother us at all, for we disapprove of its cacophony and abusive slogans. The letters of Plinius Jr may be as relevant for us as a new book by Lucian Blaga. The very fact that we do not make history, but criticism, places us in the present. For one thing, we consider the writings of Le Corbusier to be hit by caducity to a far greater extent than Alberti's commentaries on Architecture. Hence we do not believe in publicity acrobatics which, from a quarter century ago, aim to undermine basic notions in favour of false ones. Following certain study methods we are working on settling some notions. This is the reason why we think that some forgotten works must be recalled, and that there could be established rich parallels between distant publications. We are seeking for points of view which can be beneficial to the human striving for beauty. We do pursue this way, not necessarily in order to draw final conclusions, for this would be presumptuous, but to decipher the premisses of a modern harmony. This harmony lies at the heart of moral security, which is indispensable to artistic creation.

The Artist and the Freedom (1947)

To begin with, we should ask: what is social freedom? Social freedom, we believe, is the sum of all physical, moral, and spiritual bonds of society, into which the individual deliberately enters. But what is the meaning of deliberate bonds? The bonds in question are laws, moral rules, and the customs, which reason accepts due to education. For education is nothing else but a training of the individual with the purpose of making him as sociable as possible. Henceforth each society has her own views on freedom. When we compare them all, we realise that they have a common principle: the respect of man and his dignity, which we assume underlies his thoughts and deeds. Society in its turn shapes the social discipline by means of convincing education. Once an individual has been educated, the social laws and rules stop being a burden for him, for he has learnt to control his instincts and urges.

An excessive discipline, however, could threaten and even abolish freedom. This disregarding of human dignity occurs if society does impress her bonds upon man, not through reason and conviction, but through threat and horror. In such circumstances, human consciousness takes up a position of defense, mistrust and suspicion, thereby withdrawing within herself. Fear now dominates intelligence; man is trapped in a loss of freedom. Subsequently we can remark that freedom disappears when man feels his dignity is in peril.

But wherein consists dignity? Human dignity consists in man's consciousness to reflect upon his deeds and to make decisions. Society is based on a system of reason. Education shapes this system to the point that man would not interfere with the laws. They do not bother him anyway, for he has understood and accepted them, very much the same like he has understood and accepted to live within a limited landscape, which has also been shaped by reason: the city. When society threatens human dignity, man inclines to assume a revolutionary outlook and to fight that society. In such an unbalanced relationship between society and man the social bonds turn into oppression which exceeds man's capacity to accept them. Social freedom, however, is but an aspect of freedom – true, a pre-eminent one, for it is the topic of countless debates and has already shaken a great number of societies.

The notion of bonds is part of every human action, including all professions. Incessantly man undergoes the greatest efforts to learn the rules and laws of the profession he wishes to embrace. The better he will have learnt those rules, the greater will be his freedom. As a result, those rules will cease to be bonds of oppression. On the contrary, as they are a part of his knowledge, those rules will even contribute to shaping his intellectual structure. With time, new elements enrich and refine the continuous practice of those laws and rules. This striving for getting better might become the image of perfection: the ideal of the true lover of and authority on freedom. On the other hand, the more a person realises his insufficient knowledge, the more he will be constrained by the rules of his profession, which he was not able to learn. In these circumstances man will revolt, not against his profession, but rather against society. Since a society is far from being ideal, one could easily find a reason to revolt. This diversion of revolt is typical of failures – a man who failed his life from weakness. Eventually nothing is more alien to freedom then arbitrariness, for arbitrariness stems from the anarchy of instincts. Freedom, on the contrary, is based on reason. Reason and freedom complement each other.

A great deal has been said about a particular case of freedom: the freedom of the artist. By convention the artist is regarded as a privileged person. The artist is a craftsman of beauty. This activity always requires a generous disinterest. The true artist tries by all technical means at his disposal to accomplish his work and create beauty. In this striving the artist frees himself of all constraints. He works within the absolute. The question which concerns us, is to clarify the relationship between social freedom and inner freedom, which expresses the fulfillment of a work of art.

Of all arts, architecture reveals most clearly the interaction between society and artistic creation. There are two mains reasons for this: first, architecture is the very art which is closest both to social needs and technologies; second, architecture aims at creating, organizing and harmonizing the social framework. Formed by tradition (tradition as the sum of the most conclusive experiences undergone by various techniques in the course of time), the architect works entirely for the present.

Whereas Stendhal in 1830 permitted himself to say that he wrote for a reader of 1948; whereas the painter through his works might offer new artistic visions, the architect, by contrast, is bound to fulfill his commission in the very present. True, his buildings could show a certain new direction, but its full development is nonetheless a question of the future. However, the architect can improve and consolidate the vision of the present. Herein he is guided by some enduring values of proportion (which are closely related to the human body). In order to solve some present problems formulated by the society, the architect relies on the technical means provided by economy.

Architecture is an art wherein dreams and lyricism are out of place. From all sides constrained by the particular aspects of his task, the architect – if he is an artist – will try to regain his spiritual freedom: he will harmoniously co-ordinate all these aspects and fuse them into a composition. He can win the day, not by putting the problems aside, but first by going deeply into them, and then by mastering them. But even in terms of aesthetics the architect is not altogether free. Each age favours particular forms; sometimes, however, it turns them into fetishes, which it then imposes on architecture. Renewal and innovation depend upon technical possibilities and aesthetic preferences. Generally speaking, the great renewers have both understood the spirit of their time and repudiated tradition in order to adjust architecture to the needs of the present. This spirit of an age, however, can take various forms, and have manifold impacts on the architect.

In a civil society, apart from the potential uniformity of official buildings which would contribute to create a corporate identity of the state, all artistic types and nuances are possible, even the most absurd. The architect depends upon rules, the budget, and, to a certain extent, the aesthetic preferences of the client.

In a collectivist society, by contrast, the state with all his administrational ramifications is in fact the one and only client. Here, the imagination of the architect is quite heavily restricted by the regime. Such a form of collectivism, however, is not unlike, for instance, the Catholic Church in the Middle Ages or especially in late Renaissance.

At that particular time, the famous Baroque style had spread from its origins in the Jesuit schools throughout the entire sphere of influence of the Catholic Church. It is only natural that such a powerful social organisation should try to express herself through a coherent and uniform architecture. However, such a regulation and standardisation of forms cannot be a real obstacle for the creativity of the architect. Already the architects who adhered to the rigorous rules of the Graeco-Roman Classicism were capable of achieving perfection.

Basically, the state's interference should not bother the architect more than any other client's. The essential question is, whether such a regulation is performed by way of reasonable and generally acknowledged rules, or rather through police surveillance. As we have seen, the architect is anyway constrained by a variety of demands, including the diverse aspects of the programme and his own aesthetic idiom. Therefore, an architect, in order to be truly creative, must rely on a certain security. The material and moral security forms the foundation of all crafts. No matter how difficult the social conditions are, material and moral security are crucial for the artist to accomplish his work and then maybe to attain perfection.

The situation of the painter and his freedom is more complex. His vision is more personal and thus freer. It does not matter how many themes society proposes or dictates to him, for the painter's creativity is less dependent on financial safety. The burden of tradition and the call for durability play a less prominent part, as the technical revolutions are less likely to happen. The self-chosen isolation, the retreat within himself are easier to perform for a painter than for an architect. The commissions too cannot exert absolute command of the artist.

The taste, or, as we have previously mentioned, the spirit of the age and the social climate suggest certain themes to artists. At the time of Christian fanaticism the Church commissioned paintings of innumerable scenes of martyrdom, all of them competing with each other for tastelessness. Nonetheless the artists through composition and colour succeeded in turning those bloodthirsty representations into works of art. At the same time, not even the Inquisition managed to stop painters dealing with profane subjects. In the Renaissance, for instance, artists painted with the greatest sensual passion the most mundane nudes. The painter can free himself through both theme and perfection. Later on, as Church and state virtually stopped commissioning works of art, monumental painting was effectively replaced by chevalet painting which occured more or less in isolation. This art did strive, not for perfection, but for eccentricity and anarchy. True, even in anarchy the artist seeks for rules. These rules, however, are very much likely to be arbitrary. Thus the complete isolation of the artist is not recommendable at all. For such a development separates art from society and favours the emergence of an art left to the initiated. In opposition to this a number of critics have demanded that again art should be accessible to the public.

A crisis of this kind could not have occurred in architecture, since architecture depends to a much too great extent upon society. In the course of time, great art always tends to become popular – naturally on condition that the public cares to understand art, as it happened in Greece at the time of Pericles or in Renaissance Florence. And if society protects and supports the artist, it is very well entitled to demand of him the greatest efforts. All these thoughts are also true for sculptors or musicians. A harassed cannot express the soul of his community.

An artist should not be confused with a martyr. Drawing a parallel to birth pains, the poets used to say that there was no creation without sufferings. True, the creation of a work of art can raise doubts, provoke crises of conscience, or entail new beginnings in the wake of hurtful defeats, the whole of which naturally makes the artist suffer. These inner sufferings, however, are none of society's business. Even so, society should not aggravate them. The true artist knows how to create his freedom without fighting against the laws of the community he is a part of. Nonetheless he has the right to demand for security and something that Romanians call humaneness.

Letter to Marie-Lyse Cantacuzino-Ruheman
25th December 1958. Excerpt

My much beloved Marie-Lyse,

Today, twenty-five years ago, you were christened in the big drawing room at Dărmăneşti. Your god-father, Béla Szenkeresty, held you in his arms. Outside it was snowing gently. […]

I love everything you tell me: your happiness with Frank and your love of literature. You tell me in your letter that you can now read as much as you like. We never read enough because there are so many essential things we ought to know. Goethe was right when he said that we need two lives, one in which to read, and another in which to write. Life is too short for all the things we need or want to do, so one should only read what is worth reading. I am sure that you do that. It makes me so very happy that you love the same poets as I do.

I have devoted an enormous amount of time to literature and especially to poetry. But my favourite companions along the way have not necessarily been the greatest artists. The ones that never left me were the more reserved, the more mysterious ones, like Laforgue and Toulet. But there was, of course, sometimes also time for the great symphonies. I can say the same about paintings. Raphael's *Athenian School* is the height of all Art, but a modest landscape of Corot's means more to me in my daily meditations. Only Proust and Eliot are always monumental and intimate.

Each one of us creates his own Parnassus, his own spiritual family, the only family that we are able to choose ourselves … or, who knows, perhaps they choose us … these friends that live outside time.

Thanks to my accident and the long months in bed, at first in hospital and then at home, in 1955 I had the opportunity to read a great deal. So, during that time, like a Pilgrim slowly making his way through a particular country, I made my way through the great work of Sainte-Beuve: *Port Royal*. It is the most substantial work that I have ever read. It is also, essentially, the most important work written about the history of human thought. At the moment I have gone back to Proust who has played a great part in my spiritual life, as have Bergson and Rilke. To these I must also add my old friend Tudor Arghezi, he is undoubtedly, with Eminescu, the greatest Romanian artist.

Surrounded by these companions, I spend my days painting and drawing architectural plans and designs. The ancient city of Jassy is a great source of inspiration with its many turrets and its surrounding hills. I am so lucky now to have such a great project to work on. I am building a beautiful ensemble of gardens, balustrades, terraces and steps, in the midst of which there is also a library which I particularly cherish. I spend half of my time in Jassy and then I go back to my little studio in Bucarest – a small, well lit room in Marina's flat. There I find a warm family atmosphere and so you and Şerban and Sanda seem less far away in time and in space and our separation is more bearable. […]

Though I am getting older, I don't feel it, and I still hold dear the same things that I loved when I was an adolescent. I still have the same enthusiasm and the same optimism, and also the same confidence. Of course, as one gets older one becomes more critical, more objective too, and more perceptive.

"Mais ayant mis tout mon effort dans la journée même", as Gauguin wrote in a letter to Emmanuel Bibesco, and as I still expect something good from life, I manage to hold on to my serenity. People who dedicate their life to one of the arts, are somehow more priviledged. All three of us, you, Serban and I, belong to that category. But I can see what my father meant when he said: "Il y a un âge où l'on supporte plus ses contemporains." […]

In Art we find contrast – where there is light there has also to be shade or the light would not seem to us so precious and so bright. So when life seems to me a bit bitter, I think of Sanda's face that has kept all its gentle serenity, and I think of you and of Şerban, and of the beautiful way you have progressed through life – and I quickly find again some harmony and light.

I wish you a good and a happy New Year, may all your years be good and happy. And remember that happiness is a citadel that must be at all times be defended, and that "la vie est de la victoire qui dure".

Best thoughts to Frank,
Many, many kisses,

Georges

Addendum (3)
Colour plates:
Selected paintings and watercolours

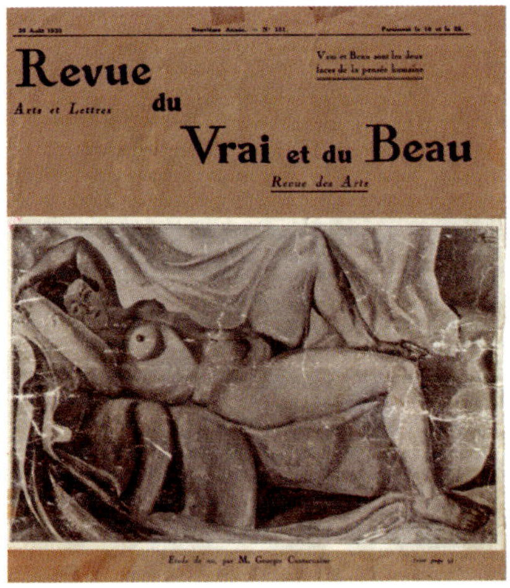
Revue
Arts et Lettres
du
Vrai et du Beau
Revue des Arts

324 GMC, *Nude*.
Revue du Vrai et du Beau, Year 9, No. 151
Paris, 25th August 1930

The selected artworks presented here are reproduced with the kind permission of GMC's children, Marie-Lyse Cantacuzino-Ruhemann and Şerban Cantacuzino. These colour plates are meant only to give a general impression of GMC's work as a painter. A proper catalogue would require further research in archives both private and public, particularly in Romania.

List of Exhibitions

1919 Group exhibition in January with Horia Teodoru, of watercolours and drawings of Moldavian landscapes and buildings,
at Casa Şcoalelor [The Schools' House] in Bucharest.

Lit.
Arhitectura 1919, No. 3/4, p. 104; Patrulius 1975a, p. 59;
Anghelescu 1977, p. 505.

1930 Contribution to the Official Salon in Bucharest

Lit.
Viala, Tancrède/Meller, André: *Le Salon Officiel de Bucarest. Etude de nu, par M. Georges Cantacuzène*. In: *Revue du Vrai et du Beau. Revue des Arts*. Year 9, No. 151. Paris 25th August 1930, title page and p. 9.

1931 Solo exhibition (62 paintings and 41 drawings), Ileana Hall of the bookshop *Cartea Românească*, opening on the 15th January 1931

Lit.
Arghezi, Tudor: *Un artist* [An Artist]. In: *Mişcarea*, Year 34, No. 46, Bucharest, 20th January 1931; Constantinescu, Mac: *Pictura lui G. M. Cantacuzino* [The Painting of GMC]. In: *Cuvântul*, Bucharest 28th January 1931, p. 1; Huzum, Virgil: *Pictorul G. M. Cantacuzino*. In: *Duminica Universului*, Bucureşti, 15th February 1931, p. 109; Masoff, Ioan: *Cochetaria unui artist* [An Artist's Flirtation]. In: *Rampa*, Bucharest, 18th January 1931; Patrulius 1975b, p. 60; Patrulius 1982, p. 92; Anghelescu 1977, p. 507

1932 Solo exhibition of drawings, opened on 4th April 1932

April-May, group exhibiition with Rodica Maniu and Perahim

Lit.
GMC, *Journal*. In: *Destin* 1962 op. cit., p. 100, entry of 5th April 1932; Ionesco, Eugène: *Cronica plastică: Rodica Maniu, Perahim, G. M. Cantacuzino*. In: *România literară*, Bucharest, No. 11, 30th April 1932, p. 5.

323 Opposite:
GMC, *Village in Lebanon*.
Watercolour, c.1935 (AMLSC).

1933 Solo exhibition, Museum *Toma Stelian*, Bucharest, opening in mid-November 1933; foreword to the catalogue by writer Camil Petrescu

Lit.
GMC, letter to Marietta Stern-Guetta, 26th Juli 1938, AMLSC;
Jianu, Ionel: *Expoziția d-lui G. M. Cantacuzino* [The Exhibition of Mr G. M. Cantacuzino]. In: *Rampa*, Bucharest, 15th November 1933; Oprescu, George: *Expoziția G. M. Cantacuzino* [The exhibition GMC]. In: *Universul*, Bucharest, 22nd November 1933; Patrulius 1975b, p. 60; Anghelescu 1977, p. 507

c.1939 Solo exhibition at Căminul Artei [The Art House], Kretzulesco Palace, Bucharest

Lit.
Patrulius 1975b, p. 60; Anghelescu 1977, p. 507

1939-1940 November 1939-January 1940
Group exhibition with Nina Arbore, Militza Pătrașcu, Mac Constantinescu and Marcel Janco, Ileana Hall of the bookshop
Cartea Românească, opening on 5th November 1939

Lit.
GMC, Letter to Sanda C., 5th November 1939; Pelin 2005, pp. 9-10.

1942 February, solo exhibition (40 paintings),
Italian Bookshop, Calea Victoriei, Bucharest

Lit.
GMC, letters to Sanda Cantacuzino, 2nd January 1942;
19th March 1942

1947 Solo exhibition at the Armand Hall, Calea Victoriei, Bucharest, in autumn.

Lit.
GMC, in: CNSAS, MAI, Dos. No. 7279/GMC, No. 5264, 3rd March 1948

1956 3rd to 5th October 1956
Solo exhibition (150 watercolours and paintings), at the Herăstrău Park Exhibition Hall, Bucharest; address by writer Tudor Arghezi

Lit.
Arghezi, Tudor: *Expoziția Gheorghe Cantacuzino din sala Parcului Herăstrău, București, 3 octombrie 1956.* [The exhibition GMC at the Herăstrău Park Exhibition Hall on 3rd October 1956] In: *Scrieri*, Vol. 29: *Proze. Pensula și dalta*, 1906-1966. Bucharest (Minerva), 1976, pp. 386-387; Patrulius 1975b, p. 60; Anghelescu 1977, p. 510.

325 *Church and palace ruin*, Moldavia. Watercolour, 28th September 1918 (AMLSC).

326 *Persepolis*, Persia. Watercolour c. 1935 (AMLSC).

327 *Kish Landscape*, Persia. Watercolour c. 1935 (AMLSC).

328 *Baghdad*, Irak. Watercolour c. 1935 (AMLSC).

329 *Street in an oriental city*. Oil on cardboard, c. 1935 (AGMC-RM).

330 *Landscape, perhaps the Colentina river at Mogoșoaia*. Oil on cardboard, 1938 (AMLSC).

331 *Landscape, perhaps the Colentina river at Mogoşoaia*. Oil on cardboard, 1938 (AMLSC).

332 *New York*. Watercolour, 25th May 1939 (AMLSC).

333 *New York*. Watercolour, 1st April 1939 (AMLSC).

334 *Koropkin, Russia*. Watercolour, 10th October 1942 (AMLSC).

335 *Construction site of the twin pavilions at the Metropolitan Church in Jassy*. Watercolour, c. 1960 (AMLSC).

336 *Flowers for Sanda*. Oil on cardboard, c. 1956 (AMLSC).

Addendum (4)
Biography of G. M. Cantacuzino

1899	Born on 23rd May in Vienna
1909-1914	Elementary school in Montreux, Switzerland
1912-1914	Summer work with Domenico Rupolo, a Venetian architect and curator of historic monuments, on the restoration of the palace and gardens of the Mogoşoaia estate (near Bucharest), which belongs to Marthe Bibesco, an aunt of GMC's
1916	High School in Bucharest
1917-1918	Military service during WW I
1919	Travels by sea to Paris via Constantza and Marseille
1920-1929	Study of architecture at the École des Beaux-Arts in Paris, especially under Georges Gromort and Roger-Henri Expert Study journeys through Romania, Italy, Austria, Germany, the Netherlands, France and Spain Private lessons in painting with Pedro Aro-Jo, Othon Friesz and Theodor Pallady
1920	Assistant to Domenico Rupolo on the Mogoşoaia restoration. During the same year Marthe Bibesco commissions GMC to take over the project
1923	Opens an architectural office with August Schmiedigen in Bucharest
1926	Marries Sanda Ştirbey First publication: *Introduction to the study of architecture*, Bucharest
1928	Birth of Şerban, a son
1929	Receives his Beaux-Arts diploma as *Architecte diplômé par le gouvernement français* (ADPGF) Independent architect in Bucharest, with interruptions until 1947
1929-1940	In addition to his architectural work, he pursues an intense activity as critic, theorist, painter, curator, professor and politician Study journeys through Romania, Italy, France, Germany, Greece, Crete, Egypt, Lebanon, Syria, Irak, Persia, Turkey and the USA. Meets the German archaeologists Professor Ernst Hertzfeld and Friedrich Krefter in Persepolis (1934-35)
1930	Enters the left-wing liberal party of young liberals headed by the historian Georges Bratiano Enters a Bucharest Freemason lodge
c. 1930	Enters the *Society of Friends of the USA* in Bucharest
1930-1944	Broadcast lectures on architectural and cultural subjects
1930-1947	Public lectures on architectural and cultural subjects
1931	Birth of Marie-Lyse, a daughter

1931	Co-founder and co-editor of the *Romanian Magazine of History* First single exhibition
1931-1937	Member of the Romanian Parliament, as representative of Dolj county in south-western Romania
1934	Enters the *Society of Promoting Urban Planning* in Romania
1934-1936	First Romanian correspondent of *L'Architecture d'Aujourd'hui*
1937-1940	Chief architect of the Romanian Railways CFR Official journey to Berlin in August 1940, where he probably meets Hans Hertlein, the chief architect of Siemens
1938	Honorary Corresponding Member of the Royal Institute of British Architects
1938-1940	Member of FRN/ *Front of the National Renaissance* party of King Charles II, enemy of the extreme right Iron Guard
1938-1941	Honorary professor of graphic arts at the Bucharest Academy of Fine Arts Architect of the official pavilion of Romania at the New York World's Fair.
1939	Lives and works for four months in New York. Meets Fiorello La Guardia, the mayor of the city. Honorary Citizen of New York Founder and main editor of *Simetria*, an annual for critic and art (eight issues until 1947)
1939-1940	His wife and children move to London Travels to London as a courier of the Romanian minister of foreign affairs, Grigore Gafencu
1940-1941	Spends six weeks in prison due to political reasons in the aftermath of the collapse in November 1940 of the Carlton building in Bucharest on ground of a massive earth-quake. Freed of all charges in 1943
1941-1943	War correspondent during the Crimea campaign
1942-1948	Professor of history and theory of architecture at the Bucharest School of Architecture Professor of graphic arts at the Bucharest Academy of Fine Arts
1944-1948	Honorary professor of landscape architecture at the Institute of Urban Planning at the Bucharest Polytechnicum
1947	Completes the first translation of Vitruvius's writings into Romanian
1945-1947	Application for visa in order to visit his family in the UK
1948	Foiled try to flee Romania
1948-1953	After a show trial, he spents five years in prison (in Jilava near Bucharest and Aiud/Transylvania)
1953-1954	Shortly after his release, he is once again imprisoned, in the labour camp at the Danube-Black Sea canal and in Piteşti/Wallachia
1954-1957	Inspector at the Department of Historic Monuments. Areas of responsibility: first Bucharest, then Moldavia
1955-1959	Public lectures on architectural and cultural subjects
1956	Last exhibition in Bucharest, closed by the communist regime only three days after the opening due to political reasons
1957-1960	Enemy of the state. Works as unofficial diocesan architect in Jassy
1960	Dies on 1st November 1960 in Jassy

Addendum (5)
Notes

Foreword – pp. 9-10
1 GMC, *Traditionalism and Modernism*
(Tradiţionalism şi modernism). Radio broad-
cast, 23rd July 1932. in: GMC 1934, p. 19.
For an English version of this essay see the
Addendum to this book.

Introduction – pp. 11-13
1 GMC, *Points of view* (Puncte de vedere). In:
GMC 2001 [1947], p. 40-41.
2 Deleuze 1988, p. 103.
3 A. Maurois, *Introduction* to Alain 1930, p. 17.
4 GMC, Letter to Marie-Lyse Cantacuzino-Ruhe-
mann, 25th December 1958 (AMLSC).

An Intellectual Biography

Family background – pp. 14-17
For the Cantacuzino background see Nicol
1 1968; Nicol 1996; J.-M. Cantacuzène 1992; J.-M.
Cantacuzino 1996; J.-M. Cantacuzène 2012;
On Pallady see Pallady1966; Lassaigne1973;
2 GMC 2010, 13th Letter.
For Marie Cantacuzène see J.-M. Cantacuzino
3 1996, plate IV; Guégan 2003, p. 350; GMC 2010,
p. 127, 7th Letter to Simon.
Löhneysen 1977; Runciman 1980; Nicol 1996.
4 5 Cf. Norwich 2007, p. 302.
5 The term Phanariots denoted initially the
6 Greek inhabitans of the Istanbul Phanar
district, and then noble Greeks, who held
high office at the Porte. From 1714 to 1821 a
number of Phanariots were posted as princes
to Moldavia and Wallachia.
On Şerban Cantacuzino as reigning prince
7 (1678-88) see e.g. Meyers 1972, vol. 5, p. 305).
Iorga/Balş 1922, p. 187.
8 C. Cantacuzino's championning of a hybrid
9 origin of the Romanians (at least Daco-Roman)
seems quite modern. See Mihăilă/Zamfirescu
1969, p. 221; J. M. Cantacuzino 1996, pp. 183-
184; Boia 2003a, p. 104; D. H. Mazilu in Kahl/
Metzeltin/Ungureanu 2006, pp. 374, 377-378;
GMC, *Fundenii Doamnei*. In: *Boabe de grâu*.
10 Bucharest, January 1931, pp. 151-154 .
See e.g. GMC, *Mogoşoaia: un palat, o grădină,*
11 *un peisaj*, c. 1955. In: INMI/FDMI, Dos. 6499
On Calea Victoriei see Crutzescu 1987 [1943];
12 Cazacu 2006.
C.-A. Cantacuzène, *Le Prince de Ligne, le dernier*
13 *grand Européen*. See *Dictionnaire diplomatique*,
Vol. 5, 1954, p. 187; GMC, *Charles Joseph de*
Ligne: Coup d'œuil sur Belœil. In: *Simetria VIII*
(1947), pp. 162-165.
J.-M. Cantacuzène 2012, chapter *La Moldavie*
14 *patriarchale*, pp. 89-92.

Childhood in Vienna – pp. 19-22
1 Gombrich 2006, p. 129.
2 Oechslin 2008, p. 321.
3 Choisy 1899.
4 Gemmel 2005.
5 On Charles-Adolphe Cantacuzène see J. M.
Cantacuzino 1996, pp. 370-372, 532.
6 Borsi/Godoli 1985, p. 13.
7 N. B. Cantacuzino 1945, p. 92. German in the
original.
8 Kraus 1990, p. 93.
9 GMC, Letter to Sanda Cantacuzino, Bucharest,
23rd October 1939, AMLSC.
10 GMC 2010, p. 29, 1st Letter to Simon.
11 Ibid.
12 Ibid.
13 Ibid.
14 Op. cit., p. 33.
15 GMC 2010, p. 159, 9th Letter; Letter to Marthe
Bibesco, Posada, 28th August 1924.
16 Pascal 1931, p. 39, *Pensées*, Fragment 139.
17 GMC 2010, p. 35, 1st Letter to Simon.
18 Ibid.
19 Ibid., German in the original.
20 Notoboom 1993, p. 67. *English in the original.
21 GMC 2010, p. 62, 3rd Letter to Simon.
22 Op. cit., p. 51, 2nd Letter to Simon.
23 GMC in *Simetria VII* (1946), p. 79.
24 GMC 2010, p. 93, 5th Letter to Simon.
25 Ibid.
26 Ibid. The verse cited by GMC in French is the
first of Baudelaire's poem *L'Homme et la mer*
[Man and the Sea], the fourteenth poem in the
series *Spleen et idéal* of the *Fleurs du Mal*. Cf.
Baudelaire 1909, p. 17. Stefan-George-Archive,
WLB Stuttgart.
27 27 GMC 2010, pp. 69-71, 3rd Letter to Simon.

Education in Montreux – pp. 23-24
1 GMC 2010, p. 75, 4th Letter to Simon.
2 Ibid.
3 Ibid.
4 Ibid.
5 GMC 2010, p. 77 4th Letter to Simon. Here GMC
interpreted a verse from Laforgue's *L'Imitation*
de Notre-Dame la Lune (1886):
"Moi, je suis laminé d´esthétiques loyales!
Je hais les trémolos, les phrases nationales ;
Bref, le violet gros deuil est ma couleur locale."
See Laforgue 1986, Vol. 2, pp. 87-88.
6 GMC 2010, p. 93, 5th Letter to Simon. On
Thérésa Tallien see e.g. Larousse 1985, Vol. 10,
p. 10,025.
7 Op. cit., p. 103, 6th Letter.
8 8 Ibid.

Years of apprenticeship – pp. 24-25
1 See Patrulius 1975a, p. 58; Ş. Cantacuzino in
GMC 1999, p. 6.
2 N. B. Cantacuzène 1940, p. 95; Morand 1990
[1935], p. 101.
3 Patrulius 1975a, p. 58; Ş. Cantacuzino in GMC
1999, p. 5. On Romania in WW I, cf. e.g. Boia
2003b, pp. 122-128; Hitchins 1994, pp. 251-291.
Arhitectura, Bucharest 1919, No. 3/4, p. 104;
4 Patrulius 1975a, pp. 58-59.
Müller in Malaparte 2005, p. 554.
5 Ibid.
6 Several titles by Alain are recorded in the in-
7 ventory list of GMC's private library (AGMC-IP).
GMC, Letter to Marthe Bibesco, Bucharest,
8 29th October 1924, AMLSC).
N. B. Cantacuzino 1944, pp. 154-155.
9 Ionesco 1968, p. 168; Boia 2001a, p. 160.
10 N. B. Cantacuzino was Romanian Vice-
11 Ambassador in Paris from 1922-1939. Cf. N. B.
Cantacuzino 1944, pp. 248-253, *Dictionnaire*
diplomatique, Vol. 5, 1954, p. 187.

Francophile Romania pp. 26-27
Boia 2001a, p. 160.
1 H. Focillon in: *La Vie des peuples*, IX, Paris,
2 10th March 1923, p. 669-685.
On Doneaud, see Rădulescu 2005, pp. 119-128;
3 Celac *et al* 2005, pp. 25, 46, 90, 130.
On Blanc, see Rădulescu 2005, pp. 129-144; Ce-
4 lac *et al* 2005, pp. 25, 46, 90, 130. On Bolomey
(1893-1947) see Rădulescu 2005, p. 134; Celac
et al 2005, pp. 94, 104, 110.
See *Monuments historiques*, No. 169, Paris 1990,
5 pp. 97-101; Machedon/Scoffham 1999, p. 23;
Fezi 2005; T. Socolescu 2004, pp. 124-134;
Criticos/Zahariade 2007; Stiller 2007, p. 25.
On Mincu, see Lascu, *Ion Mincu – Architecte*
6 *national roumain*. In: Andrieux *et al* 2003, pp.
295-302.
On Guadet, see van Zanten, *Architectural Com-*
7 *position at the Ecole des Beaux-Arts from Charles*
Percier to Charles Garnier, in: Drexler 1977, pp.
255-257; Midant, *Julien Guadet* in Turner 1996,
pp. 732-733; Kruft 2007, pp. 288-289.

Studies at the École des Beaux-Arts
Introduction, the system of studies, atelier
culture and "spirit of design" – pp. 29-31
1 Drexler 1977; *L'Architecture d'aujourd´hui* 1997,
No. 310; Jacques, *L'école des beaux-arts: Paris et*
la diffusion des modèles, in: Lortie 1995, pp. 185.
2 Chafee, *The Teaching of Architecture at the École*
des Beaux-Arts. In: Drexler 1977, p. 107.
3 B. Foucart/J.-P. Robert, *La leçon du Duban*. In:
L'Architecture d'aujourd'hui, 1997, No. 310, p. 67.

4 Egbert 1977, p. 156.
5 On the *Groupe des Architectes Modernes* see e.g. Borsi 1987; Gargiani 1992, p. 8; Frampton 1997, chap. 10: *Tony Garnier and the Industrial City 1899-1918*, pp. 100-104, and chap. 11: *Auguste Perret: the evolution of Classical Rationalism 1899-1925*, pp. 105-108;
6 Chafee 1977 op. cit., p. 88.
7 On the Beaux-Arts architect as magician, see H. Sternfeld in *NIAE Golden Jubilee Journal*, New York, 1963, p. 53 (Chafee 1977, p. 94, note 141). On the modernist architect as surgeon see Pai 2002, p. 279.
8 A. Jacques, *L'École des beaux-arts: Paris et la diffusion des modèles*. In: Lortie 1995, p. 185.
9 Dumont, *Vie et mort de l´ancienne école*. In: *L'Architecture d'aujourd´hui* 1997, No. 310, p. 91.
10 J. G. Howard, *The Spirit of Design at the École des Beaux-Arts*. In: *Architectural Review*, 1898. Cited after Pai 2002, p. 40.
11 Pai 2002, p. 43.
12 Howard 1898 op. cit. Cited after Pai 2002, p. 40.

Professors at the École – pp. 32-37

1 Oechslin 1999, p. 214. On Umbdenstock see Umbdenstock 1933; Drexler 1977, p. 501; Texier, *Gustave Umbdenstock*. In: Midant 1996, p. 899; Smet 2005, p. 83; Kruft 2007, p. 289.
2 ANFP, AJ/52/578, Dos. GMC, Letter to the École, 20th June 1925 (see Rădulescu 2005, Doc. 5). On the *atelier extérieur* run by Gromort and Expert from 1921-1925 cf Drexler 1977, p. 501; Reed in Gromort 2001, pp. 11-12.
3 On Gromort see H. H. Reed, *A Brief Biography of Georges Gromort*. In: Gromort 2001, pp. 11-12; Drexler 1977, p. 501.
4 Gromort 1950, p. 57.
5 GMC's essay in *Simetria II* (1940), pp. 97-98.
6 Cf. e.g. GMC's essays: *The Romanian Gardens* (Grădinile româneşti). In: GMC 1932, pp. 269-284; *Consideraţii despre peisaj* (On landscape). In: GMC 1993 [1956], pp. 93-106.
7 Gromort, *Préface. À Georges M. Cantacuzène*. In GMC/Schmiedigen 1929, p. 5.
8 GMC, *Palladio* 1928, pp. 16-17.
9 See Drexler 1977, p. 501; Gargiani 1992, p. 128; IFA *et al* 1983; Culot, *Roger-Henri Expert*. In: Turner 1996, Vol. 10, p. 689.
10 Borsi 1987, p. 143.
11 M. Culot 1996 op. cit., p. 689.
12 Ibid.
13 See *L'Architecture d'aujourd'hui* 5/1934, pp. 57-62.

Cantacuzino as a student, the relevance of the École for him – pp. 37-39

1 M.-J. Dumont 1997, op. cit., p. 91.
2 GMC, *Drawing* (Desen). In: *Simetria VI* (1945), p. 116.
3 A. Jacques 1995, op. cit., p. 189.
4 H. Teodoru e.g. worked with L.H. Boileau (1878-1948). The Creangă brothers and Lucia Dumbrăveanu worked with G. Umbdenstock before returning to Bucharest in 1927 (Patrulius 1980, p. 22; Rada Teodoru in a conversation with the author, Paris, 25th July 2008).
5 Posener 2004, p. 326.
6 Ibid.
7 ANFP, AJ/52/578, Dos. Cantacuzène G. M., cited from Rădulescu 2005, Doc. 3, p. 98.
8 Foucart 1997 op. cit., p. 67.
9 Ibid.
10 Pai 2004, p. 45.
11 Machedon/Scoffham 1999, p. 72. On the *Heimatstil* in Europe cf. Andrieux *et al* 2003; Crettaz-Stürzel 2005.
12 Gargiani 1992, p. 8.
13 Ibid.
14 GMC, review of *André Le Donné. L'Architecte dans la cité. Paris, Ed. Du Seuil*. In: *Simetria VIII* (1947), p. 179; GMC 2001 [1947], p. 38.
15 Gargiani 1992, p. 8; Sarnitz 2003, p. 61.
16 A. Opel, *Foreword* to Loos 1995, p. 15.

Student life and cultural circles pp. 39-43

1 On Leconte see Drexler 1977, p. 501; Egbert 1977, pp. 193-194; GMC, letter to Sanda Cantacuzino, Bucharest, 16th August 1946 (AMLSC).
2 GMC, Letter to Sanda Cantacuzino, 16th August 1946 (AMLSC). For Michau's poetry, see e.g. *Les mille vers (et Poèmes inédits)*. Paris 1936.
3 On Pingusson see *L'Architecture d'aujourd'hui* No. 9/1935, p. 72; Texier 2006; Texier 2011.
4 N. B. Cantacuzino 1944, pp. 237-238; Patrulius 1975a, p. 58; Ş. Cantacuzino in GMC 1999, p. 6.
5 GMC, Letter to Marthe Bibesco, Paris, 19th August 1931 (AMLSC).
6 Seymour-Smith/Kimmens 1996, pp. 241-242.
7 See e.g. de Diesbach 1986, pp. 233, 297, 401, 402, 406-408 etc. On Marthe see further Sutherland 1997; Wilpert (ed.) 2004, p. 209.
8 GMC 2010, p. 223, 14th Letter to Simon.
9 Larousse 1992, p. 1098.
10 On Anna de Noailles see e.g. Proust 1931; Cocteau 1963; Perche 1964.
11 On M. Ghyka see Tiegheim/Josserand 1968, Vol. 1, p. 1531; Manolescu 2003, pp. 346-349.
12 Morand 1990 [1935], p. 293. On Morand see Guitard-Auviste 1994 [1981]; M. Collomb, *Paul Morand*. Paris 2007. See also Morand's memoirs *Journal inutile*. Paris 2001.
On L. Fabre see Demougin 1992, p. 551; van
13 Tiegheim/Josserand 1968, Vol. 1, p. 1314; Truc 1926, pp. 87-95.
GMC, Letter to Marie-Lyse Cantacuzino-Ruhe-
14 mann, 25th December 1958 (AMLSC).
See Maulnier 1949; Gavoty 1982, p. 117; M.
15 Bibesco 1991; Cogeval *et al* 2003, pp. 302-304; Băjenescu 2006, p. 47; Jacob-Friesen *et al* 2008, p. 201.
16 16 GMC, Letter to Marie-Lyse Cantacuzino-Ruhemann, 25th December 1958 (AMLSC).
17 GMC, diary entry, April 1919; cited after Radu Patrulius 1975b, p. 57.
18 GMC 2010, p. 209, 13th Letter to Simon.
19 Ibid.
20 Op. cit., p. 213.
21 GMC, *Expoziţia pictorilor români cari au lucrat in Franţa*. In: *Viaţa românească*, Year 38, No. 1, 1946, p. 130, cited after GMC 1977a, p. 486.
22 GMC 2010, p. 181, 10th Letter to Simon.
23 GMC, Letter to Marthe Bibesco, Paris 1921 (AMLSC). On Charles Normand see Fiori 2012.
24 See Patrulius 1975a, p. 57.
25 Safranski 2003, p. 115.
26 Cited from J.-M. Cantacuzène 1992, p. 351.

Mogoşoaia – pp. 45-46

1 V. Fontana, *Domenico Rupolo architetto all corte di Mogosoaia (1913-1930 e segg.)*. In: Popescu 2003, p. 230; Droste 1985, p. 153.
2 Patrulius 1982, p. 89.
3 GMC, *Mogoşoaia* (1955). In: GMC 1993a, pp. 146-160; Opriş 2001, pp. 532-533.
4 GMC, Mogoşoaia (1955) op. cit.
5 Op. cit., pp. 153-154.
6 On the Romanian Department of Historic Monuments cf. Giurescu 1989; *Monuments historiques* No. 169, 1990; Opriş 2001.
7 GMC 2002 [1926], p. 22.
8 Ibid.
9 Ibid.
10 Iorga/Balş 1922; Balş 1926; Balş 1928; Ghika-Budeşti 1931.
11 Sutherland 1996, p. 180.
12 GMC 1932, pp. 214-215.
See also de la Mottraye 1727.
13 Sutherland 1996, p. 181.

Co-operation with August Schmiedigen *Architectural office and Chrissoveloni Bank – pp. 48-50*

1 On Schmiedigen, see the advertisement of Schmiedigen's company in *Arhitectura* No. 3, October 1935; Dragu Dimitriu in *Ararat, Periodic al Uniunii Armenilor din România*, Year 18, No. 1/358, Bucharest, January 2007, p. 5.
2 On J. Chrissoveloni see Guitard-Auviste 1994, p. 78-79; Kirson 2001, pp. 15-23; Morand 2001, Vol. 2, p. 468; Olteanu 2002, p. 412.
3 Kirson 2001, pp. 13-14.
4 GMC/Schmiedigen 1929, p. 8; Guitard-Auviste 1994, pp. 78-79.
5 GMC/Schmiedigen 1929, p. 8.
6 Vitruvius 2009, Book 6, Chap. 3.3, *Plans of Houses*, p. 172; Palladio1965, Book 2, Chap. 4, *Of the Tuscan Atrio, or porch*, p. 42.
7 Morand 2001, Vol. 2, p. 468.
8 GMC/Schmiedigen 1929, p. 8.
9 Ibid.
10 GMC 2002 [1926], pp. 19-20. GMC cited Valéry in French.
11 Gromort in GMC/Schmiedigen 1929, pp. 6-7.
12 GMC, cited from Patrulius 1982, p. 90.
13 GMC 1962, p. 96. On Fra Giocondo see Hootz/Dellwing 1976, p. 428; Semper 1979 [1884], p. 211; Muraro/Marton 1996, pp. 32-33.
14 Cicio-Pop 1932, pp. 142-143; Ionescu 1938, p. 18; Patmore 1939, p. 39; Celac *et al* 2005, p. 29.
15 On the start of Modernism in Romania cf. e.g. Machedon/Scoffham 1999, Chap. 3, *Pioneers of Modernism*, pp. 32-57.
16 Gromort, *Préface*, in: GMC/Schmiedigen 1929, p. 5; GMC 2002 [1926], p. 19; GMC 1927, pp. 352-353; Gr. Ionescu 1972, pp. 453-465.
17 GMC 2002 [1926], pp. 19-20; GMC, Letter to Marthe Bibesco, Tescani, 14th February 1931 (AMLSC).

Memories and design (I): on imitation – pp. 52-55

1 GMC 2010, p. 217, 14th Letter to Simon.
2 GMC 2010, p. 143, 8th Letter to Simon.
3 Proust 1993 [1922] CXI, p. 163.
4 GMC 2010, p. 143, 8th Letter to Simon.

5 Bergson 1962 [1911], pp. 69-70.
6 Op. cit., pp. 92-93.
7 Oechslin 2008, pp. 46-47.
8 Op. cit., p. 47.
9 On Quatremère de Quincy see Chafee 1977, p. 67; Egbert 1980, p. 42 ; Kruft 2007, pp. 277-279 etc.; Oechslin 2008, pp. 14-16, 45-47.
10 Quatremère de Quincy 1823, p. 3 ; cited from Oechslin 2008, p. 15.
11 Loos 1995, p. 69.
12 Kruft 2007 [1991], p. 315.
13 Ibid.
14 Ibid.
15 Sarnitz 2005, p. 10.
16 Ibid.
17 Op. cit., p. 23.
18 Op. cit., p. 11.
19 Ibid.

Memories and Design (II): Travelling – p. 56

1 GMC 2010, p. 227, 14th Letter to Simon.
2 Ibid.
3 Oechslin 2008, p. 47.
4 Gromort 1946, p. 102.
5 Bergson 1962, p. 167.
6 GMC 1928, p. 17.
7 GMC, *Un amator de artă: Goethe* (An art lover: Goethe). In: *Simetria V* (1943), pp. 59-94.

Study travels, work ethics and idleness – pp. 57-59

1 GMC 2010, p. 223, 14th Letter to Simon.
2 Ibid.
3 GMC, *Moonwatch* 1938, p. 178.
4 GMC, Letter to Marie-Lyse Cantacuzino-Ruhemann, 25th December 1958 (AMLSC).
5 GMC 2010, p. 225, 14th Letter to Simon.
6 Op. cit., p. 93, 5th Letter.
7 GMC, journal entry, July 1922, cited from Patrulius 1975b, p. 57.
8 GMC, *Goethe* (1943) op. cit., p. 65.
9 GMC 2010, p. 161, 10th Letter to Simon.
10 Op. cit., p. 215, 14th Letter to Simon.
11 Ibid.
12 Ibid.
13 Ibid.
14 Ibid.
15 Ibid.
16 GMC, Letter to Marie-Lyse Cantacuzino-Ruhemann, 25th December 1958 (AMLSC).
17 GMC 2010, p. 53, 2nd Letter to Simon.
18 Muntean 1966, p. 61.
19 GMC 2010, p. 59, 3rd Letter to Simon.
20 Op. cit. p. 79-80, 4th Letter to Simon.
21 Op. cit., p. 127-128, 7th Letter to Simon.
22 Op. cit., p. 97, 6th Letter to Simon.
23 Plotinus 1952, p. 29, Enn. I, 8[51]5.
24 GMC 2010, p. 175, 10th Letter to Simon.
25 Camus 2005, p. 112.
26 GMC 2010, p. 53, 2nd Letter to Simon.
27 Op. cit., p. 147, 8th Letter to Simon.
28 J. Guitton in Bergson 1964b, p. 31.
29 GMC 2010, p. 219, 14th Letter to Simon.
30 Camus 2005, pp. 59-61.
31 Cioran1995, p. 1349.
32 Pieper 1948, pp. 13-14.
33 Brancusi, cited from Giedion-Welcker 1958, p. 220.
34 Sainte-Beuve, *Paris*. In: *Nouveaux lundis III*. Paris, no date. Cited from Hocke 1988, p. 165.
35 GMC, *Colentina şi Plumbuita* [The Colentina river and the Plumbuita Monastery]. In: GMC 1932, p. 135. Cf. also Morand 1990 [1935], last chapter *Bucarest, ville gaie*, pp. 281-291; Patmore 1939, chap. 2, *Music in the air*, pp. 18-32.
36 GMC, *Maestrul de altă dată* [The old master]. In: GMC 1934, pp. 111-112.

The 1920s – a balance – pp. 60-63

1 GMC 2010, p. 215, 14th Letter to Simon.
2 On Charles Cuvillier see Sartori 1963, Vol. 1, p. 583; A. Lamb in Sadie 2001, Vol. 6, p. 793;
3 Letter from Olympia Zamfirescо† to the author, Cannes, 24th March 2008.
4 Morand 1990 [1935], pp. 180-181.
5 M. Ghyka c. 1961 (AMLSC).
6 GMC 2002 [1926], pp. 23-24.
7 7 Loos 1995 [1919], p. 133.
8 8 GMC, *The Romanian Gardens* op. cit. In: GMC 1932, pp. 273-275.
9 9 GMC, Moonwatch 1938, p. 177.

New start and prosperity in troubled times
The Political and economical context in the inter-war period – pp. 65-67

1 W. Lipgens, *Der Niedergang Europas*. In Hillgruber/Dülffer, 1981, pp. 26-27; W. Conze, *Internationale Entwicklung zwischen den Weltkriegen*. In: Hillgruber/Dülffer 1981, pp. 78-98; Maner 1997a, p. 516; Ziegerhofer-Prettenthaler 2004, p. 375.
2 W. Conze 1981, op. cit. pp. 78-98; W. Lipgens 1981, op. cit., pp. 26-27; F. S. Northedge, *The League of Nations: its life and times*. Leicester 1986; Ostrower 1996.
3 On the Paneurope movement, cf. W. Lipgens 1981, op. cit. p. 28; Ziegerhofer-Prettenthaler 2004.
On A. Briand, see W. Lipgens 1981, pp. 29-30; Fleury/Jílek 1998.
On the Briand-Kellog Pact (1928), see Titulesco1934; W. Lipgens 1981 op. cit. pp. 26-27; B. Roscher, *Der Briand-Kellog-Pakt von 1928*. Baden-Baden 2004.
4 Hitchins 1994, p. 377.
5 Maner 1997a, p. 503. See also J. Schmidt, *Rumänien*. In: Wende 1981, pp. 517-548; Boia 2006.
6 Hitchins 1994, p. 380.
7 Op. cit., p. 378. See also Völkl 1995, pp. 49-51, 90, 95; Maner 1997a, p. 53; Verseck 2007, p. 64.
8 Hitchins 1994, p. 379; Maner 1997, p. 521.
9 Hitchins 1994, p. 381.
10 Völkl 1995, p. 222; Scurtu et al 2002, p. 345; Cazacu 2006b, p. 6; Verseck 2007, p. 60.
11 Hitchins 1994, pp. 433-437. Cf. also Klein/Göring 1995, p. 78; Völkl 1995, pp. 110-111.
12 Hitchins 1994, p. 55.
13 Op. cit., p. 293.
14 J. Schmidt, *Rumänische Kommunistische Partei*. In: Wende 1981, pp. 536-541; Boia 2001, Chap. 4 *Romanian Communism*, pp. 111-151.
15 Hillgruber 1965; J. Schmidt, *Eiserne Garde*. In: Wende 1981, pp. 527-528; Heinen 1986; Hitchins 1994, pp. 402-405; Völkl 1995, pp. 104-106; Boia 2001, pp. 102-106.
16 Cf. B. Murgescu/M.-L. Murgescu, *Aufbruch in die Moderne?* In: Institut für donauschwäbische Geschichte und Landeskunde *et al* 2007, pp. 58-59. See also Hitchins 1994, p. 335; Völkl 1995, p. 108; Scurtu et al. 2002, pp. 342, 355; Cazacu 2006b, p. 6.
17 Hitchins 1994, p. 339.
18 Op. cit., p. 341.
19 Op. cit., p. 372.
20 Op. cit., p. 335.
21 Op. cit., p. 365.
22 Op. cit., pp. 375, 361-364. See also Durandin 1994, pp. 90-99; Völkl 1995, p. 108; Maner 1997a, p. 83, 503; Prost 2006, pp. 101-102;
23 Hitchins 1994, p. 363.
24 Ibid.
25 Ibid.
26 Hillgruber 1965, pp. 80-83; Völkl 1995, pp. 117-123, 127.
27 Maner 1997a, p. 505; 1997c, p. 344, 349-350; Völkl 1995, p. 100.
28 Maner 1997b, p. 355. Cited from Maner 1997c, p. 356, note 82.
29 Maner 1997a, p. 72; Maner 1997c, pp. 353-354; Völkl 1995, pp. 99-101.
30 Hitchins 1994, p. 432.
31 Ibid.
32 Maner 1997c, p. 371, notes 179, 180; A. Frangulis, *Titulesco, Nicolas*. In: *Dictionnaire diplomatique*, Vol. 5, 1954, p. 1121.

The reign of King Carol II (1930-40) – pp. 68-69

1 *The Times*, Monday, 9th June 1930, p. 10. Cf. also Maner 1997a, p. 73; Maner 1997c, pp. 348-349.
2 M. Schapira in Băleanu/Comănescu 2003, pp. 9, 22.
3 Maner 1997c, p. 354.
4 Cioran in Liiceanu 1995, pp. 99-104 ; Irimia-Tuchtenhagen 1997 op. cit., 324.
5 On the *rhinocerosation* of the Young generation, see Ionesco 1996 (1966), pp. 273-288; Cioran in Liiceanu 1995, pp. 99-104; Manea 1995; Irimia-Tuchtenhagen 1997, p. 323; Ornea 1999, p. 164; E. Ionesco, *Letter from Eugène Ionesco to Tudor Vianu*, 19th September 1945. In: Ornea 1999, pp. 166-167; Ţurcanu 2003.
6 Sebastian 2001.
7 Ionesco1960.
8 Völkl 1995, p. 121; Maner 1997a, p. 507.
9 Völkl 1995, p. 121. For Călinescu see also Patmore1939, pp. 15-16.
10 Maner 1997a, p. 511.

On Carol's II image in historiography – p. 69

1 Paleologu 2005, pp. 142, 145.
2 Maner 1997c, pp. 344-345, note 17.
3 Maner 1997a, pp. 87, 91, 510.
4 Schmidt 1981 op. cit., pp. 520, 528; Völkl 1995, p. 120; Maner 1997a, pp. 133, 138, 511.
5 Frangulis op. cit. c.1954, p. 1121; Durandin 1994, pp. 95, 149; Maner 1997a, p. 102; Dimitriu 2006, pp. 308-309.
6 Dimitriu 2006, Chap. 13. *Die Außenpolitik Rumäniens, Oktober 1938-September 1939*, pp. 669-751; Gafencu 1944; Gafencu 1946;
7 Maner 1997a, pp. 105, 111.

Cultural life in the 1930s – p. 70

1 Boia 2003b, p. 131.

Political attitude – pp. 71-73

1 GMC, *The Romanian Architecture after the Restauration* (1940). In: GMC 1966, pp. 119-126. See also Maner 1997c, p. 370.
2 GMC, *Form and Formalism* (1934). Cited from GMC 1966, p. 21.
3 Judt 2010, p. 123.
4 GMC, *A capital* (1934). Cited from GMC 1966, pp. 43-59.
5 GMC, *Saving Old Cities* (1934). Cited from GMC 1966, pp. 27-31.
6 GMC 1962, p. 93; GMC 1964, p. 152; Gafencu 1991, p. 146.
7 Scurtu et al 2002, p. 202; see also Schmidt 1981, pp. 527, 535.
8 GMC, Letter to Marthe Bibesco, 16th July 1930 (AMLSC).
9 GMC, Letter to Marthe Bibesco, 14th February 1931 (AMLSC).
10 GMC 1964, p. 148.
11 P.-E. Miclesco in: Rădulescu 2005, p. 302.
12 GMC 1962, p. 93.
13 Sebastian 1997, p. 307.
14 Schmidt 1981 op. cit., pp. 527, 535; Hitchins 1994, pp. 403-405; Völkl 1995, p. 117.
15 GMC, Letter to Sanda Cantacuzino, 23rd July 1939 (AMLSC).
16 CNSAS, MAI, Dos. No. 7279/GMC, No. 3677, entries, 29th January 1946 and 2nd February 1946; Bălceşti 2005, p. 124.
17 GMC, Letter to Sanda Cantacuzio, 7th December 1938 (AMLSC).
18 B. Russell, *Western Civilization*. In: Russell 2010 [1935], p. 110.
19 Ibid.

Contributions to modernising Romania– p. 75

1 GMC, *Letter to Marcel Janco*, in: *Contimporanul* 1931, p. 9.
2 GMC, *Instrucţia în problema reconstrucţiei* [The importance of education as regards the issue of reconstruction]. In: GMC 2001 [1947], p. 98.
3 GMC 2010, p. 229, 14th Letter to Simon.
4 GMC, diary entry, 22th November 1931, cited from GMC 1962, p. 92.
5 GMC, Letter to Marthe Bibesco, 30th September 1929 (AMLSC).
6 GMC, Letters to Marthe Bibesco, 23rd April and 30th September 1929. On H. Gutmann, the banker and art lover, see Rheinheimer 2007.
7 GMC, *Moonwatch* 1938, p. 177.
8 GMC 2010, p. 161, 10th Letter to Simon.
9 GMC 2010, p. 225, 14th Letter to Simon.

Architecture and Urbanism Projects – p. 76-77

1 Patrulius 1975a, S. 58
2 GMC *et al*/PMB 1935.
3 GMC, Letter to Sanda Cantacuzino, 28th March 1940 (AMLSC).
4 Rowe/Koetter 1978, p. 77.

Clients – pp. 78-79

1 See Patrulius 1982, p. 90.
2 See Duculescu 2010, p. 147.

Eforie – pp. 80-81

1 On Eforie Nord, see Cicio Pop 1932, pp. 278-279; Cicio Pop 1938, pp. 364-366; Ionescu Dunăreanu/Cristescu 1974, pp. 15-24.
2 On Blank, see Taylor 1937, p. 128; Báthory 1991; Maner 1997a, p. 104; Niţulescu 1999; Ornea 1999, p. 3; Ichim 2003 op. cit., p. 152.
3 Pârvulescu 2006, p. 74.
4 ANB/MMSOS, Dos. No. 277/1932, Eforia-Tekirghiol-Agigea, Constantza County.
5 Cicio Pop 1937, p. 365.
6 GMC, Letter to Marthe Bibesco, 30th September 1929 (AMLSC).
7 GMC, Letter to Marthe Bibesco, Bucharest, 11th March 1930 (AMLSC).
8 Patmore1939, p. 40.
9 Ileana Tilea-Troiano in a conversation with the author, London, 28th November 2008.

Mamaia – pp. 84-85

1 Prager 1979, pp. 284-286.
2 Dan Corneliu and Gheorghe Vecerdea in a conversation with the author, Constantza, 11th September 2006; Letter from G. Vecerdea, 25th September 2008.
3 Cicio Pop 1938, p. 78; Prager 1979, pp. 284-286; Iordănescu/Georgescu 1986, Vol. 1, p. 546.
4 GMC, Letter to Marietta Stern, Mamaia, 5th August 1937 (AMLSC).
5 Patmore 1939, p. 40.

Architectural Office – pp. 86-87

1 Dan Marinescu, Paul Marinescu's son, in a conversation with the author, Bucharest, 1st August 2007; P. Marinescu, Letter to Şerban Cantacuzino, c.1990 (AMLSC).
2 GMC, Letter to Sanda Cantacuzino, 25th November 1939 (AMLSC).
3 GMC, diary entry, 22nd April 1933, in GMC 1964, p. 158; Ileana Tilea-Troianu in a conversation with the author, London, 28th November 2008.
4 Gh. Vecerdea in a conversation with the author, Constantza, 11th September 2006; G. Vecerdea, letter to the author, 25th September 2008.
5 GMC, Letter to Marietta Stern, Bucharest, 31st March 1938 (AMLSC).
6 A. Marcu 1993, p. 8.
7 GMC, Letter to Marietta Stern, Constantza, 2nd April 1938 (AMLSC).
8 GMC, Letter to Marietta Stern, Câmpulung, 4th August 1938 (AMLSC).

Ethos, Friendship and Romanian Modernism – pp. 88-92

1 GMC, *Letter to Marcel Janco* (1931) op. cit.
2 Ibid.
3 Ibid.
4 Janco 1931.
5 Manaila 2003, p. 33.
6 Machedon/Scoffham 1999, p. 72.
7 Creangă, *Anarhia stilurilor şi arta viitorului* (The Anarchy of Styles and the Art of the Future). Public Lecture, Bucharest (1935). In: UAR 1992, pp. 193-196.
8 Morin 1988, pp. 126-127.
9 M. Janco, cited from Patrulius 1980, p. 32.
10 Patrulius 1980, p. 65.
11 Orsenna 2001, p. 63.
12 On Lord Burlington and his circle see e.g. Harris 1994; Barnard/Clark 1995.
13 On the friendship between Goethe and Schiller cf. e.g. Safranksi 2009.
14 Taylor 1935, pp. 211-212; Machedon/Scoffham 1999, p. 248; Olteanu 2002, p. 406; Pârvulescu 2006, pp. 211-217.
15 Patrulius 1980, pp. 126-129.
16 Patrulius 1980, p. 127; UAR 1992, p. 203.
17 Morand 1990 [1935], pp. 163-164. On Capşa see also Patmore 1939, p. 10; Ioniţă 2000.
18 UAR 1992, pp. 55-58.
19 UAR 1996, pp. 123, 254.
20 Ilk 1997, p. 53, K245.
21 GMC, Letter to Sanda Cantacuzino, Bucharest, 16th August 1946 (AMLSC); G. Opresco 1935, p. 51; Patrulius 1980, p. 59; Deac 1996, p. 123.
22 GMC, *The Official Pavilion of Romania at the New York World's Fair*, Bucharest, broadcast lecture, 13th December 1938, pp. 2-5 (ASRR).
23 On Militza Pătraşcu see Opresco 1935, pp. 52, 53, 180; Cristea-Vieru1982; Ilk 1997, p. 124; Bach 1998, pp. 339, 359.
24 GMC, Letter to Marietta Stern, 27th March 1938; Letters to Sanda Cantacuzino, 23rd March 1940, 14th July 1942 (AMLSC).
25 Bach 1998, pp. 78-85, 91-98, 347.
26 On Brancusi's project in Târgu-Jiu see e.g. Bach 1998, pp. 171-173.
27 27 S. Tattarescu-Negropontes in Centre Pompidou 1995.
28 GMC to Marietta Stern-Guetta, 21st August 1938 (AMLSC).
29 GMC to Marietta Stern-Guetta, 8th October 1938 (AMLSC).

Painting and Drawing – p. 93

1 Patrulius 1975b, p. 60; A. Anghelescu in GMC 1977a, p. 507.
2 GMC, Letter to Sanda Cantacuzino, 5th November 1939 (AMLSC).
3 Seiwert 1993, p. 25; UAR 1996, p. 254; Pelin 2005, pp. 9, 10.
4 GMC, Letter to Marietta Stern, Bucharest, 11th February 1938 (AMLSC); GMC in CNSAS, MAI, Dos. No. 7279/GMC, No. 5264, 3rd March 1948.
5 GMC, Letters to Marietta Stern, Bucharest, 12th February & 31st March 1938 (AMLSC). On Cadorin cf. Collarcho 1968, Vol. 1, pp. 65-66; Saur 1997, Vol. 15, p. 489.
6 Patrulius 1982, p. 91, note 11.
7 Letter to Sanda Cantacuzino, Bucharest 28th March 1940 (AMLSC).
8 The two manor houses belonged to the Ştirbeys. The Dărmăneşti manor was built to the designs of Nicolae Ghika-Budeşti (see GMC 1927, p. 356; Narcis 2007, pp. 130-135).
9 Letter to Marietta Stern, Mamaia, 27th June 1937 (AMLSC).

Criticism and study travels – pp. 95-97

1 On *Revista Fundaţiilor Regale* see Gusti 1937, pp. 39-41; Ichim 2003 op. cit., p. 162.
2 On *Viaţa românească* see Hurezeanu 1986; Irimia-Tuchtenhagen 1997, pp. 326-327.
3 On *Revista Istorică Română* see Cernovodeanu 1977, pp. 25-26.
4 GMC 1964, p. 153.

5 On the *Romanian Broadcasting Company* SRR see Denize 1999; Acatrinei 2005. For the beginnings of radio broadcasting see e.g. Douglas 2001; Braun/Kaiser 2003, Vol. 5, pp. 152-158.
6 Denize 1999, pp. 185-256.
7 GMC, *Romania's Appearance in the USA*, broadcast lecture, 31st August 1939 (SRR, Dos. 8/1939).
8 GMC, *Mănăstirea Văcărești*, in GMC 1932, pp. 81-93.
9 For Romania and the *Orient Express* see for instance Cars/Caracalla 1984.
10 GMC, Letter to Sanda Cantacuzino, 29th May 1938 (AMLSC).
11 Patrulius 1975a, S. 59.
12 GMC, *Moonwatch* 1938, pp. 212-218.
13 See e.g. M. Sebastian, *Notă despre o carte de călătorie* [Notes on a Travelling Book] (1938).
14 GMC, Letter to Sanda Cantacuzino, aboard the *Normandie*, 29th Mai 1938 (AMLSC).
15 GMC in *L'Architecture d'Aujourd'hui*, No. 5/1934, pp. 57-62.
16 See *L'Architecture d'Aujourd'hui*, from No. 7/1934 to 1/1937.
17 See *Bibliographie: Kurt Hielscher: La Roumanie. Leipzig 1931*. In: AA, 10/1934-1935, p. 82; *Sanatorium à Prédéal, Roumanie. Architectes: Marcel et Jules Jancu et P. Feldman*. In: AA, 10/1936, p. 64; *Halles centrales de Ploești, Roumanie. Architecte I. S. Socolesco*. In: AA, 11/1936, pp. 44-45.
18 GMC, Letter to Marietta Stern 30th July 1937 (AMLSC).
19 See *Simetria I* (1939).
20 GMC *et al*, *Simetria I-VIII*. Bucharest 1939-1947. Contributors to *Simetria* included architects like M. Cotescu, H. Creangă, T. Evolceanu, H. Georgescu, P.-E. Miclesco, N. Nedelescu, T. Socolescu; civil engineer M. Hangan; artists A. I. Brătescu-Voinești, H. Catargi, Ș. Constantinescu, D. Ghiulamila, D. Iovănescu, P. Miracovici, T. Pallady, M. Râmniceau M. Constantinescu, P. Grant; further intellectuals such as D. Cotaru, M. Ghyka, I. Pillat, T. Vianu, G. Opresco, N. B. Cantacuzino, C. Noica, G. Constandaky, P. Florescu, M. Radulescu and E. Ciomac.
21 *Simetria VI* 1945, pp. 65-76. See Patmore's memoirs Patmore 1960, and O. Mitchell, *Room to Improve*. In: *The New York Times*, 26th January 2006.
22 GMC, Letter to Sanda Cantacuzino, 29th October 1939 (AMLSC).
23 *Simetria VII* 1946, pp. 53-67. On Dard see e.g. Larousse 1982, Vol. 3, p. 2950; Mouton 1991, pp. 33, 43, 61; de Weck 2001, p. 467.
24 Letter to Sanda Cantacuzino, 19th November 1939, AMLSC.
25 On *Cartea Românească* see e.g. Pârvulescu 2006, pp. 219-284.
26 See *Simetria I-VIII*, Bucharest 1939-1947.
27 Curtius 1973, p. 170. Cf. also Harding 2002, p. 207.
28 T. S. Eliot, *A Commentary*. In: *Criterion*. London, August 1927, p. 99. Cited from Harding 2002, p. 209.
29 T. S. Eliot, *A Commentary*. In: *Criterion*, April 1926, p. 222. Cited from Harding 2002, p. 225.

Diplomatic architecture

British Institute at Bucharest – pp. 99-101

1 Lungu 1989, pp. 161, 162, 173.
2 Tilea 1998, pp. 85, 180; *London Diplomatic Changes. Chile, Turkey and Rumania. Rumanian Anglophile*. In: *The Times*, 25th January 1939, p. 11.
3 Cicio Pop 1932, pp. 52, 5; Cicio Pop1938, pp. 57-59.
4 Myss 1968; Myss 1993, pp. 448, 460; Wagner 1990, pp. 71-77; Hausmann 2002, p. 65.
5 See *Romania to broadcast news in English*. In: *The Times*, 2nd April 1938, p. 11.
6 See *Romanian National Exhibition*. In: *The Times*, 29th April 1938, p. 14.
7 See *An Anglo-Rumanian Festival*. In: *The Times*, 29th March 1938, p. 19.
8 On Sir Reginald Hoare see *Dictionnaire diplomatique*, Vol. 5, Paris 1954, p. 489; Barker 1976, pp. 22, 29, 75-77; Lungu 1989, pp. 113-114, 164; Tilea 1998, pp. 166-167, 224-226.
9 9 See Tilea 1998, p. 181; *The Times*, 13th October 1938, p. 13; *The Times*, 23rd November 1938, p. 13; Charles Bridge of the British Council, Letter to Lord Lloyd, 28th October 1938, NAL BW53/1.
10 See Briend/Thomine 2004, p. 21.
11 Sutherland 1996, p. 221; Parusi 2007, p. 516.
12 Olteanu 2002, p. 417.
13 Cicio Pop 1932, p. 418; Benz/Otto/Weissmann 1998, p. 14; Hausmann 2002, pp. 61-99; Michels 2005.
14 Tilea 1998, p. 181. On Lord Lloyd see Donaldson 1984, pp. 46-54; Atherton 1994; Tilea 1998, pp. 236-237.
15 Lord Lloyd of Dolobran, cited from Donaldson 1984, p. 60.
16 *The Times*, 15th November 1938, p. 15.
17 E. D. O'Brien of the British Council, note of 22nd November 1938, NAL BW53/1; *British Institute for Bucharest: Grant of a site*. In: *The Times*, 23rd November 1938, p. 13.
18 GMC, Letters to Sanda Cantacuzino, 1st and 2nd March 1938 (AMLSC).
19 *The Times*, 16th May 1938, p. 20; GMC's nomination paper, 29th March 1938 (RIBA/IA).
20 Letter from Charles Bridge to Lord Lloyd, 28th October 1938 (NAL BW53/1).
21 GMC, Letter to Sanda Cantacuzino, Bucharest, 15th October 1939 (AMLSC).
22 GMC, Letter to Margareta Roman, London, 8th March 1939 (AMLSC).
23 Ibid.
24 GMC, Letter to Sanda Cantacuzino, Bucharest, 25th November 1939 (AMLSC).
25 Jones/Woodward 2000, p. 97.
26 Taylor 1937, p. 118.
27 Pevsner 1992, p. 389; Frampton 1995, pp. 182-183; Brown 1996, p. 130 etc; Jones/Woodward 2000, pp. 147, 297.
28 See Duculescu 2010, p. 59; UAR-AOD, No. 76.
29 Marthe Bibesco, Letter to Lord Lloyd of Dolobran, 18th January 1939, NAL BW53/1.
30 GMC, Letter to Sanda Cantacuzino, Bucharest 19th November 1939 (AMLSC).
31 Cf. e.g. Barker 1976, p. 76; Porter 1989, p. 66.

The 1939 New York World's Fair – pp. 105-109

1 GMC, Letter to Sanda Cantacuzino, New York, 1st June 1938 (AMLSC).
2 GMC, Letter to Sanda Cantacuzino, New York, 2nd June 1938 (AMLSC).
3 GMC, *The Official Pavilion of Romania at the 1939 New York World's Fair*, broadcast lecture, 13th December 1938, SRR. On the 1939 New York World's Fair 1939 see Wurts/Appelbaum 1977; Zim *et al* 1988.
4 Wurts/Appelbaum 1977, p. 3.
5 GMC, *Romania's Appearance in the USA* (1939), op. cit., p. 2.
6 See GMC's Bibliography.
7 GMC, *Romania's Appearance in the USA* (1939) op. cit., p. 4.
8 Ibid.
9 GMC, *The Official Pavilion of Romania at the 1939 New York World's Fair* (1938), op. cit., p. 2.
10 Cicio Pop 1938, pp. 310-311.
11 GMC, *Romania's Appearance in the USA* (1939) op. cit., p. 4.
12 GMC, *The Official Pavilion of Romania at the 1939 New York World's Fair* (1938), op. cit., p. 2.
13 GMC, *Moonwatch* 1938, p. 116. On the mashrabiyas see Belting 2008, p. 272.
14 GMC, *Romania's Appearance in the USA* (1939) op. cit., p. 5.
15 Op. cit., p. 6.
16 Ibid.
17 Palladio 1965, p. 37. Book II, Chapter 1.
18 GMC, *Romania's Appearance in the USA* (1939) op. cit., p. 6.
19 GMC, *The Official Pavilion of Romania at the 1939 New York World's Fair* (1938), op. cit.
20 GMC, Letter to Sanda Cantacuzino, Bucharest 29th September 1940 (AMLSC); *Haiti Unparalleled Fair*. In: *Time Magazine*, Monday, 17th October 1949; Duculescu 2010, p. 71.
21 Hootz/Vătășianu 1986, pp. 403-404; W. Myss, *Kronstadt, Schwarze Kirche*. In: Myss 1993, pp. 284-285.
22 Moravánszky 1988, p. 64.

New York – p. 109

1 GMC, *The American Experience* (1939). Cited from GMC 1966, p. 113.
2 Op. cit. p. 109.
3 GMC, Letter to Sanda Cantacuzino, New York, 2nd June 1938 (AMLSC).
4 Holli/Jones 1981, p. 205.
5 GMC, Letter to Sanda Cantacuzino onboard the *Normandie*, 29th May 1938 (AMLSC).
6 GMC, Letter to Sanda Cantacuzino, New York, 9th June 1938 (AMLSC).
7 Cf. *The Fair Today*. In: *The New York Times*, 5th May 1939, p. 19.
8 GMC, Letter to Sanda Cantacuzino, Bucharest, 14th December 1939; P. Derer in Doicescu 1983, p. 11.
9 *The New York Times*, 6th May 1939, p. 7.
10 GMC, Letter to Sanda Cantacuzino, Bucharest, 29th October 1939 (AMLSC).
11 On A. Călinescu see Patmore 1939, pp. 15-17; Hitchins 1994, pp. 420-423; Ichim 2003, p. 177.
12 GMC, Letter to Sanda Cantacuzino, Bucharest, 29th October 1939 (AMLSC).

The late 1930s – pp. 113-114

1 1 See Tismăneanu 1996, pp. 48-58.
2 GMC, Letter to Sanda, 28th September 1939 (AMLSC).
3 GMC, Letters to Sanda, Posada, 3rd September 1939; 5th November 1939 (AMLSC).
4 Marie-Lyse Cantacuzino-Ruhemann in a conversation with the author, London, 16th August 2013.
5 A. Cooper, *Introduction* to Fermor 2004, p. 3. See also Fermor 2004 [1986], p. 13.
6 Cooper 2012, p. 119. See chap. 6, *Balasha*, pp. 99-199.
7 Ibid.
8 Marie-Lyse Cantacuzino-Ruhemann in a conversation with the author, London, 30th November 2008.
9 GMC, Letters to Sanda, 3rd September 1939; 12th September 1939; 30th January 1941 (AMLSC).
10 GMC, Letter to Sanda Cantacuzino, 3rd December 1939 (AMLSC).
11 GMC, Letter to Sanda, 29th September 1939 (AMLSC).
12 GMC, Letter to Sanda Cantacuzino, 15th October 1939 (AMLSC).
13 GMC, Letter to Sanda Cantacuzino, Bucharest, 29th September 1939 (AMLSC).
14 GMC, *The Industrial Architecture and Hans Hertlein*. In: *Simetria III* (1940-1941), pp. 133-135.
15 See Ribbe/Schäche 1985.
16 Marie-Lyse Cantacuzino-Ruhemann in a conversation with the author, London, 30th November 2008.

Under three dictatorships (1940-60)
Fascism, Carlton collapse, imprisonment and war – pp. 117-118

1 *Curentul*, Bucharest, 13th November 1940, p. 1; Pelin 2005, p. 60.
2 A. Marcu 1993 op. cit., p. 8; P.-E- Miclescu in Rădulescu 2005, pp. 302-303; A. Magheru in Dragu Dimitriu 2006, p. 25.
3 On the crimes of the Iron Guard in 1940-41 see Scurtu 1992 (1), pp. 12-14; Völkl 1995, pp. 127-128, 145-146; Maner 1997b, p. 358; Ioanid 2000, pp. 43-51, 52; Balta 2005, pp. 147 etc; Pelin 2005, p. 83.
4 A. Magheru in Dragu-Dimitriu 2006, p. 25.
5 GMC, Letter to Sanda Cantacuzino, 30th January 1941 (AMLSC); Diesbach 1986, p. 492.
6 GMC, Letter to Sanda Cantacuzino, Bucharest, 30th January 1941 (AMLSC).
7 GMC, Letter to Sanda Cantacuzino, 9th December 1943 (AMLSC); Patrulius 1975a, p. 59; Anghelescu in GMC 1977a, p. 509; Marcu 1993, p. 8; Magheru in Dragu-Dimitriu 2006, p. 25;
8 On the analysis of the Carlton collapse see: Beleş 1941; Sieberg 1941; Prager 1979, p. 451.
9 See *L'Architecture d'aujourd'hui* 5/1934, p. 60.
10 GMC, Letter to Sanda Cantacuzino, Bucharest, 14th July 1942 (AMLSC); GMC's military identity card 1945, p. 6 (AGMC-IP).
11 GMC, Letter to Sanda Cantacuzino, 29th December 1944, AMLSC.

Professional activity 1942-1948
Architecture – pp. 119-123

1 GMC, Letter to Sanda Cantacuzino, Bucharest, 19th March 1942 (AMLSC).
2 Adela Bărbulescu, chief-manager of the *Institute of Agricultural Research Băneasa* SCDP, in a conversation with the author, Bucharest, 21th September 2006.
3 See Păcurariu/Pandele, DCCPCNG Dos. No. 437, 8th August 2005.
4 M.-L. Cantacuzino-Ruhemann/Ş. Cantacuzino in GMC 2006, p. 5.
5 AMLSC.
6 M. Kühn, *Foreword* to Peschken 1979, p. IX.
7 On Schinkel's transformation of the Tegel Palace see Grisebach 1924, pp. 100-101; Forssman 1981, pp. 174-179; Bergdoll 1994.
8 GMC, *Simetria VII* (1946), p. 197-203.
9 See Machedon/Scoffham 1999, p. 165.

Lecturing in Bucharest – pp. 123-124

1 GMC, Letters to Sanda Cantacuzino, Bucharest, 19th March 1942; 14th July 1942 (AMLSC); CNSAS, MAI, Dos. No. 7279/GMC, No. 5264, 3rd March 1948.
2 GMC, 7th Letter to Simon (1956), translated by Ş. Cantacuzino. In: GMC 2006, p. 3.
3 S. Eleutheriadis, Rio de Janeiro/Brazil, in a letter to the author, 31st July 2007.
4 See BAR A-2658 a-e.
5 GMC, Letter to Sanda Cantacuzino, Bucharest, 13th September 1958; Patrulius 1975b, p. 60.
6 See Patrulius 1975b, pp. 57-58.
7 Panofsky 1979, p. 20.
8 A. Marcu 1993, p. 8.
9 Patrulius 1975b, p. 58.
10 Ibid.
11 Patrulius 1982, p. 93.
12 Patrulius 1975b, p. 57.
13 D. Corneliu, in a conversation with the author, Constantza, 19th September 2006.
14 S. Eleutheriadis, Rio de Janeiro, in a letter to the author, 31st July 2007.
15 E. Greceanu, in a conversation with the author, Bucharest, 31st August 2011.
16 E. Greceanu in OAR 2007, pp. 111-142.
17 Zucker 1987, p. 30.
18 I. M. Enescu, in a conversation with the author, Bucharest, 5th September 2006.

Journalism and Criticism – pp. 125-126

1 GMC, Letter to Sanda Cantacuzino, Bucharest, 30th January 1941 (AMLSC).
2 GMC, Letter to Sanda Cantacuzino, Bucharest, 7th July 1945 (AMLSC); Patrulius 1975b, p. 56.
3 See CNSAS, Bucharest, Dos. 12482/42, 12166, note, 14th January 1947. On the Holocaust in Romania see e.g. Ioanid 2000; Prost 2006, p. 15.
4 Vianu's contributions to *Simetria* included *Admirație* [The Admiration]. From the series *Dicționar*. In: *Simetria III* (1940-1941), pp. 89-91; *Formă* [Form]. Op. cit., pp. 91-95; *Gogenos and Gignomenon*. Op. cit., pp. 95-100.
5 Sebastian 2001, p. 331.
6 M. Celac in GMC 2001, p. 105.
7 CNSAS, Dos. 7279, 12482/42, 12166, notes, 14th January 1947; 9th August 1947.
8 Kapuściński 2007, p. 6.
9 Plotinus 1952, p. 71, Enn. II, 9[33]9. Cited by GMC in *Simetria VII* (1946), p. 20.
10 K. Jaspers, *Foreword* to Milosz 1953, p. 7.
11 B. Russel, *Scylla and Charybdis, or Communism and Fascism*. In: Russell 2010 [1935], p. 74.
12 E. Greceanu 2007 op. cit., p. 126.
13 Ibid.
14 R. Barthes, *Politisation de la Science en Roumanie*. From a letter to the French Foreign Minister, 21st July 1949. Cited from Guénard 1994, pp. 26-27.
15 GMC, *Simetria VIII* (1947), pp. 101-107.
16 GMC, Letters to Sanda Cantacuzino, Bucharest 19th March 1942; 14th July 1942 (AMLSC).
17 See Kapuściński 2007, p. 5.
18 Cited from M. Adams, *Preliminary Note* to Ortega y Gasset 1973, p. 7.

Hopes of democratisation – pp. 127-128

1 Porter 1989, p. 139.
2 Marie-Lyse Cantacuzino-Ruhemann, in a conversation with the author, London, 30th November 2008.
3 GMC, Letter to Sanda Cantacuzino, Bucharest, 7th July 1945 (AMLSC).
4 GMC, Letter to Sanda Cantacuzino, Bucharest, 4th March 1946 (AMLSC). On Le Rougetel cf. e.g *Dictionnaire diplomatique*, Vol. 5. Paris 1954, p. 604.
5 Taylor 1935, p. 1063; de Weck 2001, pp. 247, 467.
6 Mouton 1991.
7 Guénard 1994, p. 22; CNSAS, MAI, Dos. No. 7279/GMC, No. 5264, Decision No. 549/33, 1948.
8 GMC, Letter to Sanda Cantacuzino, Bucharest, 7th July 1947 (AMLSC); conversation with Marie-Lyse Cantacuzino-Ruhemann and Şerban Cantacuzino, London, August 2013. Correspondance of the author with Diane de la Bruchollerie, the pianist's daughter, July and August 2013. On M. de la Bruchollerie see Harden/Willmes 2008, pp. 105-107.
9 Klein/Göring 1995, pp. 99-100.
10 GMC, Letter to Sanda Cantacuzino, 7th April 1946 (AMLSC).
11 Ibid.
12 Ibid.
13 Cooper 2012. Cited from the caption for a photograph of Balasha Cantacuzene, reproduced in the first section of images, between pp. 112-113.
15 P. Groza, cited after Völkl 1995, p. 167.

Imprisonments (1948-1954) – pp. 129-130

1 GMC, Letter to Sanda Cantacuzino, 16th August 1946 (AMLSC).
2 GMC, Letter to Sanda Cantacuzino, 7th April 1946 (AMLSC).
3 GMC, Letters to Sanda Cantacuzino, 16th August 1946, 2nd February 1947 (AMLSC).
4 Cretzianu 1956, p. 359.
5 CNSAS, Dos. No. 7279, 12482/43/358, note, 15th January 1947.
6 GMC, Letter to Sanda Cantacuzino, 1946, cited from M.-L. Cantacuzino-Ruhemann, 22nd March 2013. Translated from the French by Marie-Lyse Cantacuzino-Ruhemann.

7 GMC, Letter to Sanda Cantacuzino, 4th March 1946 (AMLSC).
8 Völkl 1995, pp. 169-170.
9 CNSAS, Dos. No. 7279/GMC.
10 GMC, Letter to Sanda Cantacuzino, 16th August 1946 (AMLSC).
11 Professor Peter Derer in a conversation with the author, Bucharest, 1st September 2005; Ş. Cantacuzino in a conversation with the author, London, 4th November 2005; CNSAS, MAI, Dos. No. 7279/GMC, No. 5264 (3rd March 1948).
12 John VI Cantacuzino, *Message aux Valaques de Thessalie* (1342). In: *Ioannis Cantacuzeni ex-Imperatoris Historiarum Libri IV*. Vol. 3, chap. 53. French translation by M. Cousin. Paris 1685. Cited from J. M. Cantacuzène 1992, p. 433.
13 CNSAS, MAI, Dos. No. 7279/GMC, No. 5264, note, 25th July 1950; MJTMT/BAS, No. 1183C, 12th October 2004 (AMLSC); Aiud prison, GMC's personal prison file no. 145/52, 2158 (1954); Ş. Cantacuzino, in GMC 1999, p. 11.
14 A. Marcu 1993, p. 8. Translated from the Romanian by M.-L. Cantacuzino-Ruhemann.
15 CNSAS, MAI, Dos. No. 7279/GMC, personal file, note, 8th June 1953.
16 GMC, Letter to Sanda Cantacuzino, 15th August 1953 (AMLSC).
17 MAI, *Serviciul Penitenciare, Bilet de eliberare* (Release Document) No. 428/953, 21st June 1954 (AGMC-IP); A. Marcu 1993 p. 8; MJTMT/BAS, No. 1183C, 12th October 2004 (AMLSC).
18 A. Marcu 1993, p. 8.
19 N. Valéry 1978, chap. 6, *Die Hölle am Donau-Schwarmeer-Kanal*, pp. 180-216.
20 GMC, Letter to Sanda Cantacuzino, Bucharest, 11th August 1955 (AMLSC).
21 MAI, *Serviciul Penitenciare* (1954) op. cit.
22 See Ierunca1996.
23 MAI, *Serviciul Penitenciare* (1954) op. cit.

Inspector at the Department of Historic Monuments – pp. 131-133

1 Patrulius 1975a, p. 62; Ş. Cantacuzino in GMC 1999, p. 11.
2 T. Kitzulescu, in a conversation with the author, Bucharest, 24th September 2006.
3 See INMI/FDMI, Bucharest, Dos. No. 2480.
4 Patrulius 1982, p. 93.
5 Patrulius 1975a, p. 62.
6 Ibid.
7 GMC, Letter to Sanda Cantacuzino, 11th April 1955 (AMLSC).
8 Patrulius 1975a, p. 59; Ş. Cantacuzino in GMC 1999, p. 11; INMI/FDMI, Bucharest, Dos. No 8783.
9 GMC, Letters to Sanda Cantacuzino, 11th April 1955; 11th August 1955 (AMLSC).
10 GMC, Letter to Marie-Lyse Cantacuzino-Ruhemann, 25th December 1958 (AMLSC).
11 Ibid.
12 See GMC 1993a.
13 Patrulius 1975a, p. 62.
14 GMC, cited from Patrulius 1982, p. 93.
15 *On landscape*. In: GMC 1993a [1956], p. 104.
16 Greceanu 2000, p. 11.
17 GMC, Letter to Sanda Cantacuzino, 11th August 1955 (AMLSC).
18 Ibid.
19 GMC, Letter to Sanda Cantacuzino, 26th January 1957 (AMLSC).
20 T. Kitzulescu in a conversation with the author, Bucharest, 24th September 2006.
21 Patrulius 1975b, p. 60. Translation by Marie-Lyse Cantacuzino-Ruhemann and Şerban Cantacuzino. In: GMC 2006, p. 3.
22 T. Kitzulescu in a conversation with the author, Bucharest, 24th September 2006; M. Cantacuzino in a conversation with the author, Brussels, 27th November 2008.
23 GMC, Letter to Sanda Cantacuzino, 26th January 1957 (AMLSC).
24 Rusan 2008, p. 43.
25 CNSAS, MAI Dos. 7279/GMC, no. 526, entry of 29th January 1957; Ş. Cantacuzino in GMC 1999, p. 12.

Informal diocesan architect in Jassy – pp. 134-137

1 Leon 1979, p. 50.
2 GMC, Letter to Marie-Lyse Cantacuzino-Ruhemann, 25th December 1958 (AMLSC); GMC, Letter to Oscar Han. In: GMC 1977a; Leon 1979, p. 49.
3 M.-L. Cantacuzino-Ruhemann/Ş. Cantacuzino, *Art is in itself an act of love and love cannot be learnt. Introduction* to GMC 2006, p. 4.
4 Ibid.
5 GMC, Letter to Sanda Cantacuzino, 13th September 1958 (AMLSC).
6 See GMC/Ionescu 1964.
7 See GMC 1993a.
8 GMC 2010, p. 201. GMC cited from Baudelaire's poem *Semper Eadem*. In: Baudelaire 1909, p. 28. WLB Stuttgart, Stefan-George-Archive.
9 GMC, Letter to Sanda Cantacuzino, 9th November 1958 (AMLSC).
10 GMC, Letter to Marie-Lyse Cantacuzino-Ruhemann, 25th December 1958 (AMLSC).
11 GMC 1927, p. 354.
12 M. Steinbach in Gebhard/Sauerländer 2007, p. 111.
13 GMC, Letter to Jean David, 2nd May 1960 (AMLSC).
14 Cf. de Ligne in Burg 1965, pp. 11-64; 178-182.
15 See GMC 1993a, p. 141.
16 Ibid. See de Ligne 1795, Vol. 1, pp.100-101.
17 GMC, *Jassy, an urban landscape*, 1955 (AMLSC).
18 Ibid. First published by Dr E. Greceanu in *Hierasus 1981, anuarul Muzeului județean Botoșani. Sesiunea științifică de comunicări și referate "Permanențe ale istoriei" (21-22 November 1981)*, pp. 385-398. Dr Greceanu accompanied GMC's text with a substantial introduction, both of which she re-published in *Revista Monumentelor Istorice*, Bucharest, Year LXIX, Nr. 1-2/2000, pp. 11-12 (introduction), pp. 13-16 (GMC's text).)
19 Op. cit. p. 12.
20 Ş. Cantacuzino in GMC 2006, p. 5.
21 See Giurescu 1990.
22 GMC 1932 op. cit. pp. 37-40.
23 GMC 1993a [1958], p. 145.
24 Ibid.
25 P. Mihail in: GMC 1993a, p. 331; Ş. Cantacuzino in GMC 1999, p. 12.
26 Shakespeare 2001, p. 24. Sonett LXV, last line.

On the *classical attitude*

Explanatory Note – p. 139

1 GMC Simetria II (1940), p. 57.
2 Ibid.
3 GMC 2002 [1926], pp. 30-31).

Attempt at explaining the classical attitude

Understanding of the classical attitude – p. 140

1 Scruton 2001, p. 8.
2 GMC 2002 [1926], p. 30.
3 GMC 2002 [1926], p. 30.
4 GMC, *Classicism*. In: *Simetria II* (1940), p. 63.

Notion of history and tradition

1 GMC *et al*, *Foreword* to *Revista Istorică Română*. Bucharest 1931, Vol. 1, Faks. 1, p. 3.
2 Adamson 2008, p. 314.
3 M. Steinbach, *Rappel à l'ordre. Zum Traditionsverständnis im Richtungsstreit zwischen den Weltkriegen*. In: Gebhardt/Sauerländer 2007, p. 110.
4 P. Schöttler, *Marc Bloch (1886-1944)*. In: Raphael 2006, Vol. 1, pp. 242-243.
5 GMC 1993a [1947], p. 17.
6 GMC 2010, p. 179, 10th Letter to Simon.
7 Montesquieu 1952, p. 276.
8 GMC 2002 [1926], p. 22.
9 Op. cit., p. 23.
10 Catullus, cited by GMC in Romanian, in: GMC 2002 [1926], p. 21. This is a line from Poem 22: "The fact is we're all self-fooled, we've all got
A streak of Suffenus in us, some blind spot.
Every man has his vanity assigned him,
But no one sees the pack that's strapped behind him." (Catullus 1982, p. 47, Poem 22).
11 GMC, *Classicism*. In: Simetria II 1940, p. 57.
12 Ibid.
13 GMC 2002 [1926], p. 22.
14 On conservatism, the Golden Age, and the reluctance to worship the future instead of the past, see Scruton 1980b, pp. 120-121.
15 Scruton 1980a, p. 14.
16 T. S. Eliot, *Tradition and the individual talent (1919)*. In: Eliot 1963, pp. 22-23.
17 T. S. Eliot, *Tradition (1934)*. In: Eliot 1963, pp. 20-21.
18 S. Wiedenhofer, *Tradition*. In: Brunner/Conze/Kosselek (eds) 1997, pp. 646-647.
19 J. Guitton, *Leben und Werk von Henri Bergson*. In: Bergson 1964b, p. 33.
20 See Eliade 1969.
21 See Wittgenstein 1922.
22 De Bruyn 2008, p. 21.
23 Gombrich 2006, p. 214.
24 GMC, *Classicism* 1940, p. 57.

The classical attitude, the Aristotelian theory of the mean state, and Palladio – pp. 144-146

1 GMC, *Classicism* 1940, p. 57.
2 Ibid.
3 Ibid.
4 Aristotle 1906, p. 46/NE, Book II, Chap. VI.
5 Op. cit., p. 47.
6 Nerdinger 2003, p. 50. Semper delivered this lecture on March 4th, 1869 in Zurich's City Hall. See G. Semper, *Ueber Baustile*. In: Semper 1979 [1884], pp. 395-426.

7 GMC, *Notes on Bessarabia and Transnistria.* In: *Simetria IV* (1941-42), p. 187.
8 T. Vianu, *Material aesthetics.* In: *Simetria IV* (1941-1942), pp. 53-64.
9 GMC, *Byzantium-bizantine – Dictionary.* In: *Simetria V* (1943), pp. 127-132.
10 Klopfer 1911, pp. 1-2.
11 Focillon 1989, pp. 54-55.
12 Chamfort, cited from Schalk 1995, p. 349.
13 GMC 1993 [1947], p. 71.
14 Goethe 1994, Vol. 3, p. 92.
15 GMC 1928, p. 63.
16 Hertzberger (1991, p. 5) cited Brancusi in French, from Giedion-Welcker 1958, p. 219: "Les choses ne sont pas difficiles à faire, ce qui est difficile, c'est de nous mettre en état de les faire. »
17 Oechslin 2008, p. 322.
18 Wölfflin 1968 [1899], p. XII.
19 Wölfflin, *Italien und das deutsche Formgefühl.* Munich 1931, p. 157. Cited after Oechslin 2008, pp. 321, 335.
20 GMC 1928, p. 30. See also Kruft 1994, p. 88; Oechslin 2008, p. 321, 335.

The recourse to antiquity – pp. 146-149

1 Oechslin 2008, p. 321.
2 Morávanszky 1998, p. 365. See chap. 9: *Classicism as Style, Classicism as Attitude*, pp. 365-408.
3 Ibid.
4 Ibid.
5 Op. cit, p. 377.
6 Ibid.
7 A. Loos, *Der Architekt* (1898). Cited from Steiner, *The strength of the old masters: Adolf Loos and antiquity.* In: Safran/Wang 1985, p. 21. See also Morávanszky 1988, pp. 74-75.
8 GMC/Doicescu, *Declaration.* In: *Simetria I* (1939), p. 11.
9 M. Steinbach in Gebhard/Sauerländer 2007, pp. 100-102.
10 Cf. *Simetria I* (1939), p. 5.
11 Ortega y Gasset 1973, p. 104.
12 Ibid.
13 GMC 1928, p. 18.
14 Wittgenstein 1922, p. 37.
15 Oechslin 2008, p. 66.
16 GMC 1928, p. 63.
17 Höffe 2008, p. 68.
18 Noteboom 1993, p. 59.
19 Plotinus 1952, Enn. V, 8[31]1, pp. 239-240.
20 Scruton 1980a, p. 52.
21 Gombrich 2006, p. 10.
22 GMC, *Explanatory note.* In: *Simetria VII* (1946), pp. 208-209.
23 GMC 1926, p. 19.

Concept of architecture and its invariants – pp. 149-153

1 GMC, *Letter to Marcel Janco* (1931), op. cit.
2 Gromort 1946, p. 104.
3 Moravánszky 2003, p. 15.
4 GMC 2002 [1926], p 31.
5 Frank 1931, p. 22.
6 GMC 1928, pp. 82-83.
7 GMC 2002 [1926], pp. 19-20. GMC cited Valéry in French. For the English version cited here see Valéry 1956, p. xiii.
8 GMC, Letter to Sanda Cantacuzino, Bucharest, 16th August 1946, AMLSC.
9 GMC *et al*/PMB 1935, p. 17.
10 Bergson 1964b, p. 50.
11 GMC, *The critical attitude of André Gide.* In: *Simetria IV* (1941-42), pp. 128-129. GMC cited in French from Gide's *Journal 1889-1939.* Paris 1940, p. 661.
12 Valéry 1932, p. 72.
13 Á. Moravánszky, *Introduction* to Morávanszky/ Gyöngy 2003, p. 1.
14 C. Wilson, *The ethics of architecture.* In: Wilson 2000, p. 21.
15 Op. cit., pp. 29-30.
16 Aristotle 1906, pp. 182-183. NE Book VI, Chapter IV.
17 GMC 1966 [1934], p. 19.
18 Blondel 1771-77, Vol. 1, p. 450. Cited from Kruft 1994, p. 149.
19 GMC, Letter to Sanda Cantacuzino, Bucharest, 20th July 1947 (AMLSC).
20 GMC, Letter to Sanda Cantacuzino, Bucharest, 1st January 1946 (AMLSC).
21 GMC, *The critical attitude of André Gide* (1941-42) op. cit., p. 133.
22 Ibid.
23 GMC 2010, p. 79, 4th Letter to Simon.
24 GMC, *Art and technology.* In: *Simetria II* (1940), p. 35.
25 GMC 2002 [1926], p. 27.
26 GMC, *Art and technology* (1940) op. cit., p. 33.
27 Palladio 1965, pp. 25-26. Book I, Chapter XX, *Of Abuses.* On tectonic culture cf. e.g. Frampton 1995.
28 GMC 2002 [1926], p. 33.
29 GMC, *The critical attitude of André Gide* (1941-42) op. cit., p. 127.
30 Goethe, *Baukunst 1795.* In: Goethe 1999, p. 62.
31 Moravánszky 1988, p. 63.
32 Schinkel, in: Peschken 1979, p. 150. Cited from Moravánszky 1988, p. 63.
33 Moravánszky 1988, p. 67.
34 Ibid.
35 Op. cit., p. 68.
36 Naredi-Rainer 2001, p. 143. From a protocol "of a session on the construction site of the Milan cathedral" (1400). For Mignot, "sciencia" meant a geometry based on right proportioning.
37 GMC 1993 [1947], p. 81.
38 Toynbee 1949, p. 42.
39 Op. cit, p. 44.
40 Ibid.
41 Op. cit., p. 42.
42 Op. cit., p. 43
43 Op. cit. 44
44 Op. cit. 43.
45 Ibid.
46 Op. cit. pp. 43-44.
47 GMC 1993 [1947], p. 45.
48 Ibid.
49 Op. cit. p. 55.
50 Ibid.

Ethics and Aesthetics

Features of the relationship between Aesthetics and transcendental Ethics - pp. 154-155

1 Moravánszky 1998, p. 78.
2 Wittgenstein 1922, p. 183.
3 Camus 2005 [1942], p. 38.
4 Op. cit., pp. 46-47.
5 Wittgenstein 1922, p. 183.
6 Op. cit., p. 187.
7 GMC 2010, p. 123, 7th Letter to Simon.
8 GMC, *Simetria VII* (1946), p. 18.
9 Plotinus 1952, pp. 9-10, Enn. I, 2[19]7.
10 Aristotle 1906, p. 47, NE Book II, Chapter VI.

Features of the relationship between Aesthetics and practical Ethics – pp. 155-159

1 Wittkower 1949, p. 134.
2 Op. cit., p.135.
3 K. Bauch, *Klassik, Klassizität, Klassizismus* (1932). In: Bauch 1967, p. 43.
4 GMC 2002 [1926], p. 26.
5 See Naredi-Rainer 2001, p. 102, note 120.
6 GMC 1993a [1947], p. 85.
7 Forssman 1965, p. 60.
8 Naredi-Rainer 2001, p. 18.
9 Ibid.
10 Kruft 1994, p. 26.
11 Ibid.
12 GMC, Letter to Marie-Lyse Ruhemann-Cantacuzino, 25th December 1958 (AMLSC).
13 GMC 2002 [1926], pp. 27, 33.
14 Giacometti 1995 [1946], p. 33.
15 GMC 1993 [1947], pp. 44, 58, 59.
16 GMC, *Goethe.* In: *Simetria V* (1943), pp. 77-78.
17 GMC/Doicescu, *Orient – Occident?* In: *Simetria IV* (1941-42), p. 15.
18 Op. cit., p.16.
19 Moravánszky 1988, p. 64.
20 GMC, *A Capital* (1934). Cited after GMC 1966, pp. 45-46. GMC cited Montaigne in French. See Montaigne 1952, p. 471, Essays III/9: *Of vanity.*
21 GMC 2001 [1947], p. 15.
22 Höffe 2008, p. 64.
23 Ibid.
24 Ibid.
25 GMC, *Architecture as a theme of thought* (1940) op. cit., pp. 97-98.
26 Mies, cited from Conrads 1970, p. 123.
27 Ibid.
28 *Die Form*, 5th year, No. 15, 1st August 1930, p. 406; Year VII, No. 10, 15th October 1932.
29 M. Cotescu, *Spiritul artei de a clădi de Fritz Schumacher.* In: *Simetria IV* (1941-42), pp. 169-175.
30 GMC 1993 [1947], p. 77. He cited from Plotinus, Enn. II, 9[33]18. See Plotinus 1952, p. 77.
31 GMC 1993 [1947], p. 49.
32 Vitruvius 2009, Book 1, 1.7, p. 9.
33 C. Horn, *Plotin.* In: Höffe 2008, Vol. 1, p. 106.
34 GMC 1993 [1947], p. 28.
35 C. Tornau, *Introduction to* Plotin 2001, p. 7.
36 Horn 2008 op.cit., p. 108.
37 Ibid.
38 GMC 1993 [1947], p. 80.
39 Ibid.
40 Wittgenstein, *Culture and Value.* London 1930. Cited from Wilson 2000, p. 21.
41 Anders 1980, Vol. 2, §3, p. 18.
42 GMC 1993 [1947], p. 81.

A noble banality and the concept of being an architect – pp. 160-164
1 Plotinus 1952, p. 6, Enn. I, 2[19].
2 GMC 1928, p. 63.
3 Plotinus 1952, p. 7, Enn. I, 2[19].
4 GMC 1993 [1947], p. 21.
5 Eliot 1950, p. 8.
6 Ortega y Gasset 1973, p. 193.
7 Egbert 1980, p. 127.
8 GMC, *Puncte de vedere* (Points of view). In: GMC 2001 [1947], p. 43.
9 Valéry1972, p. 12, Marginal Note.
10 Valéry 1929, p. 9.
11 Cioran 1976, p. 37.
12 A. Loos, *Architektur* (1910). In: Safran/Wang 1985, pp. 107-108.
13 GMC, Palladio 1928, p. 88.
14 Morávanszky 1998, p. 365.
15 GMC 1928, p. 88.
16 GMC 1928, p. 30.
17 Valéry 1929, p. 9.
18 Eliot 1963 (1919) op. cit., p. 25.
19 Trempler 2007, p. 215.
20 A. Loos, *Principle of cladding*. In: Loos 1987, pp. 67-68.
21 Patmore 1939, p. 40.
22 GMC 1966 [1934], p. 61. See an English version in the appendum of this book.
23 Cioran 1976, p. 39.
24 GMC, *The Romanian dwelling* (1937) In: GMC 1977a, p. 65.
25 I. Nicolau in Dragu-Dimitriu 2006, p. 424.
26 Gromort 1983, pp. 151-152.
27 A. Loos, *Architektur* 1985 [1910] op. cit. Translation by Wilfried Wang, pp. 107-108.
28 Wilson 2000, p. 34.
29 GMC, *On Classicism*.
In: *Simetria III* (1940-41), p. 148.

Tradition and Modernism
On the motivation to formulate a classical attittude – p. 165
1 See Moravánszky 1998.
2 GMC 2002 [1926], p. 19.
3 Müller in Malaparte 2005, p. 557.
4 GMC, *Moonwatch* 1938, p. 317.
5 Sieburg 1967, p. 363.
6 GMC 1966 [1937], p. 101-108.
7 See GMC1993a [1947], pp. 66-67.
In 1926 Focillon also gave lectures on St Francis of Assisi in France, the Netherlands and Switzerland (see Briend/Thomine 2004, p. 23).

The classical attitude as a means for Cantacuzino to establish himself within the Romanian architectural scene – pp. 165-166
Groys 2004, p. 115.
1 Op. cit., p. 119.
2 Op. cit., pp. 70, 84.
3 Op. cit., pp. 44, 87-88.
4

Arch-traditionalism and arch-modernism – pp. 167-168
GMC 1966 [1934], p. 64.
1 GMC, *The Confusion of notions*.
2 In: GMC 2001 [1947], p. 19.
GMC/Doicescu, *Usefulness and Symbol*.
3 In: *Simetria I* (1939), p. 18.
GMC, *Letter to Marcel Janco* (1931), op. cit.
4 Oechslin 1999, pp. 46 and 70, note 1.
5 GMC 1966 [1937], p. 108.
6 GMC, *Traditionalism and Modernism*.
7 In: GMC 1934, p. 16. For an English version see the addendum to this book.
GMC, *Letter to Marcel Janco* (1931) op. cit.
8 GMC, *Tendances dans l'architecture roumaine*.
9 In: AA 5/1934, p. 57; *Traditionalism and modernism,* in GMC 1934, p. 19.
GMC 1966 [1936], p. 93; GMC 1966 [1940], p.
10 121; see also N. Ghika-Budeşti 1927; Vătăşianu, *Foreword* to Hootz/Vătăşianu 1986, p. 56.
GMC, Fountains, wells and stopovers.
11 In: GMC 1934, pp. 24-25.
See Eliade 1943 (French edition 1994).
12 GMC, *On a reconstruction programme.*
13 In: GMC 2001 [1947], p. 25.
Irimia-Tuchtenhagen 1997, p. 319.
14

Arguments for a synthesis between Tradition and Modernism – pp. 168-170
GMC, *Traditionalism and modernism* (1934),
1 op. cit., p. 16.
Op. cit. 1934, p. 17.
2 Bergson 1964a, p. 6-7.
3 GMC 1966 [1940], p. 124.
4 Cocteau 1926, pp. 115-116.
5 Rilke 2011, pp. 23-24. Taken from Letter 4,
6 16th July 1903.
GMC 1966 [1935], p. 68.
7 GMC, *Traditionalism and modernism* (1934),
8 op. cit., pp. 17-18.
Op. cit., pp. 18-19.
9 GMC 1966 [1936], p. 92.
10 GMC 1966 [1936], p. 92.
11 See also Mango 1975, pp. 342-350.
GMC 1966 [1936], p. 93.
12 Op. cit. pp. 92-94.
13 GMC 1966 [1934], p. 26.
14 H. Creangă, *Răspunsul domnului arhitect Horia*
15 *Creangă* (The Answer of Mr Creangă). In: *Arta şi omul* (Art and Man), III, No. 19-22, Bucharest 1935, p. 337. Cited after UAR 1992, p. 199.
On the Italian rationalist movement, see
16 Mallgrave 2005, pp. 261-262, 459, notes 136, 137. On the importance of the vernacular for modernism see Moravánszky 2002, pp. 95-124.
GMC, *Traditionalism and modernism* (1934),
17 op. cit., pp. 18-19.
On history as an enemy, see H. R. Jauss,
18 *Ästhetische Normen und geschichtliche Reflexion in der Querelle des anciens et des modernes*. In: Perrault 1964; Wiedenhofer, *Tradition*. In: Brunner/Conze/Koselleck 1997, Vol. 6, p. 629; Lecoq 2001; Gebhard/Sauerländer 2007;
GMC, *Traditionalism and modernism* (1934),
19 op. cit., p. 19.
Ricœur 1974, p. 290.
20 Safranski 2003, pp. 109-118.
21 GMC, *Traditionalism and modernism* (1934),
22 op. cit., p. 19.
Ibid.
23 See GMC, *Considérations générales sur la genése*
24 *de l'art moldave*. In: RIR, 1933, vol. 3, Faks. I, pp. 1-10; F. Engelberg, *Bilderbibel im Freien. Bemalte Kirchen im nördlichen Moldawien (Bukowina)*. In: Sielemann 2003, pp. 328-329.

Thoughts on the classical attitude
Cantacuzino's architecture, Romania, and Critical Regionalism – pp. 171-173
Ierunca, *Introduction* to GMC 1966, p. 9.
1 Morand 1990 [1935], p. 293.
2 GMC 2010, p. 129, 7th Letter to Simon.
3 GMC, Letter to Sanda Cantacuzino, Bucharest,
4 20th July 1947 (AMLSC).
GMC, *Explanatory Note*. In: *Simetria VII* (1946),
5 pp. 208-209.
N. Nedelescu, *On Le Corbusier*. In: *Simetria VII* (1946), pp. 135-146.
GMC, *The Artist and the Freedom*. In: *Simetria*
6 *VIII* (1947), p. 104. For an English version of this essay see the addendum to this book.
M. Ghyka c. 1961 (AMLSC).
7 GMC, *Palladio* 1928, p. 33.
8 Cf. e.g. Gavoty 1982, pp. 123-124.
9 H. F. Mallgrave, *Foreword* to Frampton 1995,
10 p. xi.
See e.g. Duculescu 2010.
11 Frampton 2007, p. 314.
12 Ibid., p. 326.
13 Borsi 1987, p. 10.
14 Ricœur1974, p. 292.
15

Further connotations to the classical attitude – pp. 176-179
1 Ortega y Gasset 1973, p. 159-160.
2 Schöttler, *Marc Bloch*. In: Raphael 2006, p. 242.
3 Christiaanse 1994, p. 48.
4 Bergson 1964a, p. 54.
5 Hart 2011, p. 31.
6 Op. cit., p. 7.
7 Schinkel, cited after Peschken 1979, p. 71.
8 De Bruyn 2008, p. 162.
9 GMC, *Points of view*.
In: GMC 2001 [1947], pp. 40-41.
10 Schinkel, cited from Hermann 1977 [1932], Vol. 1, p. 64.
11 Perret 1986, p. 51.
12 Oechslin 2008, p. 322.
13 Ibid.
14 Rowe/Koetter 1978, p. 106.
15 Op. cit., p. 49.
16 Groys 2004, pp. 87-88.
17 C.-H. Roquet, *Foreword* to Eliade 1987, p. 8.
18 Pascal 1931 [, p. 98. *Pensées*, Fragment 353.
Albert Camus used this maxim as the motto of his *Letters to a German Friend* (1943-44).
For these four essays see Camus 1988, p. 7.
19 Cacciari 1993, p. 199.
20 GMC 2010, p. 221, 14th Letter to Simon.
21 GMC 2010, p. 55, 2nd Letter to Simon.
22 *Simetria I-VIII* (1939-1947).
23 Rowe/Koetter 1978, p. 106.
24 Benda 1978 [1946], p. 20, *Introduction* to the 1946 edition.
25 Morin 1988, p. 127.
26 Valéry 1929, p. 32.
27 *Introduction to the Writings of Vitruvius*.
In: GMC 1993 [1947], p. 64.

Addendum (6)
Bibliography, archives, index
Primary sources

Unpublished manuscripts

Books

Vitruv. Despre arhitectură. Prezentat, tradus, adnotat și ilustrat de G. M. Cantacuzino [Vitruvius. On Architecture. Presented, translated, anotated and illustrated by GMC], 1947. Contributions to the illustrations by Paul Marinescu. This manuscript has not appeared as a whole yet.
See BAR, A-2658 a-e.

Directive pentru restaurarea și întreținerea monumentelor istorice [Guiding Principles for the Restoration and Maintenance of Historic Monuments], Bucharest c.1956.
See Patrulius 1975a, p. 62; Patrulius 1982, p. 93.

Orașe și monumente din Moldova de Nord
[Cities and historic monuments in Northern Moldavia].
Bucharest c.1956. See Patrulius 1975a, p. 62; Patrulius 1982, p. 93.

Unpublished Broadcast Lectures 1930-1944
Provenance: Text archive of the Romanian Broadcasting Company SRR,
62 General Berthelot St, 70747 Bucharest
Most of these lectures had been given in the series *Radio University*.

1930
Mobila românească în artă [Handcrafted Furniture in Romania],
26th June
Introducere in istoria artei românești: Metode generale [Introduction to the History of Art in Romania], 1st October.
Istoria artei românești: Izvoarele [Romanian Art History: The Sources], 15th October.

1932
Catapesmele [The Iconostases], 3rd March.

1933
Monumente bizantine în România [Byzantine Monuments in Romania], 4th April. Typoscript in French.
Formația orașelor românești [The Urban Development in Romania],
26th July.
Egiptul: Oale de lut, morminte de piatră
[Egypt: Earthenware, Stone Graves], 28th September.
Memphis – arta [Memphis – the Art], 12th October.
Teba [Thebes], 16th November.
Cultul soarelui [The Sun-Cult in Ancient Egypt], 30th November.
Epoca saită și transformarea noțiunii de personalitate
[The Saite Epoch and the Change of the Notion of Personality],
7th December.
Arta și religia [Art and Religion], 21st December.

1934
Egeea [The Aegean], 1st February.
Conacurile Cretei [The Cretan Palaces], 31st May.
Șantierul de la Bod al Postului Național de Radio [The Construction Site of the Romanian Broadcasting Company in Bod], 16th October.
De la sat la capitală [From a village to a capital], 21st November.

1935
Planul de sistematizare (însemnări)
[On the Urban Masterplan of Bucharest], 20th May.
Abdel Nur, 20th June.

1937
O casă la țară [A Country House], 8th July.
O biserică la țară [A Country Church], 12th August.
Cum ar putea fi o școală la țară
[Thoughts on a Country School], 13th November.
România in cadrul expoziției internaționale de la Paris
[Romania at the Paris World's Fair], 9th August.

1938
Construirea unei ferme [The Construction of a Farm], 12th May.
Conferință cu titlu neprecizat [Lecture of unprecise title], 7th July.
Arhitectura religioasă și peisajul românesc [The Religious Architecture and the Romanian Landscape], 13th October.
Pavilionul național al României la Expoziția din New York [The Official Pavilion of Romania at the New York World's Fair], 13th December.

1939
Bucarest, broadcast lecture for France, 24th August, in French.
Afirmarea românească peste ocean
[Romania's Appearance in the USA], 31st August.

1940
Athena [Athens], 22nd June.

1944
Stilul bizantin [The Byzantine Style], 7th March.

Public Lectures
Iași [Jassy], in Bucharest, 2nd October 1955 (AMLSC)

Private correspondance (AMLSC)
Letters to Marthe Bibesco, 1924-1932.
Letters to Sanda Cantacuzino, 1938-1958.
Letter to Marie-Lyse Cantacuzino-Ruhemann, 25th December 1958.
Letters to Marietta Guetta-Stern, 1937-1938.
Letter to Margareta Roman, London, 8th March 1938 or 1939.
Letter to Jean David, 2nd May 1960.

Published Writings

1926-1947
Introducere la studiul arhitecturii [Introduction to the Study of Architecture]. Bucharest (Atelierele grafice SOCEC & Co.), 1926
Palladio. Essai Critique. Avec douze dessins de l'auteur. Bucharest (Cartea Românească), 1928.
G.-M. Cantacuzène/Aug. Schmiedigen, architectes: Palais de la Banque Chrissoveloni, Bucarest. Un texte et 64 planches. With a Preface by Georges Gromort. Paris (Vincent Fréal et Cie), 1929.

Documents d'architecture, Petits édifices, 7e série: Roumanie. Recueillies par G.-M. Cantacuzène. 56 planches. Acompagnées de huit dessins au crayon de Charles Cuvillier. Paris (Vincent Fréal et Cie), 1931

Arcade, firide şi lespezi [Arcades, Niches and Flagstones]. Bucharest (Cartea Românească), 1932 (GMC 1932)

Izvoare şi popasuri [Sources and Breaks/Stopovers]. Bucharest (Fundaţia pentru Literatură şi Artă Regele Carol II), 1934 (GMC 1934).

Bolomey, R./GMC/Davidescu, I./Marcu, D./Rădulescu, T./PMB (Primăria Municipiului Bucureşti) [City Hall of Bucharest] (ed.): *PDSMB/Planul director de sistematizare al Municipiului Bucureşti decretat la 9. mai 1935. Memoriu justificativ şi planuri*. [The Urban Masterplan for Bucharest, passed on the 9th May 1935. Explanatory Note and Plans]. Bucharest (Ed. Bucovina), 1935.

Pătrar de veghe [Moonwatch]. Bucharest (Cartea Românească),1938 (GMC 1938).

Despre o estetică a reconstrucţiei [On the Aesthetics of Reconstruction]. Bucharest (Cartea Românească), 1947.

1947-1989

GMC/Ionescu, Gr./Costa, T.: *Vitruviu. Despre arhitectură* [Vitruvius. On Architecture]. Bucharest 1964.

Scrieri [Writings]. Introduction by Virgil Ierunca. Paris (Fundaţia Regală Universitară Carol I), 1966 (GMC 1966)

Simetrii [Symmetries]. Introduction by Virgil Ierunca. Paris (Ethos/Ioan Cuşa), c. 1971 (GMC 1971).

Izvoare şi popasuri [Stops and Breaks]. Edited by Adrian Anghelescu. Bucharest (Editura Eminescu), 1977 (GMC 1977a).

Pătrar de veghe [Moonwatch]. Edited by Adrian Anghelescu. Cluj (Editura Dacia), 1977 (GMC 1977b).

Since 1990

Introducere la opera lui Vitruviu. Scrisori către Simon [Introduction to the Writings of Vitruvius. Letters to Simon]. Edited by Zamfira Mihail. Bucharest (Editura Meridiane), 1993 (GMC 1993a).

Scrisori către Simon [Letters to Simon]. Edited by Ileana Corbea. Cluj (Editura Dacia), 1993 (GMC 1993b).

Izvoare şi popasuri. Edited by Şerban Cantacuzino. Jassy (Editura Timpul), 1999.

Despre o estetică a reconstrucţiei. Edited by Augustin Ioan. Bucharest (Editura Paideia), 2001 (GMC 2001) .

Introducere la studiul arhitecturii. Edited by Mariana Celac. Bucharest (Editura Paideia), 2002 (GMC 2002).

Letters to Simon/Scrisori către Simon. Edited by Marie-Lyse Canta-cuzino-Ruhemann and Şerban Cantacuzino. Bucharest (Simetria), 2010.

Articles in newspapers and periodicals

* denotes three unsigned contributions on Romanian topics to *L'architecture d'aujourd'hui* which were published during GMC's activity as AA-correspondent. These contributions could be attributed to GMC.

1927

L'architecture roumaine d'aujourd'hui. In: *L'architecture*, Vol. XL, No 10. Paris, pp. 351-357

1931

Fundenii Doamnei [The Church Fundenii Doamnei near Bucharest]. In: *Boabe de grâu. Revistă de cultură*. Bucharest, January 1931, pp. 151-154.

Brătianu, Gh. I./Cantacuzino, G. M./Cartojan, N./Giurescu, C. C./Lambrino, S./Panaitescu, P. P./Rosetti, Al.: *Cuvânt înainte* [Foreword. Editorial]. In: *Revista Istorică Română* (RIR) [Romanian Review of History]. Bucharest (Universitatea din Bucureşti), 1931, Vol. 1, Faks. I, pp. 3-6.

Paul Henry, Les églises de la Moldavie du Nord des origins à la fin du XVIe siècle. Architecture et peinture. Contribution à létude de la civilisation moldave. Book Review. In: RIR op. cit., pp. 416-421.

Scrisoare către Marcel Jancu [Letter to Marcel Janco]. In: Janco, Marcel (ed.): *Contimporanul*, Year 10, No. 96-98, Bucharest 1931, pp. 9-10.

1933

Considérations générales sur la genèse de l'art moldave. In: RIR, Vol. 3, Faks. I, pp. 1-10.

1934

Arhitectura modernă [Modern Architecture]. In: *Arhitectura*, No. 1, Bucharest 1934, pp. 3-4.

Cronica plastică [The Art Column]. In: *Revista Fundaţiilor Regale* (RFR), Year 1, No. 7, 1st July, pp. 188-191. Republished as *Formă şi formalism* [Form and Formalism] in GMC 1966, pp. 17-22.

Cronica plastică. In: RFR, Year 1, No. 8, 1st August, pp. 428-430. Republished as *Artele populare* [Popular Art] in GMC 1966, pp. 23-26.

Cronica plastică. In: RFR, Year 1, No. 9, 1st September, pp. 665-667. Republished as *Salvarea vechilor oraşe* [Saving Old Cities] in GMC 1966, pp. 27-32.

Cronica plastică. In: RFR, Year 1, No. 10, 1st October, pp. 195-198. Republished as *Despre stilul modern* [On the Modern Style] in GMC 1966, pp. 33-36.

George Balş. In: RFR, Year 1, No. 11, 1st November, pp. 424-426. Republished in GMC 1966, pp. 37-42.

O capitală [A Capital]. In: RFR, Year 1, No. 12, 1st December, pp. 580-591. Republished in GMC 1966, pp. 43-60.

Cronica plastică. In: RFR, Year 1, No. 12, 1st December, pp. 671-673. Republished as *Prejudecăţi* [Prejudices] in Scrieri, pp. 61-64.

Tendances dans l'architecture roumaine. In: AA, 5e année, No. 5/1934, Paris, pp. 57-62. Republished in GMC 1966, pp. 207-214.

**Bibliographie: Kurt Hielscher: La Roumanie. Leipzig: F. A. Brockhaus, 1931*. In: AA, No. 10/1934-1935, Paris, p. 82.

1935

Consideraţiuni asupra arhitecturii funcţionale [On Functionalism]. In: RFR, Year 2, No. 1, 1st Januar, pp. 192-194. Republished in GMC 1966, pp. 65-68.

Modernismul şi arhitectura românească [Modernism and Romanian Architecture]. In: RFR, Year 2. Jg., No. 3, 1st March, pp. 683-686. Republished in GMC 1966, pp. 69-76.

Cronica plastică. In: RFR, Year 2, No. 8, 1st August, pp. 445-447. Republished as Iaşii [Jassy] in GMC 1966, pp. 77-82.

Cronica plastică. In: RFR, Year 2, No. 10, 1st October, pp. 207-210. Republished as *Muzeul Naţional* [The National Museum] in GMC 1966, pp. 85-88.

Arcul de triumf [The Triumphal Arch in Bucharest]. In: RFR, Year 2, No. 10, 1st October, p. 209. Republished in GMC 1966, pp. 83-84.

Planul de sistematizare [The Urban Masterplan for Bucharest]. In: RFR, Year 2, No. 10, 1st October, p. 210. Republished in GMC 1966, pp. 89-90.

1936

Impas şi temă [Blind Alley and Theme]. In: RFR, Year 3, No. 5, 1st May, pp. 426-427. Republished in GMC 1966, pp. 91-94.

Bagdadul [Bagdad]. In: RFR, Year 3, No. 10, 1st October, pp. 103-110.

Cronica plastică. In: RFR, Year 3, No. 11, 1st November, pp. 441-444. Republished as *Câteva probleme: material şi formă. Tradiţie şi formă* [Some Topics: Material and Form. Tradition and Form] in GMC 1966, pp. 95-100.

**Sanatorium à Prédéal, Roumanie. Architectes: Marcel et Jules Jancu et P. Feldman*. In: AA, No. 10/1936, Paris, pp. 64.

**Halles centrales de Ploeşti, Roumanie. Architecte T. S. Socolesco*. In: AA, No. 11/1936, Paris, pp. 44-45.

1937

Despre posibilităţile unei arhitecturi româneşti [On the Development of Romanian Architecture]. In: RFR, Year 4, No. 1, 1st January, pp. 129-134. Republished in GMC 1966, pp. 101-108.

Deşertul [The Desert]. Excerpt from *Moonwatch* (1938). In: RFR, Year 4, 1st April, pp. 71-88.

Apele Tigrului [The Waters of the Tigris]. Excerpt from Moonwatch (1938). In: RFR, Year 4, 1st August, pp. 297-307.

Şiraz [Shiraz]. Excerpt from *Moonwatch* (1938). In: RFR, Year 4, 1st October, pp. 59-67.

1938

Note de drum [Travelling Notes]. Excerpt from *Moonwatch* (1938). In: *Artă şi tehnică grafică*, No. 3, Bucharest, March 1938, pp. 19-25.

1939

Arhitectura românească de azi [The Contemporary Architectural Scene in Romania]. In: *Viața Românească* (VR), Year 31, No. 4, April, Bucharest, pp. 54-57.

Experiența americană [The American Experience]. In: RFR, Year 6, No. 9, 1st September, pp. 582-588.

1940

Arhitectura românească dupa Restaurație [The Romanian Architecture after the Restauration]. In: RFR, Year 7, No. 6, 1st June, pp. 740-744. Republished in GMC 1966, pp. 119-126.

1941

Pavilionul oficial și casa românescă la Expoziția Internațională din New York,1939 [The Official Pavilion and the Romanian House at the World's Fair in New York, 1939]. In: *Arhitectura*, Bucharest, No. 1/1941, pp. 166-169.

1944

Cronica plastică. In: VR, Year 36, No. 11, November, pp. 89-90. Reprinted as *Un fel de bilanț* [Taking a Sort of Stock] in GMC 1966, pp. 127-132.

Cronica plastică. Expozițiile de la Căminul Artelor: Magdalena Rădulescu și Siegfried. [The Art Column. The Exhibitions at the Arts House: Magdalena Rădulescu and Siegfried]. In: VR, Year 36, No. 12/December, pp. 106-107. Reprinted in GMC 1966, pp. 133-135.

Cronica plastică. Expoziția Voinescu [The Voinescu Exhibition]. In: VR op.cit., p. 107. Reprinted in GMC 1966, p. 137.

Hendryk van Loon, Istoria artelor [Hendryk van Loon, The History of Art]. In: VR op. cit., pp. 108-110. Book Review.

1945

Cronica plastica: Salonul oficial (alb și negru). Sala Dalles [The Official Salon (Black and White). Dalles Hall]. In: VR, Year 37, No. 1-2, pp. 140-141. eprinted in GMC 1966, pp. 147-150.

Expoziția Pallady, Pătrașcu, Tonitza, Șirato (Căminul Artelor) [The Exhibition of Pallady, Pătrașcu, Tonitza, Șirato (The Arts House)]. In: VR op. cit. Reprinted in GMC 1966, pp. 151-153.

Expoziția sculptorului Medrea (Facultatea de arhitectură) [The Exhibition of the Sculptor Medrea at the School of Architecture]. In: VR op. cit., pp. 141-143. Reprinted in GMC 1966, S. 155-156.

Pallady – text de Ionel Jianu, Ed. Căminul Artei: Maeștrii ai picturii contemporane [Ionel Jianu: Pallady. Masters of Comtemporary Painting, The Arts House Edition]. In: VR op. cit., pp. 177-178.

Cronica plastică: M. Olarian, Scherer (Sala Universul). Țipoia, Risa Probst Kreid (Căminul Artei). Lydia Macovei, Edith Mayer, Ghiață (Sala Dalles). In: VR, Year 37, No. 3-4, pp. 163-165.

Realismul în artă și subiectul in pictură [Realism in Art and the Subject Matter of Painting]. In: VR op. cit., pp. 165-166. Reprinted in GMC 1966, pp. 157-160.

Reclădirea Teatrului Național [The Reconstruction of the National Theatre]. In: VR, Year 37, No. 5-6, May-June, pp. 110-112. Reprinted in GMC 1966, pp. 167-170.

Pictură – Câteva tablouri de Campigli la Librăria Italiană. Expoziția Ciucurencu, M. Nistor, Iser, la Căminul Artelor [Painting – Some Paintings by Campigli in the Italian Bookshop. The Exhibition Ciucurencu, M. Nistor, Iser at the Arts House]. In: VR op. cit., pp. 112-113. Republished in GMC 1966, pp. 171-173.

Cronica plastică: Expoziția de la Fundația Dalles: Marilena Pătrașcu-Riegler, Dna Diaconu [The Exhibition Marilena Pătrașcu-Riegler and Frau Diaconu at the Dalles Foundation]. In: VR op. cit., p. 109. Republished in GMC 1966, pp. 161-162

Cronica plastică: Căminul Artelor. Galeria Krețulescu. Sculptură: Militza Pătrașcu. Pictura: Bălașa Cantacuzino, Elvira Geblescu, Rodica Maniu [The Arts House. The Kretzulesco Gallery. Sculpture: M.Pătrașcu. Painting: B. Cantacuzino, E. Geblescu, R. Maniu]. In: VR op. cit., pp. 109-110. Reprinted in GMC 1966, pp. 162-165.

Cronica plastică: Expoziții. Pictură: Nutzi Acontz Hasefer; Salonul oficial: Pictură și sculptură [Exhibitions. Painting: Nutzi Acontz Hasefer. The Official Salon: Painting and Sculpture.]. In: VR, Year 37, No. 7-9, July-September, pp. 138-140. Reprinted in GMC 1966, pp. 175-180.

Note de vacanță. Despre peisajul românesc [Holiday Notes. On the Romanian Landscape]. In: VR, Year 37, No. 11-12, November-December, pp. 109-111.

Academia de Arte Frumoase [The Academy of Fine Arts]. In: VR op. cit., pp. 111-113.

1946

Cronica plastică. Pictură: Cazul Damian, Salonul tinerimii, Salonul oficial de toamna (alb și negru) [Painting: The Damian case, in the Youth Salon, official Autumn Salon (Black and White)]. In: VR, No. 1, January.

Expoziția pictorilor români cari au lucrat în Franța [The Exhibition of Romanian Painters who worked in France]. In: VR, Year 38, pp. 128-130.

Cronica plastică: O expoziție ideologică: Maxy (sala Dalles) [An ideological Exhibition at the Dalles Hall: Maxy]. In: VR, Year 38, No. 2, February, pp. 118-120.

Cronica plastică: Ateneul român: Ileana Rădulescu. O. Angheluță; Căminul Artelor: Sorin Ionescu. [Exhition at the Romanian Athenaeum and at the Arts House]. In: VR, Year 38, No. 3, pp. 134.

Construirea operei române [The Construction of the Romanian Opera House]. In: VR, 38. Jg., No. 4-5, pp. 128-131.

Cronica plastică: Pictură [The Art Column: Painting]. In: VR, Year 38, No. 6-7, pp. 175-177.

Urbanism. In: *Lumină și coloare, revistă de artă plastică*. Bucharest (Ed. Cultura Națională), Year 1, No. 2, December 1946, p. 55.

1962-1964

Jurnal. Journal Fragment from 17th November 1931 to 6th May1933. Introduction by Virgil Ierunca. In: *Destin* No. 12/1962 and No. 13-14/1964, Madrid.

1964

Giotto (fragment) [On Giotto. A Fragment]. In: *Revista scriitorilor români*, Munich, No. 3, pp. 49-53.

Contributions to GMC et al.: *Simetria. Caiete de artă și critică* [Symmetry. Notebooks of art and criticism], No. I-VIII, Bucharest (Cartea Românească), 1939-1947.

Simetria I, Autumn 1939

Declarație [Declaration], pp. 11-13, co-authored by Octav Doicescu.
Utilul și simbolul [Usefulness and Symbol], pp. 17-18, co-authored by Octav Doicescu.
Arhitectura și peisajul [Architecture and Landscape], pp. 21-31.
Spre Washington [On the way to Washington], pp. 43-49.
Proporția – Dicționar [On Proportion - Dictionary], pp. 60-64.
Despre o arhitectură românească [On a Romanian Architecture], pp. 65-67.
Învățământul plastic (propuneri pentru o nouă metodă) [Suggestions: A New Method for Art Education], pp. 73-75.
Pe marginea unei cărți a lui Cocteau [Notes on a Book by Cocteau]. *Le secret professionel. Paris (Sans pareil), 1925.* pp. 77-79.
Comentarii la un capitol. Artă și valoare de Lucian Blaga [Commentaries to Art and Value by Lucian Blaga], pp. 81-83.

Simetria II, Summer 1940

Contra mașinismului [Against Machine-Worship], pp. 15-16.
Arta și tehnica [Art and Technology], pp. 33-47.
Armonie – Dicționar [Harmony – Dictionary], pp. 51-52.
Atena – Dicționar [Athens – Dictionary], pp. 52-56.
Clasicism – Dicționar [Classicism – Dictionary], pp. 57-63.
Ritm – Dicționar [Rhythm – Dictionary], pp. 64-66.
Temă – Dicționar [Theme – Dictionary], pp. 66-67.
"Actar" sau despre discriminarea formelor, pp. 71-76. Book Review of: Maria Tuduri Rubió-Tudurí, *Actar. Discrimination des Formes de Quiètude des Formes de Mouvement dans la Construction. Traduit du Catalan. Paris 1931.*
Amateorism în urbanism [Amateurism in Urban Planning], pp. 85-87.
Mitocanul ca factor al civilizației românești [The "Mitocan" as a factor in Romanian Civilisation], pp. 89-90.
Despre pictura bisericească [On Church Painting], pp. 93-95.
Book Review: *Lucian Blaga, Diferențialele Divine* [The Divine Differentials], pp. 91-93, signed "S."

Simetria III, Winter 1940-Spring 1941

Coordonare [Coordination], pp. 13-15, co-authored by Octav Doicescu
Catedrala din Chartres [The Chartres Cathedral], pp. 61-85.
Moldova – Dicționar [Moldavia – Dictionary], pp. 103-104.

Profil – Dicționar [Profile – Dictionary], pp. 104-127.
Arhitectura industrială și Hans Hertlein [Industrial Architecture and Hans Hertlein], pp. 133-135.
Tema în artă [The Theme in Art], pp. 139-140, signed "S."
Despre influențe [On Influences], p. 143, signed "S."
Despre clasicism (Titu Maiorescu – de Eugen Lovinescu) [On Classicism. Eugen Lovinescu: Titu Maiorescu], pp. 147-148.
O carte uitată [A Forgotten Book], pp. 149-150.

Simetria IV, Winter 1941-1942
Orient-Occident [East-West], pp. 15-22, co-authored by Octav Doicescu.
Atitudinea critică a lui André Gide [The Critical Attitude of André Gide], pp. 125-143.
Extrados-Intrados – Dicționar [Exterior-Interior – Dictionary], pp. 145-148.
Cupola – Dicționar [The Dome – Dictionary], pp. 148-165
Note despre Basarabia și Transnistria [Notes on Bessarabia and Transnistria], pp. 179-188.
Aerofuturismul lui Marinetti explicat de Wolf von Aichelburg [Marinetti's Futurism explained by Wolf von Aichelburg], pp. 189-190.
V. Beneș – o metodă a criticii [V. Benes – a Method of Criticism], pp. 191-192.
Arhitectura. Revista Societății Arhitecților Români [Arhitectura. The Review of Union of Romanian Architects], No. 3-4, July-December 1941, pp. 193-194.
Despre personalitatea în artă [Personality and Art], pp. 201-203
Despre întrebuințarea unor motive [On the Usage of Some Motifs], p. 211.

Simetria V, Autumn 1943
Orașe și sate românești [Romanian Cities and Villages], pp. 15-31, co-authored by Octav Doicescu.
Obituary: Horia Creangă, pp. 33-35.
Un amator de artă: Goethe [An Art Lover: Goethe], pp. 59-94.
Axa – Dicționar [The Axis – Dictionary], pp. 125-127.
Bizanț-bizantin – Dicționar [Byzantium-Byzantine – Dictionary], pp. 127-132.
Coloană – Dicționar [Column – Dictionary], pp. 132-138.
Ordin – Dicționar [The Orders – Dictionary], pp. 138-142.
Roma – Dicționar [Rome – Dictionary], pp. 142-147.
Laugen, Albert: Die festliche Weltreise des Dichters Dauthendey (Eine Auswahl aus seinen Werken). München: Georg Müller. Book Review, pp. 161-164.
Note [Notes], pp. 167-173.
Despre stilul românesc [On the Romanian Style], pp. 181-182.
B. A. Kouftine, Locuința tătarilor din Crimeea în raport cu istoria colonizării peninsulei (Materiale și probleme) [The Dwelling Typology of the Tartars in Crimea as placed in the context of the colonisation of the Peninsula (Materials and Problems)]. Mémoires de la Section Ethnographique de la Société des Amis des Sciences Naturelles, d'Anthropologie et d'Ethnographie, Moscou 1925. Book Review, pp. 191-201.
Ce e o gradină [What is a Garden], p. 203.

Simetria VI, Frühling 1945
Omul și orașul sau urbanismul efemer [The Man and the City or the Transient Urban Planning], pp. 13-19, co-authored by Octav Doicescu.
Desen – Dicționar [Drawing – Dictionary], pp. 115-118.
Formă – Dicționar [Form – Dictionary], pp. 119-120.
Compoziție – Dicționar [Composition – Dictionary], pp. 120-121.
Anton Dumitriu: Orient și Occident [Anton Dumitriu: East and West], pp. 126-132.
Corpul arhitecților – note [The Institution of Romanian Architects – Notes], pp. 143-144, co-authored by Octav Doicescu.

Simetria VII, Summer 1946
Valori permanente [Permanent Values], pp. 13-17, co-authored by O. Doicescu.
Valéry sau arhitectul [Valéry or the Architect], pp. 68-79.
Convențional (formă convențională) – Dicționar [Conventional Form– Dictionary], pp. 175-177.
Plastică – Dicționar [The Sculpture – Dictionary], pp. 177-181.
Notă explicativă [Explanatory Note], pp. 208-209.
Discobolul lui Lucian Blaga [Lucian Blaga: The Discus Thrower]. Book Review, pp. 212-214.
Leo Ferrero, pp. 220-223.
Peisajul românesc și pictorii săi [Painters of the Romanian Landscape], pp. 223-224.

Simetria VIII, 1947
Artistul și prezentul [The Artist and the Present], pp. 17-19, co-authored by Titu Evolceanu.
Artistul și libertatea [The Artist and the Freedom], pp. 101-107.
Progres – Dicționar [Progress – Dictionary], pp. 136-140.
Problemă. Temă – Dicționar [Problem. Theme – Dictionary], pp. 140-142.
Tehnică – Dicționar [Technology – Dictionary], pp. 143-145.
Cărți despre grădini [Books on Gardens]. *Mgr. le Duc d'Harcourt: De l'art des Jardins en général. Paris 1919.* Book Review, pp. 159-162. *Charles Joseph de Ligne: Coup d'œuil sur Belœil. Paris 1930.* Book Review, pp. 162-165. *Le Donné: L'Architecte dans la cité.* Book Review, pp. 178-179.
Revistele franceze de artă [The French Art Reviews]. Review, pp. 179-182.
Muzeele [The Museums], pp. 184-185.
Petre Antonescu la Academia Română [The Architect Petre Antonescu at the Romanian Academy], p. 185.
Notă [Note], p. 197.

Published Letters

Letter to Marcel Janco. In: *Contimporanul*, Year 10, No. 96-98, Bucharest, June-August 1931, pp. 9-10.
Letter to the sculptor Oscar Han, 25th Januar 1960. In: GMC 1977a.

Public Lectures

1932
Pictura românească [The Romanian Painting]. Lecture at the High School Carol I, Craiova, 20th February 1932. Announced in *Arhivele Olteniei*, Year 11, Craiova, January-April 1932, p. 100.

1933
Renașterea italiană [The Italian Renaissance]. Lecture at the High School Carol I, Craiova, 20th February 1932. Announced in *Arhivele Olteniei* , Year 12, Craiova, January-April 1933, p. 130.

1938
Artă și naționalism [Art and Nationalism], Craiova, 13th February 1938. Announced in GMC's letter to Marietta Stern, 12th February 1938.

1939
Criza spiritului clasic [The Crisis of the Classical Spirit], Bukarest, Dalles-Saal, 30th October 1939. Announced in GMC's letter to Sanda Cantacuzino, Bucharest, 29th October1939, AMLSC.
Răspîndirea stilului gotic in Anglia [The Spread of the Gothic Style across England], Bucharest, 29th November 1939. Announced in GMC's letter to Sanda Cantacuzino, Bucharest, 19th November 1939, AMLSC.

1946
Artele plastice în SUA [The Fine Arts in the USA]. Lecture at the Asociația Amicii Statelor Unite [Association of the Friends of the USA]. In: GMC 1947 (2001).

1947
Degas. Lecture in the series *Masters of French Painting in the nineteenth Century*, The Arts House, March 1947. Announced in *Lumină și coloare*, Year 1, No. 2, Bucharest, December 1946, p. 65.

1955
Orașul Iași, un peisagiu [Jassy, an Urban Landscape]. Lecture in Bucharest, 2nd October 1955 (AMLSC).
Considerații asupra artei populare [On Popular Art]. 3rd Dezember 1955. In: GMC 1993a, pp. 176-192.

Mogoşoaia: un palat, o grădină, un peisaj [Mogoşoaia: a Palace, a Garden, a Landscape]. In: GMC 1993a [1955], pp. 146-160 (INMI/DMI, Dos. No. 6499).
Palatele şi casele brâncoveneşti [The Brancovan Palaces and Houses]. In: GMC 1993a [1955], pp. 160-176.

1956
Consideraţii asupra influenţelor în arta românească [On influences on Romanian Art], 20th January. In: GMC 1993a, pp. 106-120.
Consideraţii despre peisaj [On Landscape]. In: GMC 1993a [1956], pp. 93-106.
Bisericile pictate din Moldova [The Painted Churches in Moldavia]. In: GMC 1993a [1956], pp. 120-130.

1957
Ce este un monument istoric? [What is a Historic Monument?]. Lecture at the University of Bucarest, 20th January. In: GMC 1993a, pp. 82-93.

1959
Oraşul Iaşi, un peisagiu [Jassy, an Urban Landscape]. Lecture at the University of Jassy, 21st March. In: GMC 1993a, pp. 130-146.

Published broadcast lectures (1931-1944)
(in addition to those printed in GMC 1932 and GMC 1934)

1931
Consideraţiuni asupra artei româneşti [On Romanian Art]. In: *Mişcarea*, Bucharest, 9th Dezember, pp. 1-2.

1933
Locuinţa românească [The Romanian Dwelling], 26th January. In: GMC 1977a, pp. 312-315.
Oraşele româneşti de mâine [The Romanian Cities of Tomorrow], 10th August. In: GMC 1977a, pp. 316-320.

1937
Lumina românească [The Romanian Light], 21st January. In: GMC 1977a, pp. 349-352.
Valea Jiului [The Jiu-Valley], 11th February. In: GMC 1977a, pp. 352-356.
Locuinţa românească [The Romanian Dwelling], 1st April. In: GMC 1977a, pp. 63-65.
Satul românesc [The Romanian Village], 29th September. In: GMC 1977a, pp. 356-361.

1938
Şcoala satului [What Can We Learn From Villages?], 10th March. In: GMC 1977a, pp. 361-365.
Pe drumurile Orientului [On the road in the Middle East], 23rd November. In: GMC 1977a, pp. 365-369.

1939
Impresii din America [American Impressions], 21st July. In: GMC 1977a, pp. 372-375.

1940
Pe marginea pădurii getice [On the Edge of the Thraco-Getian Wood], 21st March. In: GMC 1977a, pp. 378-382.
Oraşe eline şi sate getice [Hellenic Cities and Thraco-Getian Villages], 30th May. In: GMC 1977a, pp. 382-386.

1942
Mogoşoaia. 11th May. In: GMC 1977a, pp. 411-415.

Writings on GMC

Unpublished Writings

Essays
Ghyka, M.: *Georges Cantacuzène, Homme de la Renaissance.* Typewritten obituary, 2 pp., c. 1961 (AMLSC).
Lykiardopol, M.: *G. M. Cantacuzino – un vizionar* [GMC – a Visionary]. Bucharest, 10th October 1999, 6 pp. (AMLSC).

Letters
Marinescu, P.: *Letter to Şerban Cantacuzino.* Bucharest, c.1990 (AMLSC).

Letters, post cards and E-Mail messages to the author
Dan Bolomey/Lausanne; Matei Cantacuzino/Brussels; Marie-Lyse Cantacuzino-Ruhemann/London; Dr Constantin Cheramidoglu/Constantza; Joëlla de Couëssin/École des Beaux-Arts, Paris; Dr Eugenia Greceanu/Bucharest; Stefan Eleutheriadis/Rio de Janeiro; Prof. em. Dr. Petre Năsturel/Malakoff, Paris; Suzana Paleologu-Stere/Paris; Gheorghe Vecerdea †/Constantza; Olympia Zamfirescu †/Cannes.

Writings on GMC until 1960

Books (mentions of GMC)
Patmore, D. 1939, pp. 39-40,113-114.
Gromort, G.: *Préface*. In: GMC/Schmiedigen 1929, pp. 5-6.
Morand, P. 1990 (1935), pp. 180, 181, 293.

Period articles in newspapers and periodicals
(for reviews of GMC's exhibitions see *Addendum, Colour Plates*)

Călinescu, G.: *G. M. Cantacuzino – Pătrar de veghe* [GMC – Moonwatch]. In: *Adevărul literar şi artistic*, Year 18, Series 3, No. 908, Bucharest 1st May 1938, pp. 17.
Janco, M.: *Scrisoare (către G. M. Cantacuzino)* [Letter (to GMC)]. In: *Contimporanul* No. 99, Bucharest, September 1931. Cited after UAR 1996, pp. 228-229.
Perpecissius (Panaitescu, D.): *G. M. Cantacuzino – Arcade, firide şi lespezi* [Arcades, Niches and Flagstones]. In: *Opere*, Vol. 5, Bucharest 1972, pp. 360-364.
Petrescu, Camil: *G. M. Cantacuzino*. In: *România literară*, No. 87, Bucharest, 9th December 1933, p. 1.
Sebastian, M.: *Cronica literară: G. M. Cantacuzino – Arcade, firide şi lespezi* [The Literary Column: GMC, Arcades, Niches and Flagstones]. In: *România literară*, No. 22, Bucharest, 16th July 1932.
___: *Notă despre o carte de călătorie* [Notes on a Travelling Book]. In: RFR, Year 5, No. 7, Bucharest, 1st July 1938.

Writings published after 1961

Anghelescu, A.: *Studiu introductiv* [Introductary Study]. In: GMC 1977a, pp. 5-61.
Cantacuzino, Ş./Cantacuzino-Ruhemann, M.-L.: "Art is in itself an act of love and love cannot be learnt". In: Stoica, D.: *Moldavie ... tout ce que j'aime. 99 de acuarele de George Matei Cantacuzino* [99 Watercolours by GMC]. Iaşi: Printco, 2006, pp. 1-5.
Cantacuzino, Ş.: *On being Romanian*. In: Machedon/Scoffham 1999, pp. VIII-XVIII.
Celac, M.: *Timpul fracturii* [The Breaking Time]. In: GMC 2001, pp. 103-119.
Florescu, N.: *Prefaţă* [Preface]. In: GMC 1993b, pp. 5-14.
Ierunca, V.: *Notă introductivă* [Introduction]. In: *Destin* No. 12, Madrid 1962, pp. 85-91.
___: *Introducere. Un cavaler al privirii* [Introduction. A Chevalier of the Art of Seeing]. In: GMC 1966, pp. 7-16.
___: *Prefaţă* [Preface]. In: GMC 1971, pp. 7-14.

Ioan, A.: *Cuvânt înainte* [Foreword]. In: GMC 2001, pp. 5-12.
Mihail, P.: *Postfaţă* [Epilogue]. In: GMC 1993a, pp. 327-333.
Mihail, Z.: *Cuvânt înainte* [Foreword]. In: GMC 1993a, pp. 5-16.
Stoica, D.: *Differents kinds of love. What will we see in this book of water-colours?* In: GMC 2006, pp. 17-18.

Studies on GMC

Cantacuzène, J.-M.: *Une vie en Roumanie. De la Belle Époque à la République Populaire 1899-1960*. Paris (L'Harmattan), 2011. Romanian version *O viaţă in România. De la Belle Époque la Republica Populară. 1899-1960*. Ed. Fides, 2012. Translation from the French by Petruţa Spanu.
Duculescu, M.: *G. M. Cantacuzino (1899-1960). Arhitectura ca temă a gândirii/ Architecture as a subject of thought*. Bucharest (Simetria), 2010. Study based on the diploma thesis of the same title at the University of Bucharest, Department of Art History, 2000.
Roman, L.: *G. M. Cantacuzino. Studiu monografic*. [Monographic Study]. PhD thesis at the Department of Literature at the University Babeş-Bolyai Cluj, 2008.
Teodorovici, D.: *G. M. Cantacuzino (1899-1960). Dialogik zwischen Tradition und Moderne*. PhD thesis at the Faculty of Architecture and Urban Planning at the University of Stuttgart, 2010.

Articles in newspapers, periodicals and dictionaries

Beldiman, Al.: *Filiaţii* [Affinities]. In: *Arhitecţii şi Bucureştiul. Buletin informativ al filialei teritoriale Bucureşti a ordinului arhitecţilor din România*, No. 19, Bucharest, 2008, pp. 20-22.
Bocăneţ, A.: *Cantacuzino, George Matei*. In: Midant, J.-P. (ed.): *Dictionnaire de l'architecture du XXe siècle*. Paris (Hazan/Institut Français d'Architecture), 1996, p. 171.
Chihaia, P.: *Comtes rendus. G. M. Cantacuzino, Izvoare şi popasuri*. In: *Revue Roumaine d'Histoire d'Art, Série Beaux-Arts*, Vol. 15, pp. 143-146. Bucharest 1978.
___: *G. M. Cantacuzino, Izvoare şi popasuri*. In: *Scrieri din ţară şi din exil*. Bucharest (Institutul Naţional pentru Memoria Exilului Românesc), c. 1995.
Guţanu, L.: *O scrisoare a lui G. M. Cantacuzino* [A Letter from GMC]. In: *România literară* No. 41, 20th-26th October 2004. Bucharest 2004.
Marcu, A.: *G. M. Cantacuzino*. In: *Litere, Arte, Idei. Cotidianul, Supliment cultural, No. 3/87, Year III*. Bucharest, 18th January 1993, p. 8.
Mihail, Z.: *Afinităţi elective* [Elective Affinities]. In: *Manuscriptum* No. 2, 1982, pp. 131-132. Bucharest 1982.
Mitican, I.: *Moştenirea ieşeană a arhitectului G. M. Cantacuzino* [The Jassy Legacy of the Architect GMC]. In: *Lumina*. Jassy, 14th July 2007, p. 8.
Noica, C.: *Timpul artei la G. M. Cantacuzino* [GMC´s Art], c. 1977, AMLSC.
Onofrei, V.: *Centenar G. M. Cantacuzino* [A Symposium commemorating the centennial of GMC's birth]. In: *Istoria restaurării, restaurarea istoriei*. Jassy 1999, pp. 4-9.
Patrulius, R.: *Înaintaşii noştrii – George Matei Cantacuzino* [Our Predecessors – GMC]. In: *Arhitectura*, No. 4/1975a, pp. 57-62; No. 5/1975 b, pp. 53-60. Bucharest1975.
___: *George Matei Cantacuzino*. In: *Monumente istorice şi de artă. Revista muzeelor şi monumentelor*. Year 13, No. 1, 1982, pp. 89-93. Bucharest (Consiliul culturii şi educaţiei socialiste), 1982.
Păcurariu, P./Pandele, V.: *Referat privind propunerea de exercitare a dreptului de preemţiune asupra înstrăinării unor imobile cuprinse în LMI/2005* [Report on the proposed misappropriation of historic monuments, listed in the 2005 Inventory]. Doc. No. 437, 8th August 2005. Giurgiu 2005.
Popescu Ţurlea, C.: *G. M. Cantacuzino*. In: Noica, N. St. (ed.): *Banca naţională a României şi personalităţi din istoria construcţiilor* [The National Bank of Romanian and its Architects]. Bucharest (Ed. Maşina de scris), 2006, pp. 257-270.
Rădulescu, M.-S.: *L'architecte G. M. Cantacuzène et l'École des Beaux-Arts de Paris*. In: *Anuarul institutului de cercetări socio-umane Gheorghe Şincai*, No. V-VI, 2002-2003, pp. 86-100, Târgu-Mureş, 2003.
Tiegheim, P./Josserand, P. (ed.): *Cantacuzino (G. M.)*. In: *Dictionnaire des Littératures*. Vol. 1. Paris (Presses Universitaires de France), 1968, pp. 723.

Memoirs (mentions of GMC)

Dragu Dimitriu, V.: *Alice Magheru, G. M. Cantacuzino* [A Conversation between Victoria Dragu Dimitriu and Alice Magheru]. In: Dragu Dimitriu, V.: *Poveşti ale Doamnelor din Bucureşti* [Stories of the Bucharest Ladies]. Bucharest (Editura Vremea) 2004, pp. 23-29.
Enescu, I. M.: *Haralambie Georgescu, G. M. Cantacuzino, Octav Doicescu*. In: Ordinul arhitecţilor din România (ed.): *Arhitecţi în timpul dictaturii. Amintiri* [Architects under Communist Dictatorship. Memories]. Bucharest (Paideia), 2007, pp. 27-36.
Greceanu, E: *Cuvânt înainte. G. M . Cantacuzino, Orasul Iaşi: Un Peisagiu* [Foreword. GMC, Jassy: An Urban Landscape]. In: *Hierasus 1981, anuarul Muzeului judeţean Botoşani* [The annual Cultural Periodical of the Botoşani County], pp. 385-398. Republished along with GMC's text by E. Greceanu in: *Revista Monumentelor Istorice*, Bucharest, Year LXIX, No. 1-2/2000, pp. 11-12.
___: *Sovietizarea învăţământului de arhitectură* [The Sovietisation of the Architectural Education]. In: OAR (ed.) 2007, pp. 111-142.
Jurgea-Negrileşti, Gh.: *Troica amintirilor. Sub patru regi* [Under four kings. Memories.]. Bucharest (Cartea Românească), 2002, pp. 278-81, 292-93, 390-91.
Leon, A.: *G. M. Cantacuzino*. In: Leon, A.: *Umbre*. Jassy (Junimea), 1979, pp. 48-55.
Voinescu, A.: *Jurnal*. Bucharest 1997, p. 482. Diary entry, 12th Dec. 1944.
Vulcănescu, M.: *Nae Ionescu aşa cum l-am cunoscut* [Nae Ionescu – like I knew him]. Bucharest (Humanitas), 1992, pp. 136-37.
Zamfirescu, I.: *G. M. Cantacuzino*. In: Zamfirescu, I.: *Intâlniri cu oameni, intâlniri cu viaţa* [Encounters with People, Encounters with Life]. Bucharest (Editura Eminescu), 1990, pp. 80-89.

Abbreviations of periodical titles

AA	*L'Architecture d'aujourd'hui*
RFR	*Revista Fundaţiilor Regale*
RIR	*Revista Istorică Română*
VR	*Viaţa Românească*

Bibliography

Secondary sources

Académie Diplomatique Internationale (ed.): *Dictionnaire diplomatique.* Paris, Vol. 1&2 1933, Vol. 3 c.1937; Vol. 4 1947, Vol. 5 1954.

Acatrinei, F.: *Radiodifuziunea Română de la înființare la "etatizare" (1925-1948)* [The Romanian Broadcasting from its foundation to the nationalization]. Bucharest (Tritonic), 2005.

Achleitner, F.: *Region, ein Konstrukt? Regionalismus, eine Pleite?* Basel/Boston/Berlin (Birkhäuser), 1997.

Ackermann, J.: *Palladio.* London etc. (Penguin), 1991.

Adamson, N.: *To regenerate painting: letters, 1934-48, between Jean Bazaine and André Lhote.* In: *The Burlington Magazine*, May 2008, CL, pp. 312-321.

Aderca, F.: *Mărturia unei generații* [The Declaration of a Generation]. Bucharest (Editura pentru literatură), 1967 (1929).

Alain: *Mars or the truth about war.* Translated from the French by Doris Mudie and Elisabeth Hill. London etc. (Jonathan Cape), 1930.

Anania, L. et al: *Bisericile osândite de Ceaușescu, București 1977-1989* [The Churches in Bucharest destroyed by Ceașescu from 1977 to 1989]. Bucharest (Editura Anastasia), 1995.

Anders, G.: *Die Antiquiertheit des Menschen.* 2 Vol. Munich (C. H. Beck), 1980.

Andrieux, J./Chevalier, F./Nevanlinna, A. (eds): *Idée nationale et architecture en Europe 1860-1919. Finlande, Hongrie, Roumanie, Catalogne.* Rennes (Presse Universitaire Rennes), 2003

Aragon, L. et al.: *Wege zu Giacometti.* Munich (Matthes & Seitz), 1987.

L'Architecture d'aujourd'hui: *The École des beaux-arts in Paris. L'Architecture d'aujourd'hui,* No. 310, Paris, April 1997.

Argetoianu, C.: *Memorii. Pentru cei de mâine. Amintiri din vremea celor de ieri* [For those in the world of tomorrow. Memories from the world of yesterday], 4 Vol. Bucharest (Humanitas), 1990-2003.

Aristotle: *The Nicomachean Ethics.* Translated by J. E. C. Welldon. London (Macmillan and Co., Ltd.)/New York (The Macmillan Company), 1906.

Atherton, L.: *Lord Lloyd at the British Council and the Balkan Front, 1937-1940.* In: *The International History Review*, No. 16, New York, 1st Feb. 1994, pp. 25-48.

Aurelius, M.: *Meditations.* Translated by Maxwell Staniforth. London (Penguin Books Ltd.), 2004.

Ayers, A.: *The Architecture of Paris.* Stuttgart/London (Axel Menges), 2004.

Bach, F. T.: *Constantin Brancusi.* Köln (DuMont), 1988.

Balș, G.: *Începuturile Arhitecturii Bisericești din Moldova* [The Beginnings of the Religious Architecture in Moldavia]. In: *Academia Română. Discursuri de recepție.* Bucharest (Cultura Națională), 1925.

___: *Bisericile lui Ștefan cel Mare* [The Churches of Stephen the Great]. Bucharest 1926.

___: *Bisericile Moldăvinești din veacul al XVI-lea.* [The sixteenth century Moldavian Churches]. Bucharest 1928.

Balta, S.: *Rumänien und die Großmächte in der Ära Antonescu (1940-1944).* Stuttgart (Franz Steiner Verlag), 2005.

Barker, E.: *British Policy in South-Eastern Europe in the Second World War.* London etc. (The Macmillan Press Ltd), 1976.

Barnard, T. /Clark, J. (eds): *Lord Burlington: Architecture, Art and Life.* London/Rio Grande, Ohio (Hambledon Press), 1995.

Báthory, L.: *Prominent Jewish Businessmen from Romania: 1890-1940. Mauriciu and Aristide Blank.* In: *Studia Judaica*, Cluj, 1/1991, pp. 94-103.

Bauch, K.: *Studien zur Kunstgeschichte.* Berlin (de Gruyter), 1967.

Baudelaire, C.: *The Flowers of Evil.* Translated into English by Cyril Scott. London (Elkin Mathews), 1909. WLB Stuttgart, Stefan-George-Archive.

Bauwelt: *Bukarest. Bauwelt issue 36/1996, StadtBauwelt* No. 131. Berlin, Year 87, 27th September 1996.

Bălcești, H. N.: *Enciclopedia ilustrată a Francmasoneriei din România* [Illustrated Dictionary of the Freemasonry in Romania]. Bucharest (Phobos), 2005.

Băleanu, D./Comănescu, R.: *Iluștri franc-masoni ai României. Interviuri și documente* [Important Romanian Freemasons. Interviews and Documents]. Bucharest (Editura Europa Unită), 2003.

Beck, H.-G.: *Das byzantinische Jahrtausend.* Munich (C. H. Beck), 1978.

Becker, A./ Bloch, É. (eds): *Marc Bloch: L'Histoire, La Guerre, La Résistance.* Paris (Gallimard), 2006.

Behring, E. (ed.): *Texte der rumänischen Avantgarde 1907-1947.* Leipzig (Reclam), 1988.

Behring, E.: *Rumänien und die deutsche Klassik.* Aus der Südosteuropa-Forschung, Vol. 4. Munich: Südosteuropa-Gesellschaft, 1996.

___/Richter, L./Schwarz, W. (ed.): *Geschichtliche Mythen in den Literaturen und Kulturen Ostmittel- und Südosteuropas.* Stuttgart (F. Steiner), 1999.

___: *Rumänische Schriftsteller im Exil 1945-1989.* Stuttgart (F. Steiner), 2002.

Beldiman, I.: *Sculptura franceză în România* [The French Sculpture in Romania] (1848-1931). Bucharest (Simetria), 2005.

Beleș, A.: *Cutremurul și construcțiile.* In: *Buletinul Soc. Politecnice.* Year 55, No. 10/11. Bucharest, October/November 1941, pp. 1172-1180.

Belting, H.: *Florenz und Bagdad: eine westöstliche Geschichte des Blicks.* Munich (C. H. Beck), 2008.

Beltramini, G./Padoan, A. (ed.): *Andrea Palladio. The Complete Illustrated Works.* Introduction by Howard Burns. New York (Universe Publishing), 2001.

Beltramini, G.: *Palladio. Lebensspuren.* Berlin (Wagenbach), 2009.

Benda, J.: *The Great Betrayal (La Trahison des Clercs).* Translated by Richard Aldington. London (George Routledge & Sons, Ltd.), 1928

___: *Der Verrat der Intellektuellen.* With a preface by Jean Améry. Munich/Vienna (Carl Hanser), 1978.

Benz, W./Otto, G./Weismann, A. (ed.): *Kultur – Propaganda – Öffentlichkeit: Intention deutscher Besatzungspolitik und Reaktionen auf die Okkupation.* Berlin (Metropol), 1998.

Bergdoll, B./Centre Canadien d'Architecture (ed.): *Le Panthéon. Symbole des révolutions. De l'Église de la Nation au Temple des grands hommes.* Paris (Picard Éditeur), 1989.

___: *Karl Friedrich Schinkel. An Architecture for Prussia.* New York (Rizzoli), 1994.

Bergson, H.: *Matter and Memory.* Authorised translation by Nancy Margaret Paul and W. Scott Palmer. London (George Allen & Unwin Ltd.), 1962.

___: *Creative Evolution.* Translated by Arthur Mitchell. London (MacMillan & Co Ltd.), 1964 (Bergson 1964a).

___: *Schöpferische Entwicklung.* Zürich (Coron), c.1964 (Bergson 1964b).

___: *Materie und Gedächtnis. Eine Abhandlung über die Beziehung zwischen Körper und Geist.* Hamburg (Felix Meiner), 1991.

Bernabei, G.: *Otto Wagner.* Zürich (Artemis), 1986.

Bibesco, M.: *Begegnung mit Marcel Proust.* Frankfurt a. M. (Suhrkamp), 1991.

Binder Iijima, E./Dumbrava, V. (eds): *Stefan der Große – Fürst der Moldau. Symbolfunktion und Bedeutungswandel eines mittelalterlichen Herrschers.* Leipzig (Leipziger Universitätsverlag), 2005.

Bloch, M.: *Aus der Werkstatt des Historikers. Zur Theorie und Praxis der Geschichtswissenschaft.* Ed. by Peter Schöttler. Frankfurt/New York (Campus); Paris (Éditions de la Fondation Maison des Sciences de l'Homme), 2000.

___: *Apologie der Geschichtswissenschaft oder der Beruf des Historikers.* Ed. by P. Schöttler. Preface by J. Le Goff. Stuttgart (Klett-Cotta), 2008.

Blondel, J. F.: *Discours sur la nécéssité de l'étude de l'architecture. De l'utilité de joindre l'architecture à l'étude de l'architecte celle des sciences et des arts qui lui sont relatifs.* Genève (Minkoff Reprint), 1973 [Paris 1754 and 1771].

Bock, R.: *Adolf Loos. Works and Projects.* Milan (Skira), 2007.

Böhringer, H./Söntgen, B. (ed.): *Wilhelm Worringers Kunstgeschichte.* Munich (Wilhelm Fink), 2002.

Boia, L./Nore, E./Hitchins, K./Iggers, G. (ed.): *Great Historians of the Modern Age. An International Dictionary.* New York/Westport, Connecticut/London (Greenwood Press), 1991.

Boia, L.: *La Mythologie Scientifique du Communisme.* Paris 2000.

___: *History and Myth in Romanian Consciousness.* Budapest (Central European University Press), 2001 (Boia 2001a).

___: *Romania. Borderland of Europe.* London (Reaktion Books), 2001 (Boia 2001b).

___: *Historische Wurzeln der politischen Kultur Rumäniens.* In: Bundeszentrale für politische Bildung (ed.): *Aus Politik und Zeitgeschichte*, 27/2006, 3rd July 2006: *Rumänien und Bulgarien. Beilage zur Wochenzeitung* Das Parlament. Bonn/Frankfurt am Main 2006.

Bollon, P.: *Cioran, l'hérétique.* Paris (Gallimard), 1997.

Borch, C./Stäheli, U. (eds): *Soziologie der Nachahmung und des Begehrens. Materialien zu Gabriel Tarde.* Frankfurt a. M. (Suhrkamp), 2009.

Borchhardt-Birbaumer, B.: *Der Funktionalismus im "Paris des Ostens".* In: *Wiener Journal. Das Magazin der Wiener Zeitung*, No. 25, 23rd Oct. 2004, pp. 14-15.

Borsi, F.: *The Monumental Era. European Architecture and Design 1929-1939.* London (Lund Humphries Publishers Ltd.), 1987.

Borsi, F.: /Godoli, E.: *Wiener Bauten der Jahrhundertwende.* Hamburg (Nikol), 1985.

Brachlianoff, D. (ed.): *Puvis de Chavannes au musée des Beaux-Arts de Lyon.* Lyon (Réunion des Musées Nationaux/Musée des Beaux Arts de Lyon), 1998.

Bracker, J. (ed.): *Bauen nach der Natur – Palladio. Die Erben Palladios in Nordeuropa.* Ostfildern-Ruit (Gerd Hatje), 1997.

Braun, H.-J./Kaiser, W.: *Propyläen Technikgeschichte.* 5 Vol. Berlin 1997-2003.

Brătianu, G. I.: *La mer Noire: Des origines à la conquête ottomane.* Munich (Societas Academicas Dacoromana), 1969.

Briend, C./Thomine, A. et al. (eds): *La vie des formes. Henri Focillon et les arts.* Lyon (Musée des Beaux-Arts de Lyon)/Paris (Institut national d'histoire de l'art/ INHA), 2004.

Brockhaus: *Der große Brockhaus in 20 Bänden.* F. A. Brockhaus: Leipzig, Vol. 3, 1929; Vol. 10, 1931; Vol. 18, 1934.

___: *Brockhaus Enzyklopädie in 30 Bänden.* Leipzig/Mannheim: F. A. Brockhaus, 2006, Vol. 9, 14, 21.

Brown, J.: *Lutyens and the Edwardians. An English Architect and his Clients.* London (Viking), 1996.

Bruch, R./Müller, R. (ed.): *Historikerlexikon. Von der Antike bis zur Gegenwart.* Munich (C. H. Beck), 2002.

Brunner, O./Conze, W./Koselleck, R. (eds): *Historisches Lexikon zur politisch-sozialen Sprache in Deutschland.* Stuttgart (Klett-Cotta), 1997.

Bruyn, G. de: *Die enzyklopädische Architektur. Zur Reformulierung einer Universalwissenschaft.* Bielefeld (transcript), 2008.

Burg, H.-H. (ed.): *Gestalten und Ideen. Aus den Schriften des Fürsten Karl Joseph de Ligne.* Graz/Vienna/Cologne (Styria), 1965.

Burckhardt, J.: *Der Cicerone.* Leipzig (Kröner), 1924 [1855].

Burkhardt, F./Eveno, C./Podrecca, B./Centre de Création Industrielle (eds): *Jože Plečnik Architecte 1872-1957.* Paris (Centre Georges Pompidou), 1986.

Bussmann, K.: *Paris und die Ile de France: die Metropole und das Herzland Frankreichs; von der antiken Lutetia bis zur Millionenstadt.* Köln (DuMont), 1980.

Butcher, D./Aittouarès, O. (eds): *Othon Friesz. Le fauve baroque 1879-1949.* Paris (Gallimard), 2007.

Cacciari, M.: *Architecture and Nihilism: On the Philosophy of Modern Architecture.* New Haven and London (Yale University Press), 1993.

___: *Gewalt und Harmonie. Geo-Philosophie Europas.* Munich/Vienna (Carl Hanser), 1995.

___: *Wohnen. Denken. Essays über Baukunst im Zeitalter der völligen Mobilmachung.* Klagenfurt/Vienna (Ritter), 2002.

Carol II: *Între datorie şi pasiune. Însemnări zilnice* [Between Duty and Passion. Daily notes]. Vol. 1, 1904-1939. Edited by Marcel Dumitru Ciucă and Narcis Dorin Ion. Bucharest (Editura Silex), 1995.

Camus, A.: *Fragen der Zeit.* Hamburg (Rowohlt), 1988 (1960).

___: *The Myth of Sisyphus.* London: Penguin Books Ltd, 2005. Original edition *Le Mythe de Sisyphe.* Paris: Gallimard, 1942.

Canetti, E.: *The Tongue Set Free. Remembrance of a European Childhood.* London (Granta Books), 2011.

Cantacuzène, Ch.-A. (ed.): *Le Prince de Ligne.* Paris (Mercure de France), 1934.

Cantacuzène, J.-M.: *Mille ans dans les Balkans. Chronique des Cantacuzène dans la tourmente des siècles.* Paris (Éd. Christian), 1992. Romanian edition: Bucharest (Albatros), 1996.

Cantacuzino, N. B.: *Vieux Temps – Vieilles Figures.* Bucharest/Isvor 1940. Romanian edition *Amintirile unui diplomat român.* Foreword by Nicolae Iorga. Bucharest (Cartea Românească), 1944.

Carothers, D. F.: *Radio broadcasting from 1920 to 1990: an annotated bibliography.* New York/London (Garland Publishing, Inc.), 1991.

Cars, J. des/Caracalla, J.-P.: *100 Jahre Orient-Express.* Zürich/Schwäbisch Hall 1984.

Castello Branco dos Santos, A. G./Georgescu, H./Levy, P.: *Moderne in Bukarest. Ein Architekturführer.* Edited by Winfried Nerdinger/ Architekturmuseum der TU München. Salzburg (Pustet), 2001.

Catullus: *The Poems of Catullus.* Translated by James Michie. Introduction and notes by Robert Rowland. London (Granada), 1982 [1969].

Cavalieri, G.: *Antiquarium Statuarum Urbis Romae.* Rome c. 1609.

Cazacu, M.: *Calea Victoriei/Victoria Avenue. Interbellum Bucharest.* Bucharest (NOI Media Print), 2006 (Cazacu 2006a).

___: *România interbelică/Interbellum Romania.* Bucharest (NOI Media Print), 2006 (Cazacu 2006 b).

Călinescu, G.: *Istoria literaturii române de la origini până în prezent* [A History of the Romanian Literature from its Origins up to the Present]. Bucureşti (Minerva), 1982 [1941].

Celac, M./Carabela, Oc./Marcu-Lăpădat, M.: *Bucureşti, arhitectură şi modernitate. Un ghid adnotat/ Bucharest, architecture and modernity. An annotated guide.* Bucharest (Simetria), 2005.

Centre national d'Art et de Culture Georges Pompidou (ed.): *L'œuvre d'art est un crime parfait. Témoignages sur Constantin Brancusi.* CD-Rom. Paris (Centre Georges Pompidou), 1995.

___: *Jean Cocteau, sur le fil du siècle.* Paris (Centre Georges Pompidou), 2003.

Cernovodeanu, P.: *Revista Istorică Română. Bibliografie critică* [The Romanian Review of History. A critical bibliography]. Bucharest (Editura ştiinţifică şi enciclopedică), 1977.

Chinezu, C.: *Provocarea Europei. Exilul elveţian al lui Grigore Gafencu 1941-1957* [The Provocation of Europe. The Swiss Exile of Grigore Gafencu 1941-1957]. Bucharest (Pro Historia), 2004.

Choisy, A.: *Histoire de l'Architecture.* 2 Vol. Paris 1899.

Christiaanse, K. *Entwerfen ist Navigieren.* In: *Arch +*, No. 122, Berlin 1994, pp. 48-49.

Cicio Pop, Al./Nemeth, Z.: *Reiseführer durch Rumänien.* Bucharest (Editura Ghidul României), 1932.

___/Puşcariu, Val./Badautza, Al.: *Guide de la Roumanie.* Bucharest (Editura Ghidul României), 1938 and 1940.

Cioran, E. M.: *The Trouble with Being Born.* Tranlated from the French by Richard Howard. New York (The Viking Press/Richard Seaver), 1976

___: *History and Utopia.* Translated from the French by Richard Howard. New York (Seaver Books), 1987.

___: *Œuvres.* Paris (Gallimard), 1995.

Cocteau, J.: *A call to order. Written between the years 1918 and 1926 and including Cock and Harlequin, Professional Secrets, and other critical essays.* Translated from the French by R. H. Meyers. London (Faber and Gwyer), 1926.

___: *Essai de critique indirecte.* Paris (Bernard Graset), 1932.

___: *La comtesse de Noailles oui et non.* Paris 1963.

Cogeval, G./Jones, K./Cars, L./Stevens, M. A. (eds): *Edouard Vuillard.* New Haven and London (Yale University Press), 2003.

Cohen, J.-L./Eleb, M.: *Paris. Architecture 1900-2000.* Paris (Norma), 2000.

Collarcho, J. (ed.): *Artisti italiani contemporanei.* Vol. I: *Emilia, Liguria, Toscana, Veneto.* Firenze (La Ginestra), 1968.

Comnène, P./Tataresco, G.: *Roumanie (république de).* In: *Dictionnaire Diplomatique* Vol. 4, Paris c.1948, pp. 963-976.

Conrads, U. (ed.): *Programmes and manifestos on 20th-century architecture.* Translated by M. Bullock. London (Lund Humphries), 1970.

Constant, C.: *The Palladio Guide.* New York (Princeton Architectural Press), 1993.

Constantin, P.: *Dicţionar universal al arhitecţilor* [Universal Dictionary of Architects]. Bucharest (Editura Ştiinţifică şi Encicopedică), 1986.

Cooper, A.: *Patrick Leigh Fermor. An Adventure.* London (John Murray), 2012.

Crettaz-Stürzel, E. (ed.): *Heimatstil: Reformarchitektur in der Schweiz 1896-1914.* Frauenfeld (Huber), 2005.

Cretzianu, A. (ed.): *Captive Rumania. A decade of Soviet rule.* New York 1956.

Cristea-Vieru, M.: *Militza Pătraşcu sau modernitatea clasicului.* Bucharest 1982

Criticos, M./Zahariade, A.-M.: *Modelul francez în arhitectura românească* [The Importance of the French Model for Romanian Architecture]. In: *Dilema veche*, Year 4, No. 157, Bucharest, 9th February 2007.

Crutzescu, Gh.: *Podul Mogoşoaei* [The Mogoşoaia Avenue]. Bucharest (Meridiane), 1987 (1943).

Curinschi, Gh. V.: *Istoria arhitecturii din România* [The History of Architecture in Romania]. Bucharest (Ed. Tehnică), 1981.

Curtius, E. R.: *Essays on European Literature.* Translated by Michael Kowal. Princeton (Princeton University Press), 1973.

Dahrendorf, R.: *Versuchungen der Unfreiheit. Die Intellektuellen in Zeiten der Prüfung.* Munich (C. H. Beck), 2006.

Deac, M.: *Jean Al. Steriadi.* Bucharest (Meridiane), 1962.

___: *50 ani de pictură 1890-1940. Dicţionarul pictorilor din România* [50 Years of Painting. The Dictionary of Paintings in Romania 1890-1940]. Bucharest 1996.

Dean, D.: *The Thirties: Recalling the English Architectural Scene.* London (Trefoil Books/RIBA Drawings Collection), 1983.

Deletant, D.: *Ceauşescu and the Securitate. Coercion and Dissident in Romania, 1965-1989.* London (Hurst & Company), 1995.

Deleuze, G.: *Bergsonism.* New York (Zone Books), 1988.

Demougin, J. (ed.): *Dictionnaire des Littératures françaises et étrangères.* Paris (Larousse), 1992.

Denize, E.: *Istoria Societății Române de Radiodifuziune* [The History of the Romanian Broadcasting]. 3 Vol. Bucharest (Casa Radio), 1999.

Descartes, R.: *Die Leidenschaften der Seele.* Edited and translated by Klaus Hammacher. French-German edition. Hamburg (Felix Meiner), 1996. Original edition *Traité des passions de l'âme*, Paris 1649.

Diamond, R./Wang, W. (ed.): *On Continuity. 9H Publications, No. 9.* Cambridge, Mass./Oxford, England (Princeton Architectural Press), 1995.

Diehl, C./Grousset, R./Guilland, R./Oeconomos, L.: *Histoire du Moyen Age. Tome IX, Première Partie: L'Europe Orientale de 1081 à 1453.* Paris: Presse Universitaires de France, 1945.

Diehl, C.: *Byzance. Grandeur et décadence.* Paris (Flammarion), 1919.

____: *Venise. Une république patricienne.* Paris (Flammarion), 1925.

Diesbach, G.: *La Princesse Bibesco 1886-1973.* Paris (Perrin), 1986.

Dimitriu, R.: *Die Außenpolitik Rumäniens 1918-1939 zwischen Solidarität und Sacro egoismo.* Frankfurt am Main etc. 2006.

Dini, F./Mazzoca, F./Sisi, C. (eds): *Boldini.* Venice (Marsilio), 2005.

Dobrescu, D.: *Psihologia Bucureşteanului* [The Psychology of the Bucharester]. In: *Gazeta Municipală*, Bucharest, 8th January 1939.

Doicescu, O: *Despre arhitectură. Scrieri, cuvântari* [On Architecture. Writings and Lectures]. Edited by Peter Derer. Bucharest (Ed. Tehnică), 1983.

Djuvara, N.: *O scurtă istorie a românilor povestită celor tineri* [A Short History of the Romanians told to the Youth]. Bucharest (Humanitas), 2006.

Doinaş, Ş. A. (ed.): *Bucureşti Secolul XX.* Bucharest (ARCUB), 1997.

Donaldson, F.: *The British Council. The First Fifty Years.* London (Jonathan Cape Ltd), 1984.

Donzel, C.: *Paquebots.* Paris (Éditions Solar), 2005.

Douglas, G. H.: *The Early Days of Radio Broadcasting.* Jefferson, North Carolina/London (McFarland & Company, Inc.), 2001.

Dragu Dimitriu, V.: *Poveşti ale Doamnelor din Bucureşti* [Memories of the Ladies from Bucharest]. Bucharest (Vremea), 2006.

Drăguţ, V./Florea, V./Grigorescu, D./Mihalache, M.: *Romanian Painting.* Bucharest (Meridiane), 1977.

Drexler, A. (ed.): *The Architecture of the Ecole des Beaux-Arts.* London (Secker & Warburg), 1977.

Droste, T.: *Venedig.* Köln (DuMont), 1985.

Dudescu, R.: *Salvamar. Societatea de salvare a naufragiaților în apele teritoriale române* [Salvamar. The Society of the Sea Rescue in Romania]. In: *Arhitectura* No. 2/1942, Bucharest, pp. 26-27.

Durandin, C.: *Histoire de la nation roumaine.* Brussels (Éd. Complexe), 1994.

___: *Histoire des Roumains.* Mesnil-sur-l'Estrée (Éd. Fayard), 1995.

___: *Bucureşti. Amintiri şi plimbări* [Bucharest. Memories and Strolls]. Piteşti (Ed. Paralela 45), 2006.

Durth, W.: *Deutsche Architekten. Biografische Verflechtungen 1900-1970.* Munich (Deutscher Taschenbuch Verlag), 1992.

___/Gutschow, Niels: *Träume in Trümmern. Stadtplanung 1940-1950.* Munich (Deutscher Taschenbuch Verlag), 1993.

Eckermann, J. P.: *Conversations of Goethe with Eckermann. Translated by John Oxenford.* Edited by J. K. Moorhead, with an introduction by Havelock Ellis. London/Toronto (Everyman's Library), 1930.

Egbert, D. D.: *The Beaux-Arts Tradition in French Architecture.* Edited by David van Zanten. Foreword by Robert Venturi. Princeton, New Jersey (Princeton University Press), 1980.

Elbin, G. (ed.): *Literat und Feldmarschall. Briefe und Erinnerungen des Fürsten Charles Joseph de Ligne 1735-1814.* Stuttgart (DVA), 1979.

Eliade, M.: *The Quest.* Chicago (University of Chicago), 1969.

___: *Die Prüfung des Labyrinths. Gespräche mit Claude-Henri Roquet.* Translated from the French by Eva Moldenhauer. Frankfurt a. M. (Insel), 1987.

___: *Commentaire sur la légende de maître Manole.* Paris (L'Herne), 1994. Original edition *Comentarii despre legenda Meşterului Manole.* Bucharest 1943.

Eliot, T. S.: *Selected Essays.* New York (Harcourt, Brace & Company), 1950.

___: *The Unity of European Culture.* Kiel (Lipsius & Tischer), 1950.

___: *Selected prose.* Harmondsworth, Middlesex (Penguin), 1963.

Fabre, L.: *Les théories d'Einstein. Une nouvelle figure au monde.* Paris (Payot & Cie), 1922.

Favaretto Fisca, G./Sindaco di Venezia (eds): *Catalogo della XXXIV Esposizione Biennale Internazionale d'Arte Venezia 1968.* Venice 1968.

Fechtrup, H./Schulze, F./Sternberg, T. (eds): *Aufklärung durch Tradition. Symposium der Josef Pieper Stiftung zum 90. Geburtstag von Josef Pieper, Mai 1994 in Münster.* Münster (Lit), 1995.

Félibien, J. F.: *Des Principes de l'Architecture, de la sculpture, de la peinture, et des autres arts qui en dépendent. Avec un dictionnaire des termes propres à chacun de ces Arts.* 3rd edition. Paris (La Veuve & Jean Baptiste Coignard, fils), 1699.

Fermor, P. L.: *A Time of Gifts.* London (John Murray), 1977.

___: *Between the Woods and the Water. On Foot to Constantinople: the Middle Danube to the Iron Gates.* London (John Murray), 2004.

___: *Words of Mercury.* Edited by A. Cooper. London (John Murray), 2004.

Fezi, B. A.: *Bucarest et l'influence française: entre modèle et archétype urbain, 1831-1921.* Paris 2005.

Fiori, R.: *L'Invention du Vieux Paris. Naissance d'une conscience patrimoniale dans la capitale.* Wawre (Mardaga), 2012.

Fleury, A./Jílek, L. (eds): *Le plan Briand d'union fédérale européenne.* Bern etc. 1998.

Focillon, H.: *The Life of Forms in Art.* Translated by Charles B. Hogan and George Kubler. Introduction by Jean Molino. New York (Zone Books), 1989.

___**/Gilson, E./Jordan, E./Hauvette, H./Masseron, A./Sabatier, P. :** *L'influence de Saint François d'Assise sur la civilisation italienne.* Paris 1926.

Forssman, E.: *Palladios Lehrgebäude. Studien über den Zusammenhang von Architektur und Architekturtheorie bei Andrea Palladio.* Stockholm/Göteborg/Uppsala (Almquist & Wiksell), 1965.

___: *Karl Friedrich Schinkel. Bauwerke und Baugedanken.* Munich/Zürich (Schnell & Steiner), 1981.

Frampton, K.: *Studies in Tectonic Culture: The Poetics of Construction in Nineteenth and Twentieth Century Architecture.* Cambridge, Mass./London, England: MIT Press, 1995

___: *Modern Architecture. A Critical History.* London (Thames & Hudson), 1997.

___: *Labour, Work and Architecture. Collected Essays on Architecture and Design.* London/New York (Phaidon), 2002

Frank, H. (ed.): *Fritz Schumacher. Reformkult und Moderne.* Stuttgart (Gerd Hatje), 1994.

Frank, J.: *Die Architektur als Symbol. Elemente Deutschen Neuen Bauens.* Vienna (Anton Schroll & Co.), 1931.

Freigang, C.: *Auguste Perret, die Architekturdebatte und die Konservative Revolution in Frankreich 1900-1930.* Munich/Berlin (Deutscher Kunstverlag), 2003.

Fremdsprachiger Verlag Bukarest (ed.): *Rumanian Architecture. L'architecture roumaine. Rumänische Architektur.* Bucharest 1956.

Fuhrmann, M.: *Der europäische Bildungskanon des bürgerlichen Zeitalters.* Frankfurt am Main/Leipzig (Insel), 1999.

___: *Bildung. Europas kulturelle Identität.* Stuttgart (Reclam), 2006.

Fustel de Coulanges, N. D.: *Der antike Staat. Studie über Kultus, Recht und Einrichtungen Griechenlands und Roms.* Essen (Phaidon), 1996 [Paris 1864].

Gafencu, G.: *Europas letzte Tage. Eine politische Reise im Jahre 1939.* Zurich (Amstutz, Herdeg & Co.), 1946.

___: *Însemnări politice* [Political notes]. Bucharest (Humanitas), 1991.

Galbraith, J. K.: *The Great Crash.* London (Penguin), 1992 [1954].

___: *Die Geschichte der Wirtschaft im 20. Jahrhundert.* Hamburg (Hoffmann und Campe), 1995.

Gargiani, R.: *Paris. Architektur zwischen Purismus und Beaux-Arts 1919-1939.* Braunschweig/Wiesbaden (Vieweg & Sohn), 1992.

Garleff, J.: *Die Ecole des Beaux-Arts in Paris. Ein gebautes Architekturtraktat des 19. Jahrhunderts.* Tübingen/Berlin (Ernst Wasmuth), 2003.

Gavoty, B.: *Les Souvenirs de Georges Enesco.* Paris (Flammarion), 1955.

Gebauer, G./Wulf, C.: *Mimesis. Kultur, Kunst, Gesellschaft.* Reinbek bei Hamburg (Rowohlt), 1992.

Gebhard, H./Sauerländer, W. (eds): *Feindbild Geschichte. Positionen der Architektur und Kunst im 20. Jahrhundert.* Göttingen (Wallstein), 2007.

Gemmel, M.: *Die Kritische Wiener Moderne. Ethik und Ästhetik. Karl Kraus, Adolf Loos, Ludwig Wittgenstein.* Berlin (Parerga), 2005.

Geretsegger, H./Peintner, M./Pichler, W.: *Otto Wagner 1841-1918. Unbegrenzte Groszstadt. Beginn der modernen Architektur.* Foreword by Richard Neutra. Salzburg/Vienna (Residenz), 1978.

Ghiţulescu, M. (ed.): *Goga la Ciucea* [Goga in Ciucea]. Cluj 1975.

Ghika-Budeşti, N.: *Evoluţia arhitecturii în Muntenia şi în Oltenia* [The architectural development in Wallachia]. Bucharest 1931.

Ghyka, M.: *Le Nombre d'Or. Rites et rythmes pythagoriciens dans le développement de la civilisation occidentale.* Paris (Gallimard), 1952 (1931).

___: *Couleur du monde.* 2 Vol. Paris (Éditions de La Colombe), 1956. English version *The World Mine Oyster* (London 1961), with a preface by P. L. Fermor.

Giacometti, A.: *Écrits. Présentées par Michel Leiris et Jacques Dupin.* Paris (Hermann, éditeurs des sciences et des arts), 1995.

___: *Paris sans fin.* Ed. by Sylvie Wuhrmann. Paris (Buchet/Chastel), 2003.

Gide, A.: *Journal 1889-1939.* Paris (Gallimard), 1948.

___: *Tagebuch 1889-1939.* Stuttgart (DVA), 1950-1954.

___: *Journals 1889-1949.* Translated, selected and edited by Justin O'Brien. Harmondsworth, Middlesex etc. (Penguin Books), 1984

___: *Journal 1889-1950.* 2 Vol. Paris (Gallimard), 1996/1997.

Giedion-Welcker, K.: *Constantin Brancusi.* Basel (B. Schwabe & Co.), 1958.

Giurescu, D. C.: *The raising of Romania's past.* Washington D. C. (World monuments fund), 1989.

Godin, A.: *Une passion roumanie. Histoire de l'institut français des Hautes Études en Roumanie (1924-1948).* Paris (L'Harmattan), 1998.

Gönna, G. (ed.): *Giovanni Pico della Mirandola. Oratio de hominis dignitate. Rede über die Würde des Menschen.* Stuttgart (Reclam), 2001.

Goethe, J. W.: *Italian Journey.* Translated by W. H. Auden and Elizabeth Mayer. London (Penguin Books), 1970.

___: *Collected Works in 12 Volumes. Vol. 3: Essays on Art and Literature.* Edited by John Gray. Translated by Ellen von Nardroff and Ernest H. von Nardroff. Princeton, N. J. (Princeton University Press), 1994.

___: *Schriften zu Kunst und Literatur.* Stuttgart (Reclam), 1999.

___: *Dichtung und Wahrheit.* Frankfurt am Main/Leipzig (Insel), 2000.

Gombrich, E. H.: *The Story of Art.* London (Phaidon), 2006 (1949).

___: *Die Kunst, Bilder zum Sprechen zu bringen. Ein Gespräch mit Didier Eribon.* Stuttgart (Klett-Cotta), 1993.

Gordon Smith, T.: *Vitruvius on Architecture.* New York (The Monacelli Press), 2003.

Grabar, A.: *La peinture byzantine.* Genève (Albert Skira), 1990.

Graf, O. A.: Otto Wagner. Vol. 1. *Das Werk des Architekten 1860-1902.* Vienna/Cologne/Graz (Hermann Böhlaus Nachf.), 1985.

Gray, R.: *The Imperative of Modernity. An Intellectual Biography of José Ortega y Gasset.* Berkeley/Los Angeles/London (University of California Press), 1989.

Grebing, H.: *Wilhem Worringer – Abstraktion und Einfühlung. Ein Beitrag zur Stilpsychologie.* Munich (Wilhelm Fink), 2007.

Greceanu, E.: *Puncte de vedere asupra noţiunii de valorificare a monumentelor şi ansamblurilor istorice* [Points of view on the appreciation of historic monuments and urban fabrics as a cultural value]. In: *Revista Monumentelor Istorice,* Bucharest, Year LIX, No. 1/1990, pp. 52-61.

___: *Demilitarea zonelor protejate urbane în România în timpul regimului comunist* [The Delimitation of Protected Areas in Communism]. In: *Arhitext Design* AD Bucharest, No. 5/1998, pp. 26-29; and No. 6/1998, pp. 28-31.

Grigorescu, D.: *Dicţionarul Avangardelor* [The Dictionary of Avant-gardes]. Bucharest (Editura Enciclopedică), 2005.

Grisebach, A.: *Carl Friedrich Schinkel.* Leipzig (Insel Verlag), 1924.

Gromort, G.: *Essai sur la Théorie de l'Architecture. Cours professé à l'Ecole Nationale Supérieure des Beaux-Arts de 1937 à 1940.* Paris (Vincent, Fréal & Cie), 1946 [1942]. 3rd edition Paris (Massin), 1983.

Gromort, G.: *Lettres à Nicias. Entretiens familiers sur l'enseignement de l'architecture.* Paris (Vincent, Fréal & Cie), 1950.

___: *Small Structures. French Architecture of the Early Nineteenth Century.* New York (Van Nostrand Reinhold Company), 1986.

___: *The Elements of Classical Architecture.* Edited by H. H. Reed. New York 2001.

Groys, B.: *Über das Neue. Versuch einer Kulturökonomie.* Frankfurt am Main (Fischer Verlag), 2004.

Guégan, S./Pomarède, V./Prat, L.-A. (ed.): *Théodore Chassériau (1819-1856): The Unknown Romantic.* New York (The Metropolitan Museum of Art), 2003.

Guénard, A.: *De la reconstruction à l'eviction. Entre 1944 et 1949, une politique culturelle française en Europe centrale et orientale confrontée à l'organisation du Bloc communiste.* In: *Matériaux pour l'histoire de notre temps.* Nanterre (BDIC), No. 36, October-December 1994, pp. 21-27.

Guilheux, A./Cinqualbre, O./Toutcheff, N. (eds): *Tony Garnier. L'œuvre complète.* Paris (Centre Georges Pompidou), 1990.

Guitard-Auviste, G.: *Paul Morand (1888-1976). Légende et vérités.* Paris 1994.

Gusti, D.: *Les Fondations Culturelles Royales de Roumanie.* Bucharest 1937.

Gusti, G.: *Arhitectura în România. Die Architektur Rumäniens.* Bucharest (Meridiane), 1965.

Habermann, G.: *Freiheit oder Gleichheit. Ein Alexis-de Tocqueville Brevier.* Bern (hep; Ott), 2005.

Haldon, J.: *Byzantium. A History.* Gloucestershire (Tempus), 2000.

Han, C.: *Ästhetik der Oberfläche. Die Medialitätskonzeption Goethes.* Würzburg (Königshausen & Neumann), 2007.

Harden, I./Willmes, G.: *PianistenProfile. 600 Interpreten: ihre Biografie, ihr Stil, ihre Aufnahmen.* Kassel etc. (Bärenreiter), 2008.

Harding, J.: *The Criterion. Cultural Politics and Periodical Networks in Inter-War Britain.* Oxford (Oxford University Press), 2002.

Harhoiu, D.: *Bucureşti, un oraş între orient şi occident/Bucharest, a City between Orient and Occident.* Bucharest (Simetria), 2001.

Harris, J.: *The Palladian Revival: Lord Burlington, His Villa and Garden at Chiswick.* New Haven & London 1994.

Hart, V.: *Inigo Jones. The Architect of Kings.* New Haven and London (Yale University Press), 2011

Hausmann, F.-R.: *Auch im Krieg schweigen die Musen nicht: die Deutschen Wissenschaftlichen Institute im zweiten Weltkrieg.* Göttingen (Vandenhoeck & Ruprecht), 2002.

Hautecœur, L.: *L'Architecture française.* Paris (Boivin), 1950.

Heinen, A.: *Die Legion* Erzengel Michael *in Rumänien. Soziale Bewegung und politische Organisation. Ein Beitrag zum Problem des internationalen Faschismus.* Munich (R. Oldenbourg Verlag), 1986.

Heinrichs, H.-J.: *Grenzgänger der Moderne. Essays.* Hamburg (Europäische Verlagsanstalt), 1994.

Hellenthal, M.: *Eklektizismus. Zur Ambivalenz einer Geisteshaltung und eines künstlerischen Konzepts.* Frankfurt a. M. etc. (P. Lang), 1993.

Heppner, H. (ed.): *Die Rumänen und Europa vom Mittelalter bis zur Gegenwart.* Cologne/Weimar/Vienna (Böhlau), 1997.

Herrmann, W.: *Deutsche Baukunst des 19. und 20. Jahrhunderts.* 2 Vol. Basel/Stuttgart (Birkhäuser), 1977.

Hertlein, H.: *Das Schaltwerk Hochhaus in Siemensstadt. Architektur und bautechnische Einrichtungen.* Berlin (Ernst Wasmuth), 1927.

___: *Siemensbauten. Neue Fabrik- und Verwaltungsgebäude, Wohlfahrtsanlagen des Siemenskonzerns.* Berlin (Ernst Wasmuth), 1931.

Hertzberger, H.: *Lessons for students in architecture.* Translated from the Dutch by Ina Rike. Rotterdam (Uitgeverij 010 Publishers), 1991.

Heuss, T.: *Profile. Nachzeichnungen aus der Geschichte.* Tübingen (Rainer Wunderlich Verlag Hermann Leins), 1964.

___: *Hans Poelzig: Bauten und Entwürfe. Das Lebensbild eines Baumeisters.* Stuttgart (Deutsche Verlags-Anstalt), 1985.

Hielscher, K.: *Österreich. Landschaft und Bauten.* Berlin (Wasmuth), 1931.

___: *Rumänien. Landschaft, Bauten, Volksleben.* Leipzig (Brockhaus), 1933.

Hillgruber, A.: *Hitler, König Carol und Marschall Antonescu. Die deutsch-rumänischen Beziehungen 1938-1944.* Wiesbaden (Franz Steiner) 1965.

Hillgruber, A./Dülffer, J. (eds): *Ploetz. Geschichte der Weltkriege. Mächte, Ereignisse, Entwicklungen 1900-1945.* Freiburg/Würzburg (Ploetz), 1981.

Hitchins, K.: *Romania 1866-1947.* Oxford (Claredon Press), 1994.

Hocke, G. R. (ed.): *Der französische Geist. Geistesgeschichtliche Untersuchungen der französischen Essayistik nebst Meisteressays in zweisprachigem Text.* Zürich (Diogenes), 1988.

Höffe, O. (ed.): *Klassiker der Philosophie.* Munich (C. H. Beck), 2008.

Hoffmann, W.: *Rumänien von heute. Ein Querschnitt durch Politik, Kultur und Wirtschaft.* Bucharest (Cartea Românească)/Leipzig (Felix Meiner), 1942.

Holli, M. G./Jones, P. (eds): *Biographical Dictionary of American Mayors 1820-1980. Big City Mayors.* Westport, Con./London, England (Greenwood Press), 1981.

Hootz, R./ Vătăşianu, V. (eds): *Kunstdenkmäler in Rumänien.* Munich/Berlin (Deutscher Kunstverlag), 1972.

___/Dellwing, H. (ed.): *Kunstdenkmäler in Italien. Ein Bildhandbuch.* Darmstadt (Wissenschaftliche Buchgesellschaft), 1976.

Hulten, P. (ed.): *Berlin & Paris 1900-1933. Rapports et contrastes France-Allemagne.* Paris (Centre Georges Pompidou), 1978.

___/Dumitresco, N./Istrati, Al.: *Brancusi.* Paris (Flammarion), 1995.

Hurezeanu, D.: *La revue Viața românească et les traditions radicales-démocratiques de Roumanie.* In: *Revue roumaine d'histoire.* Bucharest 1986/25, pp. 331-341.

Ierunca, V.: *Fenomenul Pitești* [The Pitești Case]. Bucharest (Humanitas), 2007. French edition *Pitești, laboratoire concentrationnaire.* Paris 1996.

Ilk, M.: *Brâncuși, Tzara und die rumänische Avantgarde.* Bochum (Museum Bochum/Kunsthal Rotterdam), 1997.

Institut Français d'architecture/L'Académie d'architecture/Culot, M. (eds): *Roger-Henri Expert 1882-1955.* Paris (Editions du Moniteur), 1983.

Institut für Auslandsbeziehungen (ed.): *Erste Schritte. Rumänische Kunst der 90er Jahre.* Stuttgart (IFA), 1993.

Ioanid, R.: *The Holocaust in Romania. The Destruction of Jews and Gypsies under the Antonescu Regime, 1940-1944. With a foreword by Elie Wiesel and a preface by Paul A. Shapiro.* Chicago (Ivan R. Dee, Inc./The United States Holocaust Memorial Museum), 2000.

Ionescu Dunăreanu, I./Cristescu, M.: *Eforie Nord, Eforie Sud, Techirghiol.* Bucharest (Verlag für Tourismus), 1974.

Ionesco, E.: *Rhinoceros: a play in three acts.* Translated by Derek Prouse. London (Samuel French), c. 1960.

___: *Présent passé, passé présent.* Paris (Gallimard), 1968.

___: *Notes et contres-notes.* Paris (Gallimard), 1996 [1966].

Ionescu, Gr.: *Istoria arhitecturii românești din cele mai vechi timpuri până la 1900* [The History of Romanian Architecture from the Beginnings to 1900]. Bucharest (Cartea Românească), 1937.

___: *București, ghid istoric și artistic* [A Historic and Travelling Guide]. Bucharest (Fundația pentru Literatură și Artă Regele Carol II), 1938.

___: *Rumänische Bautätigkeit in Siebenbürgen 1919-1940.* Excerpt from *Siebenbürgen.* Bucharest (Institut für rumänische Geschichte), 1943, pp. 593-608.

___: *L'histoire de l'architecture en Roumanie.* Bucharest 1972.

___: *Arhitectura românească. Tipologii, creații, creatori.* Bucharest 1986.

Ionescu, Ș.: *Who's who in twentieth century Romania.* New York (Columbia University Press), 1994.

Ioniță, M.: *Casa și familia Capșa în România modernă 1852-1950* [The Capșa Company and Family in modern Romania 1852-1950]. Bucharest, 2000.

Iordănescu, D./Georgescu, C.: *Construcții pentru transporturi în România* [Traffic Constructions in Romania]. Bucharest, 1986.

Institut für donauschwäbische Geschichte und Landeskunde/ Landesarchiv Baden-Württemberg (eds): *Brechungen. Willy Pragher: Rumänische Bildräume 1924-1944.* Ostfildern (Jan Thorbecke), 2007.

Institutul Cartografic Unirea (ed.): *Planul Unirea. Municipiul București și împrejurimile* [The Unirea Map of Bucharest and its Surroundings]. Brașov, 1938.

Iorga, N. /Balș, G.: *Histoire de l'Art roumain ancien.* Paris (Boccard), 1922.

Irimia-Tuchtenhagen, S.: *Ideologische Aspekte im Rumänien der Zwischenkriegszeit im Spiegel der wichtigsten Kulturzeitschriften.* In: Südost-Forschungen, Vol. 56, Munich 1997, pp. 319-340.

Jacob-Friesen, H./Reuter, A.: *Edouard Vuillard.* Edited by the Staatliche Kunsthalle Karlsruhe. Heidelberg (Kehrer), 2008.

Jaeger, M.: *Fausts Kolonie. Goethes kritische Phönomenologie der Morderne.* Würzburg (Königshausen & Neumann), 2004.

Jannière, H.: *Politiques éditoriales et architecture moderne. L'emergence de nouvelles revues en France et en Italie (1923-1939).* Paris (Ed. Arguments), 2002.

Jens, W. (ed.): *Kindlers Neues Literaturlexikon.* Munich (Kindler), 1988.

Jianu, I./Carp, G./Covrig, A. M./Scânteie, L.: *Artiști români în occident* [Romanian Artists in the West]. Bucharest (Institutul Național pentru Memoria Exilului Românesc), 2005.

Jones, E./Woodward, C.: *A Guide to the Architecture of London.* London (Seven Dials, Cassell & Co.), 2000.

Jünger, H.-D.: *Die kulturelle Krise.* Munich (Matthes & Seitz), 1998.

Judt, T.: *Ill Fares the Land.* New York etc. (Penguin), 2010.

Kahl, T./Metzeltin, M./Ungureanu, M. (ed.): *Rumänien.* Sonderband der Österreichischen Osthefte, Year 48, 2006. Vienna/Berlin (LIT), 2006.

Kähler, G.: *Architektur als Symbolverfall: Das Dampfermotiv in der Baukunst.* Braunschweig/Wiesbaden (Vieweg), 1981.

Kapuściński, R.: *Travels with Herodotus.* London (Penguin), 2007.

Kemp, M. (ed.): *Leonardo da Vinci: On Painting.* An anthology of writings by Leonardo da Vinci with a selection of documents relating to his career as an artist. Selected and translated by Martin Kemp and Margaret Walker. New Haven/ London (Yale Nota Bene/Yale University Press), 2001.

Kirson, S. P.: *Banca Chrissoveloni. Societate Anonimă Română 1920-1948. Documente* [The Chrissoveloni-Bank. A Romanian Company Ltd 1928-1948. Documents]. Bucharest (Ed. Fundației Culturale Magazin Istoric), 2001.

Klein, H./Göring, K.: *Rumänische Landeskunde.* Tübingen (Narr),1995.

Kleinstück, H. (ed.): *Griechisch-römische Lyrik. Dichtung der Antike.* Wiesbaden (Emil Vollmer), c. 1960.

Klopfer, P.: *Von Palladio bis Schinkel. Eine Charakteristik der Baukunst des Klassizismus.* Esslingen a. N. (Paul Neff Verlag Max Schreiber), 1911.

Knöfel, T./Sander, K. (ed.): *E. M. Cioran "Cafard". Originaltonaufnahmen 1974-1990.* With an epilogue by Peter Sloterdijk and a conversation between Hans-Jürgen Heinrichs and E. M. Cioran. CD-Rom. Cologne (c+p supposé), 1998.

Kraus, F.: *Paestum – die griechischen Tempel.* Berlin (Gebr. Mann), 1984.

Kraus, K.: *Pro domo et mundo.* Frankfurt am Main (Suhrkamp), 1990.

Krautheimer, R.: *Ausgewählte Aufsätze zur europäischen Kunstgeschichte.* Köln (Dumont), 2003 (1988).

Kroner, M.: *Die Hohenzollern als Könige von Rumänien. Lebensbilder von vier Monarchen 1866-2004.* Heilbronn (Johannis Reeg), 2004.

Kruft, H.-W.: *A History of Architectural Theory from Vitruvius to the Present.* New York (Princeton Architectural Press), 2007 [1991].

Laforgue, J.: *Œuvres complètes.* Lausanne (L'Age d'Homme), 1986.

Lampugnani, V. M./Schneider, R. (ed.): *Moderne Architektur in Deutschland 1900-1950. Reformen und Tradition.* Stuttgart (Gerd Hatje), 1992.

Lampugnani, V. M. (ed.): *The Thames and Hudson Dictionary of 20th-Century Architecture.* London (Thames & Hudson), 1997.

Langmuir, E.: *The National Gallery Companion Guide.* London (National Gallery Company/Yale University Press), 2004.

Larousse: *Grand Dictionnaire Encyclopédique.* Paris (Larousse), 1985.

Lassaigne, J.: *Théodor Pallady 1871-1956.* Paris 1973.

Laurent, C./Lambert, G./Abram, J. (eds): *Auguste Perret. Anthologie des écrits, conférences et entretiens.* Paris (Le Moniteur), 2006.

Lăpușan, A./Lăpușan, Ș./Stănescu, Gh.: *Album cu amintiri Mamaia 1906-2006* [Photographic Album with Memories of Mamaia 1906-2006]. Constanța (Ed. Dobrogea), 2006.

Le Corbusier: *Journey to the East.* Cambridge, Massachusetts/ London, England (The MIT Press), 1987.

Leahu, Gh.: *Bucureștiul dispărut* [The lost Bucharest]. Bucharest (Editura Arta Grafică), 1995.

Lebesque, M.: *Albert Camus.* Reinbek bei Hamburg (Rowohlt), 1991.

Lecca, O.-G.: *Familiile boierești române* [The Aristocratic Families of Romania]. Bucharest (Muzeul Literaturii Române), 2000 (1899).

Lecoq, A.-M. (ed.): *La Querelle des Anciens et des Modernes.* Preface by Marc Fumaroli, epilogue by Jean-Robert Armogathe. Paris (Gallimard), 2001.

Lefrère, J.: *Jules Laforgue.* Paris (Fayard), 2005.

Lemny, D./Velescu, C. (eds): *Brâncuși inedit. Însemnări și corespondență românească* [Unknown Brancusi. Notes and the Romanian Correspondence]. Bucharest (Humanitas), 2004.

Lemoine, B./Rivoirard, P.: *Paris/L'Architecture des années trente.* Paris (La Manufacture/Délégation à l'Action artistique de la Ville de Paris), 1987.

Lemoine, S. (ed.): *Da Puvis de Chavannes a Matisse e Picasso. Verso l'Arte Moderna.* Venice (Bompiani), 2002.

Lepenies, W.: *Sainte-Beuve. Auf der Schwelle zur Moderne.* Munich/Vienna (Carl Hanser Verlag), 1997.

Ligne, C. J.: *Coup d'œil sur Belœil et sur une grande partie des jardins de l'Europe, 2 tomes.* Dresden (Les Frères Walther), 1795.

Liiceanu, G.: *Itinéraires d'une vie: E. M. Cioran. Suivi de Les continents de l'insomnie. Entretien avec E. M. Cioran.* Paris (Michalon), 1995.

Livezeanu, I.: *Cultural Politics in Greater Romania. Regionalism, Nation Building and Ethnic Struggle, 1918-1930.* Ithaca etc. (Cornell University Press), 1995.

Löhneysen, W. v.: *Mistra. Griechenlands Schicksal im Mittelalter.* Munich (Prestel-Verlag), 1977.

Loos, A.: *Spoken into the Void. Collected Essays 1897-1900.* Translated by Jane O. Newman and John H. Smith. Introduction by Aldo Rossi. Cambridge, Mass. (The MIT Press), 1987.

___: *Über Architektur. Ausgewählte Schriften. Die Originaltexte.* Edited by Adolf Opel. Vienna (Georg Prachner), 1995.

Lord, J.: *Giacometti – A Biography.* London etc. (Faber & Faber), 1986.

Lortie, A. (ed.): *Paris s'exporte. Modèle d'architecture ou architectures modèles.* Paris (Éditions du Pavillon de l'Arsenal/Picard), 1995.

Lovinescu, E.: *Istoria civilizației române moderne* [The History of the Modern Romanian Civilisation]. Bucharest (Editura Minerva), 1997.

Lozek, G. (ed.): *Geschichtsschreibung im 20. Jahrhundert. Neuzeithistoriographie und Geschichtsdenken im westlichen Europa und in den USA.* Berlin (Fides), 1998.

Lungu, D. B.: *Romania and the Great Powers 1933-1940.* Durham and London (Duke University Press), 1989.

Lungu, V.: *Viața lui Tudor Vianu* [Das Leben Tudor Vianus]. Bucharest (Editura Minerva), 1997.

Machedon, L./Scoffham, E.: *Romanian modernism – the architecture of Bucharest, 1920-1940.* Cambridge, Mass./London, England (The MIT Press),1999.

Majetschak, S.: *Ästhetik zur Einführung.* Hamburg (Junius), 2007.

Malaparte, C.: *Kaputt. Roman.* Vienna (Paul Zsolnay), 2005.

Mallgrave, H. F.: *Gottfried Semper. Ein Architekt des 19. Jahrhunderts.* Zürich (gta), 2001.

___: *Modern Architectural Theory. A Historical Survey, 1673-1968.* Cambridge etc (Cambridge University Press), 2005.

Manaila, I.: *Marcel Iancu. Architekt.* Master thesis in History and Theory of Architecture at the ETH Zürich under Professor Dr Werner Oechslin, Dr Simone Rümmele and Sylvia Claus. Zürich 2003.

Manea, N.: *Felix Culpa. Erinnerung und Schweigen: Mysterien bei Mircea Eliade.* In: *Lettre International*, No. 28, Berlin, 1/1995, pp. 30-36.

Maner, H.-C.: *Parlamentarismus in Rumänien (1930-1940). Demokratie im autoritären Umfeld.* Südosteuropäische Arbeiten, No. 101. Mainz, Univ., Diss., 1996. Munich (Oldenbourg), 1997 (Maner 1997a).

___: *Rumänien von 1859 bis 1989: Eine Geschichte von Krisen, Staatsstreichen und verhinderten Revolutionen?* In: *Österreichische Osthefte. Zeitschrift für Mittel-, Ost- und Südosteuropaforschung.* Year 39, No. 3, Vienna 1997, pp. 345-367 (Maner 1997b).

___: *Die Rückkehr Carols aus dem Exil. Macht und Herrschaftspolitik in Rumänien gegen Ende der 20er Jahre.* In: Südost-Forschungen, Vol. 56, Munich 1997, pp. 341-372 (Maner 1997c).

___: *Multikonfessionalität und neue Staatlichkeit.* Stuttgart (Franz Steiner), 2007.

Mango, C.: *Byzantinische Architektur.* Stuttgart (Belser)/Milan (Electra), 1975.

Manolescu, F.: *Enciclopedia exilului literar românesc 1945-1989* [The Encyclopaedia of the Writers Exiled from Romania 1945-1989]. Bucharest (Compania), 2003.

Mansbach, S. A.: *Modern Art in Eastern Europe.* Cambridge/ New York/Melbourne (Cambridge University Press), 1999.

Marcel, L.-A.: *Tudor Arghézi.* Paris (Pierre Seghers), 1963.

Marcu, D.: *Arhitectură. 50 lucrări executate sau proiectate de la 1912-1960* [Architecture. 50 works, which had been built or designed from 1912-1960]. Preface by Tudor Vianu. Bucharest (Ed. Tehnică), 1960.

Maulnier, T. (ed.): *Lettres de Marcel Proust à Bibesco.* Lausanne 1949.

Mayer, H.: *Outsiders. A Study in Life and Letters.* Translated by Denis M. Sweet. Cambridge, Mass./London, England (MIT Press), 1982.

Merian: *Bukarest und Rumäniens Schwarzmeerküste.* No. 6/XIX, June 1966. Hamburg (Hoffmann & Campe), 1966.

Meyers: *Meyers Enzyklopädisches Lexikon*, vol. 5, 1972.

Michels, E.: *Von der Deutschen Akademie zum Goethe-Institut. Sprach- und auswärtige Kulturpolitik 1923-1960.* Munich (Oldenbourg), 2005.

Midant, J.-P. (ed.): *Dictionnaire de l'architecture du XXe siècle.* Paris (Hazan/Institut Français d'Architecture), 1996.

Mihăilă, G. /Zamfirescu, D. (eds): *Literatura română veche.* Vol. 1, 1402-1647. Bucharest 1969.

Milosz, C.: *Verführtes Denken. Preface by Karl Jaspers.* Cologne/Berlin (Kiepenheuer & Witsch), 1953.

Möbuß, S.: *Plotin zur Einführung.* Hamburg (Junius), 2000.

Montaigne, M.: *The Essays.* Translated by Charles Cotton, Edited by W. Carew Hazlitt. Chicago/London/ Toronto/ Geneva (Encyclopaedia Britannica, Inc.), 1952.

Montesquieu, C. S.: *The Spirit of Laws.* Translated by T. Nugent, revised by J. V. Prichard. Chicago etc. (Encyclopaedia Britannica, Inc.), 1952.

Monuments historiques: *Roumanie/Roumania. Monuments historiques* No. 169. Paris, June/July 1990.

Morand, P.: *Papiers d'identité.* Paris (Bernard Grasset), 1930.

___: *Bucarest.* Paris (Plon), 1990 (1935).

___: *Journal inutile.* Paris (Gallimard), 2001.

Moravánszky, Á.: *Die Erneuerung der Baukunst. Wege zur Moderne in Mitteleuropa.* Salzburg/Vienna (Residenz Verlag), 1988.

___: *Competing Visions. Aesthetic Invention and Social Imagination in Central European Architecture, 1867-1918.* Cambridge, Mass./London, England (The MIT Press), 1998.

___(ed.): *Das enfernte Dorf. Moderne Kunst und ethnischer Artefakt.* Vienna/Köln/Weimar: Böhlau, 2002.

___/Györgny, Katalin M.: *Architekturtheorie im 20. Jahrhundert. Eine kritische Anthologie.* Vienna/New York: Springer, 2003.

___/Langer, B./Mosayebi, E. (eds): *Adolf Loos. Die Kultivierung der Architektur.* Zürich (gta), 2008.

Morin, E.: *Europa denken.* Frankfurt a. M./New York (Campus), 1988.

Mottraye, A. de la: *Voyage en Europe, Asie et Afrique.* 2. Vol., Den Haag 1727.

Mouton, J.: *Journal de Roumanie. La collection "Les chemins effacés". La IIe guerre mondiale vue de l'Est.* Lausanne (L'Age d'Homme), 1991.

Müller, M.: *Architektur und Avantgarde.* Frankfurt (Athäneum), 1987.

Muntean, G.: *Apa trece, pietrele rămân. Proverbe românești* [Water Flows, but Stones Stay. Romanian Proverbs]. Bucharest (Editura pentru literatură), 1966.

Muraro, M./Marton, P.: *Villen in Venetien.* Köln (Könnemann), 1999.

Myss, W.: *Fazit nach achthundert Jahren. Geistesleben der Sieben-bürger Sachsen im Spiegel der Zeitschrift Klingsor (1924-1939). Studien zur Kultur- und Geistesgeschichte der ältesten inseldeutschen Volksgruppe.* Munich (Verlag des Südostdeutschen Kulturwerks), 1968.

___(ed.): *Lexikon der Siebenbürger Sachsen. Geschichte, Kultur, Zivilisation, Wissenschaften, Wirtschaft, Lebensraum Siebenbürgen (Transsilvanien).* Thaur bei Innsbruck (Wort und Welt Verlag), 1993.

Nagy-Talavera, N. M.: *Nicolae Iorga. A Biography.* Jassy/Oxford/Portland (The Center for Romanian Studies), 1998.

Narcis, D. I.: *Mogoșoaia. Trei secole de istorie 1702-2002* [Mogoșoaia. Three Hundert Years of History 1702-2002]. Bucharest (Tritonic), 2002.

Narcis, D. I.: *București. In căutarea micului Paris* [Bucharest. Tracing the former "Little Paris"]. Bucharest (Tritonic), 2003.

___: *Residences and Families of the Nobility in Romania.* Bucharest (Romanian Cultural Institute), 2007.

Naredi-Rainer, P.: *Architektur und Harmonie. Zahl, Maß und Proportion in der abendländischen Baukunst.* Köln (DuMont), 2001.

Neagoe, S. (ed.): *Enciclopedia istoriei politice a României* [The Encyclopaedia of the Political History of Romania]. Bucharest 2003.

Nenițescu, Ș. I.: *Catargi. Maler und Werk.* Dresden (VEB Verlag der Kunst), 1975.

Nerdinger, W./Oechslin, W.: *Gottfried Semper 1803-1879. Architektur und Wissenschaft.* Zürich (gta); Munich etc. (Prestel), 2003.

Neumeyer, F.: *Mies van der Rohe. Das kunstlose Wort. Gedanken zur Baukunst.* Berlin (Siedler), 1986.

___/Cepl, J.: *Quellentexte zur Architekturtheorie.* Munich 2002.

The New York Times: *Foreign Exchange Rates*, 1st May 1939, p. 34.

___: *The Fair Today.* 5th May 1939, p. 19.

___: *Rumanian Ideals are Praised at Dedication of Fair Pavillon.* 6th May 1939, p. 7.

Nicol, D. M.: *The Byzantine Family of Kantakouzenos (Cantacuzenus) c. 1100-1460. A Genealogical and Prosopographical Study.* Dumberton Oak Studies XI. Washington D. C. 1968.

___: *The reluctant Emperor. A biography of John Cantacuzene, Byzantine Emperor and monk, c. 1295-1383.* Cambridge (Cambridge University Press), 1996.

Nițulescu, C.: *Aristide Blank.* In: *Magazin Istoric*, Bucharest 1999, No. 5, pp. 61-64.

Noica, N. Ș.: *Emil Pragher – un model. Din istoria constructțiilor românești* [Emil Pragher – a Model. A Contribution to the History of Civil Engineering in Romania]. Bucharest (Mașina de Scris), 2004.

___: *Banca Națională a României și personalități din istoria construcțiilor* [The National Bank of Romania and its History]. Bucharest 2006.

Nooteboom, C.: *Wie wird man Europäer.* Frankfurt a. M. (Suhrkamp), 1993.

Norberg-Schulz, C.: *Genius loci. Landschaft, Lebensraum, Baukunst.* Stuttgart (Klett-Cotta), 1982.

Norwich, J. J.: *The Middle Sea. A History of the Mediterranean.* New York (Vintage Books), 2007.

Nowka, D.: *George Enescu und die Entwicklung der rumänischen Musik.* Sinzheim (Pro Universitate Verlag), 1998.

Oechslin, W.: *Moderne entwerfen.* Cologne (DuMont), 1999.

___: *Otto Wagner, Adolf Loos, and the Road to Modern Architecture.* Translated by Lynnette Widder. Cambridge (Cambridge University Press), 2002.

___: *Palladianismus. Andrea Palladio – Kontinuität von Werk und Wirkung.* Zürich (gta), 2008.

Oficiul Național de Turism (ONT) (ed.): *Călăuza oficială a stațiunilor balneare și climaterice din România 1937* [The Official Guide to the Resorts of Romania 1937]. Bucharest/Craiova (Scrisul românesc), 1937.

Ofrim, Al.: *Străzi vechi din Bucureștiul de azi* [Old Streets in present Bucharest]. Bucharest (Humanitas), 2007.

Olteanu, R.: *București în date și întâmplări* [A History of Bucharest according to important Dates and Events]. Bucharest (Paideia), 2002.

Oprea, M.: *Brașov.* Bucharest: NOI Media Print, 2004.

Oprescu, G.: *Roumanian Art from 1800 to our days.* Malmö (John Kroon), 1935.

Opriș, I.: *Monumentele istorice din România* [The Historical Monuments in Romania]. Bucharest (Vremea), 2001.

Ordinul architecților din România (ed.): *Arhitecți în timpul dictaturii. Amintiri.* [Architects under the Communist Dictatorship. Memories]. Bucharest (Paidea), 2007.

Ornea, Z.: *The Romanian extreme-right. The nineteen thirties.* New York (Columbia University Press), 1999.

___: *Vârsta de aur dintre cele două războaie* [The Golden Age between the World Wars]. In: *Dilema veche*, No. 304, Bucharest, 27th November 1998-3rd December 1998.

Orsenna, É.: *André le Nôtre. Gardener to the Sun King.* Translated from the French by Moishe Black. New York (George Braziller), 2001.

Ortega y Gasset, J.: *An Interpretation of Universal History.* Translated by Mildred Adams. New York (W. W. Norton & Company, Inc.), 1973.

Ostrower, G. B.: *The League of Nations.* New York 1996.

Oudard, G.: *Portrait de la Roumanie.* Paris (Plon), 1935.

Pagano, G./Guarniero, D.: *Architettura rurale italiana.* Milan (Ulrico Hoepli), 1936.

Pai, H.: *The Portfolio and the Diagram. Architecture, Discourse, and Modernity in America.* Cambridge, Massachusetts/London (The MIT Press), 2002.

Paleologu, Al.: *Breviar pentru păstrarea clipelor. Dialoguri cu Filip-Lucian Iorga.* Bucharest (Humanitas), 2005.

Palladio, A.: *I quattro libri di architettura.* Venice 1601. WLB Stuttgart, Sch. K. Fol. 173.

___: *The Four Books of Architecture.* With an introduction by Adolf K. Placzek. New York (Dover Publications),1965.

Pallady, Th.: *Jurnal.* Bucharest (Meridiane), 1966.

Palmer, A.: *Dictionary of Twentieth-Century History 1900-1991.* London (Peguin), 1992.

Panofsky, E.: *Renaissance and Renascences in Western Art.* Stockholm (Almquist & Wiksell/Gebers Förlag AB), 1960. German edition *Die Renaissancen der europäischen Kunst.* Frankfurt am Main (Suhrkamp), 1979.

Parusi, Gh.: *Cronologia Bucureștilor. 20 septembrie 1459-31 decembrie 1989* [A Chronology of Bucharest from 20th September 1459 to 31st December 1989]. Bucharest (Compania), 2007.

Pascal, B.: *Pensées.* Translated by W. F. Trottler. Introduction by T. S. Eliot. Everyman's Library No. 874. London (J. M. Dent & Sons Ltd.)/New York (E. P. Dutton & Co., Inc.), 1931.

Patmore, D.: *Invitation to Romania.* New York (Macmillan), 1939.

___: *Private History. An Autobiography.* London 1960.

Patrulius, R.: *Horia Creangă. Omul și opera* [Horia Creangă. Life and Work]. Bucharest (Editura Tehnică), 1980.

Pavord, A.: *The Tulip.* London (Bloomsbury), 1999.

Pârvulescu, I.: *Întoarcere în Bucureștiul interbelic* [Return to the Bucharest of the interwar period]. Bucharest (Humanitas), 2006.

Pehnt, W./Schirren, M.(eds): *Hans Poelzig 1869 bis 1936. Architekt, Lehrer, Künstler.* Munich (Deutsche Verlags-Anstalt), 2007.

Pelin, M.: *Deceniul prăbușirilor (1940-1950). Viețile pictorilor, sculptorilor și arhitectilor români între legionari și staliniști* [The Decade of Break-downs (1940-1950). The Lifes of the Romanian Painters, Sculptors and Architects between Legionaires and Stalinists]. Bucharest (Compania), 2005.

Perche, L.: *Anna de Noailles.* Paris (Pierre Seghers), 1964.

Perrault, C.: *Parallèle des anciens et des modernes en ce qui regarde les arts et les sciences.* Edited by Max Imdahl, Wolfgang Iser, Hans Robert Jauss, Wolfgang Preisendanz and Jurik Striedter. Munich (Eidos), 1964. Perrault's original editions were published in Paris 1688, 1690 and 1692.

Perret, A.: *Zu einer Theorie der Architektur.* Berlin (Verlag der Beeken), 1986. Original edition *Contribution à une théorie de l'architecture.* Paris 1952.

Peschken, G.: *Karl Friedrich Schinkel. Das Architektonische Lehrbuch.* Munich/Berlin (Deutscher Kunstverlag), 1979.

Pevsner, N.: *An Outline of European Architecture.* Harmondsworth, Middlesex (Penguin), 1951.

___/Honour, Hugh/Fleming, John: *Lexikon der Weltarchitektur.* Munich (Prestel), 1992.

Philipp, K. J.: *Der Gänsemarsch der Stile. Skizzen zur Geschichte der Architekturgeschichtsschreibung.* Stuttgart (DVA), 1998.

___: *Karl Friedrich Schinkel. Späte Projekte. Late Projects.* 2. Vol. Stuttgart/London (Edition Axel Menges), 2000.

Philippi, P. (ed.): *Siebenbürgen als Beispiel europäischen Kulturaustausches.* Köln/Weimar/Vienna (Böhlau), 1975.

Pieper, J.: *Muße und Kult.* Munich (Kösel), 1948.

Plotinus: *The Six Enneads.* Translated by Stephen MacKenna and B. S. Page. Chicago/London/Toronto/Geneva (Encyclopaedia Britannica, Inc.), 1952.

___: *Ausgewählte Schriften.* Edited by C. Tornau. Stuttgart (Reclam), 2001.

Plowden, D.: *Bridges. The Spans of North America.* New York/London (W. W. Norton & Company), 2002.

Poëte, M.: *Introduction à l'urbanisme.* Paris (Sens & Tonka), 2000 (1929).

Popa, R.: *Mogoșoaia. Palatul și muzeul de arta brâncovenească* [The Palace and Museum of Brancovan Art]. Bucharest (Meridiane), 1962.

Popescu, C.: *Le style national roumain. Construire une nation à travers l'architecture 1881-1945.* Rennes (Presse Universitaire de Rennes), 2004.

Popescu, Gr. A. (ed.): *Dall'Adriatico al Mar Nero: Venezia e Romeni, Tracciati di Storie Comuni.* Roma (Consiglio Nazionale delle Ricerche), 2003.

Porter, I.: *Operation Autonomous. With S.O.E in Wartime Romania.* London (Chatto & Windus), 1989.

Posener, J.: *Aufsätze.* Braunschweig/Wiesbaden (Vieweg), 1981.

___: *Heimliche Erinnerungen. In Deutschland 1904 bis 1933.* Munich (Siedler), 2004.

Prager, E.: *Betonul armat în România* [The Reinforced Concrete in Romania]. Bucharest (Editura Tehnică), 1979.

Pragher, W.: *Bukarest. Stadt der Gegensätze – București. Orașul contrastelor.* Berlin (Wiking Verlag), 1943.

Prechtl, P./Burkhard, F.-P. (ed.): *Metzler Philosophielexikon.* Stuttgart/Weimar (Metzler), 1996.

Prost, H.: *Destin de la Roumanie.* Paris (Éd. Berger-Levrault), 1954.

Proust, M.: *Lettres à la comtesse de Noailles.* Paris 1931.

___: *Correspondance. Tome XXI, 1922.* Edited by Philip Kolb. Paris (Plon), 1993.

Prügel, R.: *Im Zeichen der Stadt. Avantgarde in Rumänien 1920-1938.* Cologne/Weimar/Vienna (Böhlau), 2008.

Puppi, L.: *Andrea Palladio. Das Gesamtwerk.* Stuttgart/Munich (DVA), 2000.

Quatremère de Quincy, A.-C.: *Essai sur la Nature, le But et les Moyens de l'Imitation dans les Beaux-Arts.* Paris 1823. Reprint Brussels (Archives d'Architecture Moderne), 1980.

Radu al României, principele: *Mihai al României* [King Michael of Romania]. Bucharest (Humanitas), 2008.

Raphael, L: (ed.): *Klassiker der Geschichtswissenschaft.* Munich (Beck), 2006.

Rădulescu, M. S.: *Cu gândul la lumea de altădată* [Memories of times past]. Bucharest (Editura Albatros), 2005.

Reinalter, H.: *Die Freimaurer.* Munich (C. H. Beck), 2000.

Rezzori, Gr.: *Denkwürdigkeiten eines Antisemiten.* Berlin (Berliner Taschenbuch-Verlag), 2004.

Rheinheimer, V. J. (ed.): *Herbert M. Gutmann. Bankier in Berlin, Bauherr in Potsdam, Kunstsammler.* Leipzig (Koehler & Amelang), 2007.

Ribbe, W./Schäche, W.: *Die Siemensstadt. Geschichte und Architektur eines Industriestandortes.* Berlin (Ernst und Sohn), 1985.

Ricœur, P.: *Civilisation universelle et culturelles nationales.* In: *Esprit*, Year 29, Paris, October 1961, pp. 439-450.

___: *Geschichte und Wahrheit.* Munich (List), 1974.

Rilke, R. M.: *Letters to a young poet.* Translated by Charlie Louth. London etc. (Penguin), 2011.

Romanescu, P. (ed.): *La Roumanie vue par les Français d'autrefois.* Choix de textes et notes pas Paula Romanescu. Tirés de la sélection du livre de Paul Desfeuilles et Jacques Lassaigne, *Les Français et la Roumanie. Bucarest 1937.* Bucharest (Éditions de la fondation culturelle roumaine), 2001.

Rossholm Lagerlöf, M.: *Ideal Landscape. Annibale Caracci, Nicolas Poussin and Claude Lorrain.* New Haven/London (Yale University Press), 1990.

Roth, H. (ed.): *Studienhandbuch Östliches Europa.* Cologne/Weimar/Vienna (Böhlau), 1999.

Roulet, D.: *Le Corbusier in Vichy.* In: *tec 21*, No. 7/2006, pp. 22-25.

Rowe, C./Koetter, F.: *Collage City.* Cambridge, Mass./ London, England (MIT Press), 1978.

Rubió-Tuduri, N. M.: *Actar. Discrimination des formes de quiètude des formes de mouvement dans la construction.* Paris 1931.

Runciman, S.: *Mistra. Byzantine Capital of the Peleponnese.* London (Thames & Hudson), 1980.

Rusan, R.: *Chronologie und Geografie der kommunistischen Unterdrückung in Rumänien. Zählung der zwangsinternierten Bevölkerung (1945-1989).* Translated and annotated by Hans Bergel. Bucharest (Fundaţia Academia Civică)/Munich (Institut für deutsche Kultur und Geschichte Südosteuropas), 2008.

Russell, B.: *In Praise of Idleness.* London/New York (Routledge), 2010 [1935].

Rybczynski, W.: *The Perfect House. A Journey with the Renaissance Master Andrea Palladio.* New York (Scribner), 2002.

Sacheverell Sitwell: *Roumanian Journey.* London (B. T. Batsford Ltd.), 1938.

Sadie. S. (ed.): *The New Grove. Dictionary of Music and Musicians.* London 2001.

Safran, Y./Wang, W. (eds): *The Architecture of Adolf Loos. An Arts Council Exhibition.* London 1985.

Safranski, Rüdiger: *Wieviel Globalisierung verträgt der Mensch?* Munich/Vienna (Hanser), 2003.

___: *Goethe & Schiller. Geschichte einer Freundschaft.* Munich (Hanser), 2009.

Sainte-Beuve, C. A.: *Correspondance générale. Lettres retrouvées I (1823-1859).* Paris (Honoré Champion Éditeur), 2006.

Sandoz, M.: *Portraits et visages dessinés par Théodore Chassériau. Cahiers Théodore Chassériau, II.* Paris (Les Quatre Chemins), 1986.

Sarkowitz, H. (ed.): *Die Geschichte der Gärten und Parks.* Frankfurt am Main/Leipzig (Insel), 2001.

Sarnitz, A.: *Adolf Loos 1870-1933. Architekt, Kulturkritiker, Dandy.* Cologne etc. (Taschen), 2003.

___: *Otto Wagner 1841-1918. Wegbereiter der modernen Architektur.* Cologne etc. (Taschen), 2005.

Sartori, C. (ed.): *Enciclopedia della musica.* Milan 1963.

Săsărman, Gh.: *Gândirea estetică in arhitectura românească* [The aesthetic thinking in Romanian architecture]. Bucharest (Meridiane), 1983.

K. G. Saur Verlag, München-Leipzig: *Saur Allgemeines Künstler-Lexikon. Die Bildenden Künstler aller Zeiten und Völker.* Munich/Leipzig 1997.

Schalk, F. (ed.): *Französische Moralisten. La Rochefoucault, Vauvenargues, Montesquieu, Chamfort.* Zürich: Diogenes, 1995.

Schild, G.: *Alvar Aalto. The Complete Catalogue of Architecture, Design and Art.* London (Academy Group Ltd.)/Berlin (Ernst & Sohn),1994.

Schinkel, K. F.: *Sammlung architektonischer Entwürfe.* Heft 1-12, Berlin 1832-1835; Heft 13-24, Berlin 1835; Heft 25-28, London/Paris 1840.

Schlögel, K.: *Terror und Traum. Moskau 1937.* Munich (Carl Hanser), 2008.

Schopenhauer, A.: *Aphorismes de la sagesse. Traduction de J.-A Cantacuzène.* Paris (G. Baillière), 1880.

Schumacher, F.: *Der Geist der Baukunst.* Stuttgart/Berlin (DVA), 1938.

Schuster, O. (ed.): *Epoche der Entscheidungen. Die Siebenbürger Sachsen im 20. Jahrhundert.* Köln/Weimar/Vienna (Böhlau), 1984.

Schwefelberg, A.: *Amintirile unui intelectual evreu din România* [The Memories of a Jewish Intellectual from Romania]. Bucharest (Editura Hasefer), 2000.

Scott, G.: *The Architecture of Humanism: a study in history of taste.* London (Constable), 1914.

Scruton, R.: *The Aesthetics of Architecture.* Princeton, New Jersey (Princeton University Press), 1980 (Scruton 1980a).

___: *The Meaning of Conservatism.* Totowa, New Jersey (Barnes & Noble Books), 1980 (Scruton 1980b).

___: *England. An Elegy.* London (Pimlico), 2001.

Scurtu, I. (ed.): *Pe marginea prăpastiei, 21-23 ianuarie 1941* [On the Brink of Disaster, 21st-23rd January 1941]. 2 Vol. Bucharest (Scripta), 1992.

Scurtu, I. : *Criza dinastică din România* [The Dynastic Crisis in Romania]. Bucharest (Ed. Enciclopedică), 1996.

___: *Guverne şi guvernanţi 1916-1938.* Bucharest (Ed. Silex), 1996.

___/Alexandrescu, I./Bulei, I./Mamina, I.: *Enciclopedia de istorie a României* [A Dictionary of Romanian History]. Bucharest 2002.

Sebastian, M.: *Seit zweitausend Jahren. Roman.* Paderborn (Igel Verlag Literatur)/Bucharest (Ediţia Fundaţiei Culturale Române), 1997.

___: *Journal, 1935-44.* Translated from the Romanian by Patrick Camiller. With an introduction and notes by Radu Ioanid. London (Heinemann), 2001.

Sedlmayer, Hans: *Art in Crisis. The Lost Center.* Translated by Brian Battershaw. New Brunswick, USA/London, UK (Transaction Publishers), 2007.

Seiwert, H.: *Marcel Janco – Dadaist, Zeigenosse, wohltemperiert morgenländischer Konstruktivist.* Frankfurt a. M. 1993.

Semper, G.: *Kleine Schriften.* Edited by Hans Semper und Manfred Semper. Mittenwald (Mäander Kunstverlag), 1979 [1884].

___: *The Four Elements of Architecture and other Writings.* Translated by H. F. Mallgrave and W. Herrmann. Cambridge etc. (Cambridge University Press), 1989.

Seton-Watson, R. G.: *A History of the Romanians from Roman Times to the Completion of Unity.* Cambridge (Cambridge University Press), 1934.

Seymour-Smith, M./Kimmens, A. C. (ed.): *World Authors 1900-1950. The Wilson Authors Series.* New York/Dublin (The H. W. Wilson Company), 1996.

Shakespeare, W.: *Einundzwanzig Sonette. Deutsch von Paul Celan.* English/German edition. Frankfurt am Main/Leipzig (Insel Verlag), 2001.

Sieberg, A.: *Versuche und Erfahrungen über Entstehung, Verhütung und Beseitigung von Erdbebenschäden.* In: *Veröffentlichungen der Reichsanstalt für Erdbebenforschung in Jena*, No. 39. Berlin (Reichsverlagsamt) 1941.

Sieburg, F.: *Robespierre. Napoleon. Chateaubriand.* Stuttgart (DVA), 1967.

Sielemann, T. (ed.): *Die Natur- und Kulturwunder Europas. Alle europäischen Natur- und Kulturstätten der UNESCO-Welterbeliste.* Gütersloh/Munich (Chronik), 2003.

Smet, C. de: *Le Corbusier. Architekt der Bücher.* Baden (Lars Müller Publishers), 2005.

Socolescu, T. T.: *Fresca arhitecţilor care au lucrat în România în epoca modernă 1800-1925* [A Survey of the Architects who worked in Romania from 1800-1925]. Bucharest (Caligraf), 2004.

Staatliche Kunsthalle Karlsruhe (ed.): *Camille Corot. Natur und Traum.* Berlin/ Heidelberg (Kehrer), 2012.

Stanislawski, R./Brockhaus, C.(eds): *Europa, Europa. Das Jahrhundert der Avantgarden in Mittel- und Osteuropa.* 4 Vol. Bonn (Kunst und Ausstellungshalle der Bundesrepublik Deutschland), 1994.

Stettner, R.: *"Archipel GULag" – Stalins Zwangslager: Terrorinstrument und Wirtschaftsgigant. Entstehung, Organisation und Funktion des sowjetischen Lagersystems 1928-1956.* Munich etc. (F. Schöningh), 1996.

Stiegemann, C. (ed.): *Byzanz. Das Licht aus dem Osten.* Mainz (Zabern), 2001.

Stiller, A. (ed.): *Architektur im Ringturm XII. Josef Plecnik, Architekt in Wien, Prag und Laibach.* Salzburg/Vienna (Anton Pustet), 2006.

___: *Architektur im Ringturm XIII. Rumänien. Momente der Architektur vom 19. Jahrhundert bis heute.* Salzburg/Vienna (Anton Pustet), 2007.

Streidt, G./Feierabend, P. (eds): *Preußen. Kunst und Architektur.* Cologne (Könemann), 1999.

Sutherland, C.: *Enchantress. Marthe Bibesco and her world.* London (John Murray Publishers Ltd.), 1996.

Ştephănescu, M. I.: *Un arhitect uitat* [A forgotten Architect]. *Victor G. Ştephănescu.* In: *Anticart* No. 18, Bucharest, May 2007, pp. 15-20.

Tabacu, G.: *Revista "Arhitectura". Studiu monografic şi indici, 1906-1944* [The *Arhitectura* Review. Monographic Study and Register, 1906-1944]. PhD thesis, University of Architecture Ion Mincu Bucharest. Bucharest 2006.

Tarde, G.: *Die Gesetze der Nachahmung.* Frankfurt a. M. (Suhrkamp), 2009. Original edition *Les lois de l'imitation*, Paris 1890.

Tavernor, R.: *Palladio and Palladianism.* London (Thames & Hudson Ltd.), 1991.

Taylor, S.: *Who's Who in Central and East-Europe 1933/34.* Zürich (The Central European Times Publishing Co. Ltd.), 1935.

___: *Who's Who in Central and East-Europe 1935/36*, Zürich 1937.

Texier, S.: *Georges-Henri Pingusson Architecte (1894-1978). La poétique pour doctrine.* Paris (Éditions Verdier), 2006.

___: *Georges Henri Pingusson.* CH-Gollion (Infolio)/ Paris (Éditions du Patrimoine), 2011.

Tiegheim, P./Josserand, P. (ed.): *Dictionnaire des Littératures*. 3 Vol. Paris (Presses Universitaires de France), 1968.

Tilea, V. V.: *Envoy Extraordinary. Memoirs of a Romanian Diplomat.* Edited by Ileana Tilea. London (Haggerston Press), 1998.

The Times: *An Anglo-Rumanian Festival*. London, 29th March 1938, p. 19.

___: *Romania to broadcast news in English*. 2nd April 1938, p. 11.

___: *Romanian National Exhibition*. 29th April 1938, p. 14.

___: *British Institute For Bucharest. Grant Of A Site*. 23rd November 1938, p. 13.

___: *London Diplomatic Changes. Chile, Turkey and Rumania. Rumanian Anglophile*. 25th January 1939, p. 11.

Tismăneanu, V.: *Rumäniens mystische Revolutionäre*. In: *Sinn und Form*, Year 48, No. 1, January-February 1996, pp. 48-58. Berlin (Aufbau Verlag), 1996.

___/Comisia prezidențială pentru analiza dictaturii comuniste din România (ed.): *Analiza dictaturii comuniste din România. Raport final* [The Analysis of the Communist Dictatorship in Romania. Final report]. Bucharest 2006.

Titulesco, N.: *Le pacte de la Société des Nations dans sa liaison avec le pacte Briand-Kellog*. In: *Dictionnaire diplomatique*, Vol. 2, 1934, pp. 826-828.

Toynbee, A.: *Civilization on Trial*. London/New York (The Oxford University Press), 1947.

Trempler, J.: *Schinkels Motive*. Berlin (Matthes & Seitz), 2007.

Turner, J. (ed.): *The Dictionary of Art*. London (Macmillan Publishers Ltd.)/ New York (Grove's Dictionaries Inc.), 1996.

Țurcanu, F.: *Mircea Eliade. Le prisonnier de l'histoire*. Paris (Édition la Découverte), 2003.

Umbdenstock, G.: *Œuvres architecturales, 1897 à 1933*. Strasbourg 1933.

Uniunea architecților din România (ed.): *București, anii 1920-1940. Între avangardă și modernism* [Bucharest 1920-1940. Between Avantgarde and Modernism]. Bucharest (Simetria), 1994.

___: *Horia Creangă. Catalogul expoziției organizate la împlinirea a 100 de ani de la naștere* [Horia Creangă. Catalogue of the exhibition commemorating his 100th Birthday]. Bucharest (Simetria), 1992.

___: *Centenar Marcel Iancu, 1895-1995*. [Marcel Janco. Catalogue of the exhibition commemorating his 100th Birthday]. Bucharest (Simetria), 1996.

___: *La Biennale di Venezia – Romania 1996. 6a mostra internazionale di architettura*. Bucharest (Simetria), 1996.

Vaida-Voevod, M.: *Lucian Blaga. Ein rumänischer Dichter und die deutsche Literatur*. Hildesheim/Zurich/New York (Georg Olms), 1992.

Valéry, N.: *Zelle 24. "Gelobt seist du Gefängnis"*. Uhldingen/Seewis (Stephanus Edition), 1978.

Valéry, P.: *Introduction to the Method of Leonardo da Vinci*. Translated from the French by Thomas McGreevy. London (John Rodker), 1929.

___: *Eupalinos*. London 1932.

___: *Dialogues*. Translated by William McCausland Stewart. Bollingen Series XLV, 4. NewYork (Bollingen Foundation, Inc./Pantheons Books), 1956.

___ et al.: *Études Bergsoniennes. Hommage à Henri Bergson (1859-1941)*. Paris (Presse Universitaires de France), 1942.

Valéry, P.: *Leonardo, Poe, Mallarmé*. Translated by M. Cowby and J. R. Lawler. Bollingen Series XLV, 8. Princeton, New Jersey (Princeton University Press), 1972.

___: *Werke*. 7 Vol. Edited by J. Schmidt-Radefeldt. Vol. 6: *Zur Ästhetik und Philosophie der Künste*; Vol. 7: *Zur Zeitgeschichte und Politik*. Frankfurt am Main/Leipzig (Insel), 1995.

Vecerdea, Gh.: *Constanța. Influența architecturii franceze în prima etapă de dezvoltare a orașului modern (1860-1916)* [Constantza. The French Influence during the First Phase of Development of the Modern City (1860-1916)]. In: *Valori ale civilizației românești în Dobrogea* [Romanian Cultural Values in the Dobrodgea]. Constanța, 1993, pp. 345-355.

Verseck, K.: *Rumänien*. Munich (C. H. Beck), 2007.

Vitruvius: *On Architecture. Translated by Richard Schofield with an introduction by Robert Tavernor*. London (Penguin), 2009.

Völkl, E.: *Rumänien. Vom 19. Jahrhundert bis in die Gegenwart*. Regensburg (Pustet)/Munich (Südosteuropa-Gesellschaft), 1995.

Vossen, J.: *Bukarest. Die Entwicklung des Stadtraums*. Berlin (Reimer), 2004.

Wagner, E.: *Geschichte der Siebenbürger Sachsen. Ein Überblick*. Thaur bei Innsbruck (Wort und Welt), 1990.

Waldeck, R. G.: *Athene Palace*. New York 1942.

Wang, W./Schneider, R. (ed.): *Moderne Architektur in Deutschland 1900 bis 2000. Macht und Monument*. Ostfildern (Gerd Hatje), 1998.

Wasmuth, G. et al. (ed.): *Wasmuths Lexikon der Baukunst*, Vol. 3. Berlin (Wasmuth), 1931.

Watkin, D.: *Morality and Architecture Revisited*. Chicago (The University of Chicago Press)/London (John Murray Publishers Ltd.), 2001.

Weck, R.: *Journal de guerre (1939-1945). Un diplomat suisse à Bucarest*. Edited by Simon Roth. Fribourg (Société d'Histoire de la Suisse Romande), 2001.

Weiss, A.: *Paris war eine Frau. Die Frauen von der "Left Bank": Djuna Barnes, Janet Flanner, Gertrude Stein & Co.* Dortmund (Edition Eberbach), 1996.

Weiss, P.: *Die Ästhetik des Widerstands. Roman*. Frankfurt am Main (Suhrkamp), 1988.

Weithmann, M. W.: *Balkan-Chronik. 2000 Jahre zwischen Orient und Okzident*. Regensburg (Pustet); Graz/Vienna/Köln (Styria), 2000.

Welzer, Harald (ed.): *Der Krieg der Erinnerung. Holocaust, Kollaboration und Widerstand im europäischen Gedächtnis*. Frankfurt am Main (Fischer), 2007.

Wende, F. (ed.): *Lexikon zur Parteiengeschichte in Europa*. Stuttgart (Alfred Kröner), 1981.

Werndl, K. (ed.): *Rumänien nach der Revolution. Eine kulturelle Gegenwartsbestimmung*. Vienna (Wilhelm Braumüller), 2007.

Wilpert, G. von (ed.): *Lexikon der Weltliteratur*. Stuttgart 2004.

Wilson, C. St J.: *The Other Tradition of Modern Architecture. The uncompleted Project*. London (Academy Editions), 1995.

___: *Architectural Reflections. Studies in the Philosophy and Practice of Architecture*. Manchester/New York (Manchester University Press), 2000.

Wischermann, H.: *Paris. Architekturführer*. Ostfildern (Gerd Hatje), 1997.

Wittgenstein, L.: *Tractatus Logico-Philosophicus*. With an introduction by Betrand Russell, F. R. S. German-English edition. London (Kegal Paul, Trench, Trubner & Co. Ltd)/New York (Harcourt, Brace & Company, Inc.), 1922.

___: *Vorlesungen 1930-1935. Cambridge 1930-1932. Aus den Aufzeichnungen von John King und Desmond Lee*. Edited by Desmond Lee. *Cambridge 1932-1935. Aus den Aufzeichnungen von Alice Ambrose und Margaret Macdonald*. Edited by Alice Ambrose. Frankfurt am Main (Suhrkamp), 1984.

Wittkower, R.: *Architectural Principles in the Age of Humanism*. London (The Warburg Institute, University of London), 1949.

Wölfflin, H.: *Classic Art. An Introduction to the Italian Renaissance*. Translated from the German by Peter and Linda Murray. Introduction by Herbert Read. London/New York (Phaidon), 1968.

Wolzogen, A. (ed.): *Aus Schinkels Nachlass. Reisetagebücher, Briefe und Aphorismen*. Berlin (R. Decker), 1863.

Woodhouse, J.: *Gabriele D'Annunzio, Defiant Angel*. New York (Oxford University Press), 2001.

Woolfield, R. (ed.): *The Essential Gombrich. Selected Writings on Art and Culture*. London (Phaidon), 1996.

Worringer, W.: *Abstraction and Empathy. A Contribution to the Psychology of Style*. Translated by Michael Bullock. London (Routledge & Kegan Paul Ltd), 1953

Wurts, R./Applebaum, S.: *The New York's World Fair 1939/1940*. New York (Dover Publications, Inc.), 1977.

Wyss, B.: *Der Wille zur Kunst. Zur ästhetischen Mentalität der Moderne*. Köln (DuMont), 1997.

Zadow, M. Al.: *Karl Friedrich Schinkel. Leben und Werk*. Stuttgart/London (Axel Menges), 2003.

Zahariade, A. M.: *Moderne in Bukarest*. In: *Werk, Bauen + Wohnen*, No. 1/2, 1994, pp. 60-63.

Ziegerhofer-Prettenthaler, A.: *Botschafter Europas. Richard Nikolaus Coudenhove-Kalergi und die Paneuropa-Bewegung in den zwanziger und dreißiger Jahren*. Cologne/Weimar/ Vienna (Böhlau), 2004.

Zim, L./Lerner, M./Rolfes, H.: *The World of Tomorrow – the 1939 New York World's Fair*. New York (Harper & Row), 1988.

Zschokke, W./Hanak, M. (ed.): *Nachkriegsmoderne Schweiz. Architektur von Werner Frey, Franz Füeg, Jacques Schader, Jakob Zweifler = Post-War Modernity in Switzerland. Architecture by Werner Frey, Franz Füeg, Jacques Schader, Jakob Zweifler*. Basel/Boston/Berlin (Birkhäuser), 2001.

Zub, Al.: *Istorie și istorici în România interbelică* [History and Historians in Romania between the world wars]. Jassy (Junimea), 1989.

Zucker, P.: *Die paradoxe Entwicklung der Architekturtheorien zu Beginn der Modernen Architektur*. In: *Archithese* 2/1987, pp. 27-32.

Zwijnenberg, R.: *The Writings and Drawings of Leonardo da Vinci. Order and Chaos in Early Modern Thought*. Cambridge (Cambridge University Press), 1999.

Archives

ADAGP	Société des Auteurs dans les Arts Graphiques et Plastiques, Paris
ADT	Archive Dan Teodorovici, Stuttgart
AGMC-IP	GMC archive at Irina Patrulius, Bucharest
AGMC-PM	GMC archive at Paul Marinescu, Bucharest
AGMC-RM	GMC archive at Ruxandra Munteanu, Bucharest
AMB-JG	Archive Marthe Bibesco/Judy Ghyka, London
AMLSC	Archive Marie-Lyse Cantacuzino-Ruhemann and Şerban Cantacuzino, London
ANB	Arhivele Naţionale ale României [The National Archives of Romania, Bucharest]
ANDJC	Arhivele Naţionale ale României Direcţia Judeţeană Constanţa [The National Archives of Romanian, Department of Constantza County]
ANDJD	Arhivele Naţionale ale României Direcţia Judeţeană Dolj (Craiova) [The National Archives of Romanian, Department of Craiova County]
ANFP	Archives Nationales de France, Paris
ATT	Archive Tilea-Troiano, London
BAR	Biblioteca Academiei Române [Library of the Romanian Academy]
BNF	Bibliothèque Nationale de France, Paris
BNR	Biblioteca Naţională a României, Bucharest [National Library of Romania]
CLADRA	CLADRA Architects, Bucharest
CNSAS	Consiliul Naţional pentru Studierea Arhivelor Securităţii [National Department of the Study of the Securitate Archives]
DCCPCNG	Direcţia pentru Cultură, Culte şi Patrimoniul Cultural Naţional a judeţului Giurgiu [Department of Culture, Religions and Historic Monuments of Giurgiu County]
INMI/FDMI	Institutul Naţional al Monumentelor Istorice, Fond Direcţia Monumentelor Istorice [Department of Historic Monuments, Record DMI], Bucharest
MJTMT/BAS	Ministerul Justiţiei, Tribunalul Militar Teritorial, Birou Arhivă Specială [Ministery of Justice, Military Court of Justice, Special Archive Office], Bucharest
NAL	National Archives London
PMB	Primăria Municipiului Bucureşti [The City Hall of Bucharest]
RIBA/IA	Royal Institute of British Architects / Institutional Archives, London
SRR	Societatea Română de Radio, [Romanian Broadcasting Company], Bucharest
UAR-AOD	Uniunea Arhitecţilor din România, [Union of Romanian Architects], Archive Octav Doicescu, Bucharest

Illustration Credits

Every effort has been made to approach all copyright holders. The author would be thankful if copyright holders whom he has not been able to contact would make themselves known.

Archives

Académie d'architecture, Paris: 40.
ADAGP, Paris: 284.
ADT: Front cover, 3, 7, 11, 22, 27, 28, 29, 32, 34, 35, 37, 38, 46, 47, 49, 52, 54, 55, 57, 76, 77, 79, 82, 98, 105, 127, 129, 130, 134, 139 , 140, 142-145, 149, 154, 155, 157, 158, 183, 184, 185, 188, 189, 191, 195, 196, 197, 199, 201, 204, 220-222, 225, 233-238, 261, 263, 272, 279, 285, 294, 302, 308, 310, 312, 315, 318-321, W6, W10, W12, W32, W36-38, W41, W42, W44, W49, W51, W54-56, W58, W61, W63, W67, W74, W75, W82, W92, W94-96, W99, W103.
AGMC-IP: 95, 171, 177, 274, 275, 281, 289, 292.
AGMC-PM: 26, 45, 99, 100, 101, 102, 125, 126, 128, 132, 133, 135, 137, 138, 141, 146, 148, 150, 193, 202, 203, 205, 209, 210, 300, 303-305, 316, 317, W3, W11, W13, W14, W16, W17, W22, W25, W27, W29-31, W34, W53, W64, W76, W81, W93.
AGMC-RM: 329.
AMB-JG: 9, 68, 69, 72, 73, 103, 104, W1.
AMLSC: 1, 2, 15, 16, 18, 20, 21, 23, 24, 25, 31, 50, 61, 92, 96, 97, 116, 152, 166, 169, 170, 174, 194, 207, 214, 215, 223, 224, 226, 244, 248, 250, 252, 255, 257, 258, 259, 260, 264, 265, 266, 276, 291, 313, 323, 325-328, 330-336.
ATT: 111, 113, 124, W19, W23.
BNF: 251.
Diane de la Bruchollerie, Paris: 246.
Brukenthal Museum, Sibiu/Hermannstadt: 65.
CLADRA, Bucharest: 227, 228, 229, W88.
C. Hamann/W. Henkel (K. Hielscher): 17, W5.
Foto Marburg: 19.
IC-CD – Gabinetto Fotografico Nazionale, Rome: 282.
Alberto Giacometti Estate, Paris: 284.
Dr Heiko Krefter: 176.
Landesarchiv Baden-Württemberg, Staatsarchiv Freiburg (W. Pragher): 118, 119, 208.
Astrid von Lutitz: 301.
picture alliance/AP Images: 180.
PMB: 75, 153.
RIBA Library Drawings & Archives Collections, London: 186.
SAEML Parisienne de Photographie/ Roger-Viollet: 59.
SRR: 173, W7, W45, 322.
Staatsgalerie Stuttgart: 93, 284.
Éditions Stock, Paris: 273.
UAR-AOD: 179, 190, 192, 198.
Emil Dinu-Popa, Bucharest: 151.
Thorsten Stelter, Frankfurt/Stuttgart: 286.
VG Bild-Kunst, Bonn: 33, 58, 62, 63, 156, 159, 162, 165, 213, 299.
Marius Voica, Bucharest: 277, W47, W48.
W. Weiss, period photographs: 99, 100, 101, 102, 120, 125, 132, 133, 137, 138, 141, 160, 164, 254, 300, 303-306, W3, W11, W13-17, W22, W27, W29-31, W34, W53
WLB Stuttgart: 42, 80, 230, 239, 240, 288.

Publications by GMC

GMC 1928 (1932): 4, 94, 187, 271, 290, 311.
GMC/Schmiedigen 1929: 78, 81, 83, 84, 85, 86, 88, 91, 293, W2
GMC 1931: 254, 295, 297, 298, W102.
GMC 1934: 296.
GMC 1934 (AA): 307, 309.
GMC 1938: 175.
Simetria I-VIII (1939-1947): 51, 66, 168, 178, 200, 211, 212, 213, 219, 231, 232, 241, 243, 245, 247, 249, 267, 268, 269, 270, 280, 287, 314.
GMC 1947: 242.

Furthers Publications

AA 1934: 48, 120, 160, 172, 307, 309.
Arhitectura 1941: 163.
Bach 1988: 165.
Bergson 1964b: 60.
Bernabei 1986: 90.
Cantacuzène, Ch.-A. /de Ligne 1934: 8, 262.
Cavalieri c. 1609: 288.
Choisy 1899: 13.
Cicio Pop 1938:106, 107, 108, 109, 112, 114, 117, 131, 136, 147, 167, 206.
Dictionnaire Diplomatique 1933: 110.
Donaldson 1984: 182.
Drexler 1977: 36.
Fabre 1922: 56.
Gafencu 1946: 122.
Geretsegger/Peintner/Pichler 1978: 14, 87.
Graf 1978: 89.
Gromort 1922: 43.
Gromort 1938: 39.
Gromort 1946: 41.
Gromort 2001: 40.
Gusti 1937: 115.
Hertlein (Wasmuth) 1927: 216, 217.
Hertlein (Wasmuth) 1931: 218.
Hootz/Vătăşianu 1972: W100.
Iorga/Balş 1922: 70.
Iorga 1926: 6, 30.
Letarouilly 1857: 239, 240.
Merian 1966: 256, 301.
Narcis 2007: 74, 123, 181.
Oprescu 1935: 64, 164, W15.
Patrulius 1980: 156, 159, 161, 162.
Palladio 1601: 80.
Popa 1962: 67, 71.
Revue du Vrai et du Beau. Revue des Arts. Year 9, No. 151. Paris 25th August 1930: 324.
Runciman 1980: 4.
Safran/Wang 1985: 53, 278.
Schinkel 1831: 230.
Sebastian 2005: 121.
Stefănescu 1928: 5, 283.
UNESCO 1962: 253.
VEB Verlag der Kunst Dreseden 1975: 10.
Wölfflin 1899: 12.

Index of people

Figures in **semibold** refer to illustration numbers

Author's Note

When visiting Romania I love walking down the Magheru Boulevard in Bucharest, one of the most urban places I know in Europe. This ritual goes back to my first visit to Romania as an adult in 1996. Then I like to browse through bookshops with no real purpose. One sunny morning in that summer of 1996, in a second-hand bookshop on Magheru Blvd, I picked up a thick volume of selected essays by a man called G. M. Cantacuzino. I had no idea who he was, but I felt a strong attraction, as if I knew him. But I also felt as if there were uncountable thick curtains between us. Then I devoured *Sources and Stopovers* (edited by Adrian Anghelescu in 1977) and thought to translate it into German. But it was not until autumn 2004, when I was in my second year as assistant professor at the Chair of Urban Design at the University of Stuttgart, that I seriously contemplated pulling the curtains apart. And that is what I did.

Dan Teodorovici is an architect and curator living in Stuttgart. He was born in Brașov/Kronstadt in 1972 to a German mother and a Romanian father. In 2010 his PhD thesis *G. M. Cantacuzino (1899-1960): Dialogik zwischen Tradition und Moderne* received *summa cum laude* at the University of Stuttgart.